ONE WEEK LOAN

PRENTICE HALL
HARVESTER WHEATSHEAF

London   New York   Toronto   Sydney   Tokyo   Singapore
Madrid   Mexico City   Munich

First published 1996 by
Prentice Hall/Harvester Wheatsheaf
Campus 400, Maylands Avenue
Hemel Hempstead
Hertfordshire, HP2 7EZ
'A division of
Simon & Schuster International Group

Typeset in 10/12pt Palatino
by Hands Fotoset, Leicester

Printed and bound in Great Britain by
T. J. Press (Padstow) Ltd

Library of Congress Cataloging-in-Publication Data

Tierney, John.
    Criminology : theory and context / John Tierney.
        p.   cm.
    Includes bibliographical references and index.
    ISBN 0-13-380155-1 (pbk. : alk. paper)
    1. Criminology—History.   2. Criminology—Great Britain—History.
3. Crime—Sociological aspects   4. Crime—Sociological aspects—
Great Britain.   I. Title.
HV6021.T54   1996
364—dc20   95-49474
                                                          CIP

British Library Cataloguing in Publication Data

A catalogue record for this book is available from
the British Library

ISBN 0-13-380155-1

    2   3   4   5   ·   00   99   98   97

For Ben, Dominic and Christian

Contents

Preface

This book is written as an introduction to criminology, or, more specifically, sociological criminology. The aim has been to write an accessible and comprehensive text, but one that does not shirk from engaging with what are sometimes complex issues and debates. The approach is based on a good many years experience teaching criminology and related subjects to a wide range of groups. Now some thanks.

Writing this book has meant a frequently obsessive preoccupation with a century of criminological thought, and lengthy sojourns in, if not quite a garret, at least an attic room where I watched the seasons roll by through a Velux window. My thanks to my wife and sons for putting up with the resultant disruptions to family life, and for continuing to provide much appreciated encouragement. I hope that I can make up for all those games of Subbuteo I should have played with my youngest son, but didn't because I was consorting with various criminal and criminological miscreants. A welcome respite from writing, especially during those periods when my brain seemed to be turning into taramasalata, was provided by the Thursday night folk music sessions at the Colpitts pub in Durham, which offered comradeship and an incentive to work out some new guitar tunings.

My thanks to those colleagues at New College Durham and at the University of Northumbria who provided encouragement. For various reasons my thanks are also due to the following people – some of whom I've never met. To Stan Cohen for *Folk Devils and Moral Panics*, and to the person who a while ago lent me a copy and got me started; to Colin Sumner for helping to keep key conceptual debates alive; to the late Steven Box for writing the best Preface to a criminology book (Box, 1981); to Mike Brogden who has been a friendly face at some dire conferences; to Martin Scorsese for the film *Goodfellas*, which should be part of a criminology starter pack; to the anonymous reviewer of the original book proposal who generously described me as not part of the mainstream; and to Dick Hobbs, Barbara Hudson and Mike Maguire, who offered extremely useful criticisms and comments on an earlier draft of the book. Needless to say, I take responsibility for the final product.

Introduction

Since the late 1960s the area of study broadly described as criminology has expanded enormously in Britain. Nowadays all sorts of writers, researchers and teachers make many and varied contributions to issues of crime and social control, and represent various political and theoretical positions. Within academic criminology contributions come from many different discipline areas: psychology, psychoanalysis, geography, history, economics, political science, jurisprudence, biology, sociology, and so on. Clearly, given the vast army of participants in the 'criminological project', there are competing views regarding the agenda to be followed. In fact, one of the central questions that will accompany the discussion of criminology's history here is what is it *for*? The book is as much about criminology's history as an academic discipline as it is about criminological theory.

Although important ideas and pieces of research from other disciplines will be referred to, the primary focus is unashamedly sociological criminology. The book is also unashamedly concerned with important *theoretical* developments. There is little detailed discussion of specific forms of crime such as ram-raiding, burglary or bank robbery, though there are plenty of references to research based upon these themes. At the risk of disappointing the reader before we have begun, the argument here is that we can only make sense of specific types of contemporary crime by having a grasp of the theoretical ideas and debates that have sprung up over the years. Essentially, the book reflects what was found in a recent review of criminology in British universities and colleges: 'Theoretical criminology . . . is what British criminologists continue to teach. Variously called criminology and the sociology of deviance, it looms over all else' (Rock, 1994).

A central dimension to the book is an engagement with conceptual debates over 'what things mean'. Our everyday worlds are filled with references to crime, criminals, punishment, discipline, the law, and so forth, but what do these terms *mean*? How have these meanings and understandings been constructed? What impact does crime have on people's lives? To what extent are meanings and understandings shared by society's members? How have these phenomena been approached within academic criminology? Throughout the book, therefore, the reader will be invited to consider seriously a range of questions and issues that are often taken for granted.

Although I have attempted to present these debates and issues in such a way as to make them accessible, I have also been concerned to avoid simplifying them to the point of distorting the material and patronizing the reader. One of the things I've noticed whilst researching this book is that sometimes the ideas and theories of classic, or at least frequently referred to, writers suffer the fate of messages in Chinese whispers: the original message becomes distorted, or caricatured, or oversimplified. This book, therefore, is an invitation to the reader eventually to read those original texts, so that they can judge them for themselves.

This is also a book about social and political history, in so much as the main concerns and general shape of criminology as it has developed over the years cannot be understood without considering the context provided by that history.

The organization of the book

The book is structured around two central themes:

1. The historical development of criminology as an academic discipline, primarily within a British context.

2. The main criminological theories that have emerged as the discipline grew during this century. This will involve drawing on theoretical work from countries other than Britain, especially the United States.

The material is organized on the basis of five parts, each made up of a number of chapters.

Part I comprises three chapters. Chapter 1 sets the scene by identifying some problems associated with defining terms such as crime and deviance. In particular, the role of criminology in challenging accepted commonsense understandings of these phenomena, is discussed. Chapter 2 takes us into a discussion of some of the difficulties faced when measuring the amount and distribution of crime in society; these difficulties are both 'technical' and 'conceptual'. Chapter 3 introduces a historical dimension by examining the history of criminology from the nineteenth century through to World War Two. Unlike the rest of the book, in this chapter the theme of criminology's development as an academic discipline within specific social and political contexts, and the theme of developments in criminological theory, are combined.

In Parts II, III, IV and V, however, as sociological influences begin to appear, these two themes are, for analytical purposes, separated out for each historical period. Each Part thus addresses a particular historical period. The first chapter in each Part aims to provide an introduction to the social and political changes over that period, and their impact on the nature and social organization of criminology as a discipline. This not only allows an appreciation of the importance of these external influences but, by focusing on criminology as a discipline, it establishes a framework within which the discussion of theory in subsequent chapters in that Part can be situated. By analogy, it is rather like walking the Wembley turf and acclimatizing to the stadium before actually playing in a Cup Final. Where there has been 'delayed action' regarding the influence of a particular theory on British criminology, then reference will be made to earlier periods.

Selecting material

There are some interesting problems in writing an introductory text such as this. One specific problem is that over the years the amount of published work in criminology has grown enormously, assuming a kind of wedge shape, with the thin end receding into the past. Why, we might ask, should introductory texts continue to reproduce this work from the past?

One can often pick up a modern author's sensitivity to the recycling of older theories. They almost apologize for reproducing a well-known and well-used quotation, or revisiting some well-trodden ground. There are no apologies here, though: most of the major passages are quoted in an effort to provide a comprehensive introduction. This earlier material is often interesting in its own right, and what is well-trodden ground to the professional criminologist may be entirely new to the reader. Furthermore, this material is important in that it will have influenced subsequent criminologists, and may continue to exercise a powerful influence in some quarters. An understanding of modern criminological theory presupposes familiarity with what has gone before. Although this clearly involved making judgements, I have dwelt on certain theoretical ideas and debates from the past because I feel that they have an important contemporary resonance. Acknowledging that they may not mean much to the reader at this stage, some examples to look out for are: in the nineteenth century, Durkheim on modernity; in the 1920s and 1930s, discussions of disorganization and the urban criminal area by the Chicago School; and, in the 1960s, the conceptual problems raised by new deviancy theory. In the final analysis, of course, any introduction to criminology would be glaringly incomplete if it did not discuss the earlier work. Having said that, a large portion of the book concerns itself with more recent developments in terms of the discipline and its context, and its theories.

Part I

Preliminaries and early history

1 | Criminology, crime and deviance: some preliminaries

Good old common sense

One of the tasks of criminology should be to question taken-for-granted assumptions regarding what crime and deviance *are*, what criminals are *like*, and so on. It should, in other words, question common-sense knowledge. However, as Howard Becker has pointed out, the term 'common sense' is used to mean two different things. Sometimes common sense describes an approved quality of mind:

> the common man (*sic*), his head unencumbered by fancy theories and abstract professional notions, can at least see what is right there in front of his nose. Philosophies as disparate as pragmatism and Zen enshrine a respect for the common man's ability to see, with Sancho Panza, that a windmill is really a windmill. (Becker, 1974: 50) [From now on, rather than clutter up the text with '*sic*', whenever a quoted author uses such genderized language, disapprobation can be taken as given.]

This meaning of common sense is found in injunctions such as 'Use your common sense', and, expressed like this, is difficult to criticize. In reality, though, it is not always easy to distinguish this common sense from the second type, though we all like to think of ourselves as Sancho Panza. This second, less estimable, way in which the term 'common sense' is used is described by Becker as follows:

> Common sense, in one of its meanings, can delude us. That common sense is the traditional wisdom of the tribe, the *mélange* of 'what everybody knows', that children learn as they grow up, the stereotypes of everyday life. (Ibid. 49)

Defined in this way, common sense refers to generally held views about the social world which in some cases can, and should be, contradicted, or at least questioned by the social sciences. As Becker describes it, there is the possibility of delusion, of being misled by common sense. This is congruent with this observation made by the anthropologist Alfred Kroeber: 'That a belief is common is as likely to stamp it as a common superstition as a common truth' (Kroeber, 1952: 27). From this perspective, generally held beliefs about the nature of crime, criminals, deviance and associated themes, need to be carefully scrutinized and, if necessary, challenged. This challenge, though, involves more than just setting the record straight by providing 'factual' information. Fundamentally, it is to do with the taken-for-granted meanings of these categories. They are not neutral objects, given in nature, but are social constructions, and as such are the outcome of processes involving relationships of power. As Pat Carlen says: 'the very task of theory is to engage in a struggle over the "meaning of things" (including all material and ideological constructs)' (Carlen, 1992: 62).

Common sense is particularly active in debates about crime and criminals, and participants will, of course, insist that theirs is the 'no nonsense' rather than the 'delusion' variety. Over the years a steady stream of politicians, journalists, researchers and practitioners have, sometimes tentatively, sometimes confidently, explained the 'causes of crime', or announced a treatment/punishment package that they believe will actually work. We have had a bewildering galaxy of causal explanations, taking in bad genes, chromosome deficiencies, deformed personalities, unemployment, deprivation, trendy parents, lone parents, trendy lone parents, simple greed, blocked opportunities, peer group pressure, status frustration, too much money, too little money and artificial colouring in fish fingers. Suggested treatment/punishment regimes have been equally wide ranging, and some of them have been tried out. Thus offenders have been incarcerated in hulks on the river Thames, transported to Australia, hanged, pelted with eggs in village stocks, tortured in dungeons, given short sharp shocks in detention centres, injected with mind altering drugs, sterilized, made to face their victims, sent on safari to Africa and locked up in prison. Each of these wildly varying causes and treatments may very well represent common sense for some people.

Setting the scene

This first chapter will indicate some of the basic conceptual debates within criminology. This will entail a preliminary examination of how the academic terrain of criminology may be mapped out, and some of the attendant difficulties involved in defining the core terms 'crime' and 'deviance'. The chapters that follow will examine these issues in greater detail.

One of the tasks of criminology is to unravel, or deconstruct, the concept of crime and in the process challenge common-sense understandings that are taken for granted. It is not uncommon for politicians and journalists, for instance, to ignore the complex structures and processes within which crime and criminality are constituted, and to rely instead on a dangerous rhetoric whereby crime is reduced to a simple causal factor (see, for example, current debates about lone parents and absent fathers). Critically questioning what is meant by 'crime' opens up a whole range of questions lying at the heart of the criminological enterprise such as:

1. *What type of crime?* It is commonplace for crime to be discussed as if it was more or less one specific type of behaviour, and the emphasis is usually on 'conventional' crime such as burglary and robbery. 'Crime', though, covers a vast number of quite different sorts of activities, including white-collar and corporate crime, domestic violence, ram-raiding, child sexual abuse, and rape.

2. *Explanations of crime?* Clearly, given the wide range of possibilities, it is futile to believe that one explanation can be found which covers all crime. Furthermore, even if one particular type of crime is examined, the problems involved in seeking out an explanation are still enormous. In fact, if we narrowed it down to one particular person who stole a bar of chocolate from a store, trying to explain why they did it raises immensely complex issues.

3. *Who decides what is a crime?* On one level, crime only exists because laws exist; therefore crime is not a fixed, absolute quality of an act. Over the years laws change and vary from one society to another. On another level, given that certain laws exist, we have to consider the processes involved whereby certain crimes and criminals are selected by enforcement agencies and dealt with by the courts.

4. *When does a crime exist?* This is an intriguing question. Some criminologists, loosely described as 'realists' – and not to be confused with left realists discussed later – approach crime statistics as if there exists a real, objective amount of crime 'out there'. The task, then, is to develop suitable methods for accurately measuring these crimes. Others take an 'institutionalist' view and argue that crime rates are socially constructed: that is, they are produced by organizational behaviour and various subjective processes on the part of, say, the police. More extreme versions go further and argue that 'crime' itself does not have an independent existence, but is socially constructed. Thus crime is

seen as a social entity created not by an offender, but by control agents who, in specific cases, designate an act as 'criminal'. Using this reasoning they reject, for example, the view that last night a certain number of cases of 'threatening behaviour' occurred in the town centre, and yet only some were discovered, the remainder forming part of the 'dark figure' of crime. For institutionalists, because this offence is dependent on interpretations by, say, the police, it cannot exist as a 'real' thing detached from these interpretive processes. Crime is therefore not conceptualized in the same way that, for instance, the number of individuals carrying the Aids virus is conceptualized. Some have argued that a crime only exists as a social entity when a court finds a person guilty.

It is important to appreciate that debates regarding the definition of key terms are not merely semantic quarrels, a luxurious digression from the real business of criminology. Because phenomena such as crime and deviance are not theoretically neutral objects waiting 'out there' to be identified and analyzed, it is necessary to consider seriously how best to conceptualize these areas of study. How they are conceptualized will have profound implications for the types of theories developed. Unfortunately, for a large part of its history academic criminology has often not suspended what Colin Sumner calls 'a commonsensical acceptance of these categories' (Sumner, 1990: 26). As a result, many analyses have proceeded within a conceptual framework built upon 'what everyone knows', with crime and deviance treated as if they were non-problematical, ahistorical categories of harmful/immoral behaviour. This is not necessarily because criminologists have been, or are, unaware of the conceptual difficulties inherent in these categories. In practice, the tendency nowadays is for the criminologist to put the debate to one side because it is not thought relevant to the particular project in hand. The bracketing off of these fundamental conceptual debates is, perhaps, most vividly apparent when the mass media – say, television – invite a criminologist to comment on a crime-related issue. Due to the structural constraints imposed by the genre itself, with its demands for bite-sized nuggets of sagacity, the criminologist who launches into a detailed critique of the concept of crime is unlikely to be asked back again.

The complexity of these definitional issues makes life difficult for writers of introductory textbooks, and for those delivering introductory lectures in criminology. Usually the problems are resolved, or at least temporarily ameliorated, by offering a brief discussion on why defining criminology is complex, and why basic terms such as 'crime' and 'deviance' are difficult to define and measure. Following an overview, *en passant*, of 'problems with crime statistics', and 'crime as a socially constructed entity', the rest of the chapters or lectures may proceed, sustained by a few working definitions.

This partly accounts for the heavy use of inverted commas in such texbooks (or, in the case of a lecture, the frequent use of jiggling fingers as sign language for inverted commas). The vocabulary of criminology is replete with terms requiring this treatment, for example, 'true' or 'real' crime rates, the 'dark figure' of crime, 'deviant', 'mad', 'bad', 'pervert', 'immoral', 'meaningless violence', 'hooligan', 'undersocialized', 'sick', 'maladjusted', 'hyperactive', and so on. Essentially, the message being transmitted, quite correctly, is that these are risky concepts.

Criminology

It would be reasonable for students of criminology to ask at the outset: What is criminology and what do criminologists do? The complexities surrounding this apparently simple enquiry can be indicated by noting that it is not unusual for elderly criminologists still to be debating these questions as they head for their dotage. The term 'criminology' obviously suggests that 'crime' lies at its core, and the *Shorter Oxford Dictionary* stretches the definition to 'the scientific study of crime'. This, however, merely points the student in a general direction. As a definition it is loaded with interesting epistemological problems. From a more academic viewpoint, *A Dictionary of Criminology* defines criminology as:

> The study of crime, of attempts to control it, and attitudes to it. Crime is interpreted in its widest sense, so as to include minor as well as major law-breaking, and also conduct which, but for the special status or role of those involved, would be regarded as law-breaking; e.g. excessive punishment of children by parents, antisocial practices of commercial undertakings. (Walsh and Poole, 1983: 56)

Moreover a glance at the recently published *The Oxford Handbook of Criminology* (Maguire, Morgan and Reiner, 1994), indicates the wide range of activities in which criminology takes an interest: the politics of law and order; crime data; violent, white-collar, professional and organized crime; crime prevention; policing; pre-trial processes; sentencing policies; probation and community sanctions; prisons; 'race', gender and mental disorder and crime; victims.

And what of 'deviance'? If criminology is the study of crime, can criminologists study deviance and still work within recognized academic parameters? During the 1960s a large number of academics, some of whom had previously described themselves as criminologists, began to call themselves sociologists of deviance. This signalled a shift from the study of crime, as such, to the study of a broader range of rule-breaking activities, some illegal, some not. Today there are those who continue the sociology of deviance tradition, but academics have on the whole reverted back to the preferred label of criminologist, though they may well engage in the study of what they see as non-criminal forms of deviance.

Although there are clearly basic parameters whereby criminology has an identity and recognizable shape, it is by no means a totally integrated, theoretically homogeneous discipline. Internal divisions and disputes can be outlined as follows.

A range of disciplines

Over the years, those describing themselves as criminologists have based their work on many different academic disciplines, first one, then another, becoming dominant. As Stan Cohen puts it: 'Somewhat like a parasite, criminology attaches itself to its host subjects (notably, law, psychology, psychiatry, and sociology) and drew from them methods, theories and credibility' (Cohen, 1988: 4). At the same time, representatives of the various disciplines have given temporary attention to issues of crime and criminality, without, as it were, leaving their original discipline and emigrating to criminology. Frances Heidensohn (1989: 3) paints a suitable image:

> crime has sometimes featured as a social science tourist attraction, a Taj Mahal or Tower of Pisa, which everyone visits – once. Hence major theorists such as Durkheim, Parsons or Merton have made key but brief appearances on the crime scene.

Competing focuses

Criminologists continue to debate whether the proper focus of criminological study should be the offender, the offence, reactions to offending, the victim, or various combinations.

Competing agenda

There are extensive debates within criminology regarding what the discipline should really be aiming to achieve. Should it, for example, concern itself in the main with investigating the causes of crime, or with providing data and ideas useful in terms of penal or policing policy? Or should it be part of a struggle for civil liberties or reform of the criminal justice system? The range of possibilities is immense.

Rival theories

Reflecting broader debates within the social sciences, criminologists have over the years subscribed to rival theoretical schools such as functionalism, Marxism, interactionism and phenomenology, to take sociological criminology as an example.

Varieties of methodology

Again reflecting more general debates and developments within the social sciences, criminologists have argued the case for a range of different research methods: quantitative and qualitative; positivist and phenomenological; dispassionate and politically committed, and so on.

Political orientations

Although not always explicitly stated, criminology, like any social science, is an academic terrain containing various competing political orientations. Disputes are not always restricted to traditional political antagonists: sometimes the most vitriolic exchanges are found among those ostensibly situated within the same political grouping.

Crime

Standard definitions of crime equate it with behaviour that breaks the criminal law. The term is also used to denote a single event, for example, 'a crime was committed last night', or such events collectively, as in 'crime today is a major problem'. Dictionary definitions will generally add an evaluative dimension such as 'evil act'. Although at first glance these statements may appear uncontroversial, they are in need of some discussion. Indeed, there are significant conceptual issues at stake here, though as I have said, they are not always addressed, even within criminology. In this context we can endorse what Colin Sumner (1990: 26) has written:

> The first step of any intellectually rigorous enquiry into matters of crime and deviance must be to suspend a commonsensical acceptance of these categories and to investigate the social relationships, ideologies and contexts which combine to form them and give specific historical meaning.

Writers sympathetic to this view will endeavour to challenge generally accepted assumptions regarding what crime and deviance are, what criminals are like, and so on. This does not mean that all criminologists are agreed on how best to conceptualize these phenomena. In an analysis of criminology and the state, Robert Reiner (1988: 138) raises one of these conceptual debates. He begins by giving a standard legal textbook definition of crime as: 'an illegal act, omission or event . . . the principle consequence of which is that the offender, if he is detected and it is decided to prosecute, is prosecuted by or in the name of the State'. Following this he quotes an often cited and, from the perspective of jurisprudence, definitive statement by Lord Atkin in a 1931 case:

> The domain of criminal jurisprudence can only be ascertained by examining what acts at any particular period are declared by the State to be crimes, and the only common nature they will be found to possess is that they are prohibited by the State. (Ibid. 138)

Reiner uses these statements as a vehicle for making the point that lawyers have for a long time accepted that no human activity is, in an absolute sense, criminal. On the same theme, he also notes a famous observation made by the labelling theorist Howard Becker, which caused a stir among criminologists in the 1960s: 'deviance is *not* a quality of the act the person commits, but rather a consequence of the application by others of rules and sanctions' (Ibid. 138). This, says Reiner, 'may have been news to criminology, but it was platitudinous to criminal lawyers'.

There are a number of important conceptual issues lying just below the surface here, which take us beyond the point that Reiner is making. The observant will have noticed, for instance, that though Reiner is referring to crime, in the quotation Becker uses the term 'deviance'. This raises the question, to what extent can these two terms be used interchangeably? However, the specific point being made by Reiner can be commented on. It is true that the judge, Lord Atkin, and the sociologist, Becker, are both stressing that crime and deviance respectively are relative concepts. In other words, that no act possesses an inherent quality of 'crime' or 'deviance'. A close scrutiny of what Atkin and Becker are saying, though, shows that they are approaching this idea from different directions, so that it means different things. Atkin is saying that what is defined as criminal depends upon the nature of the criminal law in that society. And, by inference, within a particular society the law changes over time, and also varies between one society and another at the same moment in time. So, although law may be necessary, at least as far as the eye can see into the future, the nature of that law – what is in a legal sense banned – is always contingent on the nature of that society. The law, therefore, does not express absolute moral strictures. As it happens, this idea (in the context of deviance) is discussed by Becker (1963: 9) a few pages on from the quotation given by Reiner above: 'deviance is created by society . . . social groups create deviance by making the rules whose infraction constitutes deviance.' In the passage quoted by Reiner, Becker is looking at the relative nature of deviance from a different point of view to this. In the earlier passage the focus is on *specific* acts which are labelled as 'deviant', not because they are inherently deviant, but because of a process of interaction between the 'deviant' and those in a position to apply the label. Unlike Atkin, Becker is going further than simply referring to the defining framework created by an already existing set of rules at a general level. He is referring to particular cases and the processes at work whereby deviance is socially constructed. This is to shift the emphasis away from the factors that 'cause' the behaviour in the first place, to the dynamics involved in the definition of *some* of these behaviours as 'deviant'.

This discussion of Becker directs attention to the actual processes of criminalization and deviantization: that is, to how the law operates in practice. This was not what Lord Atkin was referring to. Although the law may appear to be a tightly formulated and impersonal set of codified legal rules, it is often ambiguous and less clear-cut. Furthermore, in practice the criminal law is locked into a whole series of organizational demands and processes, as well as being subject to individual interpretations. All of this will have enormous implications for the way in which crime is constructed within a particular society. The policing of the 1984–85 miners' strike, for instance, illustrates well how legal statutes and common law powers can, via police discretion, provide an extremely flexible resource. The highly discretionary dimension continued into the courts:

> The role of judges and the courts during the strike have been equally questionable. With regard to the criminal law, most controversial of all has been the systematic use by magistrates of restrictive bail conditions to prevent miners from effectively picketing or participating in the strike. Magistrates have forged close relationships with the police, have declared their hostility to striking miners and have accepted the wide discretion used by the police in defining offences. (Fine and Millar, 1985: 14)

Measuring crime

Finally, as part of this preliminary look at the notion of crime, it will be useful to examine briefly attempts to measure the amount, nature and distribution of crime in society. At this stage questions of reliability and usefulness need not concern us (these will be part of the more detailed discussion of criminal statistics in the next chapter). The main aim is to indicate the sources of information available and to relate these to conceptualizations of crime.

Official crime statistics

Criminal statistics for England and Wales are published annually by the Home Office (in the publication *Criminal Statistics*). These are the crime figures that are reproduced in the mass media accompanied by, if the figures show a decrease on the previous year, a sigh of relief – or, if they show an increase, by a sigh of anxiety. For a government, a decrease will signal an opportunity for self-congratulation that its criminal justice policies are working; an increase is obviously more of a problem, and can stimulate wonderous verbal sorcery from government sources in an effort to vindicate their policies.

The figures themselves are based on what are called 'notifiable offences' recorded by the police forces of England and Wales, which means that if someone was charged with such an offence, they could elect to be tried in a Crown Court. Thus the more serious offences are meant to be in this category. However, although offences such as homicide and rape are included, some of the offences so classified will be seen by many people as not particularly serious. Supposedly less serious 'summary offences' (made up largely of motoring offences), which are dealt with by the magistrates' courts, are not recorded in the crime statistics. There are, however, figures available for 'persons proceeded against', and these add up to about three times the number of persons convicted or cautioned for notifiable offences. The latest figures in *Criminal Statistics* (for 1994) show that in England and Wales just over five and a quarter million offences were recorded by the police.

Victim surveys

These have become increasingly popular over the last few years in Britain and in the United States. They can be incorporated into a conservative or a radical criminological tradition, and they reflect a growth in that field of criminology called victimology (cf. Walklate, 1989). Victim surveys are based on asking people if they have been the victim of a crime, usually over a twelve-month period, and whether they reported this to the police. Various supplementary questions may then be asked. In this country the largest victim surveys are the British Crime Surveys carried out under the auspices of the Home Office in 1982, 1984, 1988 and 1992 to date. As well as these national surveys, a number of smaller-scale, localized surveys have been carried out, and these purport to provide more detailed in-depth data on victim experiences.

One of the aims of a victim survey is to gather supplementary or alternative information to that provided by official statistics, and, in particular, to obtain some idea of the number of offences that are not reported to the police by the public, and therefore not recorded. In this context it should be noted that in some cases crimes are reported, but are then not considered to be crimes by the police. Inevitably, and using common-sense language, all victim surveys show that there is more crime committed than appears in official statistics. The concept used here is the 'dark figure' of crime.

It is frequently pointed out that the British Crime Surveys indicate that, because of a lack of reporting by the public, only around one in four crimes committed are recorded in official statistics. This is an average figure derived from a widely varying propensity to report, depending on the nature of the offence as perceived by the victim. Criminal damage (vandalism), for instance, is much less likely to be reported than the theft of a car. The one-in-four ratio, though, has to be treated with caution, in that some categories of offence used in the British Crime Surveys are different to those used by the police, and there are certain offences which, by definition, will not be picked up by such surveys, for example, shoplifting and fraud. In fact, Sparks, Genn and Dodd (1977), suggest that about eleven times more crime is committed than is recorded in official statistics; this gives an enormous 'dark figure' of crime.

Self-report studies

These are questionnaires asking people if they have committed any of the offences listed. Clearly it is asking a lot of someone to admit to breaking the law, and so self-report studies strive to minimize potential problems by stressing anonymity, and by using back-up data from official records and even polygraphs (lie detectors). Depending on the sample used, researchers will attempt to correlate amounts and types of offending behaviour with variables such as class and age.

Since their inception self-report studies have consistently discovered significantly more widespread offending among the general public than official information would suggest. Again, though, it has to be stressed that this kind of blanket statement is in need of qualification. The seriousness of offence and frequency of offending have to be considered, along with the actual methods of research used, before reaching too many conclusions.

Police and court records

These provide another, official, source of information for criminologists. Unlike the sources above, here we are dealing directly with individuals who have been defined and processed by the criminal justice system, this procedure culminating in a conviction or a caution. Maguire (1994: 271) mentions an eye-catching piece of information derived from these sources:

> not many more than one in ten offences recorded by the police result in a caution or a conviction: in other words, in the vast majority of cases, nothing is officially

known about those responsible. Indeed, it has been further calculated . . . that only about one in fifty of the comparable crimes identified by the British Crime Survey result in a conviction – a figure which drops as low as one in 200 where 'vandalism' (criminal damage) is concerned.

Varieties of crime

With the above as a backdrop, we can return to a discussion of the concept of crime. It should be apparent that the word 'crime' can crop up in various contexts, and refer to a variety of phenomena. This can be illustrated further by listing some of the chief ways in which 'crime' is used, though in each case it is describing different phenomena:

1. Crimes deemed to be such by a court finding a defendant guilty.

2. Crimes recorded by the police as notifiable offences.

3. Crimes reported to the police by the public.

4. Crimes reported to, or discovered by, the police, but not recorded by them.

5. The dark figure of crime.

6. Crimes actually committed.

7. There is a seventh, rather different category that could be added. This is where the term 'crime' is used to describe activities that are not at present against the law, but from the perspectives of some observers are wrong or immoral. Thus someone might say, 'It's a crime the way he treats his wife', meaning that although not illegal, the husband's behaviour is 'wrong', and perhaps should be made illegal. On a more complex level, this principle has been applied to such things as racism, sexism and imperialism (see Schwendinger and Schwendinger, 1975).

When discussing the measurement of crime in society, some criminologists have used the iceberg analogy, in which recorded crime is seen as merely the tip of the iceberg. Whatever the ultimate value of this analogy, it can be used as a basis for illustrating graphically the seven ways of conceptualizing crime noted above (see Figure 1.1). Proportions are based upon artistic licence rather than reality.

This discussion can be extended to include the notion of a 'crime rise' and the notion of a 'criminal', to point to similar conceptual problems when using these terms.

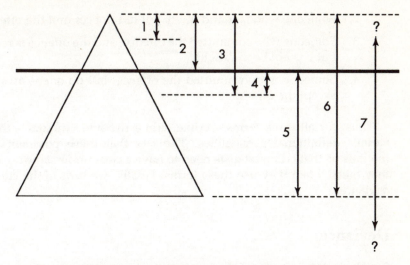

Figure 1.1 Profile of the seven conceptions of crime.

Varieties of crime rise

As Jason Ditton (1979) has shown, the notion of a 'crime rise' can mean a number of things:

1. As a result of new laws, acts that were previously non-criminal now become criminal.

2. More criminal acts are discovered.

3. Methods of classification change so that acts previously defined as non-criminal are now criminal.

4. There is more mass media coverage of crime.

5. More criminal acts are committed.

Varieties of criminal

As with 'crime' and 'crime rises', the term 'criminal' can also be used to mean different things. An interesting question (with an answer that is less obvious than might be thought) is, what is a criminal? Here are a number of possible answers:

1. Someone who really committed the offence and is found guilty by a court.

2. Someone who is found guilty but did not commit the offence.

3. Someone who committed the offence, and the offence is recorded, but has not been caught.

4. Someone who committed the offence, but no one is aware of it, except the offender.

Thus, for all three terms – crime, crime rise and criminal – there are various definitional possibilities. The fact that these possibilities exist reminds us that criminologists need to have a clear understanding of what they mean when they use these terms. Finally, we turn to the concept of deviance.

Deviance

Sociological definitions of deviance generally contain two elements: non-conforming behaviour with respect to accepted norms, and strong disapproval of such behaviour. Deviance can therefore be criminal or non-criminal. This view of deviance is illustrated by the following examples: 'Deviance may be defined as non-conformity to a given norm, or set of norms, which are accepted by a significant number of people in a community or society' (Giddens, 1993: 116); 'behaviour which somehow departs from what a group expects to be done or what it considers the desirable way of doing things' (Cohen, 1971: 9); 'the violation of the accepted norms or social rules of a group or society . . . the reaction to them is invariably one of disapproval, fear, suspicion, hostility or outrage' (Bilton et al., 1981: 563).

The advent of a sceptical – and, on one level, radical – 'new deviancy theory' in the 1960s marked the beginning of an attempt seriously to interrogate the concept of 'deviance', though by then the concept had had a relatively short lifespan. Although they were not necessarily answered, this led to a number of critical questions being placed on the agenda:

• Whose rules are being broken?

• In whose interests do these rules operate?

• Why are the rules there in the first place?

• Who is doing the disapproving?

The last question, asking *who* is doing the disapproving, is a good starting point for a discussion of the concept of deviance. One of the central sociological problems in this context concerns the issue of a consensus: that is, a general agreement or majority view over what is considered acceptable behaviour. Traditional criminologists have tended to assume that there is a consensus, which is then translated into phrases such as 'public opinion'. Functionalist approaches to deviance, for example, have built their work around the assumption of a consensus as the product of socialization processes. Those outside the posited consensus are then viewed as either deviant themselves, or marginal groups whose opinions are perverse and therefore unimportant.

For radical criminologists, or radical sociologists of deviance, especially Marxists, the notion of consensus has proved to be particularly awkward. This is because a capitalist society such as Britain or the United States is seen as being composed of different classes and groups, giving a plurality of cultural formations with different understandings of 'accepted behaviour'. Developing an interactionist perspective, new deviancy theorists such as Edwin Lemert (1967), for instance, saw deviant behaviour as being more or less evenly distributed throughout society. The search for the initial causes of deviance is seen as futile, because causes will vary enormously from one individual or group to another. The emphasis is therefore on reactions to some of the behaviour, reactions which lead to the application of the label 'deviant'. From this perspective, only some of the rule breakers are discovered and labelled. Sociologically, then, these are 'deviants', and it is their behaviour and reactions to it that should be the proper concern of sociology. Consequently, notions of consensus are spirited away, and attention is turned to the labelling process and the unfortunates who are unlucky enough to be selected by those possessing the power to label.

However, the arbitrariness inherent in this model suggests that in theory literally anyone could be selected for doing anything. In practice, though, behaviours earmarked as deviant are not randomly selected. Therefore, consideration should be given to the nature and distribution of the power to accomplish labelling, and the structural settings within which specific labelling processes operate. And there is still the thorny issue of consensus. If a plurality of cultures and subcultures exists in society, each with their own quite different feelings about acceptable and unacceptable behaviour, how is the public labelling of individuals and groups to be made palatable? Outside a totalitarian society, presumably there has to be a degree of public disapproval, some congruence of opinion among the various groups regarding the labelled behaviour. The issue then becomes one of determining the nature and source of this disapproval, by examining, for example, the role of ideology.

Radical criminologists wishing to develop a Marxist approach to understanding deviance also had to grapple with the idea of consensus. This was apparent in the 'new criminology' of Ian Taylor, Paul Walton and Jock Young (1973), where they presented a radical Marxist alternative to new deviancy theory. They rejected the view that a consensus existed, but met problems when actually defining what 'deviance' was. In fact, in this study no definition was forthcoming. They attempted to solve the problem of a consensus by arguing that although there was none, people thought there was, because of the influence of the mass media and education. This suggested that individuals did not really disapprove of certain behaviours that are labelled 'deviant', but at the same time believed that most people did.

In the mid-1970s the Marxist Colin Sumner (1976) developed a different approach. He argued that deviance was best conceived of as a social censure – an adverse judgement – existing at the level of ideology. This is to depart from conceptualizing deviance in terms of actual behaviour. To complicate matters further, at about the same time another Marxist writer, Paul Hirst (1975a), rejected out of hand the project of developing a 'Marxist perspective' on deviance. For him, deviance was a pre-given bourgeois concept, not a Marxist theoretical object, and therefore was not a proper area for study, except in the form of revisionism. So, by the mid-1970s the debates were beginning to intensify.

More recently, so-called left realist criminology has accepted the existence of a consensus with respect to certain sorts of 'conventional' crime. Put simply, this position states that it is absurd to believe that large numbers of people, and especially those who are victims, do not strongly disapprove of crimes such as rape, burglary and robbery. To many people, though, this will appear to be a pretty unremarkable statement. In fact, presented in this way such statements mask complex theoretical issues pertaining to the deviantization of certain defined criminal acts.

The left realist position takes us back to the notion of 'strong public disapproval' whereby deviance is defined, but can deviance be conceived of in crude numerical terms? Furthermore, how do we know that people in general strongly disapprove of a particular type of behaviour or person? Obviously, it is reasonable to make this assumption with respect to some behaviour. However, can we say the same about all examples of so-called deviance as defined in the literature of criminology? Certainly, research does point to a significant consensus among the public with regard to the core areas of the criminal law as generalized categories (cf. Braithwaite, 1989). And West (1982) found that even known offenders disapproved of their children's delinquent behaviour. On the basis of localized crime surveys left realists have argued that 'the major crimes *as presently defined in criminal law*, are agreed upon by the mass of the population' (Young, 1987: 355, original emphasis).

However, even if we accept this proposition uncritically, the range of behaviours constituting the academic study of deviance over the years is much broader than this. A quick glance at the books in the criminology section of a university or college library, where the author has designated the activities as 'deviant', will indicate the possibilities: the blind, Mods and Rockers, Hell's Angels, those with learning difficulties, 'Paki'-bashers', homosexuals, naturists, 'obese' people, school truants, marijuana users and 'topless' barmaids. If a consensus is the lynchpin of a definition of deviance, how is that consensus to be measured? The danger is that a researcher may simply feel, using common sense, that a consensus exists; indeed, they might create a stigmatized group as a result of doing the research. How could feelings of disapproval over a vast range of potential behaviours be ascertained anyway? No national survey, for instance, has been instituted asking people what they feel about all these behaviours; and it would be of only limited value. How do we discover what people 'really' feel, and what does that mean? An individual may nominally be against some behaviour, and yet do it themselves. On the other hand, they may feel that they should pretend to be against something because they believe that everyone else is.

The difficulties surrounding this issue can be summed up with this, albeit crude, scenario. Imagine a sociologist of deviance decides to do research on a specific type of deviant behaviour. How is he or she to know that this *is* an example of deviance? Are they to be debarred from doing this research because deviant status cannot somehow be objectively assessed? Does it matter? Given these sorts of problems we can perhaps understand how tempting it is to dispense with the definitional niceties, and just get on with studying an activity because it can be reasonably assumed that someone, somewhere, will disapprove of it. Unfortunately, as well as ignoring the central conceptual problem, this criterion probably applies to any activity. The question remains: how is deviance to be recognized?

Debates about how deviance and crime should be conceptualized bubbled to the surface with the radicalism of new deviancy theory, post-new deviancy theory, and left criminology, which became influential during the 1960s and 1970s. Many of the writers involved dispensed with the concept of crime because it was so problematic. As Heidensohn (1989: 8) says:

> Since the concept (of crime) is so flexible and the records so unreliable, and so far outside of the control of researchers, there has been a tendency to avoid confrontation, to argue against any engagement with the concept or especially with official records.

And as she points out, for some the solution was to focus on deviance – though the problems are still there in abundance. From the mid-1970s, however, the focus in the main shifted back to 'crime', and conceptual debates about 'deviance' have tended to be shelved. In a recent analysis, Sumner (1990: 15) begins with this telling observation: 'Students still ask "Whatever happened to the theoretical debate about deviance in the early 1970s?" ' He goes on to say that within radical criminology there has been a failure to 'reconceptualize "deviant behaviour" '. Certainly, more recent work has been concerned with reconceptualizing crime rather than deviance.

2 | Measuring crime and criminality

Official statistics
The 'dark figure' of crime
Public reporting
Changes in the law
The role of the police
Ways of seeing
The implications for criminal statistics
Victim surveys
The usefulness of criminal statistics
Local crime surveys and left realism

Official statistics

How much crime?
How many criminals?
How many victims?
It is impossible to give any accurate or straightforward answers to the questions
posed . . . Not only does everything depend on what is meant by 'crime',
'criminals' and 'victims', but even if there were to be broad agreement on the
definition and scope of these basic terms, it is very apparent that most of the
extant methods of measuring the nature and amounts of crime, criminality and
victimization would be inadequate to the task. (Bottomley and Pease, 1986: 1)

Give or take a few qualifications, all criminologists would probably go along
with this sobering assessment, which appears on the first page of an
important analysis of crime data. Criminologists can answer questions (or
find the information) regarding such things as the number of people
residing in HM prisons in England and Wales at a given moment, or the
number of offences of criminal damage recorded by the police in a given
year. The questions posed by Bottomley and Pease, though, refer to

qualitatively different phenomena. In fact, the quotation indicates two issues at stake here. One concerns the accuracy of data, and the other concerns the conceptual meaning of the phenomena that the data purport to represent. Put another way, it is not just a question of how close official statistics are to 'real' amounts of crime; it is also a question of what processes are involved in the construction of such figures and, ultimately, what is meant by crime anyway.

This does not mean that all statistical information pertaining to crime, either official or not, is useless and unworthy of serious attention by criminologists. It does mean, though, that such information has to be treated with extreme caution. Of course, a judicious amount of caution is not always exercised by those who comment on, and use, these statistics, for example in support of a political programme. Furthermore, as Jack Douglas (1971b) has pointed out, criminological knowledge produced by academics can be put to all sorts of nefarious uses by those representing particular ideological interests; to this extent, criminological knowledge can be 'dangerous knowledge'.

There is, however, one question that at the level of common sense may be viewed as one to which criminologists should be able to provide an answer: is there more crime now than there was in the past? This question can form the basis of a more extended discussion.

Echoing Bottomley and Pease, the immediate response has to be that no simple answer can be given, for any engagement with the question necessarily triggers layers of statistical and conceptual problems. To begin with, what is meant by 'the past'? Between the wars? A hundred years ago, or beyond? A crude reading of the official criminal statistics for this century would leave no option but an affirmative answer to the original question. Apart from a few fluctuations – notably a dip at the end of the 1940s, and between 1950 and 1955 – total amounts of crime, and crime rates based upon offences per 100,000 of the population, have continued to rise steadily.

From the turn of the century up to World War One, under 100,000 offences were recorded by the police of England and Wales for each year. In 1993 the figure was over five and a half million; in 1994 it was just over five and a quarter million. The categories of theft and handling stolen goods and burglary add up to 75 per cent of all offences recorded. Vehicle theft is at a particularly high level now; each year around 500,000 vehicles are stolen, a figure which in itself is five times the total number of offences recorded in the first part of this century. Most recorded offences are offences against property – about 95 per cent – and this has remained fairly constant throughout the century. Needless to say, all information of this nature needs careful scrutiny, and especially so if we extend the picture to include international comparisons, for then such factors as different jurisdictions and offence classification systems have to be incorporated into tortuously complicated analyses (for a more detailed up-to-date review of official crime statistics see Maguire, 1994).

Not surprisingly, many will view the increases in recorded crime in Britain, and in many other industrialized nations, with some dismay, seeing them as confirmation that there *is* more crime committed today than in the past. However, even if crimes are simply viewed as objective events waiting 'out there' to be discovered and recorded, there are still huge problems involved in interpreting criminals statistics and making comparisons across time. If conceptual problems relating to the meaning of crime are considered alongside these 'technical' problems, then analyses become more complicated. For the moment, though, it will be useful to concentrate on criminal statistics at a technical level: that is, to examine those factors that will determine their shape and 'accuracy' (there are good, extended discussions in Wiles, 1976a; Jupp, 1989; Maguire, 1994).

The 'dark figure' of crime

The concept of a dark figure of crime has been mentioned earlier, when the iceberg analogy was introduced. It refers to those 'hidden' crimes that are not recorded by the police, and are therefore absent from official statistics. Data from victim surveys are used to estimate the magnitude of this dark figure – Sparks *et al.* (1977) suggest that it is eleven times the official figure, though this latter statistic is an overall average which hides enormous variation between one offence and another.

Whether or not the 'dark figure' is an appropriate way in which to think about crime is an issue that can be left to one side for now. What has to be stressed is that it cannot be assumed that amounts of unrecorded crime have stayed constant throughout history, as the following discussion of some of the main variables determining amounts of recorded crime will illustrate.

Public reporting

Given that about 80 per cent of crime known to the police comes to their attention as a result of information from the public, the willingness of the public to report crime is a crucial factor. Obviously, statistical comparisons across time will need to take this into consideration. As a result of motor insurance being legally compulsory, we can expect very high levels of public reporting and police recording of vehicle theft. Likewise, the spread of household contents insurance, and the requirement to notify the police of loss of property before a claim can be made, will increase the reporting of burglary. With other types of offence – for example, sexual offences, domestic violence and child abuse – the evidence from victim surveys suggests substantial underreporting. Finkelhor's (1979) study of American students, for instance, found that 19.2 per cent of women and 8.6 per cent of men had experienced sexual molestation as children, though only rarely had they disclosed this to another person.

In more recent years there have been increases in amounts of these offences recorded by the police. A plausible argument is that this results as much from such things as greater publicity and improvements in police procedures as from increases in the incidence of such offending.

Other factors to note in the context of public reporting are the spread of telephones, making contact with the police easier, and neighbourhood watch schemes, whose *raison d'être* is to encourage public reporting. There is also the degree of public tolerance of certain sorts of behaviour. If a more sensitized public exists, with a lowered tolerance threshold, then we can expect reporting to increase. Thus the official crime rate can go up as members of a society become more demanding in terms of notions of civility and propriety.

Changes in the law

This factor in itself illustrates the massive problems involved in determining whether or not there is 'really' more crime today than in the past. Over the years new laws are introduced, and others repealed, which means that legal rules are in a constant state of flux. Compared to the early part of this century, the net of criminalized behaviour has widened considerably – for example, with respect to the use of drugs, the treatment of children and commercial fraud. In general terms, then, the further back one goes in history, the more difficult it is to make judgements about the moral health of a society on the basis of criminal statistics, On the other hand, providing there have been no significant recent legislative changes, comparisons between the present and the recent past are more valid.

Changes in the law also involve changes in the counting rules and the classification of offences as imposed upon the police by the Home Office. A most striking, and consequently often referred to, example of this characteristic concerns the offence of criminal damage (vandalism). According to official statistics, in 1976 there were 93,000 offences of criminal damage in England and Wales, whilst in the following year this had increased to 297,400. One explanation might be that during this twelve-month period there was a huge upsurge in criminal damage, an anarchic festival of paint spraying and property destruction. Needless to say, this was not the case. The real reason for the increase was that the 1976 figure excluded criminal damage valued at £20 and under, whilst in 1977 the police had been instructed by the Home Office to record instances of criminal damage valued at this figure and under as well. Of course, relying on monetary value, for any class of offence, will mean that all subsequent figures are influenced by inflation.

The role of the police

In view of the fact that criminal statistics are derived from information supplied by the various police forces, the 'gatekeeping' role of the police is of central importance. The nature of this role will vary over time, as well as between one force (and even one officer) and another. This introduces yet more variables into the process of constructing crime statistics.

The importance of the police can be outlined by distinguishing between a reactive and a proactive dimension. Reactive policing refers to responses to specific incidents by the organization or individual officers. The incident may come to light because of information from the public, or through direct experience. The proactive dimension to the police role is usually associated with general policing policies based upon a mix of Home Office directives, discussions within the police at a national level (for example, via the Association of Chief Police Officers, ACPO), and policies emanating from a particular force. A proactive dimension, however, can exist at the level of the individual too, such as when an officer develops local contacts, or keeps an eye on certain establishments.

All of these various aspects of the police role need to be situated within an organizational as well as broader social structural context. In terms of the organization, note would have to be taken of, for instance, management styles and resources available to a particular police force. The broader social structural context will include the social composition and policing problems pertaining to that forces' area, political pressures from government, legal powers and constraints, modes of accountability, and so on.

Thus we can see that a whole range of factors will be at work shaping the manner in which offences and offenders are dealt with by the police. Obviously, it is absurd to assume that these have been constant through history. All of these factors will, in various ways and in varying degrees, affect the actual decision-making process with respect to amounts and types of offences that are eventually included in the national criminal statistics. This can be illustrated by taking a few key examples.

Fundamentally, the police have to decide if an indictable crime has taken place, and, if so, within which particular category of offence it should be included (remembering that the counting rules are subject to periodic change by the Home Office). For instance, in those cases where no suspect is apprehended it is by no means always unambiguously clear what type of offence is being dealt with. In an assault case, how severe are the victim's injuries? Did the shopper really have a wallet containing £1,000 picked from their pocket? How serious has the criminal damage to be before it is recorded? Furthermore, as we shall see, police officers are part of a complex interactional and interpretive process whereby particular understandings of reality are negotiated (e.g. Bittner, 1967; Cicourel, 1968; Manning, 1977; Tierney, 1987).

At a national and local level police forces will set priorities regarding the targeting of particular types of offence. These law enforcement priorities will be derived from various sources: the Home Office and central government, perceived public anxieties, and plans drawn up by senior officers. At specific moments, the result of this may be a sudden statistical increase in the incidence of a targeted offence, or what appear to be startlingly high levels of illicit drug use and child sexual abuse, or appalling standards of driving in certain police force areas. Hence the necessity of seeing such information as the artefacts of police organization and practice, rather than as a statistical photograph of objective reality. In this context we can note Maguire's (1994: 249) comment that:

> Prior to 1968, there was little consistency between police forces on how many offences were to be recorded when events of these kinds came to their notice. Following the recommendations of the Perks Committee in 1967, clearer 'counting rules' were established . . . which tidied up some of the discrepancies between forces, but at the same time they appear fairly arbitrary and, undoubtedly, understate the relative frequency of some offences.

Other factors associated with the police which could increase or decrease amounts of crime that are recorded, irrespective of 'actual' amounts taking place, can be listed briefly, as follows:

- The number of police officers – this has risen from about 110,000 in 1980 to just under 130,000 today.

- The use of increasingly sophisticated technology, such as computers.

- More efficient systems of administration.

- More expenditure on policing – in England and Wales, 1992–93, total spending on the police was £5.42bn, an 87 per cent rise in real terms since 1979.

Ways of seeing

Having established a broad analytical framework within which policing operates, we can now examine in more detail what is often referred to as 'cop culture' and the bearing that this has on the production of criminal statistics:

An understanding of how police officers see the social world and their role in it – 'cop culture' – is crucial to an analysis of what they do, and their broad political function. It is a commonplace of the now voluminous sociological literature on police operations and discretion that the rank-and-file officer is the primary determinant of policing where it really counts – on the street. (Reiner, 1992: 107)

As a result of the nature of the occupation and the structural pressures to which it is subject, police officers construct shorthand characterizations pertaining to types of public, location and event. In particular, the public become 'dramatis personae' persons of the drama. This process is predicated on the necessity of gathering together the elements of what could be a chaotic and confusing world in order to make sense of it, as well as control it – and sometimes this involves crude stereotyping. In different ways, of course, we are all caught up in this kind of process. However, with respect to the police it is a fundamental occupational requirement, and has important implications for the rest of us. It is well summed up by Cicourel (1968: 67), who says that the police develop:

theories about individuals and groups, morality and immorality, good and bad people, institutions, practices and typifications of community settings, and such theories or conceptions are employed in routine ways . . . the officer's preconstituted typifications and stock of knowledge at hand lead him to prejudge much of what he encounters . . . particular ecological settings, populated by persons with 'known' styles of dress and physical appearance, provide the officer with quick inferences about 'what is going on'.

In this way chaos is transformed into order. There may be rioting in progress at the time, but police typifications allow all events to be understood, meaningfully interpreted, and thus at least mentally ordered:

People are expected to fill categorical niches and fall into line with the commonsense police theory about human nature. The observed facts are assembled under the umbrella of a commonsense theory. The facts are not taken as a means to disconfirm the police theory of human nature. (Manning, 1977: 237)

Broadly speaking, members of the public tend to get assigned to one of two categories: 'respectable' or 'non-respectable'. According to the Policy Studies Institute (PSI) report on the Metropolitan Police: 'In this scale the "respectable" working class and the suburban middle class stand highest, while the "underclass" of the poor and the rootless, together with groups regarded as deviant, such as homosexuals or hippies, stand lowest' (Smith and Grey, 1985: 435). Phil Scraton discusses how these understandings become part of police practices: 'The regular, institutionalized use of these images leads to their incorporation into the general ideology of police operations and practices. They . . . form a central part of the political management of communities' (Scraton, 1985: 105). So what, from a police point of view, does the *ideal* citizen look like? This question is perhaps answered most succinctly by the PSI report. Referring to police culture, the report says: 'It is a milieu in which people who do not speak with a London or other regional accent and men who do not dress like football managers are definitely made to feel out of place' (Smith and Grey, 1985: 435).

The implications for criminal statistics

Taken together, the cirumstances outlined above constitute a complex mix of factors shaping police policies and practices across the board. The nature and impact of these factors, for example, political and public pressure, organizational and managerial demands, and police ideologies and culture, will not, of course, remain constant in terms of their contribution to the construction of recorded crime. If changes in the law, methods of classifying offences and the propensity of the public to report crime to the police are also taken into account, then the hazards inherent in using official criminal statistics from different moments in history as a measure of the moral health of a society become apparent.

Although the primary focus of this section is on amounts of crime as represented by these statistics, we might note that the issues raised in our discussion of policing will have important ramifications for other aspects of crime and criminality as socially constructed phenomena. The types of offences that end up in the statistics and act as one representation of the 'crime problem' – for example, conventional property crime rather than corporate fraud – will be partly a function of the activities of the police. So too will be the types of offenders who are officially labelled and processed by the criminal justice system. We will return to these issues at a later stage. For the moment what our discussion illustrates is that the criminal statistics are the product of dynamic and complex processes involving the law, the police, offenders, victims and witnesses.

Victim surveys

Essentially, the analysis so far of criminal statistics has taken place within a more or less common-sensical framework, employing an accepted and familiar definition of crime. This has meant questioning the accuracy of those statistics, though there have been some hints of other, conceptual, agendas. The analysis, therefore, has been situated within the more conventional parameters associated with criminological positivism. Biderman and Reiss (1967) describe this approach as 'realism' (not to be confused with left realism). From the point of view of realism, the problems with criminal statistics are – to use the term I introduced earlier – basically technical. That is, there is an assumption that a 'real', objective amount of crime exists in society, but only some of it is actually recorded. Therefore, there is a 'dark figure' of crime. Looked at from this perspective, the task of criminology is to improve the tools of research in order to determine as accurately as possible the posited 'real' amount of crime. Institutional processes involving interpretation and negotiation, whereby criminal statistics and the 'crime problem' are constructed, are thus neglected in these analyses.

On occasion, some researchers have taken this way of considering crime a step further and have treated recorded crime as if it is a slice of a large homogeneous cake, a representative sample of the whole. The same sort of logic has been applied to convicted offenders, leading to the conclusion that if the prisons are mainly populated by poorer people, then poorer people must be more involved in crime than the better-off. The problem is neatly summed up by Steven Box (1981: 181):

> It is as though some researchers would have approached the question of how many colours there are in Joseph's coat by placing one fragment under a microscope and declaring, after studying the fragment intensely, that the coat's multi-colouredness was a myth for only one colour had been revealed after the most elaborate scientific investigation.

In recent years victim surveys have become increasingly popular, as, indeed, has that field of study called victimology, now accepted as one of the normal concerns of criminology:

> Studying victims has become one of the growth industries of criminology. Since 1980 there has been an extraordinarily rapid increase in national and local victim surveys and in studies of the impact of crime, of victim needs and services. Academic research has been mirrored and encouraged by the growth of dynamic and influential groups set up to help victims and to promote their interests. (Zedner, 1994: 1207)

For realists there are obvious attractions in victim surveys in that they seem to offer a technique for discovering and measuring more accurately amounts of crime. At the same time, victim surveys have attracted the attention of some less conventional, more radical criminologists. One of the attractions for those with a more sceptical mind than realists, is that victim surveys appear to bypass the institutional processes and allow the researcher to get to the heart of the matter directly. Furthermore, victim surveys have been latched onto by criminologists on the right and on the left, with right-wing versions tending to mobilize findings around a 'get tough' law and order stance, whilst left-wing versions have used them to argue for general improvements in the lives of oppressed sections of society. (An awkward issue is that sometimes victims are also offenders.)

While there are many important debates and issues surrounding the uses and abuses of victim surveys, in this section the focus is (again) essentially on their value as ways of measuring amounts of crime in a society, that is, we are still operating within a more or less 'realist' framework.

Victimology

Victimology, through the use of victim surveys, is centrally concerned with gathering information on the experiences of victims of crime. Broadly speaking, two different traditions can be discerned. At its inception in the United States during the 1940s (with the work of Von Hentig, 1948, and Wertham, 1949) the emphasis was on the psychological characteristics and social circumstances – for example, 'lifestyles' – of those most likely to find themselves victims of crime. Whilst this tradition continues today, during the 1960s, and again in the United States, a second tradition focusing on measuring the extent of hidden crime developed.

Victim precipitation is perhaps the term most closely identified with the first of these traditions. This was introduced into the vocabulary of criminology by Wolfgang (1958), and arose from his analysis of homicides. For Wolfgang, victim precipitation had a very precise meaning, namely, that in a significant number of cases which he looked at, the homicide victim was the first to use force. Other writers, however, began to use the term more loosely, so that it came to refer to instances where victims actually provoked or hastened their own victimization, for example by the way they dressed or the places they visited. The classic study based upon this sort of reasoning – and for obvious reasons much criticized by feminists – is Amir's (1971) investigation of rape, where he argues that in the cases he examined, almost one-fifth of victims precipitated the assault (for example, gave out the 'wrong signals').

More recent work (e.g. Sparks *et al.*, 1977) has tried to develop more sophisticated models of victimization. Here, a range of factors such as age-linked vulnerability, lifestyle management, a lack of power to complain, and types of neighbourhood, are analyzed. This kind of research shifts the focus of attention away from the perceived culpability, or even stupidity, of the victim, towards other socially structured factors over which the victim may have little control.

The second tradition began during the 1960s in the United States with large-scale national surveys of victims' experiences. Their primary aim was to shed some light on the dark figure of crime, and such surveys are therefore particularly relevant to the theme of this section.

Surveying victims

The first British example of a victim survey at a national level is, in a modest way, found in the General Household Survey of 1972, which included a question about being the victim of a burglary. The first specialized mass survey, though only carried out in London, was by Sparks *et al.* (1977). In 1982 the first of a series of large-scale national surveys – the British Crime Survey – specifically designed to cover a wide range of offences and bring to light hidden crime, was carried out under the auspices of the Home Office (Mayhew and Hough, 1983). Since then a number of British Crime Surveys have been completed (Hough and Mayhew, 1985; Mayhew *et al.*, 1989; Mayhew and Maung, 1993).

Information is gathered by asking household members aged over 15 years a set of standardized questions. Up to the 1992 survey, the households used were chosen randomly from electoral registers; however, for the 1992 survey the postal address code was used. This change was made because of earlier criticisms that a significant minority of people are in fact absent from electoral registers. The main questions in these surveys are concerned with people's experiences as victims of crime, though other, supplementary questions are included: for instance, questions relating to the fear of crime or decisions not to report an offence to the police.

The British Crime Surveys suggest that about four times as much crime is committed as is officially recorded in the criminal statistics, though other surveys have suggested even higher figures (e.g. Sparks *et al.*, 1977). Supporters of these surveys have argued that as well as providing a more accurate picture of criminal victimization in general, they also bring to light the experiences of particularly vulnerable groups whose victimization rates were hitherto grossly underestimated by official data. As an example, the latest British Crime Survey found between 130,000 and 140,000 racial attacks for the year, though it has been suggested that the 'true figure' could be as high as a third of a million. This contrasts dramatically with the 7,793 racial attacks recorded by the police in 1991.

Because victim surveys inevitably discover relatively large amounts of previously 'hidden' crime, they can generate increased public fear of crime. This perhaps accounts for the general tone of British Crime Surveys, which has been one of balanced reassurance. Thus, in the style of the presenters of TV's *Crime Watch UK* at the end of each programme, efforts are made to point out that as individuals the chances of being a victim of a serious crime are not especially high: for example, in the words of the 1989 survey, the 'statistically average' adult will have their home burgled only once in every 37 years.

Obviously, such statistics, being averages, mask the inequalities in victimization rates between one neighbourhood and another, one type of housing and another, and one group of people and another; council house tenants, for example, are more likely to be victims of burglary than owner-occupiers. It was this sort of critique that helped to stimulate an interest in more detailed, localized victim surveys in Britain during the 1980s. By focusing on specific neighbourhoods, and using research methods that were thought to be more sensitive in nature, the aim was to gain more valuable, detailed knowledge of patterns of victimization. In the main, these localized studies have been carried out by criminologists sympathetic to the so-called left realist perspective, and have been sponsored by local Labour Party controlled councils. As such, this research has been incorporated into a left-realist call to 'take crime seriously'. This links data generated by victim surveys to what left realists see as a socialist reform programme in areas such as policing and crime prevention policies.

Findings

It is true that by their nature victim surveys show higher levels of crime than do official statistics, and so send out a message that there is even more crime being committed than we thought. However, once a number of similar surveys have been conducted, and it is possible to draw out trends over a suitable period of time, then a different picture may emerge. A good example of this is discussed by Bottomley and Pease (1986).

Between 1971 and 1981 the number of domestic burglaries in the official statistics rose from 204,560 to 349,692, confirming widespread fears that burglary was growing significantly in frequency. As Bottomley and Pease say, this could mean that the proportion of burglaries reported to, and recorded by, the police remained constant, and the increase actually happened. Or, it could mean that there was no increase, but more burglaries were reported and recorded. In this context the data from the 1972, 1973, 1979 and 1980 General Household Surveys make interesting reading. As mentioned earlier, these surveys asked if households had been the victims of a burglary during the past twelve months. Surprisingly, these surveys found no increase in the incidence of burglary in private households over the period from 1971. The first British Crime Survey was conducted in 1982 and asked for recollections from 1981. The figure for household burglaries from this survey was within 1.3 per cent of the figure from the 1980 General Household Survey (when people were interviewed in 1979, and asked to recall the previous twelve months). This suggests that there was no massive and sudden increase in burglary missed by the General Household Survey of 1980. In conclusion, Bottomley and Pease (1986: 23) state: 'This surely clinches the view that the increase in burglary during the 1970s was almost completely illusory.'

According to the first British Crime Survey, the volume of crime was four times that recorded by the police, a similar figure to that found by the latest survey. This ratio, however, only applies to those offences directly comparable with those compiled by the police; one-third of British Crime Survey offence groups are in fact not directly comparable. As a result, the survey does not purport to offer a more accurate picture of victimization rates for *all* offences. Picking up on the earlier discussion of burglaries, during the 1980s the rate of increase in burglaries found by the British Crime Surveys matched that in official statistics (this also applied to vehicle-related theft and other personal theft).

Local victim surveys

Although sympathetic to the basic principle of focusing on victims of crime, some criminologists argue that because of the large sweeps involved, mass surveys are unable to draw out deeper, more detailed information on the nature and distribution of crime:

> Inevitably, therefore, national crime surveys obscure the way in which victimization is concentrated in different communities and among particular groups within those communities . . . By drawing samples from small neighbourhoods, these (local crime) surveys have described much more accurately the experiences of different sections of the population. (Anderson *et al.*, 1991: 5)

As a consequence, since the mid-1980s there has been a parallel growth in localized crime surveys (Kinsey, 1984 (Merseyside); Jones *et al.*, 1986 (Islington, London); Crawford *et al.*, 1990 (Islington); Anderson *et al.*, 1990 (Edinburgh); Anderson *et al.*, 1991 (Edinburgh); Hartless *et al.*, 1995 (Glasgow)). One of these will be examined in order to illustrate the sort of information these local surveys generate.

The first Islington survey

According to Jones *et al.* (1986: 5) *The Islington Crime Survey* is much more focused than the national surveys and 'embraces a much greater part of the whole process of criminalization':

> the pattern of victimization, the impact of crime, the actual police response to both victim and offender, the public's requirements as to an ideal police response and the public's notions of appropriate penalties for various offences.

The survey certainly provides a great deal of detailed information on victimization patterns in Islington. It found, for instance, that victims of burglary were more likely to be young rather than old, men rather than women, and black rather than white. With theft or robbery it was the other way round, apart from black people, who were more at risk than white people. As far as assault was concerned, the survey says: 'Black people on average are almost twice as likely as other people to be victims of assault and women half as likely again as men to be assaulted' (ibid. 65).

This contrasts sharply with the British Crime Survey, 1982, which reported that young men were more likely to be the victims of assault than any other group, though this survey did pinpoint young men who regularly went out drinking a few nights per week; they were also the most likely assailants. The reason why women were at greater risk of assault than men in the Islington survey is that the researchers uncovered relatively large amounts of domestic violence against women. The Islington survey also discovered a much higher incidence of sexual assault than the British Crime Surveys. In fact, only one case of unreported attempted rape came to light in the first two British Crime Surveys, and 17 and 18 cases of sexual assault in each year of the sweep, whilst the Islington survey estimated that there were 1,200 sexual assaults in the area covered by the study. According to the authors, this discrepancy arises from the greater sensitivity of the researchers, as well as the way in which questions were phrased. The underreporting by women of rape, attempted rape and other forms of sexual assault has been highlighted by a large number of victim surveys. According to Hall (1985), for instance, only 8 per cent of rape victims informed the police.

The greater assault rate in Islington for black people when compared with white people was congruent with the national findings of the 1992 British Crime Survey. However, interestingly, the second Islington survey found very little difference in assault rate between white people and people of Afro-Caribbean background. Zedner (1994: 1215) gives some possible explanations for this disparity:

> It may be that Afro-Caribbeans in Islington are so exposed to violence that they tend to underreport assaults against them. Alternatively, it may be that the high concentration of ethnic minority populations in this inner London borough levels out disparities in the victimization of whites and blacks.

It should be appreciated that local crime surveys carried out by 'left realists' – such as the Islington survey – are not simply attempts to gather better knowledge about crimes and victims. They constitute the basis of a much broader criminological project involving the development of crime control policies, and theoretical models seeking to explain criminal behaviour. Thus left realism attempts to engage in a direct, practical way with issues of law and order. At root this means entering a terrain traditionally colonized by the political right, and in the process developing a critique of other radical left positions characterized by the left realists as 'left idealism'. This project has coalesced around the slogan 'take crime seriously', an injunction based upon the left realist view that:

1. Not only do poorer people have to cope with all the usual problems associated with relative deprivation, they also have to cope with being more at risk from crime; and

2. Following on from this, the fear of crime is not an irrational moral
    panic generated by the mass media, but a realistic assessment of
    the situation.

According to the left realists, data from local crime surveys can then be used
as a basis for developing crime control policies at a local level.

Victim surveys: limitations and problems

A whole range of criminal offences are not picked up by victim surveys. In
addition, these tend to be underrecorded in official statistics, the combined
effect of which is to give a misleading picture of the 'crime problem'. By
questioning people as individual members of households there are certain
offences that, although often creating victims, cannot be identified. The
following examples will illustrate this.

Corporate crime and organized crime

The amount of illegal profit made from multinational and national corporation
crimes, as well as the illicit gains from 'organized crime' (or crimes of the 'mafia'
or 'cosa nostra' or some other official mystifying synonym), is enormous, and,
beside it, the value of goods stolen or otherwise illegally acquired by
'conventional, ordinary' criminals drops into insignificance. (Box, 1981: 235)

Clearly, the responses of households in victim surveys will give no inkling
of the magnitude of corporate and organized crime. Leaving aside, for now,
a more detailed discussion of these aspects, it can be noted that there is a
large and important literature of 'exposé' criminology which analyzes the
illegal activities of big business (e.g. Pearce, 1976; Chambliss, 1978; Henry,
1978; Levi, 1987; Yeager, 1991) and organized and professional crime (e.g.
Taylor, 1984; Hobbs, 1988; Block, 1991).

Occupational crime

This can involve persons of high or low status within an organization.
White-collar occupational crime can be carried out *against* the company (for
example, fiddling expenses), or *for* the company, when it enters the realms
of corporate crime (the classic study is Sutherland, 1983, originally
published 1949; for a recent overview of this area see Nelken, 1994). Ditton's
(1977) study of fiddling among bread salesmen provides an example of the
criminal activities of those further down the hierarchy.

Other examples of offences hidden from victim surveys are:

- *Theft from businesses.* This will involve such things as shoplifting and insurance fraud.

- *Criminal damage.* Vandalizing public or non-household property will not, of course, be registered in victim surveys.

- *'Crimes without victims'.* This term is used to describe offences such as illicit drug use, certain illegal sexual activities, or offences connected with the Obscene Publications Act.

- *Taxation and social security fraud.* Clearly, victim surveys cannot measure offending rates in these areas.

In addition, there are likely to be instances where respondents in victim surveys have been victims of crime but, because of circumstances, or the design or conduct of the interview, their victimization will not come to light; for example:

- Where respondents are too frightened, embarrassed or ashamed to admit that they are victims (e.g. having property stolen whilst visiting a prostitute, or experiencing a sexual assault).

- Where they are simply unaware that they are victims (e.g. believing that a purse has been lost when it has been stolen).

Walklate (1989) offers a perceptive discussion of the need for research to be sensitive to the individual's understanding of his or her own victimization, and that ready-made categories used by the police or researchers may not be appropriate. In this context she quotes Kelly who, with reference to sexual violence against women, argues that the victims' experiences should be seen as forming a continuum:

> Using the concept of a continuum highlights the fact that all women experience sexual violence at some point in their lives. It enables the linking of more common, everyday abuses women experience with the less common experiences labelled as crimes. It is through this connection that women are able to locate their own particular experiences as being examples of sexual violence. (Ibid. 33)

This dimension is important, too, in a general sense, for different people will have different understandings and thresholds regarding the seriousness and harmfulness of what has happened to them. The victim's own perception of events will have implications for how he or she responds to questions in victim surveys. Furthermore, how elaborated a victim's account is will be linked to their articulacy when answering questions.

Finally, the information from victim surveys is, of course, dependent on people being honest and accurately remembering what has happened to them.

Thus, although victim surveys, national and local, do provide valuable alternative sources of information about the extent of crime and patterns of victimization, their limitations have to be acknowledged.

The usefulness of criminal statistics

The discussion so far of statistics, especially official statistics, has been quite critical. Many criminologists, though, whilst generally accepting these criticisms, would argue that this does not mean that they are therefore of no value. One example of this is associated with the *class conflict* approach to statistics. From this perspective, the fact that criminal statistics, as well as statistical information relating to the operation of the criminal justice system in general, reflect the activities of the various organizations and individuals involved, is precisely why they can be usefully employed. As the label applied to this perspective suggests, the main emphasis is on exploitative class relations in a capitalist society:

> Only by understanding that statistics are produced as part of the administration and control of a society organised around exploitative class relations can we grasp their full meaning; and only with the aid of this understanding can we determine their uses, and usefulness, in critical social research. (Miles and Irvine, 1981: 127)

Thus in a sense criminal statistics are 'rehabilitated', but only if they are read as products of conflictual class relations. The statistics may not, in terms of common sense, reflect the reality of crime, but for class conflict theorists they do provide an insight into the class-based nature of the criminal justice system. From this point of view, crime-related statistics, though manipulated to suit the interests of the powerful, do none the less provide useful indicators of the inequalities and biases inherent in the system itself, and indeed in capitalist society in general. The over-representation of the working-class, as opposed to bourgeois, crime in the statistics, and the overrepresentation of black and poorer people in the prison populations of capitalist societies, are not seen as simply the result of their greater criminality. In an unequal society, it is argued, only the naive believe that a fair and equal system of justice can be delivered. Thus, crime-related statistics can be used as the basis for developing critical explanations of these inequalities.

From a different perspective, Bottomley and Pease (1986: 159) recognize that 'criminal statistics provide few, if any, significant answers to many of the important traditional questions of evaluation' (such as, is crime under control?), but add: 'On the other hand, criminal justice statistics are informative in a variety of ways, and should not be discarded as meaningless, as has sometimes been their fate.' Indeed, they call for an increase in routine statistical information pertaining to the workings of the criminal justice system, and see such descriptive material as forming the basis for more informed discussion. As an example, they point out how this kind of information can act as an antidote to the often lurid and misleading stereotypes of crime and criminals found in the mass media and pub conversations:

> Simple descriptive studies can sometimes have a powerful influence that their lack of technical or theoretical complexity may at first belie – consider, for instance, the important effect upon public attitudes towards capital punishment of basic information about the 'typical' murderer as someone caught up in a stressful domestic situation to which no other solution is seen but a tragic murder–suicide attempt, or the important message from research that most house burglaries involve only quite modest financial losses and no violence by the burglar, and happen during the day. (Ibid. 169)

Some of the other areas identified by the authors where statistical information will be useful are as follows:

- The crime mix of particular neighbourhoods.
- Mechanisms at work whereby crimes come to the attention of the police.
- The ways in which different branches of the police service are used.
- The rates of cautioning between one force and another.
- Links between criminal activity, police clear-up rates and various community-based initiatives.
- Disparities in sentencing between one part of the country and another.

The recent Audit Commission report on the police used a range of statistical data to inform its recommendations, and controversially argued that the police should prioritize criminal investigations by concentrating on the more serious offences. In fact, although it may be controversial to suggest that the police should ignore some (minor) crime, secret trials along these lines are being developed at the moment by the Association of Chief Police Officers in several forces.

A similar argument in favour of the police prioritizing their work is contained in a 1994 report by the National Board for Crime Prevention. This report argues that 44 per cent of all reported crime is suffered by just 4 per cent of victims of crime, and that large increases in recorded crime during the 1980s was mainly due to these victims being victimized more often. The report concludes that the police should therefore concentrate on those making up the 4 per cent. Obviously data of this kind require careful scrutiny, although in the context of this discussion it is the nature of the recommendations that is of relevance.

Statistical information from other areas of the criminal justice system may also be drawn on. According to a Council of Europe survey, in 1994 Britain has the highest rate of imprisonment in Western Europe. At the time of writing, the prison population in England and Wales stands at 47,870, which is nearly 600 more than the official capacity of the prison system. The Council of Europe survey shows that there are 92.1 prisoners in British prisons for every 100,000 people in the populations; the two lowest figures were 44.4 for the Netherlands, and 44.0 for Turkey. Around 46,000 of the inmates of prisons in England and Wales are men, mostly from unemployed/working-class backgrounds, and about 15 per cent of them are black (23 per cent of female prisoners are black). Furthermore, just over 22,750 people were sent to prison in 1993 for non-payment of fines – 504 of these for not paying their poll tax and 845 for not having a television licence. According to the Home Office, fine defaulters make up a quarter of all admissions to prison, and the average number of such people in prison on any one day is just under 500. The National Association of Probation Officers estimates that in 80 per cent of cases the cost of keeping the offender in prison exceeds the amount of the fine.

Clearly, this kind of statistical information provides a useful backdrop to debates about the value of imprisonment. Likewise, the relative costs and merits of cautioning and imprisonment can only be seriously considered in the light of relevant statistical information.

Local crime surveys and left realism

Local crime surveys carried out by left realists, such as the Islington surveys, have two central aims. They seek to show first, that those people living in the area being studied see crime as a significant problem, and secondly, that this is a rational assessment on their part: that is, that crime really is a problem, and the fear of crime is therefore understandable. The corollary of this is that current official definitions of crime provide suitable anchor points, especially as they are seen to reflect a consensus, at least as far as 'conventional' crime (burglary, street robbery, for example) is concerned. This approach is at variance with a radical tradition in criminology that questions the requirement to be constrained by a particular state's definition of crime at a particular moment in history. It is also at variance with those left-wing criminologists, characterized by left realists as left idealists, who are purported to play down the harmfulness of conventional crime, to see the fear of crime as a moral panic generated by the mass media, and to emphasize corporate and white-collar crime as the real problem.

Those carrying out local surveys are aware that official/police categories are not able to accommodate the myriad experiences that various victims have. Sometimes these experiences do not at face value involve a criminal offence, but are, none the less, harmful or frightening. However, although left-realist crime surveys may sometimes spread the net beyond what are nominally criminal offences, and include other activities, these still tend to be referenced against official definitions of crime. Anderson *et al.* (1991: 37), for example, do this:

> In terms of the law, the incidents so far described are all criminal offences. In terms of young people's lives, however, there are many other examples of general harassment, abuse and frightening and stressful events which may fall outside the law, but which contribute to general levels of anxiety and fear of crime.

Relevant activities are therefore those that either, as above, contribute to 'anxiety and fear of crime', or represent a sort of mild version of a criminal offence, for example various threats. Apart from anything else, this does raise the issue of what it is that criminologists should study: where is the line to be drawn? There are other activities that are also harmful, distressing and frightening, and yet, nominally, no law breaking is involved. On the other hand, there will be criminal offences committed that do not have harmful repercussions. Furthermore, there will be many criminal activities that are harmful, and yet victims will be unaware that they are victims of that activity, for instance the adulteration of foodstuffs. Victim surveys are always dependent upon people having knowledge of their victimization.

This indicates one of the central difficulties with the local surveys of left realism. While much useful information may be forthcoming, they do tend to be rooted in a concrete, 'essentialist' framework, with positivist overtones. By concentrating on the experiences of a specific neighbourhood at a specific moment in time, and relying on a taken-for-granted set of crime-related concepts, such studies inevitably foreclose the project of developing a non-parochial theoretical criminology. In this hard-headed, 'non-idealist' world of realism there is no requirement for esoteric debates about what the criminologist should properly study: whether the capitalist state's current definition of crime is too narrow or too wide, or whether 'problematic situations' rather than crime should be the intellectual currency. Thus the Islington surveys are content to take official definitions as working categories, and to accept as satisfactory the victim's interpretation of events as 'criminal'. If the victim's account appears to match official discourse, then the reality of the crime is assumed. In this way, 'real' fears and 'real' crimes are brought blinking into the light.

This is not to say, of course, that left realism is wrong: clearly victims of crime are damaged by their experiences, and they need protecting. Rather it is that a criminological project based on questionnaires about criminal victimization is partial – the data produced are elements of a wider jigsaw.

3 | Criminology and criminologists up to World War Two

Tree of sin, tree of knowledge
The criminological tree of knowledge
Classicism and positivism
Positivist criminology
The turn of the century to the 1930s
Eugenics

The historical development of criminology as an academic discipline has been less neat and tidy than some accounts would suggest. It certainly did not achieve its modern form as a result of a straightforward, linear progression, involving the careful assembly of an agreed body of knowledge and understanding. Indeed, even how we might recognize the 'first' criminology, or a 'real' criminologist, remain contested issues.

However, there seems to be general agreement that by the beginning of the 1960s there existed in Britain a distinct, recognizable academic discipline in the shape of *modern* criminology. This chapter examines its historical development from its early stages up to World War Two.

Tree of sin, tree of knowledge

In volume 1 of Marx's (1969) *Theories of Surplus Value*, there is a frequently quoted section, only two pages in length, on the theme of crime – or rather it was frequently quoted when criminologists were, for whatever reason, less bashful about drawing on Marx. With few direct references in Marx's work to crime *per se*, it is not surprising that this section should be seized upon as a 'criminological' discussion. Unfortunately, the section – entitled

'Apologist conception of the productivity of all professions' – was often read out of context and consequently misunderstood. It was written primarily as an attack on those economists who would ascribe the quality of 'productive' to an almost infinite range of human activities. Thus it cannot be understood if it is taken out of the context of his criticisms of conceptualizations of productive labour then found in the field of political economy.

For Marx, it was not a question of whether or not some activity was 'useful' or even whether the activity created physical objects. Productive labour is labour that produces surplus value for capitalism. The veracity or usefulness of Marx's model is not at issue here, but it is necessary to make the general point. What is worth noting here is that in the process of criticizing what to him were specious and imprecise notions of productive labour, Marx (1969: 387–8) does provide the reader with a rapid sequence of observations of interest when examining the place of crime and criminology in society:

> The criminal produces not only crimes but criminal law, and with this also the professor who gives lectures on criminal law and in addition to this the inevitable compendium in which this same professor throws his lectures onto the general market as 'commodities'. This brings with it augmentation of national wealth . . . The criminal moreover produces the whole of the police and of criminal justice, constables, judges, hangmen, juries etc.; and all these different lines of business, which form equally many categories of the social division of labour, develop different capacities of the human spirit, create new needs and new ways of satisfying them. Torture alone has given rise to the most ingenious mechanical inventions, and employed many honourable craftsmen in the production of its instruments . . . The criminal produces . . . also art, belles-lettres, novels . . . The effects of the criminal on the development of productive power can be shown in detail. Would locks have reached their present state of excellence had there been no thieves? . . . Doesn't practical chemistry owe just as much to adulteration of commodities and the efforts to show it up as to the honest zeal for production?

Crude readings have seen in this passage a version of functionalism, where crime is conceived of as being functionally useful for society, and hence necessary and inevitable. In a similar vein some writers have concentrated on references further on in the text to the criminal 'arousing the moral and aesthetic feelings of the public', and breaking the 'monotony . . . of bourgeois life', thereby keeping it from 'stagnation'. Such attempts to draw out an early 'functions of crime' argument misconstrue what Marx was saying, though we might note that some of his observations do represent a remarkable precurser to what Durkheim was famously to debate a few years later. Having said this, it is equally misleading to dismiss the functionalist overtones in favour of the view that this section is nothing more than an amusing digression, an excuse for some tongue-in-cheek mockery of 'bourgeois apologists'. Marx *is* making some important points regarding the connections between criminals and their crimes, and the economic, social and cultural development of capitalism. He happens to do this by employing the device of irony.

This use of irony by Marx has been stressed by some writers, notably Taylor, Walton and Young (1973) and Hirst (1975a), though the irony goes beyond the situation where, in Hirst's words, 'The most upright citizens depend for their livelihood on the criminal classes' (ibid. 212). In fact the irony operates on two levels. First, it is used in a Socratic sense, that is, with a pretence of ignorance. Here Marx takes on the part of a bourgeois apologist and, in the manner of a devil's advocate, argues that the activities of the despised low-life criminal are somehow 'productive'. In this way he hoped to hold up for ridicule understandings of productive labour current in bourgeois political economy. Secondly, he uses irony in the sense of a perverse conjunction between the desirable and the undesirable: specifically, between crime and such things as job opportunities, increased national wealth, inventions, novels and, significantly, knowledge. This is succinctly summed up by Marx (1969: 388): 'And hasn't the Tree of Sin been at the same time the Tree of Knowledge ever since the time of Adam?' Thus for the entire history of the world, criminals and their crimes have stimulated the production of knowledge on a number of fronts, including more recently a criminological one. And in the modern world what is called the 'fight against crime' is very big business indeed. Across the globe, governments and private organizations spend vast amounts of money on efforts to prevent crime, to apprehend and deal with criminals, and so on. Furthermore, and in tandem with this, a global media devotes much of its time to fictional and factual accounts of crime and the culprits involved.

The criminological tree of knowledge: separating the tree from the wood

At the time Marx was making the above observations, no distinct discipline called criminology existed, and no one described themselves as criminologists. In fact, we had to wait until the last decade of the nineteenth century before the term criminology came into general use. Of course, the fact that no discipline was around with the name 'criminology' and no individuals were identified as criminologists, does not necessarily mean that criminology in some form or other did not exist. Obviously, what is recognized today as modern criminology did not appear overnight as a fully grown 'tree of knowledge'. The problem that historians have had is in identifying a recognizable early criminology and then tracing its subsequent development. For hundreds of years various thinkers and writers have spent a great deal of time discussing phenomena of interest to criminologists. After all, issues of defined 'bad' behaviour, immorality, social control, punishment and order, have been central to religious, political and social thought down through the ages. What, though, makes such a discussion specifically *criminological*? A contemporary criminologist who has tried to answer this question is David Garland. He proceeds by establishing initially a basic definition of modern criminology: 'Modern criminology, like other academic specialisms, consists of a body of accredited and systematically transmitted forms of knowledge, approved procedures and techniques of investigation, and a cluster of questions which make up the subject's recognized agendas' (Garland, 1994: 25).

Accepting this definition of modern criminology, we might ask if there was something in the past that, although lacking some or even all of these attributes, could none the less be classified as criminology, albeit 'old' or 'pre-modern', or whatever. Garland's answer to this is a qualified 'yes', and he offers a convincing argument to support the view that:

> Discourse about crime and punishment has existed, in one form or another, since ancient times, but it is only during the last 120 years that there has been a distinctive 'science of criminology', and only in the last fifty or sixty years has there been in Britain an established, independent discipline organized around that intellectual endeavour. (Ibid. 27)

Others have been less restrained in discovering a 'real' criminology deep in past history. Drapkin (1983), for instance, has trawled the writings of ancient scholars, latching on to any references to crime and punishment. As Garland says, though, not only do these historians operate with a notion of 'criminology' stretched beyond reasonable boundaries, they also fail to see these early discourses within their contemporary contexts, that is, situate them within particular institutional structures, involving particular assumptions and agendas.

Classicism and positivism

Over the past twenty years or so a more or less consensual reading of criminology's history grew up among British writers (e.g. Taylor, Walton and Young (1973); Roshier (1989)). In these accounts the beginning of criminology lies in the classical criminology of the eighteenth century. However, it was not until the latter part of the nineteenth century that attempts were made to develop an explicit, recognizable 'science' of criminology. This is normally given the general label of positivist criminology.

Positivism represented a quite different agenda to that of the earlier classical school. Although it would be wrong to give the impression that classicism incorporated a unified body of knowledge, with internal unanimity regarding philosophical assumptions and ideas, it did have one, fundamentally important thread running through it. Classical criminology was centrally concerned with the establishment of a reformed, equitable and efficient system of justice (the two most influential writers were Beccaria and Bentham). Classical writers concerned themselves with the creation of, they believed, a fairer, better regulated social order. Drawing on utilitarian philosophy, and in particular the pleasure–pain principle, the aim was to create a system where punishment proportional to the crime would act to deter would-be offenders. This would take place within a rational, codified legal order. The focus was therefore on the criminal act, rather than the criminal actor. Indeed, no differentiation in terms of special attributes was made between the criminal and the non-criminal.

Garland's main argument is that modern criminology grew out of a convergence between the 'governmental project' of classicism, covering a period from the late eighteenth century to the last quarter of the nineteenth century, and the 'Lombrosian project' associated with late nineteenth-century positivism. The term governmental project is used because classicism was oriented towards criminal justice administration. In contrast, the Lombrosian project of positivism is so called because of the influence of Cesare Lombroso, a criminological positivist *par excellence*. It was he who popularized the notion of genetically determined, distinct criminal types. Via a crude physiognomy, he argued that criminals were atavistic beings, that is, throwbacks to an earlier stage of human evolution, who were physically different from non-criminals. This is a fascinating, though totally discredited, idea.

The late nineteenth century saw the publication of a number of works purporting to represent 'scientific' criminology. The repercussions were felt across Europe, and the touchstone for this criminology was the positivist criminology of key writers such as Lombroso (1876), Ferri (1895) and Garofalo (1914) – the Italian school. Lombrosian anthropology, however, was less influential in Britain than in other parts of Europe. Likewise, the positivism of the French sociologist, Auguste Comte, did not find particularly fertile ground among British criminologists. However, as Garland (1994: 79) says: 'the project of positivism (in a more modest version), and its corresponding methods, formed the broad intellectual basis for the criminological programme.'

With the strongest influence coming from psychiatric medicine, and research locked into penal imperatives, this was the beginning of scientific criminology in Britain.

Using the prisons as ready-made laboratories, criminals were classified into psychological types, with the promise of finding both the causes of crime and the most efficacious ways of dealing with them. Above all, the project was to be *scientific*; research would proceed by empirical investigation and according to scientific principles, principles borrowed from earlier studies of animals and the material world. It was believed that only through science could truth be found. Thus was born a causal–corrective tradition in British criminology that was to continue largely unchallenged until the 1960s. This was the ultimate promise held out by criminology: to establish the causes of crime and then suggest ways in which society could correct the problem.

Not surprisingly, from the late nineteenth century until the 1960s a consensus was sustained which viewed the earlier classical criminology as not 'real' criminology at all. Vold (1958), for example, saw classical criminology as mere pre-scientific 'Administrative and Legal Criminology'.

By the late 1960s there had been another fundamental shift in criminological thinking, and with it a reassessment of classical criminology. Now it came to be rehabilitated as the first 'real' criminology. This reflected a move away from an increasingly derided positivist criminology, with its deterministic views on criminal behaviour. Now there was to be an emphasis on 'voluntarism', on people creating their own social worlds, and this was seen as being in accord with the 'free will' model of classical criminology.

Positivist criminology

There is always a danger of oversimplification when trying to paint in some historical background, of ending up with such broad brushstrokes that the past becomes a caricature of itself, smoothed out and shed of all those irksome details that confound an apparent coherence and elegant simplicity. Part of the problem concerns the selection of supposedly representative and influential writers in order to draw out some posited 'mainstream' or 'dominant' ideas. Do we, for instance, study only those ideas that received official recognition and became incorporated into policy? Or do we judge the importance of a text according to the manner in which it was received by contemporary academic peers?

Obviously there was no precise date, no magic moment, when modern criminology suddenly appeared. The development of criminology into a distinct academic discipline was a gradual process, and this process was linked in various ways (depending on one's reading of history) to 200 years or more of crime-related intellectual discourse. It was also linked to sweeping economic, social and political transformations that took place, as British society moved from feudalism to agrarian capitalism to mature capitalism. More recently, in the postwar period, the progress of criminology has been connected to such things as an increasingly interventionist central state, the growth of the welfare state, and the expansion of higher education. Certainly, by the beginning of the 1960s criminology was established as a modern academic discipline, with all that

that meant: full-time specialists working in university departments or in specialized institutions; an agenda of research questions and approved methodologies; its own learned journals; postgraduate programmes; and various forums for the exchange of ideas.

When discussing the history of criminological thought, it is not controversial to point to the late nineteenth century as the time when 'scientific' criminology first appeared on the scene. Neither is it controversial to describe this as positivist criminology. What is controversial, at least nowadays, is then to go on to label indiscriminately as 'positivist' the bulk of British criminology that developed since the late nineteenth century up to the 1960s, though the application of this label has not always been seen as problematic.

From the late 1960s, there grew within sociology a sustained critique of positivism among those influenced by the ideas of interpretive sociology. Specifically, this critique was aimed at functionalism, and, because functionalism was, not unreasonably, viewed as a conservative social theory, the critique was also embraced by more radical, left-oriented sociologists. The success of this onslaught in terms of the subsequent development of sociology is well known. The critique was generally successful among students too, even early on in their criminological studies. This is well illustrated by my own experiences as an 'A' Level sociology examiner during the late 1970s and early 1980s. Most of the candidates were 'anti-positivism' and 'pro-phenomenology', even those who clearly had no idea what phenomenology was. Indeed, it was not uncommon to read quite malignant, no holds barred, tirades against alleged functionalist miscreants such as Talcott Parsons.

The critique of positivism within sociology in general was paralleled with a critique of positivist criminology, for by the beginning of the 1970s sociology had become the dominant discipline within academic criminology. Garland (1994) has argued that it is misleading to characterize the period from the late nineteenth century to the 1960s as a period of positivist hegemony, with the new deviancy of the 1960s arriving on the scene to rescue the discipline from its clutches. This overgeneralized and demonizing view of history has had two important results:

1. As Jock Young (1988: 168) puts it, 'the long lineage of radical positivism in Britain was forgotten'.

2. There was a failure to appreciate the various strands of criminological thought developing from the turn of the century, and that some of the most influential work, especially in the first two decades of this century, did not easily fall into the category of positivism.

In order to assess these debates it is necessary to be reminded of what is meant by sociological positivism. Cuff and Payne (1979: 159) offer the following, standard definition based upon two propositions:

1. The kinds of explanations sociology should produce about the social world should be the same as those produced in the natural sciences, i.e. law-like statements which have the form, 'A causes B' . . .

2. Sociology should as far as possible make use of the same sorts of methods as are used in the natural sciences for constructing and testing their explanations. An essential implication is that sociologists need to model their approach on the logic of that exemplary tool of the natural sciences – the experimental method.

What are the implications of this for a specifically criminological positivism? Three central questions are associated with this type of criminology, if and when such a creature can be identified: Why do some individuals break the law? How can criminals be reformed? What can be done to prevent them wanting to break the law in the first place? According to Jeffery (1960) and Matza (1964), attempts to answer these questions proceed within a characteristic framework derived from three fundamental assumptions: determinism, differentiation and pathology.

Determinism means that factors outside of the individual's control – be they biological, psychological, sociological, or some combination – push that individual into criminal behaviour. From this perspective, crime does not result from choice, or rational decision making, but rather from force of circumstance. This model of crime contrasts sharply with that associated with classical criminology, which emphasizes the ability of members of society to make rational choices about whether or not to commit crime, similar to a cost-benefit analysis. In this formulation, the 'cost' of crime equates with punishment proportional to the crime, and ideally this acts as a deterrent. As we shall see, different sorts of causal theories developed within criminology through the twentieth century, each stressing different, more or less deterministic, factors.

There is an intriguing contradiction between positivist conceptions and conceptions built into the legal system. The courts, of course, are willing to take such things as age and mental state into consideration when judging a person's guilt. The determinism of positivism, however, removes personal culpability, by making the wrongdoer into a victim of behaviour-determining factors. This certainly does not square with notions of justice based upon just deserts or retribution, and indicates why positivism leads naturally to a 'treatment' model: that is, to attempting to 'cure' the offender. In practice, this uneasy tension has been managed by what is usually referred to as the neoclassical principle of mitigation: for example, by allowing the psychologist or social worker into the court to plead for the defendant. It *is* an important issue that continues to generate much debate within criminology, namely, to what extent, and in what ways, is the offender to blame?

The second assumption made by positivist criminology, according to Jeffery and Matza, is *differentiation*. What this means is that criminals are differentiated in kind from non-criminals. Depending on the type of criminology involved, criminals have been viewed as different because of their biological constitutions, because they possess certain abnormal or negative psychological traits, or, from a sociological direction, because they have learned attitudes and values which lend themselves to law breaking.

The third assumption, *pathology*, follows on from differentiation, in that criminals are seen as being different to non-criminals because of something going 'wrong' at a biological, psychological, or sociological level.

Before turning to developments in the first part of the twentieth century, it will be useful to note two important issues that are usually seen as featuring prominently in positivist criminology: the problematic nature of the concept of crime, and the tension between heredity and environment.

The *raison d'être* of positivism has been its promise to enlist the services of science. Discarding the deadweight of pre-scientific knowledge as mere prejudice and dilettantism, positivist criminology would apply the methods and principles of scientific thought. However, such a criminology had to resolve a crucial problem concerning the concept of crime itself. Because it was appreciated that what was defined as crime changed over time, and from one society to another, it was clear that this central concept, as legally defined, did not offer a fixed, objective, scientific anchor point. To fall back on definitions of crime current in a particular society at a particular moment in history would seem to subvert the positivist project of producing general theories. Consequently, attempts were made to arrive at some objective concept of 'natural' or 'real' crime. The magnitude of this endeavour can be readily appreciated, and positivism met serious problems on two levels. First, in practice, abstracted conceptions simply reflected a writer's personal moral feelings. Moreover, if the solution was to tap into perceived 'public sentiments', and emphasize deviance rather than crime, the problem of relativism remained unsolved, in that supposedly consensual attitudes and values in a society (if they can be identified) are themselves shaped by particular cultures. Secondly, positivist criminologists eventually tended to surrender to legally defined categories anyway, and even early on in this century they used prison inmates as subjects for research: that is, they used individuals whose criminal status was obviously derived from legal definitions. We might also add that one of the main criticisms of positivism made by the 'new deviancy' theorists of the 1960s and 1970s was that they accepted uncritically official crime statistics.

The second issue featuring prominently in positivist criminology is that of heredity versus the environment. Some positivists concentrated on what they saw as genetically determined predispositions to criminality, whilst others focused on environmental factors, and the effect of these on the individual. Hereditarians usually acknowledged, though, that the social circumstances of the individual were of *some* importance. Stressing the 'environment' can, of course, still mean subscribing to a deterministic explanation of criminality.

The turn of the century to the 1930s

It is a complex business unravelling the varieties of positivism, quasi-positivism or non-positivism prevalent in British criminology during the first three decades of this century. From the available evidence, at the end of the nineteenth century there was strong support for the notion of biological determinism, though this support tended not to follow the Lombrosian idea of linking criminality to body shape. In Britain the main stress was on genetically determined psychological traits such as 'feeble-mindedness' and 'moral degeneracy' and their links with criminality. After this early, crude attempt at 'scientific' criminology, which continued up to World War One, mapping developments during the 1920s and 1930s becomes rather more hazardous. In particular we have to be wary of making sweeping statements to the effect that British criminology simply continued along a positivist pathway. Some writers, influential during the interwar years, clearly represented the positivist tradition, but others did not. Of course, a problem here, as mentioned earlier, is deciding on which writers best represent this period.

Research carried out under the banner of 'criminology' continued to be dominated by medical practitioners employed within the prison service; usually they had received training in psychiatric medicine. The result was that much of this research was locked into the institutional requirements of the courts and prisons. Taking the individual's mental state as the starting point, criminological investigations were designed to facilitate the more effective organization of prison regimes and treatment programmes. Thus psychiatry, defined as psychological medicine, and then psychology, were the main influences in this period. Any influence from sociology was conspicuously lacking (for example, the work done by the Chicago school during the interwar years). This is not surprising given that research was largely driven by the needs of the system, and was carried out by those with a vested interest in that system. They were also concerned with legitimizing criminology as an academic discipline. This did not mean that social factors were ignored. Such things as 'inadequate' family life, poverty, single parenthood and illegitimacy were often on the agenda. However, these were invoked within a psychological frame of reference. For hereditarians, negative social factors were seen as the outcome of inborn, abnormal mental states – for example, 'inadequate' people created 'inadequate' families –

whilst environmentalists saw such things as poverty as leading to abnormal mental states.

By the beginning of the 1920s, mainstream criminology in Britain had moved away from seeing the criminal as a distinct type of human being, towards a model based upon a spectrum of mental traits and conditions. Fundamentally, these attributes were judged in terms of diagnosed pathological conditions labelled 'low intelligence', 'feeble mindedness', and so on.

We can explore this situation further by looking at a number of influential writers around in the 1920s and 1930s. This will show that a plurality of views existed within criminology, and that the appellation 'positivism' may not always apply. Garland suggests that mainstream criminology in the 1920s and 1930s was best represented by the work of W. Norwood East, a writer who, although sharing with positivism a desire to develop objective, empirically based research, did not support a deterministic approach. Neither did he take the view that all criminals were suffering from some psychological disorder. Other writers, however, such as Hamblin Smith and Grace Pailthorpe, did argue that the 'abormal' mental state of the individual led to criminal behaviour.

Those linking heredity to criminal dispositions took into account what they saw as genetically inherited mental traits. This is well illustrated by the work of Charles Goring, a medical officer in the prison service. Between 1902 and 1908 he carried out a psychiatrically based study of over 1,500 prisoners. In his report, published in 1913, he concluded that 'there is no such thing as a physical criminal type'. Although this is a clear refutation of the Lombrosian view, Goring was not seeking to suggest that criminals were 'made' rather than 'born'. In 1919, following his death, an abridged version of the report was published, and this contains an introduction by a collaborator in the research, Karl Pearson, who points out that Goring was 'much surprised' to find that there was 'relatively little influence of environment' in criminality. Goring (1919: 211–12) himself wrote:

> Relatively to its origin in the constitution of the malefactor, and especially in his mentally defective constitution, crime in this country is only to a trifling extent (if to any) the product of social inequality, of adverse environment, or of other manifestations of what may be comprehensively termed 'the force of circumstances'.

One of the most influential studies from the 1920s, carried out on delinquent youth by Cyril Burt (1925: 29), also argued the case for hereditary factors (Burt's reputation has suffered since the revelation in the 1970s that he doctored the figures in various pieces of research): 'if our inquiry is to begin at the very beginning, it must go back to influences that were operative long before the child himself was born. We must review not only his birth and early life, but his ancestry also.'

By the late 1930s, mainstream criminology was linking criminal behaviour to a range of psychological and social factors, against the backdrop of a continuing debate about the relative importance of genetic endowment. This is a tradition that has carried on into the work of modern psychologists. As Roshier (1989: 26) says:

> The quest for identifiable crime-prone personality types has included learning theorists as well as heredity theorists, psychoanalysts ('anti-social' or 'affection-less' personality theories), and studies not concerning themselves with the question of how such types come about.

By the time we reach World War Two psychology was clearly in pole position within criminological discourses, with different emphases given to 'heredity' (inborn psychological dispositions to crime, or an inborn lack of mental defences against 'proper' attitude formation), and 'environment' ('bad' social conditions detrimentally affecting psychological growth).

Interestingly, the same kind of policy-influencing framework was reflected in debates about future secondary education taking place in the late 1930s and during the war. A belief in the genetic basis of intellectual ability, derived in large part from the research of Cyril Burt, was built into the 1938 Spens Report and 1943 Norwood Report, and then enshrined in the tripartite system ushered in by the 1944 Education Act. The reform of education was, of course, only part of a massive transformation in British social policy following World War Two, and we have to appreciate the strong feelings building up during the war around a welfare theme. Here were reflected Fabian ideas pertaining to the intervention of the central and local state into the social and economic life of the country in order to improve that life. The same rationale was apparent in discussions and policy formulations relating to offenders, especially young offenders, during and after the war. Thus there was an increasing presence of social work, psychotherapy and treatment, and reformative strategies. The movement towards welfarism was, in effect, one way of resolving the tension between 'heredity' and 'environment'. Improvements in health and housing, and an end to poverty, and so on, in a sense made the debate redundant. Put crudely, whatever the importance of genetic endowment might be, society is lumbered with it. At least the social environments of ordinary people can be improved, which, it was reasoned, would minimize the unwanted effects of 'bad' environments, for example crime. Geoff Pearson refers to a 1946 Conservative Party report, called *Youth Astray*, which, from a contemporary vantage point makes startling reading: 'The behaviour of boys and girls is mainly the outcome of conditions, social, economic, and to some extent hereditary, for which they themselves cannot be blamed. The blame – for blame there is – rests largely upon society' (Pearson, 1983: 14).

Eugenics

There was during the interwar years, however, an alternative response to welfarism among some of those convinced of the importance of genetics. The frequent identification of criminality with low intelligence, feeble-mindedness, moral degeneracy and the like led some down a eugenics road and the sad attractions of sterilization. The eugenics movement achieved a significant following in Britain, as well as on the Continent and in the United States. Essentially it was concerned with improving the perceived genetic stock, which meant devising ways of preventing those defined as degenerate, of low intelligence, or otherwise deviant, from producing offspring. This mission to purify the genetic pool of what was bizarrely referred to by some as the 'British race', was rather sullied by Nazi Germany taking the arguments to their logical conclusion in the gas chambers of Auschwitz.

These various strands within criminology between World War One and World War Two are brought together in a significant book by Claude Mullins (1945). The book is significant not because it had any particular impact on policy, or because of its academic excellence, but rather because of its nature. The title, to begin with, says it all: *Why Crime? Some Causes and Remedies from the Psychological Standpoint*. In addition, because the author was a self-taught psychologist and a magistrate, he acts as a kind of melting pot for academic, lay and judicial opinion. Interestingly, he begins by referring to the lack of popular support for genetic explanations of criminality:

> The popular view among those interested in the subject is that criminals are what they are because society has made them so. This view accords with modern political tendencies and is based upon the assumption that if society had provided for all a satisfactory social and economic environment, there would be few criminals. Those holding this view find that it generates soothing feelings of anger against the scheme of things . . . they believe that the delinquent, rather than his victims or society, is really the aggrieved party. (Ibid. 2)

As the book proceeds, and his own personal opinions emerge, it is clear that Mullins was sceptical of these 'political tendencies', tendencies associated with the welfarism discussed above. While pointing out that 'No one would maintain that the inheritance, whether biological or psychological, can be directly a cause of crime', (ibid. 9), he went on to observe that 'Delinquency is closely associated with the low-grade and the mentally deficient' (ibid. 48). His conclusion was to thoroughly commend the findings of the 1934 government *Departmental Committee on Sterilization*, which stated that they were:

> impressed by the dead weight of social inefficiency and individual misery which is entailed by the existence in our midst of over a quarter of a million mental

defectives and of a far larger number of persons who, without being certifiably defective, are mentally subnormal.

This Committee said that all witnesses before them 'recognized heredity as an important factor in the causation of these conditions'.
Mullins (1945: 49) continues:

The Sterilization Committee expressed the opinion that many low-grade parents 'would be glad to be relieved of the dread of repeated pregnancies and to escape the recurring burden of parenthood, for which they are so manifestly unfitted' . . . There must be few of those who have had close contacts with such people who would disagree with this statement . . . The only practical way of preventing people of low-grade intelligence from being overwhelmed with unwanted children, to the immense detriment of such children, is by the sterilization of the fathers.

It is not worth dwelling overlong on Mullins' text, but there is a section in a chapter on 'Illegitimate Children' which manages to combine prejudice towards such children with surreal psychology and anti-trade unionism:

adoption (of illegitimate children) frequently brings severe psychological dangers . . . many medical psychologists will say that a trauma will also remain in the child's unconscious which at any time may result in a crisis. Such a trauma may produce throughout life a hostility towards some one or society generally. An excellent illustration of this was . . . a well-known miners' leader in the decades between the wars. His uncompromising nature . . . its explanation probably lay in the fact that he was a foundling, adopted into the home of a miner and his wife . . . But all his life his pugnacity and his dogged reluctance to meet the other side in any way were in all probability the legacy from his birth, and though his foster-parents' love and care doubtless had their beneficial effect, they could not eradicate what birth and the earliest reception into the world had produced. (Ibid. 102)

The views of people such as Mullins were, at the time, out of step with 'modern political tendencies', tendencies that led to the creation of the modern welfare state – but these views did not disappear. As we shall see when discussing the 1980s and 1990s, reports of the demise of the above type of criminology turned out to be greatly exaggerated.

Part II

World War Two to the mid-1960s

4 | The discipline of criminology and its context – 1

The emergence of criminology
Sociological criminology
Sociological criminology in Britain from the 1950s to the mid-1960s
Sociological criminology in the United States

The emergence of a recognized academic discipline called 'criminology' was not pre-ordained or inevitable; it was not an ology waiting to happen. Similarly, no master plan was guiding the discipline towards some 'true' state. Debates regarding what criminology *is*, or should be, continue unabated. Indeed, they have increased in intensity as time has gone on.

The academic terrain of criminology has been, and still is, colonized by theories and research projects that have their intellectual bases in a range of pre-existing academic disciplines. As we have seen in the last chapter, in Britain during the first part of the twentieth century that discipline was psychological medicine/psychology. Crime and criminality, though, have been studied from the perspective of biology, anthropology, economics, sociology, and so on. Criminologists, therefore, have either opted for a strategy of broadly based eclecticism, where they synthesize, or at least draw on, a number of disciplines, or for an approach rooted in their own academic specialism.

The choice of an eclectic approach was to a large extent a feature of the criminology that developed during the period under review in this chapter. This raises the interesting issue of whether there is an extant body of theoretical knowledge with uniquely criminological characteristics. What is the distinction, say, between the sociology or psychology of crime and criminology? After all, the specialist area of, for instance, the sociology of the family did not lead to a separate academic discipline called 'familyology'.

In the ebbs and flows of subject dominance and changing research agendas, 'criminology' became a flag of convenience, under which a motley crew could sail. Its status as a separate academic discipline derived from the institutional trappings accumulated over the years: specialist research centres and departments, parking spaces on library shelves, academic journals, professorships, conferences and the like. This allowed for a concentration of scholarship and the potential for cross-fertilization of ideas; but the work produced has always remained rooted in earlier disciplines, either as a primary focus, or some sort of synthesis.

The emergence of criminology

By the end of the 1950s criminology had achieved the status of a recognized academic discipline. Indeed, as one measure of this, according to Radzinowicz's (1961) review of this period, Britain was second only to the United States in terms of government funding for criminological research during the 1950s.

In the last chapter mention was made of Garland's distinction between two different criminological projects, first one, then the other, becoming dominant as the discipline developed in history. On the one hand, there is the 'governmental project', where criminology's *raison d'être* was its practical usefulness for administrators, and on the other, the 'Lombrosian project', where criminology was oriented towards the production of scientific knowledge. According to Garland, by the end of the 1950s there had been a convergence between these two projects: criminology lay claim to proper academic/scientific status, and at the same time offered useful knowledge for those involved in the administration of the criminal justice system.

This raises important and complex philosophical issues relating to the role of the social sciences in general, and, as we shall see, these become particularly pertinent within the context of radical criminology. For the moment, one point to make is that irrespective of whether or not one believes that criminology should be 'useful', it is necessary to consider the basic framework within which criminological research is carried out. There is a distinction between research carried out within the constraints and demands imposed by a funding body, according to an agenda they set, and research carried out because it is interesting and will further academic knowledge and understanding. Those involved in each type of research might even agree that criminology should, for instance, help in the 'fight against crime', but there is a huge difference between research that is locked into some administrative requirements and research that is not (though nowadays such freedom is increasingly difficult to come by).

In Garland's view, then, research carried out during the 1940s and 1950s satisfied both administrative and academic demands due to a happy coincidence of the two projects. On a general level this was undoubtedly the case, though a more detailed analysis shows that there were differences of opinion within criminology. Without this administrative and academic convergence, it is probably true to say that criminology's evolution into a legitimate and recognized academic discipline would have been more drawn out. Whatever the personal preferences of the criminologists involved might have been, the promise of a 'scientific' understanding of crime and its treatment was a seductive one for governments in the postwar period – a period of optimism founded on notions of social planning.

Before we examine the implications of this for criminology, it will be useful to step back a little and consider the social and political climate in British society at that time. The Fabian-influenced social reform movement referred to in the earlier discussion of the 1930s, gathered momentum as World War Two ran its course. The idea of social reform in the shape of better housing, health care and education, and freedom from abject poverty, captured the imagination of large numbers of the population, especially the working class. During the war, cinema audiences got used to seeing government information films giving glimpses of a postwar future when the quality of life would be greatly improved for everyone. Magazines such as *Picture Post* began to carry similar messages, with photographs of model council housing estates, where kids had plenty of green spaces to play in, and a trip to the lavatory was not an expedition through the elements to the outer reaches of a backyard. Many people lived in grossly inadequate housing, and dreaded the onset of illness because of the costs involved. Memories of the 1930s and the high levels of unemployment were still fresh in the minds of those once unemployed men and women now fighting for Britain. The sacrifices that people at the front and at home were being asked to make demanded a promise of something better than the prewar world that had gone before. The idea that winning the war would be rewarded merely by a return to the old days of glaring class inequality and privilege would not have been much of an incentive. Driven by welfarist principles, Britain after the war was to be a land fit for heroes.

In spite of this, many people were surprised when Churchill's wartime charisma failed to ensure a Conservative general election victory in 1945. As it turned out, the Labour Party won by a significant majority, and their manifesto committed them to a radical programme of social and economic reform. Not only was the welfare state to be established, but key sectors of the economy were to be nationalized. Clearly, the Labour Party's victory reflected the fact that a large number of voters were in accord with their plans for postwar reconstruction. An interesting explanation of their victory is attributed to my father-in-law, John Tracy. In his view it was because the men and women fighting overseas were rarely able to read the mainly Conservative supporting newspapers.

This, then, was the social landscape in which studies of crime and delinquency continued to develop in the 1940s and 1950s, and the nature of these studies became part of the *Zeitgeist* of postwar Britain. Criminology was thus infused with the ideas of social reform within a political philosophy of social democracy.

Institutional roots

One measure of criminology's growing importance during the two decades of the 1940s and 1950s is provided by looking at the institutional roots laid down by the discipline. The specialized criminology course which began at the London School of Economics in 1935 continued to develop under the leadership of Mannheim. A Department of Criminal Science was set up at the University of Cambridge in 1941, though this was concerned with research and publishing rather then teaching. Eventually the Home Office-funded Institute of Criminology grew out of this Department. The government funding of criminological research, originally sanctioned by the 1948 Criminal Justice Act, indicates the congruence between governmental social policy and the directions taken by British criminology at that time. In 1950, the Institute for the Scientific Treatment of Delinquency (ISTD), established in 1932, first published the *British Journal of Delinquency*, Britain's first specialist criminological journal. A shift in emphasis from delinquency to the broader concept of crime is reflected in the decision to alter the title of this journal to the *British Journal of Criminology* in 1960.

As criminology was trying to find its feet and establish itself as a legitimate academic discipline, debates about the types of behaviour or social problems criminology should study were joined by debates about how and why these should be studied: for example, whether research should be tailored to meet the needs of the Home Office, and whether the research should be driven by perspectives derived from psychology, psychoanalysis or sociology. One outcome of these debates was the setting up of the British Society of Criminology by a breakaway group dissatisfied with the lack of interest in theoretical analysis within the Scientific Group for the Discussion of Delinquency Problems, an organization founded in 1953 by the ISTD, and strongly influenced by psychoanalysis and a 'social problems' approach. Finally, in 1957 the Home Office Research Unit was established, and this continues to be an important centre for criminological research in this country.

Main characteristics

In his review of developments in British criminology during the postwar period, Stan Cohen (1981) argues that the institutions discussed above, within which criminology took root, exhibited four main characteristics: pragmatism, the interdisciplinary conception, correctionalism and positivism. In general terms, these describe the characteristics of criminology in this country up to the 1960s, though as Cohen concedes, there were a few individuals and pieces of research that deviated from the mainstream. However, it was not until the second half of the 1960s that significant breaks occurred, leading eventually to a new orthodoxy. Cohen's four characteristics can be examined in turn.

Pragmatism essentially refers to an approach based on empiricism and a strong orientation towards research with direct, practical consequences. In other words, a commitment to the provision of what is perceived to be useful knowledge, rather than to the construction of social scientific theory. As has been commented on earlier, promulgating the view that criminology was 'useful' was important in these early days from the point of view of gaining official acceptance and legitimation. The idea also fitted in neatly with the social reformism associated with the postwar period. This emphasis on pragmatism is, according to Cohen, well represented in the views of Radzinowicz, one of the leading criminologists at the time. Radzinowicz celebrated what he himself described as the 'pragmatic position', a position that precludes attempts to build an all-embracing theory, or theoretical schools of thought. In consequence, existing data and ideas, from whatever source, constituted an intellectual smorgasbord from which the criminologist might select as required. This again raises the question of what it is that identifies criminology as a distinct academic discipline. Can the approach recommended by Radzinowicz create something peculiarly 'criminological'? Can it fashion a legitimate, though hybrid, discipline, based as it is on dipping into the handiwork of already established academic disciplines?

Explaining why criminology was characterized by this stress on pragmatism, Cohen (1981: 222–3) points to:

> the fact that the whole idea of 'schools' of criminal law and criminology in the Continental sense is quite alien to the British legal tradition . . . The strong American socio-legal tradition was virtually absent in Britain. There was, thus, little opportunity for either a legally or sociologically based theoretical criminology to emerge.

He also refers to the argument, originally put forward by Anderson (1968), that on a different level, pragmatism has been a traditional feature of Britain's national culture. With reference to sociology, Anderson highlights a general distrust of theory and a failure to build any classical traditions at the time when European counterparts were doing just that. In Britain, sociology is historically associated with charity, social work and Fabian institutions. As Cohen (1981: 223) puts it:

In a much wider sense, the pragmatic tradition could be seen as part of the national culture; the amateur, muddling-along ethos of British life, combined with the Fabian type of pragmatism in which disciplines with obvious practical implication like criminology are located. Behind many enterprises in such fields, the attitude is: find out the right facts, then let the well-meaning chaps (for example, in the Home Office) make the obvious inferences and do the rest. Contrast, for example, the highly professional and research-based collection of information for policy-making in an American official commission with the typical Royal Commission – with its motley collection of peers, bishops, judges, very part-time experts and 'informed laymen', and its unbelievably slow rate of productivity.

The second characteristic of postwar British criminology identified by Cohen is *interdisciplinary conception*. By this he means that the empiricism and pragmatism which permeated criminology lent itself to the utilization of a broadly based mix of disciplines. This suggests that the eclectic approach was pursued not only because it apparently produced 'useful', practical knowledge, but also because it corresponded with the dominant view that it was in the nature of criminology to be an eclectic discipline. The work carried out by the big institutions of criminological research during the 1940s and 1950s, and which, as a totality, constituted 'British criminology', was based on a range of perspectives such as psychology, psychiatry, psychoanalysis, forensic science, medicine and sociology. However, an examination of these institutions individually does show that there were differences in the emphasis given to these various disciplines. While the dominant view seems to have been that no one discipline had cornered (or should corner) the market as a 'master discipline', research in specific institutions did tend to be skewed towards one or other of them. In fact, psychology and psychiatry were the most prominent. The minor role played by sociology is worthy of special note, and is returned to below.

Garland (1994) has identified three primary strands in the criminology that had emerged in the 1950s: administrative, psychoanalytical and sociological. The first of these was originally labelled 'administrative criminology' by George Vold (1958), in an effort to disparage a type of criminology lacking commitment to the development of a scientific, theoretically oriented model. This critique was mainly aimed at the Cambridge Institute of Criminology, then under the tutelage of Radzinowicz, and the Research Unit at the Home Office. Drawing on an eclectic mix of academic disciplines, administrative criminology describes a criminology that is fundamentally geared towards doing research which will be of direct practical use to government agencies concerned with criminal justice matters, for example the prisons and the courts.

The psychoanalytical strand exemplified the clinical approach to criminology. Studies set within a psychological and psychiatric framework attempted to fathom the causes of crime, to classify different types of offender, and, in the process, to develop theoretical models. Again, although these studies had scientific aspirations, they were ultimately locked into some notion of 'useful' knowledge – useful, that is, to the policy process. This kind of criminology was associated with the ISTD, the Maudsley Hospital, the Tavistock Institute, the British Society of Criminology and the *British Journal of Criminology*. According to Cohen (1981: 224), these institutions 'heavily weighted the field towards psychology and psychiatry', and 'This weighting remained despite the later contributions by sociologists'.

The sociological strand was largely associated with a growing number of sociological criminologists working under Mannheim at the London School of Economics in the 1950s. Mannheim, who came from a legal background, favoured a multidisciplinary approach, but did gradually come to develop a sociological perspective on crime and delinquency (Mannheim, 1965). Overall, however, British criminology contained relatively little written from a specifically sociological direction.

Cohen's third characteristic of postwar criminology – *correctionalism* – he describes as correction, reform and the problem of values. Although there were some exceptions, with writers such as Walker (1965) arguing for scientific detachment and a commitment to theoretical knowledge, on the whole, says Cohen, British criminology was strongly tied to government-led demands for a more efficient, albeit humanely reformed, correctional system (though there is no logical necessity for these two ambitions to coincide in practice). There was, therefore, a great stress on the treatment of offenders, and modes of intervention in the lives of predicted offenders. In essence, Cohen's reasonable complaint is that criminology had developed a largely unreflexive posture, whereby key assumptions, that should have been critically interrogated, were more or less taken for granted as 'givens'.

The fourth, and final, characteristic for Cohen (1981: 229) is what he calls the *positivist trap*, and he attributes this to the dominance of clinical interests: 'the search for clinical or statistical proof of causation, the commitment to scientific determinism, the denial of authenticity and meaning to deviance'.

This mobilization of 'scientific' criminology in the battle against recidivism and the prevention of delinquency among those 'at risk' was more of a promise than a reality. As David Downes (1978: 490) puts it: 'no clear idea had emerged of what might be inflicted on "pre-delinquents", should an adequate predictive instrument be devised, a seemingly remote possibility in any case.'

The lack of impact made by these correctionalist ideas, due to their inherent inadequacies, partly explains, says Downes, why no sustained criticisms, or indeed worries, developed during the 1950s. Put another way, the clinical alchemy feeding the correctionalist's dreams of scientific intervention into the lives of supposed 'pre-delinquents' was so underdeveloped and hazy that it was not looked upon as a real threat. However, says Downes, by the early 1960s and the advent of people such as the psychologist Hans Eysenck, these interventions on the basis of, say, aversion therapy, concentrated the minds of more liberally inclined criminologists wonderfully. Thus began a shift towards a more critical criminology impatient with the (dangerous) correctionalist principles lying at the heart of mainstream criminology.

An 'everything' of crime

Criminologists working in the postwar period obviously felt that they were engaged on a project that was distinctively 'criminological'. Using an interdisciplinary approach that entailed dipping into and borrowing from various already established relevant areas of study was precisely why criminology was seen as a distinct academic discipline. Somehow, the process of extracting the various factors – psychological, psychoanalytical, biological or sociological, etc. – in nature, viewed as acting in combination on offenders, or potential offenders, constituted the business of doing criminology. An approach anchored in a single discipline – for example, a psychology or sociology of crime – would have negated efforts to construct a separate, qualitatively different, way of studying crime and criminality. Thus, criminology became, potentially, an 'everything' of crime.

In this context Cyril Burt's (1925) prewar study, *The Young Delinquent*, is a good example. Using a sample of 400 children, Burt sought to identify those factors in a child's life that produce individual psychological variations. In particular, he was interested in those factors which in combination are associated with delinquency and, hence, can be used as predictors of future delinquency. Burt's work reflected his background in psychology and his professional role of educational psychologist in so far as he linked the various factors to psychological differences. However, the process of selecting the key factors was broadly based, relying as he did on all sorts of indices and measurement techniques: for example, psycho-analysis, IQ tests, and the investigation of social and material circumstances. It was this commitment to a multifactorial approach that endeared him to postwar criminologists. So too did his focus on the *individual* delinquent and, as a corollary, on the need to devise individually tailored treatment programmes. One other feature of Burt's work, which was to dominate much of the British criminology that followed, was its pathological frame of reference: some parents had 'defective' relationships with their children, some children had 'bad' temperaments, and so on.

Burt's study stands as a direct precursor of much of the criminology produced in the 1940s and 1950s. It concentrated on young offenders, and attempted to predict in a 'scientific' manner which children would be most likely to end up as delinquent. This endeavour to predict delinquency has been described by Stan Cohen as an 'obsession in British criminology'. Certainly, as we shall see, British criminology has been seduced by notions of 'prediction' and dominated by studies of youthful delinquency. In the immediate postwar period this was partly connected to the fact that official statistics continued to show apparent increases in amounts of juvenile crime. And, predictably, the research pathway relating to the treatment of young offenders marked out by Burt, was also followed, with research explicitly linked to the penal requirements of the Borstal system.

Sociological criminology

As criminology began to emerge as a separate discipline during the 1940s and 1950s, where was sociology? The short answer is that sociological criminology did exist and some studies were carried out within a loosely defined sociological framework. However, as a contributing discipline it played a minor role over that period in Britain, and continued to do so until the middle of the 1960s. From then on things changed and the influence of sociology increased dramatically.

In order to understand why this was so we have to take account of the central features of both the emerging criminology and sociology itself during the period under review. As we have seen, mainstream criminology made a virtue out of an interdisciplinary multifactorial approach. This, by definition, precluded embracing a specifically sociological analysis, though it did not preclude the incorporation of ideas and theories from sociology, at least in principle. However, in comparison with, notably, psychologically grounded criminology, sociological criminology was thin on the ground. Furthermore, according to Cohen (1981: 227), British criminology was operating within a fairly crude conceptual framework: 'Curious notions about sociology being concerned with "area" or "environmental" factors appear, sociology is identified with statistics, and concepts such as anomie, sub-culture or deprivation are distorted.'

It was also, as far as influences from other countries were concerned, something of a closed shop. This is particularly striking with respect to the United States where, by World War Two, a large and important body of sociological criminology had developed.

The way in which mainstream criminology coalesced around a commitment to pragmatism is also important. The desire to produce knowledge useful to criminal justice administrators, and especially to those working within the penal system, enabled criminology to achieve recognition as a legitimate discipline. Unfortunately, sociology failed to convince the pragmatists that it was able to offer much of value. The promise held out by criminology of being of practical use was predicated on a primary concern with the individual delinquent or pre-delinquent, and this clearly lent itself to a strong influence from psychiatry and psychology. In that context, even a more mature and sophisticated sociology would, because analyses are pitched at the level of the 'social', have had difficulty in gaining mainstream acceptance. The 'social problems' orientation of mainstream criminology finds a parallel with social work, with its emphasis on casework. Here, too, with knowledge evaluated on the basis of such things as 'relevance', 'practical application' and a promise to make problems 'manageable', sociology has traditionally assumed a secondary status to psychology.

This illustrates the continuing importance of the 'governmental project' (Garland, 1994) in the postwar years. Under these conditions, for sociology to become influential – and thereby earn centrally administered funds, respectable status, and a seat at the top table – it needed to prove its worth by producing what was seen as useful knowledge, which equates to knowledge that will help in the 'fight against crime'. Eventually, some sociology was able to do this, as exemplified by the research carried out at the Home Office. However, a coextensive process was at work from the late 1960s onwards which offered an alternative to this administrative route to discipline status. Some strands of sociological criminology opted out of the government project in favour of an academic – rather than 'Lombrosian' – project. Sociology was able to disengage itself from the government project to a significant degree because its discourse gathered together a large internal audience, irrespective of any claims to 'usefulness'. From the late 1960s there was a massive expansion in university, and then polytechnic, courses in sociology, and a concomitant growth in the publication of sociological texts. One outcome was increasing interest in sociological studies of crime, though at that period these were likely to be described as the sociology of deviance.

While the themes of much of this work would have shocked many of the criminologists from the 1940s and 1950s, it was just as much a product of that time in history as theirs was a product of the immediate postwar period. By the beginning of the 1970s there had been a spectacular expansion of this sociological area of study, characterized by a kaleidoscopic outpouring of bold, brash, unsettling, and sometimes wild virtuosity. As a consequence, sociological criminology (or whatever it was labelled) could to a large extent be sustained by its own internal resources, with a growing audience for the books and papers that were produced among undergraduates, post-graduates, researchers and teachers. In this way market forces began to play a part, as publishing houses became aware of the trend. Furthermore, the work produced could be as theoretical as the author wanted: it did not have to gain acceptance on the basis of some perceived usefulness to the Borstal system. Indeed, that sort of administrative criminology became the focus of criticism: disengagement from the Establishment was celebrated. Of course, one result of this disparaging attitude towards the pragmatic approach was a corresponding lack of direct political influence, a point that raises an interesting debate that has surfaced recently within the context of the growth in influence of 'left realism'. This is discussed later on.

Sociological criminology in Britain from the 1950s to the mid-1960s

Winning the World Cup made 1966 an auspicious year for English soccer: it was also an auspicious year for sociological criminology. In his short, though now classic, account of criminology over this period, Stan Cohen (1981: 227) tells us: 'there was virtually nothing before the post-1965 wave following Downes's book *The Delinquent Solution*.' Apart from being the most theoretically sophisticated sociological study of youth crime then available, Downes's research on delinquency in the East End of London arrived at a time when sociological criminology was poised to develop very significantly in Britain. The study is also important in that it was part of a lineage that over a decade or so had started (albeit spasmodically) to draw on American sources. It is ironic, though, that soon after Downes's book appeared, British criminology, under the influence of other, fresh ideas from the United States, shifted direction towards the so-called new deviancy. In a short period of time an alternative to mainstream criminology was developed by a number of young, and soon to be very influential, British criminologists.

Looking back from the vantage point of the 1990s to the time when Downes's book was published, the lack of sociological research on crime seems remarkable. Downes (1966: 100) described the situation as follows:

> What aspects of American Theorisation are substantiated by post-war findings on Juvenile delinquency in England? Any attempt to answer this question involves a revelation of the paucity of English work on the sociology of crime . . . Concentration on penology, the psychology of crime, and legal and statistical studies of delinquency . . . has involved the almost complete neglect of the very questions with which American sociologists pre-occupy themselves.

Soberingly, he suggested that sociological work, when it did begin to take off in this country in the 1950s, did so from a position established by the Victorian researcher Henry Mayhew. It was as if British painting had lain dormant since the time of the Pre-Raphaelites: 'Despite the almost single-handed efforts of Mannheim, the sociological study of crime and delinquency slowly revived only during the 1950s, almost a century after the publication in 1862 of Mayhew's massive documentation of the London "underworld" and slums' (ibid. 100–1).

Given that there was only a handful of British sociologically based studies of crime in existence by 1966, it is quite easy to list the key examples: H. D.

Willcock (1949); T. Ferguson (1952); T. Ferguson and J. Cunnison (1951, 1956); J. B. Mays (1954, 1959); M. P. Carter and P. Jephcott (1954); T. Morris (1957); H. Jones (1958); D. Lowson (1960); T. R. Fyvel (1961); J. C. Spencer *et al.* (1961). In addition to these, there were also studies essentially concerned with the statistical distribution of young offending: J. H. Bagot (1941); A. M. Carr-Saunders *et al.* (1942); W. R. Little and V. R. Ntsekhe (1959); J. W. B. Douglas (1964). Studies by P. Sainsbury (1955) and P. Scott (1956), although often referred to in this context (the former, for example, being reproduced in a set of readings on the sociology of crime by Carson and Wiles, 1971), were carried out by psychiatrists.

This meagre list, then, more or less constituted the sociology of crime and delinquency in Britain up to the mid-1960s, thus reinforcing the point made earlier: that criminology during this period was not much interested in sociology, preferring instead the pragmatic, interdisciplinary approach, with strong leanings towards clinical positivism. Clearly, sociological criminology was marginal to the concerns of the mainstream. One result was that until picked up by some of the writers listed above, the large amount of sociological criminology produced in the United States since the early 1920s was virtually ignored in this country. Cohen suggests that this was not always because of mere ignorance, or a perception of it as irrelevant. Even Mannheim, who did most in the late 1930s and the 1940s to introduce sociological perspectives into criminology, is accused by Cohen (1981: 227) of a 'certain parochialism . . . with his apparent policy of selecting for his textbook American work only when British or European work could not be found'. This situation was slowly remedied during the 1950s as two of the most influential early sociological studies of crime (Mays, 1954; Morris, 1957) introduced American ideas and research.

Although British criminology was not much interested in sociology, the reverse is also true: British sociology was not much interested in criminology. Yet in the light of what has already been said about the nature of criminology, this detachment can perhaps be easily forgiven. Criminology as it was constituted provided few attractions for the dedicated sociologist. However, a failure to appreciate the continuities between the general concerns of sociology (for example, social order) and the concerns of criminology, is less easily explained. According to Cohen, some of the reasons for this resistance to criminology derived from features internal to the discipline of sociology itself in Britain, such as a view that studying criminals or deviants was peripheral to core sociological projects. Other reasons, he says, derived from the 'other side', from the traditional framework within which crime was studied. This framework was guaranteed to put sociologists off: 'the moralistic, non-abstract ways in which deviance was studied and the early identification of this field with social work, reformative or correctional concerns' (Ibid. 231). On a more personal level, Cohen has painted an unflattering picture of sociology departments during most of the 1960s, with antagonism towards issues of crime and deviance being encountered among all political and theoretical persuasions.

The sociological studies of crime developing in the 1950s represented a move away from an interdisciplinary, clinically based mainstream criminology. Instead of juggling with a multiplicity of biological, psychological and social factors which, in one way or another, were seen as creating individual criminals, sociology explicitly focused on the social context of crime. This social context was the neighbourhood, thus sociological criminology developed within the strong British tradition of area–community studies, a tradition that has endured (e.g. Willmott (1966); Parker (1974); Baldwin and Bottoms (1976); Gill (1977); Bottoms and Wiles (1986); and Bottoms et al. (1987)).

The 'social' dimension had been acknowledged in prewar criminology, even though it had tended to be lost due to the preoccupation with clinical psychology. Mainstream criminological research at that time was littered with concepts such as 'inadequacy', 'maladjustment' and 'low intelligence', and these 'conditions' were often associated with poverty and the slum neighbourhood. On a political level, as we have seen, one important feature of postwar Britain was an increasingly interventionist state, and this included an expanding social welfare programme. Thus an emphasis was placed on the social bases of various defined social problems, among which was crime. This was clearly congruent with the concerns of a Fabian-influenced sociological criminology.

One striking characteristic of the sociological studies of crime carried out during the 1950s and first half of the 1960s, and listed above, is that they all concentrated on young people and their delinquencies. This is not surprising, perhaps, given growing panics about juvenile crime, and the message from official statistics that the peak age of offending was 14. This was also the period that saw the emergence of distinctive youth subcultures, beginning in 1953 with the Teddy Boys, as well as the social category of 'teenager'. These developments helped to accentuate the well-documented tendency to associate adolescence with unruly or troublesome behaviour (Pearson, 1983; Muncie, 1984).

During the decade up to the publication of Downes's book, then, a sociological alternative to mainstream criminology began to emerge in Britain. As we shall see when this work is examined in more detail, British criminologists were at last acknowledging, and drawing on, American research, and shifting the spotlight away from individualism towards the socio-cultural context of delinquency, towards the neighbourhoods in which delinquent youth lived. However, this type of research started much later here than in the United States, and this, combined with the facts that few sociologists were interested in the field and that there was much less money available to fund research, meant that by the mid-1960s, relatively few studies aimed at testing the explanatory models had been carried out.

While the late 1960s saw a rapid growth in the number of sociologists in this country who did have an interest in crime and deviance, this interest was by then being sustained in the main by the promise held out by a different kind of sociological criminology. The emphasis now was on the sociology of deviance, and the emerging paradigm was referred to as new deviancy theory. Inevitably, this shift had occurred originally in the United States and the work produced there provided a fecund source of ideas for British criminologists. Very quickly, and in spite of being only relatively short-lived, the earlier sociological criminology was itself labelled, disparagingly, as 'mainstream', or 'orthodox', and became the target for intense criticism. Obviously, these criticisms can only be fully appreciated after we have examined the respective models. However, the discussion so far, aimed at plotting briefly the direction taken by sociological studies of crime, does perhaps give a hint of the nature of some of these criticisms.

Fundamentally, the earlier work had made no attempt to grapple with the definitional issues surrounding the use of terms such as 'crime' and 'delinquency'; state definitions were taken as given. On a less abstract level, these studies were content to rely on official statistics regarding the distribution of crime, and this helped to concentrate research not just on youthful delinquency, but also specifically on lower-working-class males; middle-class deviance was more or less ignored, as was corporate crime. This situation links up with an assumption of a consensus over norms and values: although some studies pointed to delinquency being normal in certain areas, these areas tended to be conceived of as enclaves of criminality within a larger society founded upon a monolithic law-abiding citizenry. There was too, in these studies from the 1950s, a strong social work ethos, and a positivist orientation towards seeking out the causes of delinquency, or identifying 'at risk', 'pre-delinquent' children, with a view to devising appropriate treatment regimes. Above all else, though, earlier sociological criminology was accused of ignoring the part played by the various control agencies in the actual construction of deviance.

Before turning to these developments in British criminology from the late 1960s, it will be useful to cross the Atlantic and have a look at sociological criminology in the United States from the early part of the century up to the impact of new deviancy theory.

Sociological criminology in the United States

When sociological perspectives on crime started to appear, the discipline of criminology in the United States and in Britain was dominated by analyses pitched at the level of the individual. In extreme examples, attempts were made to trace the source of criminal behaviour directly to biological or

psychological factors within the individual. The assumption ͓
something was wrong with the individual, rather than with society. ͙͙
sociological challenge to this type of theorizing developed much earlier in
the United States than it did in this country. Although biologically and
psychologically based versions of positivism by no means disappeared, a
shift towards seeing crime as the outcome of social circumstances began as
early as the turn of the twentieth century in the United States.

It was during the 1920s and 1930s, though, that two particularly
important and influential traditions in the sociology of crime and
delinquency emerged, one based on the work of the Chicago ecologists, the
other on Robert Merton's 'strain theory'. Until the 1950s, however, this
work was 'wilfully excluded' (Cohen, 1981) by criminologists in Britain. The
situation began to change when Mays (1954) acknowledged the contribution
made by some of this American research, but Morris (1957) was the first
British criminologist to seriously tap into, and give a voice to, American
sociological criminology. From then on American research became
increasingly influential, and by the late 1960s the floodgates had opened.

The Chicago School

Some of the reasons why sociology began to influence criminological
thought in the United States much earlier than it did in Britain can be briefly
noted. To begin with, as an academic discipline, sociology had established
an institutional foothold by the end of the nineteenth century. The first
university sociology department was set up in 1892 at, significantly, the
University of Chicago. As a consequence, by the beginning of this century
sociology had already achieved a degree of legitimacy, and a power base,
including resources for research, from which to develop. For those
academics connected with the sociology department in Chicago, the city
itself stood before them like a vast social laboratory. Even by American
standards the city had grown rapidly. Only 4,100 people lived there in 1833
when the city incorporated; by the late 1890s the number had risen to 1
million. This spectacular growth continued into this century, so that by 1910
the population had doubled to 2 million. As well as indigenous Americans,
such as black people moving up from the southern states, the population
was swelled by immigrants from all over the world. Chicago was therefore
characterized by a hugely diverse range of social groups, and for many of
these the move to the city was a move into urban deprivation. Small wonder
that criminologists were fascinated by the social life of the city in which they
lived. Working within an urban sociology tradition, the Chicago School
sought to illuminate the socio-cultural dynamics of crime and delinquency
in Chicago's mean streets.

Drawing on the familiar imagery of the 'urban jungle', and equating city life with crime and other social problems, many Americans viewed the rapidly expanding cities with some apprehension. The city became an 'issue'. In this context we might note the growth of the 'progressive movement' during the first part of the century. This movement, based on liberal principles, concerned itself with the human costs of capitalist growth in America: the city slums, poor working conditions, the lack of health care provision, and so on. By the 1920s the movement had gathered a great deal of support, not just among the urban poor, but also among more powerful groups in society, who saw in its reformism an acceptable alternative to more radical groups, such as the American Communist Party. A general climate of opinion was therefore developing that was sympathetic to the work of the Chicago School: in other words, to research that stressed the social contexts of crime. In many ways this is similar to the influence exerted by Fabianism in Britain in the postwar period. At each respective time in history, reformist ideas helped to create conditions conducive to the emergence of a criminology curious about the social contexts of crime. In America the framework within which this criminology was nurtured was urban sociology; in Britain it was community studies. In each case there was a promise of gathering data and constructing explanations that would prove useful for social policy makers.

As we shall see, much of the research carried out by the Chicago School (also known as the Chicago ecologists) concerned itself with juvenile delinquency, just like the sociological criminology in Britain in the 1950s and 1960s. In general terms this meant relating delinquency (the distribution of which was derived from official statistics) to the nature of the social processes associated with the areas in which it occurred. For the Chicago ecologists, social disorganization was identified as the key explanatory concept (Shaw and McKay, 1942). They were also interested in talking to people, and in this vein carried out a great deal of pioneering work based on in-depth interviews (referred to as the 'life history' approach (Shaw, 1930)). Often there was a social policy dimension to this research. Shaw and McKay, for example, two of the most famous researchers from this period, were attached to a child guidance clinic, although they had close connections with the University of Chicago sociology department, and as such were committed to discovering ways of preventing delinquency. Indeed, Shaw established the 'Chicago Area Project' in the early 1930s, which was a community-based set of initiatives aimed at, for instance, creating better organized neighbourhoods and providing facilities that would divert youngsters away from delinquent activities. In an assessment of the Project fifty years on, Schlossman et al. (1984) credit it with achieving some success in reducing amounts of recorded delinquency in the areas concerned.

One important figure who did depart from this typical concentration on juveniles was Sutherland, who was a professor in the sociology department at Chicago from 1930 to 1935. In the 1940s Sutherland (1940, 1949) turned the spotlight onto white-collar crime (a term he coined), that is, crime commited by persons of high status. This was well in advance of any criminological research on this theme in Britain.

Early 'strain theory'

An alternative approach to explaining crime was put forward by Robert Merton (1993) in 1938. Although Merton was not a criminologist, but a notable figure in sociology, and though his original formulation covered only a few pages, his basic ideas have endured in criminological thought. Unlike the Chicago ecologists, who located the source of criminal behaviour in the socio-cultural characteristics of the neighbourhoods in which they lived, Merton located the source within the social structure of American society itself. For him, crime did not result from the deviant values of the slum neighbourhoods, but rather from mainstream, conventional values into which all Americans were socialized. He argued that the core values stressed material success, but that the problem was that not everyone was equally placed to achieve this success. Hence the existence of 'strain' in some people's lives. In essence, then, property crime resulted from a lack of equality of opportunity, and was therefore a product of social structure. The – to many – startling conclusion was that American society was criminogenic.

Given that crime, for Merton, was a function of relative deprivation, the obvious way to ease the crime problem was to create more opportunities for the poor, so that they had better chances of legitimately achieving material success. As it happens, Merton was himself brought up in a slum neighbourhood, and was well aware of the routine disadvantages experienced by those around him.

Merton's introduction of strain theory into criminology was to have a long-term and profound influence on the shape of sociological studies of crime and delinquency. In the United States, the general principles were picked up and elaborated by, for example, Cohen (1955) and Cloward and Ohlin (1960).

Strain theory and crime policy

The beginning of the 1960s saw a change in the political climate of the United States. The ideas of the strain theorists found fertile ground in a Kennedy administration that had openly embraced a policy of equal opportunities. While the country had achieved massive economic growth in the postwar period, the ideology of the American Dream was subverted by the persistence of poverty, the endemic racial discrimination and disadvantage faced by black and Hispanic people, and rising levels of recorded crime. In terms of social policy, the emphasis shifted from purely community-based schemes that attempted to divert youngsters away from crime, to broader, federally funded initiatives directed at increasing the opportunities available to the disadvantaged. There were direct links here with Merton's version of strain theory. If crime resulted from a lack of legitimate opportunities to achieve the goal of material success, then increasing those opportunities should lead to less crime.

The need to establish equality of opportunity within the education system was centre stage; improving the educational qualifications of the disadvantaged would improve their chances in the job market. Consequently, with the opening up of legitimate avenues to success, there would be less pressure to opt for the illegitimate avenues provided by crime. The aim, of course, was not the creation of a classless society; somehow, equality of opportunity was to be fashioned out of a society where the class structure remained intact. It was a profoundly liberal philosophy that aimed to create a capitalist system with a human face. Criminologists who belonged to the strain theory camp had found some powerful political allies.

There was another dimension to Merton's work that helped it to become influential at this time. By using the concept of relative deprivation, he stressed that it was not deprivation *per se* that was important, but rather the ways in which individuals subjectively experienced deprivation. Specifically, the impact of blocked opportunities was dependent upon the aspirations that people had; from this perspective, problems arise when available opportunities cannot meet these aspirations. Merton, therefore, seemed to offer a plausible explanation of why during periods of affluence recorded crime rates, puzzlingly, continued to rise.

The state-sponsored 'war against poverty' intensified when Kennedy's successor, Lyndon Johnson took office. Under the direction of the Office of Economic Opportunity – a title that summed up the prevailing ethos – large sums were spent on 'Operation Head Start' and other big initiatives, and these continued into the 1970s. While analyses vary in their explanations, the consensus appears to be that in spite of billions of dollars being expended, the programmes were not significantly successful. As far as recorded crime rates are concerned, these climbed inexorably throughout the 1960s and 1970s.

The link between theory and practice was even more explicit, and finely tuned to delinquent youth, in the case of two other strain theorists, Cloward and Ohlin. As Lilley *et al.* (1989: 79) describe it:

> their opportunity theory 'resonated well with the liberal domestic politics of John F. Kennedy,' and particularly with the president's call for equal opportunity. Indeed, the fit between strain theory and the prevailing political context was so

close that Lloyd Ohlin was invited to Washington, D.C. to assume a Health, Education and Welfare post and to assist in formulating delinquency policy.

One outcome of this was the 'Mobilization for Youth' (MFY) delinquency prevention programme; Cloward was appointed director of research. MFY eventually became more radical in its demands than many powerful groups could tolerate: 'MFY promoted boycotts against schools, protests against welfare policies, rent strikes against "slum landlords", lawsuits to ensure poor people's rights, and voter registration' (ibid. 79). And there were claims 'by the *New York Daily News* that the staff was infested with "Commies and Commie Sympathizers" ' (ibid. 80). In the end this sort of radicalism led to such programmes being allowed to die. There is a parallel here with the Community Development Projects set up in the 1970s in Britain: once they strayed too far from fairly narrow parameters – say, helping establish playgroups – complaints of 'going too far' started to appear.

5 | Social disorganization and anomie

The sociology and criminology of Emile Durkheim (1858–1917)
The Chicago School
Mertonian strain theory

The sociology and criminology of Emile Durkheim (1858–1917)

It is platitudinous to say that Durkheim's influence on sociology, including sociological criminology, has been immense. Unlike Marx and Weber, the other two giants of sociological theory, Durkheim devoted a significant amount of space to the phenomena of crime and deviance. The main links between Durkheim and subsequent developments in the field of criminology can be summarized as follows:

- His work was influential in shifting analyses of criminality away from sources rooted in the individual towards sources that were socio-cultural in nature.

- He was a proponent of the positivist school of thought, especially with reference to methodology: that is, he attempted to develop an objective, scientific understanding of society.

- He characterized societies as 'healthy' or 'unhealthy'/ 'pathological', assessed in terms of degrees of organization or disorganization, and by employing the concept of 'anomie'. These ideas were to have a considerable influence on the Chicago School and R. K. Merton in the period up to World War Two.

- His evolutionary view of social development and the application of social Darwinian principles also influenced the Chicago ecologists, who conceived of the social life of the city in terms of dynamic social processes involving interactions between the inhabitants and their environments.

- He influenced functionalist writers through his discussion of the importance of a consensus regarding norms and values, and the socialization processes through which this was achieved.

- Later writers were to utilize his argument that crime was both normal and functionally useful.

- His work also represents an interesting early precursor of labelling theory. He argued that the quality of 'crime' or 'deviance' is 'not the intrinsic quality of a given act but that definition which the collective conscience lends them' (Durkheim, 1982: 101).

- Finally, his analysis of the social bonds that secure a cohesive, integrated society, pointed the way to the emergence of control theory much later on in the twentieth century.

Durkheim's sociology

There is not the space to present a detailed discussion of the sociology of Durkheim, and in any case such discussions are widely available (e.g. Lukes, 1973; Giddens, 1978). The intention here is to examine those aspects of his work that are particularly pertinent to issues of crime and deviance, and influenced the ideas of subsequent writers.

A key contributor to functionalist sociology, and strongly committed to positivist principles based on scientific method, Durkheim sought to study human beings and their societies from a fundamentally sociological perspective. By so doing he wished to repudiate those who reduced human behaviour to individual psychological or biological impulses. This is not to say that he rejected the psychological dimension, but rather that he saw psychological states of mind as deriving from the nature of society itself. Indeed, he was centrally concerned with the effects that social forces had on the individual member of society, and sometimes the distinction between the two dimensions is not always clear-cut.

His desire to show the importance of the social dimension is exemplified in his famous study of suicide (Durkheim, 1970). Taking what appears to be one of the most personal, individualized actions, and hence ostensibly more amenable to psychological than sociological modes of analysis, Durkheim in fact located the sources of suicide not in the psyche of the individual, but in a social reality external to the individual. In this way he wished to illustrate how a society was not just a collection of individuals; that it was something more than the sum of its parts. On the basis of a comparative study of different countries, Durkheim noticed that suicide rates had, over time, assumed a definite pattern. They remained fixed at a certain level within the same society, the variation between one society and another also remained fixed, as did the suicide rates pertaining to different groups within the same society (for example, Jews and Catholics). In view of the fact that over these time periods the actual individuals living in the various societies obviously changed, he concluded that the primary source of differential suicide rates lay in an external social realm; there were, in other words, suicidogenic forces at work that were external to the individual. We will return to this below.

Achieving social order

Durkheim was fundamentally concerned with the 'problem of order', and, indeed, this is often referred to as the central 'problem' of sociology. This concern with order and regulation led him to consider issues of crime, deviance and difference. At the time Durkheim was writing, European society was attempting to come to terms with modernity. Industrialization and urbanization had profoundly altered the nature of European societies. Rapid, and sometimes abrupt social upheavals had occurred, especially in his own country, France. Not surprisingly, many social thinkers directed their energies at trying to make sense of these changes and their impact on social life. They often looked back to an earlier, pre-industrial golden age of 'community', and in the process, making unfavourable comparisons with modern life (for example, Tonnies). Others, for example Simmel, directed their worries specifically at the city, which was seen to exemplify modernity and all its ills. Durkheim also counterposed the past – in the shape of traditional, 'primitive' societies – with the present, though he took the view that whilst there was a real danger of sliding into irretrievable disorganization, those with power could actively intervene to prevent this happening. Sociology, he believed, would provide the knowledge base for such interventions, and in fact he eventually worked with the French government on the design of the state education system.

Mechanical and organic solidarity

In common with other eminent sociological theorists such as Comte and Spencer, Durkheim viewed social change from an evolutionary perspective and, applying Darwinian logic, saw societies as analogous to biological organisms. Just as animals and plants adapt to suit changing circumstances over periods of time, so human societies, as they evolve, have the potential to adapt by developing appropriate social institutions. Societies that did adapt in this way to social change would, from this perspective, be 'healthy'; those that did not, 'pathological'. However, his belief in the need for governmental intervention, guided by scientific knowledge, suggests a departure from the notion of natural selection in the social sphere, and also raises questions about the relative importance of human agency in managing social change.

Durkheim argued that in pre-industrial, traditional societies, social order was based upon a certain kind of social solidarity that he called 'mechanical solidarity'. These societies lacked the complex web of mutually dependent institutions characterizing modern societies. Instead they were composed of fragmented, small, tribal or clan-based segments. Solidarity was achieved through an all encompassing set of norms and values referred to as the 'collective conscience'. Although this constraining moral force was external to the individual – in the form of 'social facts' – through a process of socialization it became internalized by society's members:

> A social fact is every way of acting, fixed or not, capable of exercising on the individual an influence, or an external constraint; or again, every way of acting which is general throughout a given society, while at the same time existing in its own right independent of its individual manifestations. (Durkheim, 1982: 59)

In this type of society social order was fundamentally rooted in moral regulation. Unlike the situation in modern societies, there was no place for individualism: the individual was, in effect, subsumed or 'lost' within the tribe or clan. Reactions to non-conformity would be harsh and retributive in character.

On the other hand, and according to Durkheim, a central feature of modern societies was individuation. Here individual members are freed from the tyranny of 'sameness', and this illustrates how Durkheim rejected a commonplace late-nineteenth-century sentiment that bemoaned the loss of 'real community'. He did recognize, however, that freeing the individual from the constraints of mechanical solidarity brought with it its own dangers in terms of social order. In his view human nature was composed of two selves: the social self (socialized and integrated), and the egoistic self (unsocialized and unintegrated). The egoistic self, freed from constraining social forces and left to its own devices naturally possessed desires that knew no bounds. If modern societies were to stress individualism – that is, to have as a central value the right of individuals to realize their own potential – then, Durkheim argued, some restraining mechanism had to operate, otherwise disorder would reign – for example in the form of crime and deviance. For Durkheim, order in modern societies was predicated on the social integration deriving from functionally interdependent institutions, and the division of labour was to play a central role. Modern industrial society is based upon a diverse range of work tasks, tasks that continue to become increasingly specialized. He saw a 'natural' division of labour – that is, one where the individual's work task matched their talents and abilities – as the source of functional interdependency. Although treated as individuals, and perceiving of themselves as individuals, society's members would appreciate the necessity of working together for their mutual benefit. The division of labour is 'the sole process which enables the necessities of social cohesion to be reconciled with the principle of individuation' (Durkheim in Lukes, 1973: 147).

He called this type of solidarity 'organic solidarity', though his discussion of a 'forced' division of labour indicates that Durkheim was aware that modern European societies had some way to go before this happy state of social integration could be said to have arrived. In essence, a forced division of labour is one where people's jobs do not match their abilities, hence his argument that selection processes based upon equality of opportunity were a necessary pre-condition.

The increasing modernization of society, then, represented a move away from social order based upon mechanical solidarity to one based upon organic solidarity. This entailed a process of individuation, whereby the all-consuming moral regulation of the collective conscience associated with traditional societies, and encompassing all aspects of human behaviour, receded, and social integration deriving from functional interdependency emerged. This did not mean, however, that Durkheim saw no need for moral regulation via a collective conscience; quite the contrary. He believed that a lack of moral force, and adherence to a normative system, was an ever-present danger, and *in extremis* would produce a condition of 'anomie'. In an anomic society there are no moral constraints on the individual's limitless desires. Even a society with a division of labour based upon equal opportunities still needed a consensual moral force. The difference would be that in modern societies the collective conscience, whilst having a central moral core, would be flexible enough to allow a high degree of individualism. For Durkheim a modern collective conscience should be constituted by a cluster of values regarding individual dignity, equal opportunities, the work ethic, and social justice. Legal rules and rules based on custom would still be required if organic solidarity was to be maintained. With the decline in influence of religious beliefs, Durkheim saw it as imperative that governments intervened in economic and social life in order to establish suitable institutional arrangements and processes of socialization conducive to the creation of social cohesion. As Sumner (1994: 12) has pointed out in an illuminating recent discussion of the relevance of Durkheim's thought to contemporary Britain:

> By arguing that the urgent duty and task of the state was to bring the anomic condition of society to an end, Durkheim's position is rounded off and he can clearly be seen as an early theorist of what we would now call social democracy.

The two concepts egoism and anomie (together with 'altruism' and 'fatalism') also crop up in Durkheim's study of suicide mentioned earlier. Taking a specific example of 'deviant' behaviour, he links certain types of 'pathological' society, as external entities, to the state of mind of individuals living in those societies. His conclusion was that: 'Suicide varies with the degree of integration of the social group of which the individual forms a part' (Durkheim, 1970: 209).

Four different types of suicide were said to result: egoistic, altruistic, anomic and fatalistic (the last type, in fact, is only treated as a footnote, since Durkheim felt that it could be ignored because of its rarity in modern societies). *Egoistic* suicide was the product of 'excessive individualism', whereby individuals are cast adrift from other members of society and are isolated from the shared norms and expectations. At times of trouble such individuals lack the 'mutual moral support' of work, family, or community networks. There is a strong link between these ideas and a later development in criminological theory known as control theory. *Altruistic* suicide, on the other hand, occurs when the individual is overintegrated into the group, so that they cease to have a separate, personal identity, thereby denigrating their own worth. This type of suicide includes, for instance, those who take their own lives out of a sense of duty. *Anomic* suicide results from times of upheaval, when the force of moral regulation is weakened – for example, during times of economic slumps or booms – and normative constraints on behaviour cease to be effective. This is sometimes referred to as a state of 'normlessness'. In this situation there is an absence of a moral force in society through which the individual is able to accept their place in the world and the rewards they receive. Lacking this moral restraint an insatiable, though futile, desire for 'more' is released. As Box (1981: 98) puts it:

> Durkheim viewed human aspirations as naturally boundless, and, as he saw it, the trick of social control was not to give people what they want – that would be impossible – but to persuade them that what they have is about all they morally deserve.

Crime as inevitable and necessary

Durkheim is also associated with the augument that crime is both inevitable and necessary. For him crime is a social fact, just as a stable suicide rate is a social fact. If such things are found in an 'average' society, then they are normal; hence crime is normal. In order to appreciate the reasoning behind this, it is important to consider what has already been said regarding Durkheim's views on modernity and individualism. While he endorsed the high moral premium placed on individualism in modern societies, he also recognized that the existence of a flexible, less draconian collective conscience, which provided the breathing space for the individual, would inevitably lead to degrees of nonconformity, and some of this nonconformity would be criminalized. Even in a society composed entirely of saints, he hypothesized, there would still be crime. Extraordinarily high moral standards would be enshrined in the collective conscience, giving an extremely low tolerance threshold, so that what to us are negligible examples of rule breaking, become for the saintly brethren terrible acts. This suggests that in the real world it is futile to attempt to eradicate crime by introducing more repression. By closing down areas of freedom through increasingly repressive legislation, previously trivial acts of nonconformity become serious transgressions. In response, the net of legal sanctions is spread even wider, forever criminalizing more and more acts.

In order for no crime to exist there would, from Durkheim's perspective, have to be total agreement regarding norms and values among all members of society, but for him 'a uniformity so universal and absolute is utterly impossible' (Durkheim, 1982: 100). An opposite situation arises when there is a weak collective conscience, bringing with it a state of anomie. Here the limitless desires of the individual would be subject to no moral constraint. However, as Bob Roshier (1977) has pointed out, following Durkheimian logic a crime-free society is theoretically possible not only where the collective conscience is all-consuming (albeit in reality an impossible situation for Durkheim), but also where the collective conscience ceased to exist – a society of devils. In this situation there would be no basis for defining any act as criminal, and although such a society is not one that most people would consider emigrating to, it would none the less be crime-free.

An important dimension to this discussion of the inevitability of crime has been highlighted by Sumner. The framework that Durkheim developed opened up a theoretical space for the concept of 'deviance', and therefore a specialism called the sociology of deviance. By illustrating how modernity, by definition, frees the individual from the conformity of a traditional society, bringing with it an inevitable diversity of behaviour, Durkheim acknowledged that some of this diversity will, again inevitably, be socially sanctioned (or censured) as crime or deviance, or in some cases left alone as mere difference. This raises the question of how these various categories are arrived at in practice.

Of course many people would agree with Durkheim that crime is inevitable; the view that it is also necessary, though, has struck some people as very odd. Roshier has pointed out that accidents at work are inevitable, but that does not mean that they are necessary. According to Durkheim, apparently, crime is necessary because it is functionally useful: it helps to maintain a healthy society. Crime does this, he believed, by fulfilling an 'adaptive' function and a 'boundary maintenance' function.

The *adaptive* function of crime is to introduce new ideas into society, thereby preventing that society from stagnating. The criminals concerned are, therefore, innovators who help society to adapt to changing circumstances – unfortunately for the criminals their ideas are ahead of their time. From this viewpoint too much conformity – that is, too little crime – would put the brakes on a society's development. Durkheim gives as an example Socrates, who although condemned in his own time as a criminal, eventually had a beneficient and progressive influence on society through his (criminal) ideas.

In the second case, the *boundary maintenance* function, crime is seen as operating rather like a medieval morality play. Through such things as public hangings, media reporting, and conversations between people, the criminal event is inserted into people's lives and functions to reaffirm the boundary between 'good' and 'bad' behaviour. The collective nature of these responses, according to Durkheim, promotes social solidarity. In common with most supporters of the functions-of-crime argument, Kai Erikson (1966) draws on the boundary maintenance function discussed by Durkheim rather than the adaptive function. Using a dispute among members of an early Puritan group in the United States as a case study, Erikson argues that the public trial and then banishment of the dissident minority who refused to follow the elders was functionally necessary in terms of the social solidarity of the whole group. The response of the majority is seen as drawing the new moral boundaries in that society.

An important critique of what he calls the functions-of-crime myth is provided by Roshier (1977). As far as the adaptive function of crime is concerned, Roshier accepts that this is what Durkheim argued, but maintains that he was wrong. In the case of the boundary maintenance function, on the other hand, he argues that this in fact was not what Durkheim was saying, and that Erikson, therefore, has misinterpreted his original source. With respect to Durkheim's view that crime involves innovation and allows society to adapt and progress, Roshier says that to illustrate the validity of this proposition we would have to take specific examples of activities that were previously criminal and show how they eventually contributed to a healthy society, as well as demonstrate that the fact that they were originally criminal was a necessary characteristic of these activities. Roshier concludes that it is the functional value of the *ideas* associated with such activities that is important, not their criminal status. Thus, in the case of Socrates, criminalizing his ideas was not required in order to make them subsequently useful. Roshier also points out that while certain activities such as pornography or prostitution might be functionally useful for society, it is not their status as crimes (if they were criminalized) that endows them with this usefulness. In his view society could simply allow a diversity of behaviour, and this would throw up innovative ideas. Durkheim, of course, would argue that this is precisely what modern, individualistic societies do, with the inevitable consequence that some of this diversity is criminalized. His position seems to be that given the likelihood that those behaviours and ideas seen as most threatening to society will be criminalized, then, with the passage of time, there will be an inevitable tendency for diversity of a criminal nature to fulfil this adaptive function. However, this still leaves the question: Does the behaviour by necessity have to be criminal? Durkheim appears to be arguing that crime will fulfil this adaptive function *inevitably* rather than *necessarily*.

Turning to the boundary maintenance function of crime, Roshier argues that Durkheim's views have been misinterpreted by Erikson and others, and offers this as a key passage:

> If then, when (a crime) is committed, the consciences which it offends do not unite themselves to give mutual evidence of their communion, and recognize that the case is anomolous, they would be permanently unsettled. They must re-enforce themselves by mutual assurances that they are always agreed. The only means for this is action in common. In short it is the common conscience which is attacked, it must be that which resists, and accordingly the resistance must be collective. (Durkheim quoted in Roshier, 1977: 5)

According to Roshier, Durkheim is not saying that crime, as such, maintains the moral boundaries between right and wrong in a particular society, but that a collective response to crime – that is, social control – fulfils this function. If there is no crime or deviance, then by definition social solidarity exists, because there is complete consensus over norms and values. For Durkheim, though, this situation is not only impossible to achieve, but the very idea is not congruent with the values placed on individualism in a modern society. Thus, again, Durkheim is saying that the existence of crime is inevitable, and as Roshier points out, responses to it must be collective. In the specific case discussed by Erikson, it could be argued that the deviance of the dissenting group was not a necessary pre-condition for the acceptance of the new moral boundaries. If no split had occurred, then arguably the moral boundaries would have been universally agreed upon anyway.

The Chicago School

Durkheim once commented that the platform of the railway station in Paris onto which France's rural workers alighted, and made their first contact with a new life in the city, seemed to possess magical qualities. As soon as their feet touched the platform, all religious beliefs disappeared.

Throughout the nineteenth century social thinkers in Europe had been variously appalled, excited or fascinated by the consequences of urbanization, and one of the main consequences was judged to be an increase in crime. As the nineteenth century developed, studies of urban life and criminality were increasingly influenced by the ideas of positivism, though explanations of crime tended to emphasize social rather than individual factors. A positivist commitment to scientific method is well represented in the statistical work of the Belgium mathematician, Quetelet, and the French lawyer, Guerry. Referring to their endeavours as 'social physics' and 'moral statistics' respectively, they analysed official records relating to the amount and distribution of crime in the city. The published statistical results were seen as scientific measures of the moral life of the city. This sort of social scientific research eventually began to influence research in Britain. Motivated by a strong sense of a philanthropic, reforming mission, figures such as Fletcher, Mayhew and Booth amassed a wealth of highly detailed information on the dark side of city life. By the late nineteenth century, however, and especially because of the influence of Lombroso, attempts to locate the social bases of crime began to be superseded by positivistic studies oriented towards the individual.

The early social researchers produced graphic descriptions of life among the urban poor, and in the process introduced the notion of the criminal area. Cities were associated with crime, but it was in certain parts of the city that crime and deviance were seen to be concentrated. Then, and now, there are potent images of dark and 'dangerous places'. Nineteenth century accounts made reference to the undeserving poor, debauchery, disorder and insanity; nowadays it is the underclass, the inner city and deprived council estates, social disorganization and 'yob culture'. Rising levels of recorded crime and outbreaks of urban rioting in recent times have ensured a continuing interest in such areas. From Mayhew's writings on the rookeries of Victorian London to contemporary accounts of life in the deprived inner cities and outer council estates of Britain, there stretches a deep seam of criminological research.

Whilst the late-nineteenth-century shift to positivist explanations that sought to locate the sources of criminality within the individual set in motion a continuing tradition of this type of criminology, the stress on the social aspect was to re-emerge powerfully soon afterwards in the United States in the shape of the Chicago School. Some of the organizational features of the department of sociology at the University of Chicago have already been discussed. So too has the way in which the city of Chicago provided a social laboratory for these sociologists during the 1920s and 1930s; Chicago seemed to encapsulate all of the salient characteristics of the modern city.

The members of the Chicago School were clearly acquainted with, and influenced by, the work of Durkheim. This manifested itself on a number of fronts:

- Crime and crime rates were viewed as social phenomena, and were not to be explained in terms of the individual's biology or psychology.

- Crime was linked to social disorganization, whereby family and community-based bonds were weakened. Low levels of social integration were associated with high levels of crime.

- It was the social life of certain neighbourhoods that was seen as 'pathological', and not the people living in them. Criminal behaviour was regarded as a normal response to an abnormal situation; in a spirit of optimism it was viewed as a temporary phenomenon arising out of periods of rapid social change.

- Drawing on Social Darwinism, crime was seen as part of an evolutionary process of adaptation.

- A certain amount of crime in society was accepted as inevitable and of no threat to that society.

- There should be government intervention to improve the bases of social organization in the criminal areas of the city.

The key figure behind the work of the Chicago School was Robert Park, an ex-journalist who had studied sociology in Germany, and who had apparently dabbled in delinquency himself in his younger days. Park established the basic framework for research by arguing that the city was best viewed as an ecological system, comparable to the ecological systems associated with plants and animals. He also argued that in order to carry out proper research, researchers should go into the city and discover at first hand what was going on. This led to a large number of ethnographic studies being conducted by sociology department members.

As the name suggests, a social ecological perspective sees the city in terms of a web of interdependent relationships created by people as they adapt to a changing environment. These adaptations follow an evolutionary pattern and are comparable to the modes of adaptation found among species of plants and animals as they adjust to changes in their environments. Thus cities such as Chicago had not developed on a random basis, but rather this development was patterned according to 'natural' social processes. The outcome was that cities evolve their own particular types of neighbourhood, each with their own type of social life. Some of these are stable, well-organized neighbourhoods, but others are more socially disorganized, and it is here that social problems, including crime, are concentrated. Proponents of a social ecological model argued that neighbourhoods have periodically to cope with an influx of outsiders (e.g. new immigrants, or business organizations), leading to conflict and a 'struggle over space'. Eventually, equilibrium is restored, but not without winners and losers according to the Darwinian principle of the survival of the fittest. From this perspective the city is in a state of flux, as market forces and evolutionary processes lead to the the migration of people from one neighbourhood to another; those who leave then conform to the values and norms of their new neighbourhood. In the most deprived areas, characterized by transient populations who are unable to put down roots, will be found those values and norms most conducive to criminal behaviour. Thus the Chicago ecologists rejected explanations of criminality that focused on particular individuals. For them, the fact that neighbourhoods with high crime rates continued to have high crime rates even when the original inhabitants had moved out, showed that it was not the people but rather the social characteristics of the neighbourhood that led to crime – some areas were criminogenic.

In a book published in 1925 one of Park's colleagues, Ernest Burgess, attempted to map out the results of these processes in Chicago. His 'social map' of the city consisted of five zones forming concentric circles. In the middle stood the Central Business District, where banks, insurance companies, and the like, had their offices. Four residential zones then radiated out from this central area, with each zone containing various subsections. Of particular importance was the Zone of Transition, which skirted the Central Business District. It was here that most of Chicago's poorest citizens lived: new immigrants and various groups lacking access to urban survival kits. Housing was of low quality, and was largely comprised of cheap lodging houses nestling in the shadows of decaying factories. According to Burgess this was the zone in which crime was likely to be concentrated. The next zone contained the houses of the more respectable working class and was the escape route from the ghetto. The assumption seemed to be that in general, and given time, most people would be successful in their escape attempts.

Clifford Shaw and Henry McKay (1942), two researchers from a local child guidance clinic with close ties with the sociology department at Chicago, attempted to test Burgess's model by looking at the distribution of juvenile delinquency in the city. Their findings supported the ecological thesis that even when individuals living in a particular neighbourhood moved on to greener pastures, crime rates remained the same in the neighbourhood they had left behind.

The high rates of juvenile crime found in the Zone of Transition were said to be linked to the social disorganization in those areas. In the absence of strong normative controls from the family and the community, juveniles were likely to engage in delinquent activities. This was an idea that was to eventually influence the development of control theory. Although Shaw and McKay had, through their analysis of crime statistics, satisfied themselves that criminal areas existed and could be identified, they agreed with Park that in order to establish precisely what processes were at work, it was necessary to talk to and observe at first hand those involved. Thus were born two important research methods associated with the Chicago School: first, the construction of 'life histories' via in-depth interviews, and second, the use of participant observation as the basis for what Matza (1969) calls the 'appreciative' study of delinquency. This indicates the acknowledged debt that the Chicago School owed to writers in the symbolic interactionist tradition, such as Thomas, Cooley, and Mead. A research strategy that sought to present the social world from the point of view of those being studied, and to 'tell it like it is', lay at the core of symbolic interactionist methodology. The result was that the Chicago School generated a large number of detailed, appreciative studies during the 1920s and 1930s, some of which have now achieved the status of classics. Some of the more notable examples are: *The Hobo*, Anderson (1975), first published in 1923; *The Gang*, Thrasher (1963), first published in 1927; *The Jack-Roller: A delinquent boy's own story*, Shaw (1930); *The Natural History of a Delinquent Career*, Shaw and Moore (1931); *The Professional Thief: By a professional thief*, Sutherland (1937); *Brothers in Crime*, Shaw, McKay and MacDonald (1938); and in a similar vein, though set in Boston, *Street Corner Society*, Whyte (1955), written in 1930.

In their studies of juvenile offenders, Shaw and McKay extended the explanations offered by ecological theory by introducing the concept of cultural transmission. Delinquent values, they argued, became established in criminal areas, and were then passed on to a new generation of youngsters. It is, therefore, an explanation of delinquency deriving from learning theory. Criminal areas, where those sorts of values predominated, were counterposed against a mainstream, consensual culture into which law-abiding juveniles were socialized.

Shaw and McKay's ideas were picked up by Edwin Sutherland, who spent the first half of the 1930s at the University of Chicago. Sutherland's work, though, marked an important theoretical change of direction which was to permeate the Chicago School as the 1930s progressed. There had always been an inherent tension at the heart of social disorganization theory. The use of appreciative research methods had presented the social world of the delinquent as coherent and meaningful to the participants. However, by relying on the notion of social disorganization as a way of explaining that delinquency – and with it the assumption that there existed a conformist, consensual mainstream society that was by definition socially organized – the social world of the delinquent was pathologized. Sutherland's important contribution was to depathologize the criminal area. He did this by developing a model of criminality based upon assumptions of cultural plurality. Instead of social disorganization, he spoke of differential social organization, and questioned the ready acceptance of the existence of consensus. Neighbourhoods, in his view, were not disorganized, but rather organized in different ways, one outcome being differential crime rates. And with his concept of 'differential association' Sutherland analysed criminality in terms of a person's exposure to particular cultural influences, seeing this as the mechanism whereby some became criminals and others did not: 'a person becomes delinquent because of an excess of definitions favourable to violation of law over definitions unfavourable to violation of law' (Sutherland quoted in Taylor *et al.*, 1973: 126).

In this formulation Sutherland is arguing that delinquency is learned in the same way that any other type of behaviour is learned. Through differential association the individual not only learns how to commit crime – for example, how to break into a car – but also the moral outlook and motivations conducive to criminal behaviour. Through his refinement of the concept of differential association Sutherland had, by the 1940s, made a significant break with dominant explanations of criminality. For Sutherland these were too narrowly focused on deprived youth, and made an unwarranted assumption that crime was basically a product of poverty. His 1937 study of a professional thief signalled this change of emphasis, but it was his classic study of white-collar crime, first published in the late 1940s, that finally left the slum behind. Crime, he argued, was widespread among those with high status in America. Unfortunately, most of this crime remained invisible, so that official crime statistics gave a misleading impression of the nature of criminal behaviour. Sutherland believed that differential association was able to explain white-collar and corporate crime as well as the crime committed by the youth living in the Zone of Transition.

The Chicago School: an assessment

There is no doubt that the ideas generated by the Chicago School had a significant influence on subsequent sociological criminology. In particular, as we have seen, those associated with the sociology department at Chicago locked into a nineteenth-century tradition of providing accounts of life among the urban poor. By developing more sophisticated theoretical explanations and research methodologies, they were then instrumental in influencing an important modern tradition of areal studies in Britain and the United States. The use of participant observation and a 'life histories' approach has continued to influence many rich ethnographic studies. In addition, elements of what became known as control theory, and the foundations for the growth of subcultural approaches should be noted.

Looking back over the two decades of the 1920s and 1930s at the huge amount of work produced by the Chicago School, however, it is clear that it does not stand as a single, agreed body of knowledge. As Heidensohn (1989: 18–19) puts it:

> There is no single definitive view in their work; indeed, as was inevitable in such a productive group, ideas diverged between different writers and even within the work of one man . . . their work was not systematised and did not generate a 'finished system of sociology'.

In many ways those involved were finding their feet. They were caught up in a variety of theoretical influences and cross-currents. Individuals changed their mind, and sometimes contradictory ideas co-existed for a while. With reference to their use of life histories, Matza (1969) speaks approvingly of their commitment to 'appreciative' sociology, to a sociology concerned with letting people tell their own stories. And yet researchers such as Shaw and McKay were also strongly committed to pinning down the causes of crime, and to social policy-based interventions that would lead to a reduction in criminal behaviour. This is an approach that Matza disparages for being 'causal-corrective'. Likewise, although many were influenced by the ideas of symbolic interactionism, which sees individuals as actively constructing their social worlds through interactions with others, the Chicago School is frequently criticized for its positivism – for example, the deterministic view that environments determine people's behaviour. In fact, as we have seen, Sutherland's contributions during the 1930s moved the Chicago School away from seeing society as a consensus, and some localities as enclaves of disorganization and criminal values, towards a position of cultural pluralism. Again, though, this was a tension that was never fully resolved, and returns us to one of the central issues in Durkheim's work: How can social order be achieved in a modern society that places a high premium on individualism, and with it the cultural space for pluralism and diversity?

Although Sutherland went on to address the issue of white-collar crime in the 1940s, one particularly striking feature of the work of the Chicago School during the 1920s and 1930s is that with one exception (Landesco, 1968) it ignored organized crime, as well as the crimes of the powerful and the 'respectable'. This, remember, was a period in Chicago's (and America's) history that saw Prohibition, large-scale crime syndicates, gangland luminaries such as Al Capone, and significant levels of corruption among city officials and politicians. Hollywood did not miss the opportunities, but it is therefore ironic that the Chicago sociologists did. Sumner (1994: 31–2) provides one of the few discussions of the Chicago School that includes some details relating to these wider criminal activities: 'Two billion dollars' worth of business shifted from the old established brewers and the bar-owners to the bootleggers and the "hoods"; money which they continually reinvested in gambling, prostitution, labour unions, regular business and extortion.' In an interesting, and telling, footnote, he adds: 'As Harold Finestone, a doctoral student there in the 1930s, once told me in conversation, in response to my query about the lack of studies on the mob itself: the mob was the government at that time, and you don't do fieldwork on the government, do you?' (ibid. 51)

Finally, we can conclude this section by briefly outlining some of the main criticisms that have been levelled at the Chicago School:

- There was a reliance on, and faith in, official crime statistics.
- Writers such as Shaw referred to 'delinquent areas'. What was unclear, though, was the distinction between an area in which delinquents lived, and areas in which delinquency took place.
- The earlier work has often been accused of being tautological. Crime is seen as a product of social disorganization, and yet crime is an example of social disorganization.
- The ecological models of the city, with their descriptions of the 'natural area', missed out of the equation class conflict and an unequal distribution of power – for example, the actions of slum landlords.
- On the same ecological theme, there tends to be a picture of criminals as determined creatures, moulded by their environments.
- To what extent was an ecological system used merely as a metaphor, as opposed to an actual description of social life in the city?
- By concentrating on poor areas, the Chicago School overpredicted the crimes of the poor; clearly, not all poor people engaged in criminal behaviour. Thus it has been said that their work served to perpetuate dominant stereotypes.
- With reference to the later theory based upon cultural transmission, the origins of the delinquent culture being transmitted were never clearly explained.
- The notion of differential association developed by Sutherland has been criticized for not being amenable to empirical verification, because of the enormous range of experiences that individual's have.
- It has been argued that close analysis of the data shows that crime rates in particular localities were in fact not stable over periods of time.
- There are the usual criticisms of a life histories approach – for example, the truthfulness of those being interviewed.
- In common with most criminological research at that time, the victims of crime were ignored, along with the reactions of control agents and their role in the construction of deviance.

Mertonian strain theory

Robert K. Merton was a key figure in the functionalist school of thought that dominated American sociology during the 1940s and 1950s. Although not a criminological specialist, functionalism's primary interest in the nature of social order inevitably led him to consider issues of crime and deviance. The classic, and much discussed article in which Merton (1993) first presented his ideas was originally published in 1938 (and subsequently revised) in his book *Social Theory and Social Structure*. The title of this article, 'Social structure and anomie', indicates a connection with Durkheim, and it stands as the seminal work within a criminological tradition known as 'strain theory'.

In simple terms strain theory, as the name suggests, is an attempt to answer the question that common sense perhaps impresses upon us: What sorts of 'faulty' social conditions make some people act in deviant ways? (We should note in passing the presupposition in the question that deviance must be a result of something going wrong.) At the time that Merton was writing, and in spite of the contributions of the Chicago School, answers to the question 'What went wrong?' tended to focus on the individual. Merton, on the other hand, was committed to a sociological level of analysis, where the sources of deviance are traced to the nature of the social structure. Rejecting efforts to individualize, or 'atomize' the causes of deviance, he argued that deviance arose in certain groups, 'not because the human beings comprising them are compounded of distinctive biological tendencies but because they are responding normally to the social situation in which they find themselves' (Merton, 1993: 250).

For Merton this 'social situation' is the product of a disjunction between, on the one hand, culture, and on the other, social structure. Individuals living in American society, as participants in the American Dream, are, he says, socialized into desiring certain cultural *goals*; chief among these is the goal of material success. At the same time, the social structure provides various legitimate *means* through which material success can be achieved – passing examinations, working hard in business, and so on. However, when there is a lack of fit between the goals and the means – that is, when opportunities are blocked for individuals because of their social class position, even though the message is that everyone can succeed if they have the ability – then problems of 'strain' arise: there is a 'contradiction between the cultural emphasis on pecuniary ambition and the social bars to full opportunity' (ibid. 260). Merton describes this type of society – where there is a lack of equality of opportunity, coupled with a strong emphasis on material success – as 'anomic'. Deviant behaviour is seen as resulting from reactions to situations of anomie.

According to Merton, this tendency towards deviance is not simply a result of limited opportunities for some people. As he notes, there are societies where very few opportunities for social advancement exist, and the gap between rich and poor is enormous, and yet relatively little deviant behaviour occurs. The crucial factor for Merton is that socialization processes strongly emphasize the achievement of material success. He saw the United States as just such a society. A disjunction between this cultural goal and the opportunities, or legitimate means, within the social structure for achieving it, creates strains which, says Merton, individuals will adapt to in different ways. On the basis of this reasoning, he suggested the following 'ideal type' set of 'modes of adaptation', where (+) signifies 'acceptance', (−) signifies 'rejection', and (±) signifies 'rejection of prevailing values and substitution of new values':

A typology of modes of individual adaptation

Modes of adaptation	Cultural goals	Institutionalized means
I. Conformity	+	+
II. Innovation	+	−
III. Ritualism	−	+
IV. Retreatism	−	−
V. Rebellion	±	±

Apart from 'conformity', where individuals accept both cultural goals and the institutionalized means, irrespective of how they are actually performing, the categories represent various sorts of deviant adaptation. 'Innovation' describes a situation where the individual has been socialized normally into accepting the goal of material success, but, faced with a lack of legitimate means for achieving the goal, resorts to deviance. In this formulation, this constitutes the source of property crime. With 'ritualism', the individual has given up on the goals and merely goes through the motions: 'The original purposes are forgotten and close adherence to institutionally prescribed conduct becomes a matter of ritual' (Ibid. 251). Although this adaptation involves conformity to the means, it is, for Merton, deviant in so far as the individual has jettisoned the goal of material success. 'Retreatism' occurs when the individual gives up on both the goals and the means, and in effect drops out of normal society. Here Merton had in mind hobos and drug addicts. Finally, 'rebellion' applies to those individuals who reject the dominant cultural goals, together with the legitimate means for achieving them, in favour of alternative goals and means; political revolutionaries would occupy this category.

Invoking as it does notions of winning and losing, and playing or not playing according to the rules, Merton's version of strain theory has often induced commentators to search for analogies with games. In fact Merton himself mentions football, wrestling, athletics, and poker. Usually, though, a game analogy crops up within the context of a sentence such as 'in Merton's theory it is as if society was like a . . .'. The best-known British example is probably a 'fruit machine', introduced by Laurie Taylor (1971). Taylor goes on to explain how the machine is rigged (a lack of opportunities), leading different players to respond in different ways according to Merton's typology. Heidensohn (1989) prefers to use an analogy with a bowling alley. One imagines criminology lecturers worldwide bringing out their own particular favourites when they discuss Merton (readers can choose their own).

Merton's anomie

Although Merton uses the Durkheimian concept of anomie, and develops a theoretical explanation of deviance as illustrated above, the meaning that he gives to anomie is not consistent. For much of the article he in fact follows Durkheim and uses the concept to describe a society where there is a lack of moral regulation:

> contemporary American culture continues to be characterized by a heavy emphasis on wealth as a basic symbol of success, without a corresponding emphasis upon the legitimate avenues on which to march towards this goal. (Merton, 1993: 255)

A lack of moral regulation has unleashed an unrestrained desire for material success; individuals want everything, but are no longer willing to play according to the rules. Clearly, under these circumstances an increase in property crime is likely. However, as some commentators have pointed out, Merton moves away from this Durkheimian definition of anomie and gives it a rather different meaning: 'Durkheim's conception of anomie raised problems for Merton because the logical and empirical implications of it ran counter to his beliefs about the social distribution of deviant behaviour' (Box, 1981: 98-9).

If American society was anomic in the sense that Durkheim used the term, then deviant behaviour would be distributed among all social classes. Although mentioning problems with official statistics, and referring to white-collar crime, Merton (1993: 259) did none the less conclude that deviance was in general linked to poverty:

> Of those located in the lower reaches of the social structure, the culture makes incompatible demands. On the one hand, they are asked to orient their conduct toward the prospect of large wealth . . . and on the other, they are largely denied effective opportunities to do so institutionally.

Thus in order to remain true to his belief that deviance was concentrated among the deprived, Merton had to move away from Durkheim's definition of anomie, for that would apply to the whole of American society. In terms of his understanding of the distribution of deviant behaviour, he logically equated anomie with a lack of equality of opportunity. As discussed earlier, the ideas of strain theory, including Merton's version, were to influence those political administrations that saw the creation of equality of opportunity via poverty programmes as the way to solve the problem of crime.

Criticisms

While some writers have more recently attempted to rehabilitate Merton's work (see Reiner, 1984) it has over the years been subject to a barrage of criticism. Some of the main criticisms can be summarized as follows:

- There is too much reliance on official statistics.

- As a theory it predicts too much lower-class crime.

- The various modes of individual adaptation are difficult to classify in reality. Thus value judgements are likely to be used when assigning individuals to specific categories.

- Although the source of deviance lies in the social structure, responses of a deviant nature are conceptualized in individual terms. This ignores the importance of collective responses.

- It is unclear why particular individuals opt for one type of adaptation rather than another.

- The theory does not explain non-utilitarian deviance: that is, deviance such as rape or criminal damage that is not oriented towards material success.

- The theory cannot accommodate the wide variety of deviant motivations and types of deviant behaviour (e.g. domestic violence, rape, and murder).

- How and why does addiction, associated with 'retreatism', result from anomie? Could addiction not lead to anomie?

- There is an assumption of a monolithic culture oriented towards material success, and this ignores the plurality of cultural values. It may be that lower-class individuals typically set their sights on extremely modest goals in the full knowledge that to do otherwise would be unrealistic.

- Social control as a factor shaping deviant behaviour is ignored.

- The theory fails to address those situations where means exceed goals: that is, where individuals have 'too much', leading them into deviant behaviour.

- Has Merton exhausted the possibilities with respect to modes of adaptation? In other words, is it logically possible to continue his table using permutations based upon $(\pm)$ and $(+)/(-)$?

- He ignores those situations where deviant behaviour occurs prior to a lack of success in achieving cultural goals.

6 | Strain, subcultures and delinquency

A. K. Cohen: developments in strain theory
R. Cloward and L. Ohlin: opportunity knocks

A. K. Cohen: developments in strain theory

In *Delinquent Boys*, published in 1955, Albert Cohen offers his own version of strain theory. As with Merton before him, Cohen attempts to explore sociologically those features of American society that create strains for some people, leading eventually to delinquent behaviour. His conclusion is similar to Merton's in that he sees criminogenic pressures as being inherent in the society itself:

> those values which are at the core of the 'American way of life', which help to motivate the behavior which we most esteem as 'typically American', are among the major determinants of that which we stigmatize as 'pathological' . . . the problems of adjustment to which the delinquent subculture is a response are determined, in part, by those very values which respectable society holds most sacred. (Cohen, 1955: 137)

He also follows Merton by assuming that the bulk of delinquency is found within the lower working class, though unlike Merton, Cohen concentrates specifically on adolescence: 'The delinquent subculture is mostly found in the working class' (ibid. 73). Having said that, Cohen's work is riddled with caveats through which he is at pains to point out, for instance, that not all lower-working-class boys become delinquent, and that delinquency also exists among middle-class boys. He also departs from Merton by drawing on psychology and includes the notion of 'psychogenic factors'. Here again there are various caveats. He accepts that there may be different types of delinquency, each resulting from different causal processes, but he is

100

particularly interested in what he sees as those processes causally linked to most delinquent activity: 'in the majority of cases psychogenic and subcultural factors blend in a single causal process, as pollen and a particular bodily constitution work together to produce hay fever' (ibid. 17). From this we can clearly see that Cohen believed that some individuals, whatever their social circumstances, were predisposed to delinquency; he was interested in what triggered it. As a result of these various caveats, Cohen was left with a core of what he described as 'typical' adolescent delinquency, and he therefore focused on young, lower-class males committed to the delinquent values of the subculture.

There are also links between Cohen's work and Sutherland's theory of differential association, and this indicates another departure from Merton's version of strain theory. Whereas Merton conceived of deviant adaptations in individual terms, Cohen followed Sutherland and saw delinquency as a collective response; in other words, he highlights delinquent subcultures. Furthermore, although, like Merton, he invokes the idea of the American Dream, its saliency derives from differential access to status rather than to material success.

Cohen's basic argument is that American society is dominated by what he calls middle-class, mainstream norms and values, and through the mass media and the education system these permeate the whole of society. It is against these that individuals are judged. Unfortunately, lower-class boys, referred to by Cohen as 'corner boys' (a term he borrowed from William Foote Whyte (1955)) are ill-equipped, because of their socialization, to compete with middle-class boys in the status stakes. The corner boy is pictured as organizing his life around working-class values, finding satisfaction in the close-knit companionship of his mates. It is, however, a milieu that inhibits vertical mobility. The outcome is that in early adolescence such boys are faced with a 'problem of adjustment', as they are denied the status more readily given to their middle-class counterparts:

> In the status game, then, the working-class child starts out with a handicap and, to the extent that he cares what middle-class persons think of him or has internalized the dominant middle-class attitudes toward social class position, he may be expected to feel some 'shame'. (Cohen, 1955: 110)

Cohen outlines three 'ideal type' responses open to the corner boy, and again he draws on Whyte's terminology: the 'stable corner boy', the 'college boy', and the 'delinquent boy'. The stable corner boy response involves an ambivalent acceptance of one's lot in life, with individuals accommodating themselves to their situation as best they can, and this may include some mild acts of delinquency. The college boy response, as the name suggests, applies to those lower-working-class boys who, having to a significant extent internalized middle-class cultural norms, aspire to improve themselves through educational success, and hence compete with the middle class on their own terms. The delinquent boy response is the one that Cohen is particularly interested in. Using the Freudian concept of 'reaction formation', he argues that some boys, faced with a lack of status by the carriers of middle-class culture who are able to judge them, join together with others in the same situation and develop a delinquent subculture. While acknowledging that Merton's version of strain theory can explain criminal activities carried out for monetary gain, in Cohen's view it cannot explain day-to-day working-class delinquency which, he argues, is mainly non-utilitarian and negativistic (e.g. fighting and vandalism).

The psychological concept of reaction formation describes a situation where the individual who is denied something they desire, reacts by disparaging it to excess. In the context of Cohen's study the denial of status leads some to seek out others who share the same 'problem of adjustment'; the resultant subculture develops an exaggerated hostility towards middle-class values. In effect, it is a contra-culture within which middle-class norms and values are inverted; now an activity is 'right' because mainstream culture says it is 'wrong'. This raises an important issue.

For Cohen, a crucial aspect of this process of delinquency creation is that the corner boys care about their lack of status:

> most children are sensitive *to some degree* about the attitudes of *any persons* with whom they are thrown into more than the most superficial kind of contact. The contempt or indifference of others, particularly of those like schoolmates and teachers, with whom we are constrained to associate for long hours every day, is difficult, we suggest, to shrug off. (Ibid. 123, original emphasis)

The candidate for delinquency cares, according to Cohen, because:

> To the degree to which he values middle-class status, either because he values the good opinion of middle-class persons or because he has to some degree internalized middle-class standards himself, he faces a problem of adjustment and is in the market for a 'solution'. (Ibid. 119)

However, as Box (1981) has shown, this suggests that the delinquent boy can feel either resentment or shame/guilt, or both. The working-class boy may resent the low status that he is given, simply because it is difficult to be indifferent, but this does not mean that he sees his own culture as inferior and desires middle-class status. A feeling of resentment might lead to delinquency, but it might also lead to an angry resignation. The important element in Cohen's theory, though, is reaction formation, and this requires more than resentment. Reaction formation requires the shame/guilt and the rejection of something previously desired, in this case middle-class status. Thus Cohen's theory of delinquency is based upon the assumption that the typical working-class delinquent to some degree internalizes middle-class norms and values prior to the creation of the subculture. Put another way, the assumption is that middle-class culture is widely dispersed and accepted throughout all social classes. This has been picked up by some of Cohen's critics, in particular those who have developed an explanation of delinquency based upon cultural diversity. Proponents of this approach have questioned the view that middle-class norms and values are internalized by lower-working-class boys early on in their lives. There has also been much criticism of the characterization of delinquent working-class boys as vehemently anti-middle-class culture (e.g. Short and Strodtbeck, 1965; Downes, 1966). In fact, Cohen saw the values associated with the delinquent subculture as taking on a life of their own, rather as the Chicago School had done, which would put even greater pressure on some boys to become delinquent. If this is true, we might query why working-class boys need to have internalized middle-class values in the first place in order for them to become delinquent. Other critics have made the familiar claim that such studies rely too much on official statistics regarding the social class distribution of delinquency, and in so doing underestimate the extent of middle-class delinquency (e.g. Kitsuse and Dietrick, 1959).

Finally, a note about the policy implications of Cohen's work. As with Merton, the message is that crime results from strains inherent in the structure of American society, and these are basically to do with a lack of equality of opportunity. According to the logic of this formulation the way to tackle crime is to create equality of opportunity, in other words, to make the reality of life in America correspond to the ideology of opportunities for all, irrespective of social class origins. There is, though, a fundamental contradiction at the core of this type of reasoning. Although the goal of equality of opportunity may be desirable the notion of equality of opportunity to succeed implies equality of opportunity to fail; they are two sides of the same coin. In the work that we have looked at so far from strain theorists, there is no suggestion that class society should be eradicated. On the contrary, each writer is committed to an unequal class society, but people should have an equal chance to win or lose in that society. Indeed, the concept of equality of opportunity presupposes the existence of social class inequality. However, if such a divided society exists, then how are people able to line up equally? Poverty programmes, for example, may be introduced so that the chances of those at the 'bottom' are improved, but the model is predicated on the continuing existence of a 'bottom' and a 'top'.

R. Cloward and L. Ohlin: opportunity knocks

When discussing the development of criminology during the postwar period it was pointed out that the explanations of delinquency associated with strain theory fitted well with the ideas of the Kennedy administration of the early 1960s. This was particularly apparent with respect to the contribution made by Richard Cloward and Lloyd Ohlin in their study *Delinquency and Opportunity*, published in 1960. Again, the central themes of strain theory are in evidence. There is a basic assumption that delinquent behaviour results from something going 'wrong' and, as a corollary: 'under normal circumstances, that is the absence of strains and tensions, individuals will not be motivated to break the law' (Box, 1981: 103).

Furthermore, and as with Cohen, although individual psychological factors may be implicated in triggering specific types of response, the source of 'strain' lies in the nature of society itself. This, of course, does not amount to a critique of American capitalist society as such. It is, rather, a critique of the way that society is actually working. Fundamentally, strain theory lends itself to social policies oriented towards managing the opportunity structure so that the disadvantaged have a better chance to succeed, whilst at the same time ensuring that disincentives to succeed because of reduced income and status differentials do not intrude. It is a tall order. Indeed, as we have seen, by the 1970s the perceived failure of programmes such as Operation Head Start was shifting the emphasis away from 'equal opportunities' towards a rudimentary policy of control and containment.

Cloward and Ohlin had the explicit intention of forging together the ideas of Merton ('strain') and Sutherland ('differential association'), but their work also illustrates the continuing influence of Durkheim on American criminological theory. Essentially *Delinquency and Opportunity* addresses two issues: first, how the opportunity structures of mainstream American society lead some people to fail and become involved in delinquency, and secondly, how the opportunity structures within criminal subcultures create, in turn, their own failures.

When analysing the causal factors associated with delinquency Cloward and Ohlin's (1960: 32) basic research question is: 'Under which conditions will persons experience strains and tensions that lead to delinquent solutions?' Clearly, it is the impact of these conditions on the individual, conceived of in terms of strains and tensions, and leading to delinquent motivations, that they are interested in. In Mertonian fashion they begin by arguing that in modern societies such as the United States, people are socialized into believing that those with ability will 'get on'. Through qualifications gained in the education system people will be matched to the job that suits them. The actual achievement of this kind of society – a meritocracy – would create a system of functional interdependence, as envisaged by Durkheim. However, in the real world, say Cloward and Ohlin, some fail to achieve a social position commensurate with their ability; unfortunately, there are not enough higher-status jobs to go round. Faced with queues of equally able applicants, employers fall back on criteria other than ability, such as class, religion or style of dress. For Cloward and Ohlin the lower-working-class victims of these processes, who feel that they have been treated unjustly, are those most likely to become delinquent. This introduces a moral dimension and, again, makes links with Durkheim. There are no strains for those who fail and yet subjectively believe that their failure is the result of a lack of ability, for they will resign themselves to their fate. The angry failures, on the other hand, do not, and they are in a situation where they are likely to withdraw their support for conventional, legitimate norms. Although Cloward and Ohlin follow Cohen and argue that most delinquent youth will come from lower-working-class backgrounds, they point to a different source within that social class. For them delinquency is most likely to occur among those who have earlier on committed themselves to middle-class norms, given some evidence of their ability, and have therefore been encouraged in their quest for higher status. In short, it is the 'college boy' who is most at risk: 'all available data support the contention that the basic endowments of delinquents, such as intelligence, physical strength and agility, are equal to, or greater than, those of their non-delinquent peers' (ibid. 42).

Cloward and Ohlin's theory represents an application of the Durkheimian logic that social order requires the existence of a hierarchical system where each person feels that what they have achieved is all that they are morally entitled to. This raises a number of issues. For instance, they seem to assume that those working-class youth who fail to achieve success, but see themselves as being of low ability, will passively accept their failure. The possibility that they might turn to delinquency is ignored, as is the possibility of them adopting non-compliant, non-delinquent political strategies. In addition, equality of opportunity is conceived of as a system for separating the wheat from the chaff. The assumption is that the 'chaff' really exist – 'ability' is regarded as a natural, fixed level of intelligence, rather than a product of educational experiences – and what is required is a suitable system for identifying those with low ability. Importantly, though, such a system must at least appear fair to the failures; they must be convinced that their failure is morally deserved.

The main concern of Cloward and Ohlin, however, is with those working-class boys who supposedly possess high ability, but who none the less still fail. In the absence of a sufficient number of higher-status jobs to satisfy the demand represented by the pool of ability among all social classes, it is difficult to see how improving opportunities would in itself lead to a decrease in the number of angry failures. Without a corresponding expansion in actual job opportunities, social peace could only be achieved through other strategies, such as a more powerful ideology that convinced people of their morally deserved failure, or, some might say, more powerful modes of social control. There is one problematic aspect of their work that is shared with other strain theorists. This is their argument that lower-working-class delinquent boys have at a prior stage accepted middle-class norms and values.

Opportunity structures in the world of delinquency

Cloward and Ohlin argue that the social world of the delinquent contains the same sort of inequalities as the social world of the non-criminal – though we might question this neat dichotomy between 'goodies' and 'baddies'. Drawing on Sutherland's theme of differential association, they discuss the various opportunities available for learning the techniques and absorbing the motivations necessary for criminal behaviour. On this basis they suggest three different types of criminal subculture:

1. *Criminal*. This is a subculture oriented towards property crime, and will tend to be found in more socially organized lower-class neighbourhoods. Here informal social control networks centred on experienced adult criminals ensure that delinquent youth confine themselves to well-planned, utilitarian activities rather than such things as vandalism and gang warfare.

2. *Violent*. These are also referred to as conflict subcultures, and are associated with the more socially disorganized neighbourhoods which approximate to the Zone of Transition identified by the Chicago School. Delinquent activity is much less restrained than in the criminal subculture, and tends towards violent, gang-oriented behaviour.

3. *Retreatist*. This subculture is primarily associated with illegal drug use, and arises among those boys who have failed in both criminal and violent subcultures. In effect they represent the lumpen proletariat of the delinquent world.

7 | Criminology theory in Britain

American influences
Sociological criminology in Britain
Developing a British perspective
Cultural diversity theory
Schools and the 'problem of adjustment'
Subcultural theory: taking stock

American influences

We have seen that there are important differences between the Chicago School and the subcultural strain theorists, such as Cohen and Cloward and Ohlin, in their analyses of the processes that lead to criminal behaviour. They also differ in the way in which they conceptualize those areas of the city in which crime is believed to be concentrated. As we shall see, the respective positions raised an issue that influenced the early British sociologies of crime in the 1950s, and has resonated within criminology up to the present day.

On the basis of a social ecological model, the Chicago School saw the city in terms of 'natural areas'. These had their own ecological systems, and were differentiated according to the types of people living there and the relationship between their lifestyles and the physical environment. Some of these were identified as 'criminal areas'. These areas were characterized by run-down housing, transient populations, and high levels of immigration and poverty. Crime in these areas was initially linked to social disorganization, though later on, partly because of the influence of Sutherland, there was a move towards the idea of differential social organization. This acknowledged the existence of a plurality of norms and values in the city. Although the subcultural strain theorists developed different understandings of the origins of delinquency, they agreed with the Chicago

School that delinquent subcultures existed in certain lower-working-class areas. However, a central dispute concerned the relationship between such areas and the rest of the city, and indeed the rest of society.

For the Chicago School, the criminal area consisted of a delinquent culture, and inhabitants absorb the corresponding norms and values, and these are at variance with those of a supposed conformist, mainstream society. Youngsters became delinquent out of a 'natural' process of cultural transmission. Cohen and Cloward and Ohlin, on the other hand, stress the ways in which the inhabitants are connected to, and influenced by, the wider mainstream culture, described as 'middle class'. Lower-class boys, specifically, are seen as to some extent internalizing the norms and values of middle-class society:

> all their lives, through the major media of mass indoctrination – the schools, the movies, the radio, the newspapers and the magazines – the middle-class powers-that-be that manipulate these media have been trying the 'sell' them middle-class values and the middle-class standard of living. (Cohen, 1955: 124–5)

The 'reaction formation' suggested by Cohen, and the 'alienation' of Cloward and Ohlin's 'college boys' presuppose that this internalization of middle-class values has occurred. Lower-working-class youth could not be insulated from mainstream middle-class culture, for the internalization of this culture, at least to some extent, is necessary for a delinquent reaction to take place. The dispute between cultural transmission theorists and strain theorists essentially boils down to the issue of whether those living in a so-called criminal area become delinquent because they conform to the norms and values of the area, or because they have been rejected by a middle-class value system which, to a significant degree, they have internalized. The question is: Do lower-working-class lads typically desire, then are denied, middle-class status?

It is an issue that was to figure in the early British sociologies of crime, and for some time afterwards. However, leaving aside the question of delinquency-creating processes for the moment, there is one dimension to the work of these two schools of thought that is of particular interest nowadays. In the wake of rising levels of recorded crime and urban rioting, there have been powerful media images of 'no-go' areas, 'yob culture', unprecedented violence and young criminals 'laughing at the law'. Drawing on the idea of an 'underclass', some urban neighbourhoods appear to have been cut adrift from decent, law-abiding society. There are clearly strong echoes here of the Chicago School's view of the Zone of Transition, and in their formulation delinquent behaviour only ceased when the individuals concerned moved to other more 'civilized' areas. Of course, these 'criminal areas' were not associated with crime in general; they were associated with conventional crime, for example street robbery, vandalism and burglary.

Other areas of the city, where white-collar and corporate crime were concentrated, were not looked upon as criminal areas.

In these and contemporary accounts, there is a danger of constructing distorted stereotypes of what life is like among the urban poor. This is especially apparent in recent highly moralistic contributions focusing on lone parents, absent husbands, and children who are 'out of control'. In an effort to emphasize the positive, rather than negative, aspects of coping with the grim reality of unemployment and social deprivation in modern Britain, one commentator has written:

> I am sick and tired of the moral high ground being divided up between the haves and the have-nots. If this is the high ground give me the low ground anyday. I am at home in the low ground – it is where I grew up and where I see women on their own struggling to bring up their children as best they can with little money and support. It is in the moral foothills that I see people look after their dying relatives day in and day out. Amongst this misery I also see more ingenuity than in a thousand sermons. (Moore, 1995: 5)

A problem with the Chicago School's description of the working-class criminal area is that it automatically equates non-delinquent values with some posited 'mainstream' middle-class society. Concomitantly, delinquent values, and thus such things as immorality and selfishness, are equated with lower-working-class culture. It is as if this culture is intrinsically delinquent: that is, the opposite of respectable, hard-working, mainstream America, and possessing no non- or anti-delinquent resources. The move from delinquency to non-delinquency, therefore, has to be accomplished through factors on the 'outside'.

In the case of the subcultural strain theorists, it is true that they do see the lower working class as not being cut adrift from the wider society, and in varying degrees subscribing to values associated with respect for other people's property, courtesy, and nonviolence. However, these are only absorbed by the lower working class because they have a moral conduit into the wider, mainstream culture. In fact, these values are presented as middle-class values. Thus again the image is one of the less well off having no intrinsic source of 'decent', non-delinquent values. The implication is that left to their own devices, and without the benefit of middle-class morality via schools and the mass media, these working-class neighbourhoods would become irredeemably delinquent. As a description of American society, Cohen's work in particular offers a highly idealized, one-sided picture of what he calls middle-class culture. Obviously, working-class children in 1950s America were, through the education system and the mass media, exposed to a range of norms and values from outside their family and neighbourhood. With the growth in mass communications, this is even more the case today. It would, though, be misleading to see all of these influences as being, by definition, 'middle class', 'decent', and non-delinquent. In Britain the readers of some tabloid newspapers, for instance, are likely, in varying degrees, to be exposed to sexism, racism, ethnocentricity, and homophobia. It would perhaps be reckless to judge these as necessarily benign, civilizing influences on the lower working class.

Sociological criminology in Britain

It was not until the 1950s that the sociological criminology produced in the United States since as far back as the 1920s began to influence criminology in Britain. This delay was related to the fact that up to the 1960s criminology was not much interested in sociology and, conversely, sociology was not much interested in criminology. Although there were some internal disputes, the early British sociologies of crime did share certain features: they were strongly empirical, and owed more to the Chicago School than to the strain theorists; they concentrated on young offenders; they favoured an areal or community studies approach; they assumed that delinquency was in the main carried out by lower-working-class males; and they were oriented towards Fabian-influenced correctionalist principles. Importantly, though, they did represent a move away from focusing on the individual offender, via the strong influence of psychology, towards a consideration of the socio-cultural context of delinquency. The strength of individualized approaches at this time is indicated by the amount of criticism received by one major writer, Mays, for failing to carry out psychological tests to measure 'maladjustment'. This work created a framework for the subsequent development of sociological criminology in Britain.

It also provided an opportunity to assess the extent to which American ideas and explanations, based upon criminal areas and delinquent subcultures, could be transposed to a British context. Unlike conflict or labelling theory, for instance, these 'middle range' theories are, of course, potentially more culture-bound (in Britain, for example, there was an important municipal housing market, and there seemed to be an absence of American-style adolescent gangs). It is worth noting that in the early British work the same issues discussed above regarding the nature of lower-working-class culture, and its relationship to the rest of society, bubbled to the surface.

The general tendency was to follow the Chicago School, rather than the strain theories of Cohen and Cloward and Ohlin. Thus although 'criminal areas' were identified, where children were socialized into delinquent values, the delinquent subcultures were not seen as resulting from reactions to a denial of desired middle-class status. Conceptualizations of class structure and class dynamics were, however, fairly crude, and in this respect were similar to the American analyses. Non-delinquent, and by implication 'decent', values were often equated with some perceived 'middle-class' culture, as if these values were somehow intrinsic to the culture of an area where the head of the household had a job nominally corresponding to the Registrar-General's understanding of social class. Even in those cases where the writer acknowledged the existence of non-delinquent values among sections of the lower working class (e.g. Carter and Jephcott, 1954) the values were still essentially middle class; some people were poor, but middle class in lifestyle and outlook. As with the American work, it was as if lower-working-class culture was in its natural state delinquent; it only became non-delinquent when it borrowed ideas from the middle class.

The two figures in British criminology who were largely responsible for introducing American ideas into this country were John Barron Mays and Terrence Morris. Mays's (1954) *Growing Up in the City: A study of juvenile delinquency in an urban neighbourhood* was centred on an inner city slum area in Liverpool. Mays drew on the ideas of the Chicago School, but toned down the concept of social ecology. He did, though, subscribe to the idea of the criminal area in which delinquency was concentrated, and used extensive interviewing as a basis for his research. Mays's central argument was that delinquency was widespread, and involved virtually all of the adolescents living in the area. The source of this delinquency, said Mays, was not strains or tensions in the boys' lives, as Cohen had argued, but, rather, it developed 'naturally' out of normal socialization. He did, though, utilize the concept of subculture: 'This to the best of my knowledge is the first reference, in British literature at least, in which the notion of subculture is invoked to account for juvenile crime', and he argued that the bulk of delinquency was 'not so much a symptom of maladjustment as of adjustment to a subculture in conflict with the culture of the city as a whole' (Mays, 1975: 63). In spite of using the word 'conflict', he was not arguing that delinquency was a conscious rebellion against middle-class society. He found no 'reaction formation' due to a prior internalization of middle-class values, as Cohen had done. However, he did concur with Cohen to the extent that the boys in Liverpool, not surprisingly, resented being treated as inferior. Although there was a small minority who involved themselves in serious delinquency, on the whole Mays paints a picture of socially and economically deprived young people trying to make the best of a bad job. In general, their delinquent behaviour represented an attempt to inject some fun into their lives. Given the overwhelming power of the delinquent subculture found in accounts such as Mays's, a question that is often asked is: Why do all of the boys not become delinquent? The mordant answer from Mays is that they all do, but only some are unlucky enough to get caught. After leaving school, however, the boys' involvement in delinquency begins to decline and eventually, apart from a small core, ends by adulthood. He therefore repudiated the commonly held view that today's youthful delinquents are tomorrow's adult criminals.

In their study of Radby, a mining town in the Midlands, Carter and Jephcott (1954) argue that whilst working-class neighbourhoods might appear homogeneous, they were in fact socially differentiated. 'Respectable', non-delinquent families gravitated towards each other, and lived in the same streets, referred to as 'white' streets; 'rough', delinquent families lived together in the 'black' streets (forty years on their choice of colours seems strikingly unfortunate). This division into 'respectables' and 'roughs' could not, they found, be traced back to the particular jobs that people had. The general pattern, they argued, was for delinquent youth to be brought up in delinquent families; delinquency was thus culturally transmitted, both in the family and on the street. For Carter and Jephcott, these values, then, persisted into adulthood, to be passed on to children. They, in fact, criticized Mays for failing to recognize this continuity between the values of adults and the values of children. Inevitably, the 'respectables' are seen as working-class people who have actually adopted supposedly middle-class values. So, once again, these values – respect for property and people, for instance – are not conceived of as *just* values, but they are specifically identified with the 'middle class', as if they were one of the key defining features of middle classness, but not working classness.

Although he was a psychologist, Sainsbury's (1955) study of suicide in London also drew on the work of the Chicago School. In particular he refers to the 'ecology of London', and identifies what he also calls 'natural areas'. On the other hand, Sainsbury rejects the view that poverty equals social disorganization equals delinquency. He discovered that the greatest amounts of poverty did not correspond with the most socially disorganized areas. Delinquency, he argued, did correlate with poverty, but not with social disorganization, though suicide, the main focus of the study, did.

The title of Morris's (1957) book, *The Criminal Area: A study in social ecology*, indicates the direct link with the Chicago School, though as we have said, in common with British writers at this time, the full ramifications of the ecological model were not accepted. He did, however, approve of the concept of the criminal area, and used this as the framework for his areal study of delinquency in the London suburb of Croydon. For Morris, though, a deteriorating physical environment coupled with the existence of poverty did not in themselves explain why some youngsters came to be involved in delinquent behaviour. Neither did he consider areas associated with high levels of delinquency to be socially disorganized. Morris, therefore, reconceptualized the notion of a delinquent area, by seeing it as the product of two crucial variables: the housing policies of the local authority, and social class. As a result of decisions made by housing departments, and in particular decisions based upon a policy of placing 'problem' families together on the same estates, certain neighbourhoods had the 'potential' for the development of delinquent behaviour. This was an idea that stimulated a large amount of research in Britain on the theme of housing classes, and the struggle for housing space (see, for example, the well-known study by Rex and Moore (1967) of Sparkbrook in Birmingham).

Morris's explanation of delinquency owes much to Sutherland's theory of differential association. The boys living together on 'problem estates' form delinquent subcultures because of their socialization into the norms and values of the area, norms and values carried by the people living there. Unlike the argument from the Chicago School, this suggests that if such people were relocated they would take their culture with them, along with their possessions in the removal van – which approximates to a 'pollution' explanation of delinquency. In fact, in an attempt to explain why all children do not become delinquent, and arguing against Mays, Morris uses as an analogy the spread of diseases such as cholera in the nineteenth century. Some people, he says, were more resistant than others to the disease. Using the same logic, the resistance to delinquency in Croydon was explained in terms of the 'adjustment' to socio-economic factors made by the family. This contagion view of delinquency found in the theory of differential association has often been criticized, essentially because it presents a mechanistic model of becoming delinquent. The individual is pictured as in a sense soaking up the various 'bad' (or 'good') influences that they happen to come into contact with, rather like Pavlov's dogs.

Developing a British perspective

If British sociological criminology could never hope to match the sheer volume of research carried out by its counterparts in the United States, at least by the 1950s British researchers had begun to recognize and draw on this research. Furthermore, by the time the 1960s arrived, a more distinctly British approach to adolescent delinquency was building up.

One difficulty was that adolescent gangs – in the sense of identifiable, distinct groups of adolescents, whose *raison d'être* was to engage in specifically delinquent activities – proved hard to find in Britain. Research increasingly centred on the notion of youth culture, and the delinquency with which it was sometimes associated. Even in the United States the existence and nature of so-called gangs continued to generate debate within criminology. Short and Strodtbeck (1965) in their study in Chicago, for instance, were sceptical that specialized gangs existed. One's position on this matter, of course, depends upon one's definition of a 'gang'. As far back as 1927 Thrasher (1963) in *The Gang* provided a sociological definition, though too often the term has been used very loosely more or less simply to describe an 'unruly' group of individuals who spend a certain amount of time together. In order to achieve conceptual integrity, though, a sociological definition has to do better than this. Following Thrasher, therefore, a delinquent gang should more properly be seen as a collectivity possessing a number of key features such as permanence, face-to-face contact, a sense of identity among members, territoriality, usually a name, and a central concern with acts of delinquency. Unfortunately, in many studies the concept of subculture is used as if it were synonymous with gang.

Cultural diversity theory

As the discussion of the work of Mays and Morris has indicated, British sociological criminology in the main favoured an approach to delinquent behaviour that had more in common with the Chicago School than with the strain theorists, although there were moments of tension. This pedigree continued into the 1960s and came to be referred to as cultural diversity theory (it also had other names: differential association theory, cultural transmission theory, and affiliation theory). Essentially, cultural diversity argues that society is composed of a number of different cultures, these usually being linked to social class and neighbourhood. Generally there is an assumption that a dominant 'mainstream', conformist, culture exists, with other alternative delinquent cultures described as subcultures. Delinquency, from this perspective, results from normal socialization, through which individuals conform to the norms and values of these delinquent subcultures. People learn to be delinquent in exactly the same way that they learn to be non-delinquent; no pathological motivations need explaining. Unlike the subcultures described by Cohen, though, delinquent subcultures are not seen as reactive and anti the dominant mainstream culture, although they are, by definition, in conflict in a normative sense with that culture (should it exist).

The American anthropologist Walter Miller (1958) had outlined the central elements of cultural diversity theory. Focusing on lower-working-class culture as the prime source of delinquency, Miller argued that the adolescents involved were conformists rather than nonconformists or rebels. Their delinquency reflected their conformity to what he termed the 'focal concerns' of the working-class neighbourhood: trouble, toughness, smartness, excitement, fate, and autonomy. He also noted that many of the boys in his study lived in lone parent families, with that parent being a mother rather than a father. This led him to suggest that the machismo associated with delinquency functioned to express and register the boy's escape from his mother's apron strings.

Peter Willmott's (1966) study of adolescent boys living in Bethnal Green in the East End of London contains a section on the theme of delinquency. The book illustrates some of the uncertainties around at the time. Willmott is sympathetic to Cohen's status frustration theory, as well as to the cultural diversity theory of Miller. Thus he is able to write: 'Some . . . argue that the motive is above all "status frustration" – that is, the boys behave as they do to hit back at the society that has rejected them and to show their contempt for its values' (Willmott, 1966: 161). But he then goes on to say:

> there is no widespread and continuing sense of resentment, revolt or frustration among the local boys. Many boys are 'delinquent', in the sense that they sometimes break the law, and particularly steal. But, since most boys do not feel rejected or frustrated, the theory does not explain their transgressions. It can help to explain only the delinquency of the minority. (Ibid. 161)

One of the difficulties was that Willmott came across only a small minority of boys who were seriously involved in delinquency. He refers to the typology introduced by Whyte – 'corner boys' and 'college boys' – though his preferred terms are 'working class' and 'middle class' (the latter, strangely, meaning working-class boys who want to be middle class). Each represents a particular type of adjustment to a perceived lack of success in monetary and status terms. The 'working-class' boy accepts his status and financial situation; the 'middle-class' boy wishes to surmount his working-class status by trying to move into a non-manual occupation. There is also a third group identified by Willmott and he refers to members of this group as 'rebels', adding that it is 'probably from boys like this that the seriously delinquent are drawn . . . though it cannot be proved from our figures' (ibid. 168). In fact, the 'rebel', described as actively deviating from both working-class and middle-class standards, was in a small minority. In his sample of 246 boys, only 'a tenth or less' could be described as 'rebels', and he acknowledges that not all of these were necessarily delinquent. There is in Willmott's study one particularly interesting type of rebel, and it is a type of working-class adolescent rarely commented on, or even recognized, in sociological studies of youth. This is the bohemian or politicized working-class youth. Given the stereotyping of working-class culture in much of the literature, it is perhaps understandable that any serious engagement with, say, avant-garde poetry, music or painting, or with political struggle, will be overlooked in studies of this culture. In the example given by Willmott, the 'rebel' is into jazz, the novels of Kerouac and Mailer, and smokes marijuana. In short, he is nearer to what at that time was a beatnik than a delinquent tearaway or middle-class-style conformist.

Willmott's general conclusion is that serious delinquency is rare in Bethnal Green, though he estimates that one in three of the boys that he interviewed will probably end up in court before they are 21. Most of the boys in his study had no desire for middle-class status and they used their intermittent acts of delinquency as vehicles for a bit of fun and an expression of group solidarity. To this extent he sees them as belonging to a delinquent subculture.

Published in the same year, David Downes's (1966) *The Delinquent*

Solution had the distinction of being the most theoretically sophisticated British sociological study of delinquency. Not only did he provide a graphic account of working-class life in Poplar and Stepney in the East End of London, and evaluate the relevance and validity of current influential theories, but he also developed a theoretical understanding of delinquent subcultures that addressed their deeper social and cultural roots. The study did, however, appear just as criminology in Britain was about to be transformed because of the impact of the new deviancy, and it therefore soon found itself assigned to a pre-new deviancy category.

In line with cultural diversity theory, Downes argues that delinquency is fundamentally conformist, in the sense that those involved in the delinquency are conforming to the values of the lower-working-class neighbourhood in which they live; he found no evidence that these delinquent subcultures resulted fxom antagonisms towards a perceived mainstream culture. This is similar to Miller's formulation, though Miller uses the notion of 'focal concerns' rather than values. According to Downes, there was no discontent with working-class status. In general the boys wanted to be working class, and certainly had no 'problems of adjustment' of the sort discussed by Cohen. Their speech, dress, and demeanour were in many ways a celebration of their working classness. This is not to suggest that they felt no dissatisfactions. They saw school as basically a waste of time, and left at the earliest opportunity with few or no academic qualifications. When they entered the world of work there was no expectation, and rarely any realization, of 'job satisfaction'. However, they did not want to cease being working class and become middle class, though like most people they would have welcomed more money.

Downes describes working-class areas where men have often been in trouble with the law, where there is drug dealing and prostitution and where fights continue into middle age. For the boys their social space is the street, and given the normative expectations to which they conform, it is difficult for them *not* to come into conflict with the law or the norms of 'respectable' working-class and middle-class society. This was not rebellion though: the delinquent subcultures were not contra-cultures. Furthermore, Downes found no evidence of delinquent *gangs*.

As the title of the book suggests, Downes argues that delinquency provides a solution, for some boys, to the central problems they experience. The delinquent subculture provides a way of coming to terms with the profound dissatisfaction experienced in schools and work. What they have achieved:

> is an opting-out of the joint middle- and skilled working-class value-system whereby work is extolled as a central life-issue, and whereby the male adolescent of semi- or unskilled origin is enjoined to either 'better himself' or 'accept his station in life'. To insulate themselves against the harsh implications of this creed,

the adolescent in a 'dead-end' job, in a 'dead' neighbourhood, extricates himself
from the belief in work as of any importance beyond the simple provision of
income. (Downes, 1966: 236–7)

With neither of these middle-class/skilled-working-class options striking
them as particularly attractive, the non-aspirant and non-compliant
adolescent 'dissociates' himself from the two spheres of school and work,
so that they have no importance or credibility. With no educational
aspirations or commitment to seeking out a 'good' job, let alone a career,
the adolescent 'deflects what aspirations he has into areas of what has
been termed "non-work"' (ibid. 237), that is, they put their energies
into the leisure sphere. If education and work cannot provide the basis
for a meaningful life, then it is down to the opportunities provided
by the enticing space represented by leisure. The way in which leisure
is used, though, has to be seen against the backdrop of the value system
in which the boys have been brought up. It is a value system that stresses
adventure, daring, toughness and excitement. If these values cannot be
lived out in schools or factories, or some substitute attachments found, then
they have to be lived out in leisure. Indeed, as Downes puts it, there is an
'edge of desperation' about the boys' reliance on leisure. Unfortunately,
because of their class position and outlook, they have neither the money
or the inclination to engage in certain leisure pursuits that could potentially
realize their aspirations. In other words, they face blocked opportunities
in the world of leisure, opportunities that are available to their better-off
middle-class counterparts. What *is* readily available, though, for the
lower-working-class adolescent is delinquency: 'Law-breaking is the only
area of excitement to which he has absolutely untrammelled access'
(ibid. 249).

An important dimension to Downes's work is his partial incorporation
of the ideas of the American criminologists Matza and Sykes (1961) (their
work is looked at in more detail later on). Matza and Sykes argue that so-
called delinquent values are not at all peculiar to the lower working class,
but are present as leisure values throughout society. They are critical of
much criminology for, in their view, erroneously polarizing the value
systems, so that a posited middle-class value system is presented as the
normal, non-delinquent value system to which members of society in
general conform. Delinquency, they argued, was more or less evenly
distributed among all social classes; members of the lower working class just
happened to get caught more often. While agreeing with the general tenor
of this argument, and accepting as a 'criminological truism' the view that
non-delinquency is extremely rare, Downes (1966: 247) disagrees that
middle-class adolescents are as frequently and as seriously involved in
delinquency as are lower-working-class adolescents: 'Most evidence
supports the view that group delinquency is more frequent, persistent,

diversified and less amenable to control among male, working class, urban adolescents than in any other sector.'

In Downes's view it is necessary to employ the notion of differential access to leisure goals in order to make Matza and Sykes's argument plausible. Leaving school at the earliest opportunity, working-class adolescents are, he says, more likely to find themselves with 'free time', as they are not involved in studying for examinations, or pursuing apprentice-ships or a career. However, because of their dissociation from school and work, they in fact require *more* from leisure – but here they meet blocked opportunities. There is no educational preparation for, and a lack of interest in, 'constructive' hobbies, and the local youth clubs and dance halls usually fail to compensate for what is missing in education and work. In this situation delinquency offers an accessible and attractive way of achieving leisure goals.

Schools and the 'problem of adjustment'

The role of the school in the lives of working-class boys was explored in more detail by David Hargreaves (1967) in *Social Relations in a Secondary School*. The school in question was a Secondary Modern School in the North of England taking mainly working-class 11-plus failures. Hargreaves is strongly influenced by the work of Albert Cohen, drawing on the concepts of status frustration and problem of adjustment, as well as identifying an oppositional contra-culture.

By the fourth and final year, two subcultures – one 'academic', the other 'delinquescent' – had developed in the school, with the latter concentrated in the bottom D stream. While the values of the academic subculture were 'oriented to those of the school and teachers', the values of the delinquescent subculture, though not necessarily delinquent, were in opposition to those of the school. In the familiar terminology of this period, the boys in the top stream were described as conforming to middle-class values, and in Hargeaves's estimation they tended to come from homes that although working class, were themselves oriented to middle-class values. Once again it is as if those working-class families that respect people and property are honorary members of the middle class, and to that extent are actually deviant. Conversely, the delinquescent ones are merely conforming to something that is presumed to be intrinsically working class. It is as if only those working-class professional footballers who have internalized 'middle-class' values are capable of behaving themselves on and off the pitch.

In Hargreaves's account the bottom-stream boys lost status because they had failed on two counts: by not passing the 11-plus examination, and by ending up in the D stream. On top of that they were 'negatively valuated' by teachers, making them feel inferior; they lacked the privileges enjoyed by the A-stream boys; and when leaving school had only a limited range of jobs open to them. The result of all this, not surprisingly, was that the bottom-stream boys felt resentment because of status deprivation. Thus, as Hargreaves puts it, this created a problem of adjustment, leading to a collective, subcultural response, with the subculture adopting an oppositional stance towards the norms and values of the school. Within the subculture, anti-school and anti-teacher behaviour became a source of status for the boys, though in practice the opposition was limited because of the power held by teachers; much of the time the boys fell back on 'sullen compliance'.

The similarities with Cohen's work are obvious, but there is one important difference between the two studies. Unlike Cohen, Hargreaves does not argue that the oppositional subculture was composed of boys who had previously internalized middle-class values, and were then denied status. He does not see the boys' delinquescent behaviour and antagonism towards the school as an example of 'reaction formation'; feeling resentment at a perceived lack of status was sufficient. This detail raises the question of timing in studies such as these. Cohen, presumably, would argue that we would need to know if the boys concerned had at some previous stage internalized, or at least partly internalized, middle-class values. Hargreaves assumes that they have not. The top-stream boys, though, had, according to Hargreaves, internalized middle-class values, but for Cohen these were unlikely candidates for delinquency because they had, in 'college boy' style, achieved a degree of academic success, and satisfied their aspirations. Alternatively, Cloward and Ohlin would see these college boys as the prime source of delinquency, because of the blocked opportunities they would eventually face. Even if we accept the argument that lower-working-class delinquent boys typically desire, but are then denied, middle-class status, the above discussion illustrates the lack of clarity and consensus in these sorts of studies regarding precisely when status frustration, leading to delinquency, will surface. Indeed, by 1958 Cohen had moved away from the idea of reaction formation as the crucial basis of delinquency (Cohen and Short, 1958).

Subcultural theory: taking stock

Subculture has proved to be a seductive concept within criminology, whether used in the context of delinquent behaviour, or as a way of understanding youth subcultural formations (see the later discussion of the work of the Birmingham Centre for Contemporary Cultural Studies, for example). At this juncture we can take stock of the subcultural theory that grew up in the 1950s and 1960s. Frances Heidensohn (1989) has usefully summarized the limits of subcultural theory on the basis of five headings: determinism, selectivity, gender, conformity, and anomie.

Determinism indicates the strong tendency in subcultural theory, especially under the influence of functionalism, to present an 'over-socialized' view of the delinquent. Adolescents are seen as passive products of the cultural forces around them, responding rather like robots programmed by 'bad' influences. Qualities of reflection, choice and rationality are thus neglected. Under such determining conditions – for example, due to living on a 'criminal' housing estate – it is difficult to explain why *all* of the inhabitants do not become delinquent. This overprediction of delinquency arises because of what Matza (1964) calls an 'embarrassment of riches'; in a sense the theory over-explains delinquency.

Selectivity refers to the types of subculture earmarked for attention. These are the more flashy, exciting examples that in fact involve only a tiny minority of young people. Through such selectivity the mundanity, ordinariness and conformity of large sections of British and American youth are neglected. Furthermore, the much more serious crimes carried out by adults tend to be ignored.

Gender was not seriously addressed within criminology until the late 1960s: 'gender was a sociological issue which ticked away, like a time bomb in the cellars, for generations' (Heidensohn, 1989: 54). Although issues of masculinity and machismo were on the agenda, and sometimes a few pages were even reserved for a discussion of females, the (male) subcultural theorists lacked the conceptual resources to deal adequately with gender. This is not simply to do with the exclusion of girls from their delinquency studies, though. It is to do with the social construction of notions of masculinity and femininity, and the ways in which these are incorporated into the lives of adolescents, as well as the adults with whom they come into contact.

Linked to selectivity, the notion of *conformity* directs us to question critically the inability of subcultural theory to explore the reasons why so many young people do not, to any significant degree, engage in delinquency. An understanding of conformity, for example among 'college boys', may very well be an important dimension to an understanding of delinquency.

Finally, we come to the problematic concept of *anomie*. Many subcultural theorists have described the delinquent's world in terms of anomie, or a lack of moral regulation. However, this world is often presented as if it was a self-contained, more or less independent social entity. As Heidensohn says: 'Presumably all these children have homes, parents, siblings, elderly neighbours, churches and clubs. If they don't, then such information needs to be built into the picture, since it is likely to be significant' (ibid. 57).

Matza and Sykes: dissenting voices

The work of the American criminologists David Matza and Gresham Sykes has already been briefly referred to. As far as a critical reading of subcultural theory is concerned, two of their early papers are particularly important. In the first (Sykes and Matza, 1957) they introduce the concept of 'techniques neutralization', and in the second (Matza and Sykes, 1961) the concept of 'subterranean values'.

In these two papers Matza and Sykes raised awkward and provocative questions for conventional criminology, including subcultural theory. Essentially they set out to challenge the dominant view in criminology that delinquents were fundamentally different from non-delinquents: that they each inhabited separate moral universes. This formed the basis for Matza's later work in which he developed a critique of the sociological determinism with which much criminological theory was infused (Matza, 1964, 1969). Needless to say, Matza was a major influence on the new deviancy of the late 1960s and early 1970s.

Many of the writers we have looked at have stressed that for some adolescents, because they live in certain neighbourhoods, delinquency was normal. Due to their social circumstances they simply conformed (or because of strains ended up conforming) to a set of delinquent norms and values at variance with those of a supposed mainstream culture. From this perspective, society is composed of a non-delinquent majority subscribing to non-delinquent values, and a delinquent minority subscribing to delinquent values. It was this sharp differentiation between the two that Matza and Sykes rejected. The 'delinquent', they argued, had been falsely characterized as a special kind of person, inhabiting a special deviant world. Although this is a view that satisfies common-sense understandings, and is not uncommon within criminology, it is highly misleading. It depicts the delinquent as being totally and consummately committed to a delinquent way of life. It is as if they brush their teeth and make love in a delinquent way, invariably refuse to help anyone in trouble, and harm people and property at every available opportunity. Within this framework every activity appears to be undertaken without reference to any of the values supposedly associated with law-abiding, mainstream society. For Matza and Sykes this is nonsense. They argue that delinquents are routinely involved in the non-delinquent world, and only occasionally engage in delinquency. Furthermore, those who do engage in delinquency are not just aware of non-delinquent values but, to the extent that anyone else does, they actively believe in them.

Matza and Sykes's attempt to connect the delinquent to law-abiding, non-delinquent society, and thereby stress the similarities rather than dissimilarities, can be illustrated by their concept of 'techniques of neutralization'. Basically, their argument is that just about everyone breaks the law. However, in order to go ahead with the law breaking, individuals need to convince themselves that what they are doing is not actually wrong. This is different to the excuses that someone might make after they have committed an offence. It is a process through which the individual neutralizes the 'badness' or 'immorality' of their actions prior to carrying them out. It thus operates as an important feature of the motivation to commit delinquent acts, or, as Matza puts it, to 'drift' into delinquency. This was part of Matza's project to show how the delinquent is not a determined creature, but exercises, at least to some extent, free will. Techniques of neutralization indicate how individuals actively make decisions to break rules. However, according to Matza and Sykes, the fact that people have recourse to these techniques beforehand, shows that they are aware of, and subscribe to, non-delinquent values. Sone hypothetical examples will illustrate the sorts of situations they are referring to. Although they are against theft, someone fiddles their expenses at work 'because everybody does it, and it is a perk of the job'. Someone is against violence, and yet hits a man at the bar in the face because 'he said something to my wife'. Someone is in favour of a 30 mph speed limit in a built-up area, and yet travels at 40 mph in their car because 'I was in a hurry'. And so on.

This attempt to illuminate the continuities, rather than discontinuities, between the world of the delinquent and that of the non-delinquent, is also apparent in their paper on 'subterranean values'. Here they are strongly critical of studies of delinquency that feel obliged to construct a definitive standard in the shape of 'middle-class' values, against which delinquent values can be measured. For Matza and Sykes, society contains a subculture of delinquency, rather than a number of delinquent subcultures. In other words, delinquent values exist throughout society, among all social classes, and should not be specifically linked to the lower working class. Values stressing such things as hedonism, conspicuous consumption, machismo, excitement and daring are, they say, to be encountered everywhere and are so prevalent that to call them 'deviant' is absurd. However, the middle and upper classes are in a better position than the working class to live out these values in appropriate settings, or in ways that do not invite the attention of control agencies. The working-class delinquent often suffers from 'bad timing'. The notion of subterranean values at least acts as an antidote to those theories that see 'middle-class' culture as exemplifying an unqualified commitment to such things as hard work, keeping to the rules, politeness, and so forth, and its opposite designated as 'working-class' culture. As Downes says: 'far from standing as an alien in the body of society, the delinquent may represent instead a dangerous reflection or caricature' (Downes, 1966: 246).

Part III

The mid-1960s to the early 1970s

8 | The discipline of criminology and its context – 2

The development of sociological criminology in Britain
The break with orthodoxy: the new deviancy
The New Left
Radicals and the new deviancy: the impact on British criminology

The development of sociological criminology in Britain

The relatively small contribution made by sociological perspectives to criminology in Britain up to the mid-1960s effectively ensured the suppression of any significant influence from sociological criminology in the United States. During the second half of the 1960s, however, this situation changed dramatically, as British criminology began to draw increasingly on American sources for ideas and inspiration. From then on, as Downes (1988: 46) puts it: 'For two decades Britain became an off-shore laboratory for the distillation of ideas fermented in the U.S.A.'

This coincided with the expansion of sociology in British universities and polytechnics, and with it a rapid increase in the number of young sociologists interested in the field of crime and deviance. The result was that by the beginning of the 1970s the sociology of crime had shed its marginalized status, though by now the preferred term was the sociology of deviance.

The pillaging of American sources by British sociologists of deviance was not simply because there was so much of it; the innovations associated with new deviancy theory were what proved to be overwhelmingly attractive. Indeed, the apparently sudden interest in this field on the part of British academics was stimulated by new deviancy theory, though in some cases the work had actually been produced some years previously.

The break with orthodoxy: the new deviancy

The rush to embrace the ideas of new deviancy theory was the result of factors operating at both the level of criminology/the sociology of deviance, and at a wider societal level.

The new deviancy developing at that time – and variously called labelling theory, social reaction theory, transactionalism and interactionism – was subversive, though what was subverted was not so much the wider society as academic criminology. It did not provide a critique of Western capitalist societies, and generally would not have wanted to, though it did raise questions that subsequent writers utilized in the construction of a much more radical sociology of deviance/criminology. It did, however, mark an important break with earlier criminology, a criminology that was by then being called 'orthodox'.

Within orthodox criminology, debates over the conceptual language of the discipline were conspicuously lacking. Crime was by definition 'bad' because it was against the law; deviance was 'bad' because it was against the norms. Debates about the meaning of such terms became central to the new deviancy. Likewise, the sociological criminology that had grown up since the war was criticized for its causal–corrective concerns and positivist methodologies: track down the causes of crime, then decide on the most appropriate ways of dealing with the criminal. There was frustration with the constraints placed on criminology by social policy and penal and legal practices. Authoritarian versions of orthodox criminology stressed the individual's personal responsibility and the need for punitive action by the agencies of social control. More liberal versions emphasized more or less deterministic 'social factors', or individual/family 'problems' of a psychological nature; problems that could be cured, or solved, or adjusted to, providing that help was given by those with the professional expertise. When 'deviance' was mentioned in these accounts, it was assumed that it represented a pathological state, and the important questions were: What caused it? How can we stamp it out? This was the legacy of British criminology that the new deviancy theorists sought to break away from.

This critical stance was part of a much wider revolt in the social sciences against the set of assumptions underlying the, until then, dominant positivist paradigm. David Hargreaves *et al.* (1976: 1) very broadly define the debate as being between positivism and phenomenology:

> In an oversimplified form the debate can be characterised as a battle between the more traditional social scientists of this century, who are grouped together under the general label of 'positivists', and the growing supporters of the alternative paradigm, who are grouped together under the general label of 'phenomenologists' . . . Nowhere has this debate been more sharply felt than in that area of social science . . . which is traditionally referred to as deviance.

In fact, the impact of phenomenological sociology on the area of deviance petered out fairly quickly, but Hargreaves *et al.*'s observation is correct if 'phenomenology' is used in the loosest sense. For new deviancy theorists this basically entailed taking account of the subjective world of the actor, seen as the product of meanings constructed through social interaction.

Stan Cohen described the new deviancy theorists as 'sceptical theorists', and for him the new deviancy was part of a revolution:

> This reorientation is part of what might be called the sceptical revolution in criminology and the sociology of deviance. The older tradition was *canonical* in the sense that it saw the concepts it worked with as authoritative, standard, accepted, given and unquestionable. (Cohen, 1973: 12)

Many writers viewed what was happening to criminology as cataclysmic: 'The 1960s saw a Renaissance in sociological criminology in Britain' (Wiles, 1976b: 14).

In an attempt to gather together the various cultural threads which contributed to these changes in the sociology of deviance, Geoff Pearson (1975: 51) described the new perspectives gathering momentum in the 1960s as follows:

> This area of scholarship is an odd theoretical cocktail, constructed out of sociology, psychiatry, criminology, social administration, media studies, law, social work, political science, cultural criticism, social psychology, and even some strands of popular culture and music. This interdisciplinary misfit finds its focus in the study of deviants . . the sociology of labelling is only one of its elements. Within the same domain one finds what passes for 'phenomenology', and also a sort of 'Marxism'. Anti-psychiatry has left its mark . . . a theoretical jigsaw which has earned the reputation of being 'radical' . . . I call this space which opened out in social thought in the 1960s, *misfit sociology*. (original emphasis)

This gives a whiff of the hotchpotch of sometimes frenetic ideas that grew out of the wild possibilities of the new deviancy. Given the lack of interest in, or even antagonism towards, the sociology of crime/deviance within the discipline of sociology in Britain, we can understand why criminologists, or sociologists, who considered themselves as radicals, received the new deviancy as it arrived from across the Atlantic with unrestrained enthusiasm. It was a breath of fresh air, bringing with it an invigorating sense of new possibilities. There was a promise of a radical alternative to the moribund perspectives of traditional criminology. The alternative to positivist criminology offered by the new deviancy encouraged a critical frame of mind, and allowed a broader spectrum of sociological theory and method to enter the arena. Also, by focusing on 'deviance' rather than 'crime', it opened out the range of activities encompassed by research. No longer obsessed with juvenile delinquency, the new sociologists of deviance turned their attention to all sorts of groups supposedly having deviant status: nudists, the blind, the mentally ill, the mentally retarded, poolroom hustlers, Hell's Angels, drifters, dropouts, illegal drug users, blackmailers, and so on. By the early 1970s though, some new deviancy writers were becoming worried that this shift of emphasis was actually contributing to the deviantization of such groups. One example of this view is provided by Alexander Liazos (1972), who famously used the phrase 'nuts, sluts and preverts'. ('Preverts', incidently, is the correct spelling, although when used by British writers it is inevitably spelt 'pervert'. The phrase originally appeared in the 1960s film *Doctor Strangelove, Or How I Learned to Stop Worrying and Love the Bomb*. It was used by one of the redneck characters.)

After the initial burst of new deviancy activity at the end of the 1960s, the dust began to settle and more careful assessments of the impact could be made. Certainly, new deviancy theory represented a move towards a more sophisticated approach to theory, with deviant motivations and official reactions to deviant behaviour at the core. In the post-new deviancy period from the early 1970s, a number of strands in varying degrees critical of what had gone before, began to develop, and these are examined below. What we can note is that since the late 1960s the area of crime and deviance has provided an arena for a discussion of the most fundamental theoretical concerns of sociology.

In this context the issue of the relationship between the 'deviant' and the sociologist is of particular interest. The 1960s saw a move away from a situation where the criminologist in effect lined up with the rule enforcers, to one where the stance adopted was either ambivalent or even explicitly on the side of the deviant. Becker, for instance, one of the most influential American criminologists at the time, argued that the researcher should take sides. This idea had important implications for the way in which new deviancy theory was received in Britain, though there are significant differences between the more liberal sociologists, and those on the left, especially what was called the 'New Left'. For the liberal there was, somewhere within new deviancy, the promise of a more humane welfare state, where the 'outsider' was treated with dignity – dignity commensurate with a fuller appreciation of the authenticity of his or her actions. This stance was what 'law and order' letter writers to the press would describe, derogatorily, as soft. For those on the left, the promise led in a different direction, and brought to the surface what may be described as latent moral ambiguities regarding deviants and their actions. In a review of new deviancy, Jock Young (1975: 63) has written: 'Attacking a theoretical position to which one is opposed often tends towards the erection of an alternative position which is merely an inversion of one's opponent's.' The inversion of traditional criminology created an interesting situation. If crime was previously pathological, it was now 'normal'. If criminologists had previously sided with official versions of reality, they now sided with the deviant's. If previous research was aimed at correction, it was now aimed at 'appreciation'. And – wherein lies the crux of the problem – if crime was previously 'wrong', was it now 'right'? Was there something in crime/ deviance that the left could positively appreciate, that is, explicitly approve of?

Various new deviancy luminaries such as Becker (1963), Erikson (1962) and Kitsuse (1962), had replaced the 'absolutism' of earlier criminology with a new 'relativism'. No behaviour, it was argued, was inherently deviant or inherently 'bad'; deviant status depended upon the power to label. This idea was to take some criminologists on the left down some interesting highways.

During the 1960s the orthodox left, as opposed to the emerging New Left, in one sense occupied a similar position to that of the conservative criminologist. Although moral ambivalence on a personal level may have existed, publicly crime was judged to be 'wrong', though of course the respective explanations and solutions would have been different. For the New Left, however, the ideas introduced by new deviancy theory led to a fundamental questioning of common-sense distinctions between crime and non-crime and deviance and non-deviance. If nothing was inherently immoral or evil, why should official, or ruling-class definitions be accepted? Perhaps some acts labelled deviant are in fact acts that can, from a socialist point of view, be approved of. This is to move beyond the argument that some legal activities, such as arms deals, are more harmful than some illegal activities, to one where certain deviant acts are to be welcomed because they are beneficial in socialist terms. Eventually, this was to lead some radical writers to argue that crime and deviance were forms of political action.

The commitment of new deviancy theory to 'siding with the deviant' was interpreted in different ways. For some it meant organizing research and theory around the deviant's version of reality. For others it meant actually *supporting* the actions of at least some defined deviants, and it is here that the moral ambivalence enters, leading to statements such as 'the mass of delinquents are literally involved in the practice of redistributing private property' (Taylor, Walton and Young, 1973). It can also lead to a full-blooded romanticism, where all so-called deviants are viewed as courageous non-conformists fighting an evil system. If, say, members of the working class are thought to be frustratingly docile, or at best wrapped up in strategies based on economism, than it is perhaps tempting for radical criminologists to see in deviance an example of struggle against the state apparatus of capitalism. It is this that raises the important question of whether a left-wing criminologist or sociologist of deviance should, as it were, align themselves with judges, magistrates, prison governors and police officers, all of whom are in the business of maintaining the status quo, rather than with the deviant who is threatening it. This niggling problem has haunted various types of radical criminology since the 1960s, though it has not always been given explicit attention.

Wider societal factors: the counter culture

When explaining the friendly reception given to American new deviancy theory by young British sociologists and criminologists during the second half of the 1960s, we need to also consider the broader cultural and political developments that took place. On a cultural level the 1960s saw the growth of the so-called counter culture, and on a political level, an increasingly influential challenge to the old, orthodox Left from what came to be known as the 'New Left'. Sociologists and criminologists in this country were not immune to the effects of these two movements. Thus, from the mid-1960s a climate of opinion was being generated that was to prove highly conducive to the ideas of the new deviancy.

In essence the counter culture represented a disengagement with the values of mainstream, conformist culture, and an attempt to create a non-materialistic, more expressive and meaningful alternative. With a subjectivist and hedonistic frame of reference, the emphasis was on personal liberation from the constraints imposed by what was seen as a dehumanized consumer society, where *things* had become more important than people. Hence the resistance to dominant ideas regarding such things as sexuality, drug use and appropriate style of dress.

The primary source of the 'great refusal' (as Marcuse put it) represented by the counter culture of the 1960s was affluent middle-class youth, and the greatest wrath was reserved for the stultifying middle-class lifestyle associated with affluent suburbia, the land of 'little boxes' in the song sung by Pete Seeger. In fact, the little boxes from which many of them had come:

> For here were people protesting not against material hardship, but against the emotional containment of affluence, a feeling that affluence was not all that there was to life and that public success in the affluent world might be personally meaningless. (Pearson, 1975: 83)

The rejection of consumerism and conventional mores, and a corresponding commitment to cultural diversity, harmonized with the sympathetic, even celebratory, approach to deviance taken by the new deviancy theorists. This is not to say, of course, that British sociologists who latched on to the ideas of the new deviancy were dropouts, who, high on drugs, wrote their books and papers in between listening to Donovan and Jimi Hendrix in a convention-shunning hippy commune. What was important was the way in which elements of the counter culture permeated into the lives of a whole range of people, though their commitment stopped short of, say, dropping out of society. At the time, in fact, many of the sociologists concerned were undergraduate or postgraduate students, or in some cases young lecturers, and the desire to acquire qualifications and teaching posts, and to write books, indicates a degree of commitment to staying in the system. However, being a student did provide rather more opportunities than did paid employment for experimenting with ideas and lifestyles associated with the counter culture.

The influence of the counter culture on a younger generation in Britain was swift and pervasive. Ironically, the commercial interests sustaining a consumer society so vehemently rejected by the counter culture, were responsible for the dissemination of many of these ideas. Within a short space of time commercial interests were eagerly seizing and marketing in a vulgarized form anything that would sell. It is a familiar process which, in this case, was to find its nadir when, in the early 1970s, Marks & Spencer finally brought Woodstock to the High Street when they started selling pale blue trouser suits with a printed pattern of fake stitched patches. In the summer of 1967, with Scott McKenzie's *Let's Go to San Francisco* filling the air, holiday-makers in Blackpool and Southend would have seen Indian love beads, cardboard headbands and plastic daffodils by the score. In a classic review of postwar cultural movements, Jeff Nuttall (1970: 200) paints this picture:

> Nine months after the first gatherings in Haight-Ashbury girls and office workers were wandering down the Brighton and Blackpool seafronts, jangling their souvenir prayer-belts, trailing their Paisley bedspreads, brandishing daffodils and trying to look tripped out. The Beatles had gone 'flower power' and it was up to the kids to do their best to follow.

Many commentators saw members of the counter culture as harbingers of new, personally fulfilling, strategies for coping with a future based on leisure. The American sociologist Fred Davis (1967: 12), for instance, in a paper with the attention-grabbing title 'Why all of us may be hippies someday', celebrated the prophetic nature of the counter culture, suggesting that hippies were 'Rehearsing *in vivo* possible cultural solutions to central life problems posed by the emerging society of the future'.

In spite of these commendations, though, various contradictions within the counter culture began to appear, and critics on the left started to question its radical credentials. Because of its nature, however, the counter culture was hardly going to deliver a coherent political programme, let alone a socialist one. In reality, when they did participate in the activities of the counter culture, it was the Left at play rather than the Left at (class) war; the barricades in Paris in 1968 were built by politicos rather than hippies.

Ultimately, the counter culture represented a critique of, and reaction to, not so much capitalism as modern, consumer-oriented society abstracted from its economic and political structures. The dissatisfaction shown by those on the political left was eventually paralleled by a dissatisfaction with new deviancy theory among radical sociologists, and with it a corresponding shift to a much 'harder' political stance. The dawning of the Age of Aquarius signalled a romantic celebration of youth. They would lead people back to the Garden of Eden, though they could take some of the artefacts of modern technological society with them, but only some of them. Because they were identified with middle-class suburbia, such things as vacuum cleaners and food processers were frowned upon, whilst electric guitars, stereo systems and synthesizers, also products of an affluent capitalist technology, were acceptable. Youth would change society, but somehow capitalism would still exist.

The New Left

For the New Left too, modern life was characterized by a soul-destroying consumerism, though here the target was a specifically capitalist society. Day-to-day social order, the argument ran, was maintained not by overt measures of social control, but by concentrating people's minds on an overriding concern with consumer goods. Important social and political questions were relegated to second place behind questions about the best deodorant or washing machine to use. In the words of Marcuse, capitalist societies were 'one dimensional'. Of course the Left in Europe had for a long time equated capitalism with self-centred consumerism, but from the perspective of the New Left, older groups, such as the Communist Party, had become ossified: their formulations and strategies had ceased to provide a meaningful alternative vision.

The New Left also shared with the counter culture a preoccupation with subjectivism and the need for a personal liberation of thought, out of which will grow a basis for revolutionary change. In the case of the New Left, though, this was explicitly linked to the removal of capitalism. While the New Left did confront capitalism as a system, it was in a manner that many older European socialists found strange. Essentially this was because of the importance attached to the relationship between the personal and the political. Again we see how the influence of a more broadly based intellectual framework was important for the subsequent reception given to the ideas of new deviancy theory by radical sociologists.

The intellectual roots of the New Left lay in what is called the Frankfurt or 'critical' School, whose ideas were developed in prewar Germany, and during the war when its members were in exile in the United States. Undoubtedly, this School held a formidable array of intellectual talent: Adorno, Horkheimer, Fromm, Benjamin, Lowenthal and Marcuse. The Frankfurt School believed that the view of man's relationship to nature that grew out of the Enlightenment, although it discarded the naive animism of an earlier period, was not fulfilling the promise of real social progress. As human beings had manipulated nature, so those with power used technology to manipulate the less powerful. This manipulation, however, did not occur simply at a physical level, for their consciousness and senses were also manipulated, and the Frankfurt School argued that what was needed was a 'sense' liberation. Marcuse, one of the most prominent proponents of these ideas in the 1960s, saw in the sometimes serious, yet at other times silly and childish, behaviour of the counter culture the possible basis for liberation. A later member of the Frankfurt School, Habermas, commented on the political content of the counter culture:

> I consider the politicisation of private conflicts a singular result of the protest movement . . . Today, difficulties that a mere 2 or 3 years ago would have been passed for private matters . . . now claim political significance and ask to be justified in political concepts. Psychology seems to turn into politics – perhaps a reaction to the reality that politics, in so far as it relates to the masses, has long been translated into psychology. (Habermas quoted in Pearson, 1975)

Thus in the 1960s there were points of fusion between the counter culture and the New Left, and these produced definitions of 'political' notable for their extreme fluidity and flexibility – a theme that was to be picked up by sociologists of deviance in the post-new deviancy period. In a range of publications almost anything was likely to be prefixed by the term 'the politics of': the politics of ecstasy, of madness, of sexuality, of shoplifting, and so on. Those involved in making everything 'political' did so from a number of perspectives, and with varying degrees of sophistication. Poets, journalists, novelists, psychiatrists, cultural pundits, as well as sociologists of deviance, carried forward this break with traditionalism. Many of them also began to use the term 'radical' to underline opposition to traditional ways of thinking, and thus there appeared movements such as radical social work, radical education and radical philosophy.

There was an ironic subtext to all of this that has already been alluded to in the discusssion of the counter culture. This is that the 'radical', 'revolutionary', 'transforming' ideas of the New Left came to be disseminated and popularized by the very capitalist institutions against which the radicalism was aimed. A striking example of this is provided by a book published in 1968 and written by a French student prominent in the uprisings in Paris in that year. The author, Daniel Cohn-Bendit, cannot resist pointing out the contradiction:

> the publishers now come chasing after me, begging me to write about anything I choose, good or bad, exciting or dull; all they want is something they can sell – a revolutionary gadget with marketable qualities . . . publishers are falling over themselves to cash in on the May events. In our commercial world, individual capitalists are perfectly willing to pave the way for their own destruction, to broadcast revolutionary ideas, provided only that these help to fill their pockets . . . They do not even seem to be bothered by the fact that their cash will be used for the next round of Molotov cocktails. (Cohn-Bendit and Cohn-Bendit, 1968: 11)

Radicals and the new deviancy: the impact on British criminology

Against a backdrop of counter cultural and New Left influences, new deviancy theory was absorbed with relish by a generation of British sociologists. Soon, as with Cohn-Bendit, publishers were seeking out work from these radical sociologists. This was important in that, coupled with a growth in sociology in general, and the sociology of deviance in particular, it contributed to a situation where radical criminology broke free of any significant dependence on funding from institutions such as the Home Office, the police and the prisons. Criminological work that was tied to these institutional demands, and often referred to as mainstream 'administrative' criminology, did, it should be noted, continue throughout this period under review – and still continues.

David Garland (1985b) has strongly argued that since its inception criminology has always been linked to 'external' political and ideological demands. In other words, the discipline has been tied to the administrative and ideological constraints imposed upon it by its political paymasters; and we have seen something of this when looking at the nature of criminology up to the 1960s. To this extent, and in spite of pretensions to scientific status, criminological research has conformed with the requirements of the state. However, notwithstanding the validity of Garland's argument, the sociology of deviance/criminology did, at that moment in the late 1960s, provide, at least for radical practitioners, a space in which to work that was relatively free from these constraints. As Jock Young (1988: 164) has said:

> The fall-out from the new deviancy explosion has been considerable. Radical criminology has its powerbase in those areas of what one might call unsubsidised criminology. That is criminology as it is taught in the schools and polytechnics, the universities and the colleges of education. It has not held sway over those parts of criminology which are paid for directly out of central government funds.

Furthermore, many of the ideas derived from radical criminology have also had an impact in areas outside these teaching institutions and 'have entered into the general social perspective of educated sections of the population as they have influenced the thinking of establishment criminology itself' (ibid.).

An important institutional development for the new deviancy in Britain was the creation in 1968 of the National Deviancy Conference (NDC), which acted as a forum for radical criminologists. Continuing well into the 1970s, the conferences organized by the NDC quickly attracted large audiences, and played a key role in augmenting and developing alternatives to mainstream criminology. As Downes (1988: 177) says:

The great appeal of the NDC was not only to sociologists of crime in search of a congenial forum, but also to younger sociologists who saw in deviance an escape route from the positivist methods and functionalist orthodoxy of much British sociology.

That many of the main figures in British criminology today were closely involved in the NDC is a further indication of its significant contribution to the field of criminology. Achieving senior positions in universities and research centres, the influence of these criminologists on the shape of the discipline in this country has been far-reaching. In fact, the success of the assault on mainstream criminology mounted by these figures was such that their ideas were to become the new mainstream, at least as far as the teaching of criminology was concerned. Now in their forties and fifties, they have not had to withstand a comparable onslaught from the next generation of radical criminologists, though they may have themselves modified their views. The extraordinary fecundity, in terms of quantity and quality, that characterized the late 1960s and early 1970s, was not to be repeated by the new generation – but this was not because of a decline in ability. By the late 1970s cut-backs in the funding of university and polytechnic postgraduate programmes reduced the pool of rising criminologists, and teaching posts in sociology departments had become thin on the ground in the 1980s. This is an important factor when explaining the lack of any substantial paradigmatic challenge from radical criminologists on the scale of that mounted against the mainstream during the 1960s.

The 'unsubsidized criminology' associated with the new deviancy period established a particular intellectual framework, deriving from agreement – at least in the short term – regarding how criminology was to be studied, what was to be studied and why it was to be studied. At the core of new deviancy theory lay the theoretical insights of interactionism, sometimes with bits of Marxism or phenomenology added. The areas studied reflected a move away from an earlier concentration on juvenile delinquency towards a broader concept of 'deviance'. Some of the more important studies from the period illustrate this: soft drug use (Young, 1971); industrial sabotage (Taylor and Walton, 1971), suicide (Atkinson, 1971); white-collar crime (Carson, 1970); surviving long-term imprisonment (Cohen and Taylor, 1972); ideological violence (Cohen, 1969); Teddy Boys (Jefferson, 1973). The 'why' element coalesced around the notion of 'appreciation', and the need to give the deviant an authentic voice. This was a clear departure from the corrective concerns of the criminology that had gone before.

Divisions and disputes

By 1973 various divisions involving the 'how', 'what' and 'why' of criminology had begun to surface among members of the NDC. Disputes over how criminology was to be studied reflected growing criticism of interactionism and the labelling theory associated with it. Some wished to develop a more radical, explicitly Marxist criminology; others opted for the promises offered by phenomenology; some attempted to incorporate the insights offered by another theoretical development originating in the United States, control theory, with interactionism; whilst others wished to refine interactionist criminology.

Disputes over what to study were directed not so much at areas of study *per se* (e.g. skinheads versus hippies), as at the wider moral and political implications of the choices made. Ethnographic research, for instance, was accused by some of aiding the imposition of deviant statuses on marginalized groups, exploiting them in the furtherance of an academic career and providing data useful to those in power. Similar sentiments had been expressed in a famous (or infamous, depending on one's viewpoint) address to the American Sociological Association in 1968 by a young sociologist called Martin Nicolaus. At one point he scandalized his audience by telling them:

> the professional eyes of the sociologist are on the down people, and the professional palm of the sociologist is stretched toward the up people . . . he is an Uncle Tom not only for this government and ruling class but for any. (Nicolaus quoted in Gouldner, 1971: 10)

This was to a largely conservative audience. To apply a similar critique to the new deviancy theorists, as some radicals were doing, was particularly mordant.

Although these divisions began to become very public in 1973, they had been a latent feature of the new deviancy from the start; by 1973 the divisions had reached critical mass. Within a short space of time the field began to fragment, with different strands flying off in different directions. In conformity with an already established pattern, these divisions appeared first in the United States, and were then picked up shortly afterwards by British counterparts. One of the central unstable elements in new deviancy was the concept of deviance itself: How much mileage was left in it?

In the next chapter the new deviancy is discussed in detail, and in particular one of its chief components, labelling theory (though supporters came to prefer the term labelling *perspective*). This will include an examination of a critical assault on labelling theory, building up between 1968 and 1973, and pursued on two fronts: first, for treating the deviant as a passive 'underdog', and secondly, for concentrating on 'nuts, sluts and preverts' (I'll retain the original spelling).

9 | New deviancy theory: the interactionist approach to deviance

Labelling theory
Learning to become 'deviant'
Primary and secondary deviation
The amplification of deviance
Conceptualizing deviance
Criticisms of the new deviancy

As we have seen in the last chapter, new deviancy theory and the interactionist ideas on which it was based, began to have a strong impact on criminology, or the sociology of deviance as it became known, in Britain and the United States during the middle to late 1960s. With a shift away from crime towards the broader concept of deviance, interactionism continued to influence criminological thought through the 1970s and, indeed, up to the present day.

Interactionism marked an important break with the causal–corrective approach of traditional criminology, where crime was investigated and explained within the context of social policy and legal and penal processes. In the orthodox criminology looked at earlier, crime and deviance tended to be conceptualized in terms of pathology, according to some assumed yardstick of acceptable behaviour, and the search for causes (of a more or less positivistic nature) was linked to the eradication of the criminal or deviant behaviour. Many of these orthodox studies, especially where they had forgotten the lessons to be learnt from the early ethnographic work of the Chicago School, denied authenticity to the deviant's account of what they did, and thus rendered invalid subjective motivations and purposes. Importantly, this break with a causal–corrective orientation signalled by the arrival of new deviancy theory, brought with it a reconceptualization of what criminology, or rather the sociology of deviance, should be about. The development of a sceptical approach meant a disengagement from the common-sense agenda obsessed with answering the question, 'Why did they do it?' in favour of analyses of reactions to perceived deviance, and the subsequent implications for those so labelled. The new deviancy was in fact often referred to as social reaction theory.

The interactionist approach to deviance had its roots in the earlier work of George Herbert Mead and the symbolic interactionist school, though it did come in a number of guises. Following the symbolic interactionists, attention was on the individual social actor and the ways in which he or she develops perceptions of self and others through social interaction. And it was this subjectivism that allowed for the assimilation (albeit sometimes crudely) of certain ideas from phenomenology. Matza's work with Sykes was clearly relevant to this reorientation in criminology, as was the 'naturalism' of his phenomenological perspective developed later on. Matza's concept of 'appreciation' was particularly influential. Appreciation meant that the sociologist should aim for truthfulness and accuracy in their descriptions of social phenomena, rather than impose their own under-standings on them. Thus, instead of carrying out one's study on the basis of presuppositions regarding the (immoral) nature of deviant behaviour, with the hope of eradicating it, the sociologist should attempt to present the behaviour in its own terms. As Matza (1969: 17) puts it: 'These appreciative sentiments are easily summarized: We do not for a moment wish that we could rid ourselves of deviant phenomena. We are intrigued by them. They are an intrinsic, ineradicable, and vital part of human society.'

Labelling theory

Above all, interactionism is associated with labelling theory, though many have questioned its status as a theory and prefer to call it a perspective. As one of the influential members of this school put it, writing retrospectively in the 1970s: 'I have never thought that the original statements by myself and others warranted being called theories, at least not theories of the fully articulated kind that they are now criticized for not being' (Becker, 1974: 41–2). With this qualification, we will refer to it here as a theory.

Labelling theorists focused on the interactions between individuals or groups and those who label or define them as deviant. Out of these interactional encounters – say, between police and 'delinquents' – the participants will construct meanings: namely, images and understandings of both themselves and the others involved. The relationship between definers and defined is conceived of as processual: that is, individuals are involved in a process whereby they subjectively construct a symbolic world. Under certain circumstances these interactions lead to the application of a 'deviant' label. This, in turn, has psychological implications in that those so labelled may come to see themselves in terms of the label. It also has social implications in that such labelling is likely to have an impact on the way in which individuals labelled as deviant are treated by others in the future. This link between labelling and future behaviour was partly derived from Merton's idea of a 'self-fulfilling prophesy'.

From the perspective of labelling theory the quality of 'deviance' does not reside in the behaviour itself, but is, rather, the outcome of responses to that behaviour by various social audiences. Behaviour that is potentially deviant is said to occur all the time, among all sections of society (though, in effect, *all* behaviour is potentially deviant). Which behaviour actually gets labelled deviant depends upon how and where it is carried out, and on the nature of the interactional responses:

- In some instances the individual simply does not get caught. They perhaps possess the resources to cover their tracks.

- Sometimes the audience lacks the power to apply the deviant label. Clearly, relationships of power are central to labelling processes.

- Sometimes the general circumstances allow the behaviour to be normalized. In another context the behaviour may easily be defined as deviant, but contingent factors, such as being on holiday or inebriated, may allow the behaviour, although it might be odd or frightening or whatever, to be kept within the frame of normality.

- Sometimes the individual is able to resist the impact of labelling, perhaps because of others who can protect their non-deviant identity.

Out of these complex interactional processes the participants interpret and negotiate their understandings of what is going on. In short, they construct social reality. The process of becoming deviant reaches a key stage when the recipient of the label begins to accept the label and sees him or herself as deviant.

From this brief outline we can see that interactionism's focus on reactions to perceived deviance marked a radical departure from traditional criminology's concentration on the causal factors leading to deviance in the first place. This is not to say, however, that this dimension to the study of deviance had been entirely ignored in the past. The American criminologist Tannenbaum (1938) provided the first serious discussion of the effects on the young delinquent of negative judgements by the community. One of labelling theory's pivotal concepts, 'primary deviation', was originally introduced by Edwin Lemert in 1951, and Howard Becker's article 'Becoming a marijuana user', one of the most influential and widely quoted texts, was first published in 1953. It was not until 1963, though, that his *Outsiders: Studies in the sociology of deviance*, a collection of essays on marijuana use and reactions to it, first appeared.

Learning to become 'deviant'

Becker's *Outsiders* found an enthusiastic audience among more radical British and American sociologists in the late 1960s. Here was a fundamental critique of a criminological orthodoxy that conceptualized the social world in terms of the normal on one side of the moral line, and deviance/crime on the other. Becker had attempted to bring to light the continuities, rather than discontinuities, between deviant and non-deviant worlds. Significantly, instead of the concept of crime, with its connotations of moral absolutism, he used the concept of deviance, and he shifted attention away from the supposed intrinsic qualities of the rule breaker, towards the reactions of the social audience, and the interactional processes leading to the application of the deviant label.

Becker traced the processes through which an individual learns to become a marijuana user. The behaviour is not seen as resulting from deviant motivations; these come later because of the reactions of control agents and their efforts to deviantize those involved. Put another way, prior to any deviant label being applied, the individual chooses not to be deviant, but to use a drug that happens to be strongly frowned upon, and indeed, illegal. Becker aimed to show how deviant identities and understandings depended upon the labelling process. In this way he sought to infuse the user's original behaviour with authenticity – to show how choices are made. This was a challenge to traditional formulations that viewed deviant motivations as resulting from deterministic forces operating prior to any labelling. As Matza (1969: 110) says in a commentary on Becker's analysis: 'it becomes apparent that *anyone* can become a marijuana user and that *no one* has to' (original emphasis).

Two important elements of labelling theory are present in Becker's account: first, an anti-deterministic stance, allowing people to make choices and exercise their wills, and secondly, following successful labelling by control agents, the notion of a deviant 'career'. For labelling theorists, the original causes of the behaviour, as traditionally understood, are not on the agenda. Modern societies, they say, are composed of different groups with different norms and values, and deviant behaviour – or more accurately, behaviour that could be labelled as deviant – is widespread. However, only some of it becomes officially designated as deviant. More people are doing their own thing than traditional criminology had seemed to realize. And, as Edwin Lemert, another eminent writer in the labelling tradition, argued, trying to establish the original 'causes' is pointless. In his view, all that deviants have in common is that they have been labelled deviant.

As the central canon of labelling theory is that deviance is 'caused' by the reactions of a social audience, then, logically, analyses have to concern themselves with the creation of deviance at that point. The position is well summed up by Becker (1963: 9) in this widely quoted passage:

> Social groups create deviance by making the rules whose infraction constitutes deviance, and by applying those rules to particular people and labeling them as outsiders. From this point of view, deviance is *not* a quality of the act the person commits, but rather a consequence of the application by others of rules and sanctions to an 'offender'. The deviant is one to whom that label has been successfully applied; deviant behavior is behavior that people so label.

The same relativistic view of deviance had also been put forward by two other labelling theorists:

> Forms of behavior *per se* do not differentiate deviants from non-deviants; it is the responses of the conventional and conforming members of society which identify and interpret behavior as deviant which sociologically transforms persons into deviants. (Kitsuse (1962) quoted in Taylor *et al.*, 1973: 144)

> Deviance is not a property inherent in certain forms of behaviour; it is a property conferred upon these forms by the audiences which directly or indirectly witness them. (Erikson (1962) quoted in Taylor *et al.*, 1973: 144)

We can see from these quotations that the primary focus of labelling theory is on the application of already existing rules to particular people. From this perspective who gets selected, and why they get selected, become crucial, given the argument that it is not the distinctive quality of the behaviour itself that is the determining factor; no behaviour is in itself deviant. Thus rule breaking, as such, does not designate a person as deviant; a response to that rule breaking is required. According to Becker, particular individuals and groups are labelled deviant because of what he calls 'career contingencies'. These are extraneous factors, external to the actual behaviour itself, and include such things as the dress and demeanour of the participants, the neighbourhood in which they live, and police resources and policies.

Primary and secondary deviation

The impact of labelling on the deviant's future behaviour was explored by Lemert (1967), who introduced the concepts of primary and secondary deviation. In his view, traditional criminology had put the cart before the horse by assuming that deviant behaviour came first, and then triggered social control responses. At the time this seemed to many a startling proposition:

This is a large turn away from older sociology which tended to rest heavily upon the idea that deviance leads to social control. I have come to believe that the reverse idea, i.e., social control leads to deviance, is equally tenable and the potentially richer premise for studying deviance in modern society. (Ibid. v)

He illustrated this link between reaction and deviance through his research into stuttering in a number of Indian tribes in British Columbia. In some of these tribes he found that the language contained concepts relating to stuttering, and that some members of the tribe did stutter. Among neighbouring tribes, however, no such concepts existed, and stuttering seemed to be absent. Clearly, there was no physiological reason why this should be so, and it could not be connected with the contacts that the tribes had had with white people. Lemert found that in the tribes where stuttering existed, great emphasis was placed on oratory and story telling. Children were socialized into a set of norms and values that placed great stress on not stuttering, and failure to put on a 'good performance' was ridiculed. Lemert concluded that the enormous pressure placed on people to speak 'properly', and the institutionalization of the social reaction to those that didn't (to the 'deviants'), actually led to the development of stuttering: that is, the social reaction created the deviance. In tribes where these cultural expectations did not exist, there was, of course, no negative reaction, and hence no deviance of this type.

Lemert enphasized the ubiquitous nature of 'deviance'. Most of the time, he argued, individuals 'get away' with such behaviour, meaning that it remains unlabelled, and they are therefore able to maintain a non-deviant self-image, and are not treated as deviant by those around them. He describes this as primary deviation, and as such is of little interest to interactionists. However, under certain circumstances, again not dependent upon the nature of the behaviour, there is a social reaction and the individuals concerned are labelled as deviant. This is described as secondary deviation, which is seen as: 'deviant behavior, or social roles based upon it, which becomes a means of defense, attack or adaptation to the overt and covert problems created by the societal reaction to primary deviation' (ibid. 17).

An acceptance of the label, and the carrying out of further deviant acts, may therefore be mechanisms used by those labelled to cope with the problems posed by the labelling. Obviously, the imposition of the label 'deviant' involves, at its core, judgements about a person's moral worth. The label can easily become the new 'master status', superseding a range of other statuses such as mother, teacher and footballer. The early symbolic interactionists, from whom many of these ideas had been drawn, had shown that how an individual is treated by significant others has profound implications for how an individual sees him or herself; the process was encapsulated in Cooley's concept, introduced at the beginning of the twentieth century, of the 'looking glass self'. Being treated as a 'thief', 'sexual pervert', 'alcoholic', 'mad person', and so on, makes it extremely difficult for those involved to take part in the routines of normal life, and, as Becker said, they 'of necessity develop illegitimate routines'. In this situation, the individual is likely to seek out others who have been similarly labelled, which then forms the basis for mutually supporting subcultural groups.

The amplification of deviance

Leslie T. Wilkins (1964) introduced the concept of 'deviancy amplification' as a way of explaining the process outlined above. It describes those paradoxical situations where the social reaction on the part of control agents, which is aimed at stamping out or controlling the deviance, in fact leads to an increase in amounts and frequency. Amplification in this context does not simply mean that publicity given to some deviant behaviour by the mass media leads to 'copycat' behaviour on the part of others. Rather it seeks to identify a process arising from secondary deviation, where those labelled as deviant incorporate the label within their self-image. This has a knock-on effect of producing more reactions from control agents, thereby further consolidating the deviant self-image. In time, this creates a deviancy amplification spiral, as others attracted by the deviant status also become involved. Stan Cohen's (1980) classic study of the Mods and Rockers phenomenon in the 1960s set out to illustrate how deviancy amplification operated with respect to these specific youth subcultures. The title of his book, *Folk Devils and Moral Panics*, contains two further concepts popular with interactionists. Cohen argued that the very actions by police, magistrates and mass media designed to eradicate the delinquent activities of Mods and Rockers, were in reality counterproductive in that they ultimately created and sustained a much larger 'problem'.

Although interactionists agreed that none of the processes discussed above were inevitable, there was less clear-cut agreement about the nature of the relationship between the changes in self-image resulting from labelling and changes in subsequent behaviour. If secondary deviation involves a change in both thinking and acting, then it would have important implications for traditional studies that attempt to discover the causes of deviance. In such studies, samples of offenders are usually drawn from among those officially processed by the criminal justice system, namely, secondary deviants. However, this research aims at discovering why people offend in the first place: it is seeking out the causes of primary deviance. Thus it is using secondary deviants as a basis for explaining primary deviance, and is therefore somewhat flawed. If the mass of primary deviants escape apprehension, then such research may simply tell us what kind of offenders are likely to get caught and labelled.

Conceptualizing deviance

As the discussion so far has indicated, interactionism made an important contribution to the sociology of deviance by attempting to develop what is sometimes called a 'constitutive' model. From this perspective, 'deviance' does not have an independent existence, but is socially constructed through processes of interaction. This approach represented a commitment to a thoroughly sociological understanding of deviance, and marked a break with the absolutism characterizing common-sense understandings. According to the logic of this argument, no deviance can exist unless it has been labelled as such. Unfortunately, labelling theorists themselves did not always consistently adhere to the conceptual implications of this, which led to many criticisms – some of which will be examined below – and to some spirited defences (e.g. Becker, 1974; Gove, 1975; Plummer, 1979).

In Chapter 1 there was a brief discussion of Reiner's (1988) reference to Becker's statement that 'deviance is not a quality of the act'. Reiner's comment that this was merely a platitude – that lawyers had known all along that in order for crime/deviance to exist there must be rules – is highly misleading. Clearly, as Durkheim had pointed out in the nineteenth century, no behaviour is in itself intrinsically criminal or deviant, just as no painting is intrinsically beautiful. What is defined as 'bad' or 'immoral' in a society changes over time, and varies from society to society. Left like this, Becker's message is, of course, not at all novel; but it was necessary for labelling theorists to reaffirm the point that when analysing deviance we are not dealing with moral absolutes – deviance is a relative concept. However, Becker was saying more than this, as the rest of the sentence quoted by Reiner indicates: '. . . but rather a consequence of the application by others of rules and sanctions'. If he had simply said that deviance exists because rules exist, then it would have suggested that deviant behaviour can exist without a social reaction and the *application* of the rule, a proposition that labelling theorists rejected, at least when they remained faithful to their theory. The crucial argument from labelling theory was that deviance does not exist merely because a rule is broken: deviance results from the labelling of specific cases. Although consistency regarding this theoretical formulation was not always maintained (see, for example, Becker's notion of a 'secret deviant' below) it was, none the less, an insight of central importance. It alerted sociologists to the need to consider carefully the ways in which they conceptualized crime and deviance, and thus pushed them towards complex epistemological questions pertaining to the subject-matter of the sociology of deviance/criminology. These questions still stand, though contemporary criminology does not always engage with them (the issues they raise are many miles away from, say, research on how to 'design out' ram-raiding).

Criticisms of the new deviancy

Given the break with orthodoxy represented by the advent of new deviancy theory, and the nature of the questions it thrust onto the agenda of the sociology of deviance, it was inevitable that it generated much criticism.

A quality of the act?

At what point can a deviant act be said to exist? Obviously, labelling theory was correct to draw attention to the implications for self-image and future behaviour of being labelled, but is it correct to say that a rule-breaking act cannot be deviant (or criminal) until labelling has occurred, or in other words, that deviance is not a quality of the act? The 'constitutive' approach argues that 'deviance' is a social label conferred upon rule breaking. This can be illustrated with a simple example. In 1986 Diego Maradona pushed the ball into the goal with his 'hand of God' during a World Cup football match between England and Argentina. Clearly (for we can see the video evidence) Maradona broke a rule, but the referee did not see what happened and he let the goal stand: that is, the *crucial* social audience did not label the act as a foul (though England supporters might label Maradona a 'cheat'). The interesting question to ask is, was a foul 'really' committed? Can the quality of foul be given to the act in the absence of labelling? There is one further dimension to this that can be commented on. Labelling involves both a 'deviant' act and a 'deviant' person, though the distinction is not always made explicit. Thus, in the case of Maradona, we have to consider the creation of a 'foul' as well as a 'fouler'. According to the official records no foul occurred, and Maradona was not a fouler. Is it possible that rule breaking can constitute a deviant act (a foul), but the absence of a reaction, of labelling, means that the social category of a deviant (a fouler) is not created? And what are the implications of this for perceptions of self?

Criticism of labelling theory's claim that deviance is not a quality of the act is built up along two broad fronts: first, a critique of what was seen as a logical inconsistency on the part of some writers, and secondly, a critique of the idea itself. As far as the first of these was concerned, the main criticisms were aimed at Lemert and Becker. In the case of Lemert, it was the concept of 'primary deviation' that was at issue. If, as labelling theory contends, deviance results from labelling, then how can primary deviation, that is, unlabelled deviance, be possible (see Gibbs, 1966)? The same criticism has also been levelled at Becker, and arises from his categorization of different types of deviance deriving from two variables: actual behaviour, and perceptions of that behaviour by a social audience. Becker (1963: 20) thus offered the following typology:

	Obedient behaviour	Rule-breaking behaviour
Perceived as deviant	*Falsely accused*	*Pure deviant*
Not perceived as deviant	*Conforming*	*Secret deviant*

As Gibbs (1966), for example, has pointed out, according to the logic of the labelling perspective a 'secret deviant' cannot exist. Although a rule has been broken, the individual concerned has avoided being labelled, so how can it be deviance? (There is a parallel here with the example of Maradona, whose 'deviance' was not seen by the referee.) Becker, says Gibbs, is here confusing two different conceptual models: one sees deviance as rule breaking, the other views it as the result of social reaction. The same critical point is discussed by Taylor *et al.* (1973). From an ethnomethodological perspective Pollner (1974) sees Becker's concept of secret deviant as arising from a confusion between what he calls a mundane/common-sense model of deviance and a constitutive model. Although we can see what Becker meant by secret deviant, for Pollner he had retreated from a proper, constitutive model. In the same vein, Pollner says that the concept of 'falsely accused' is illogical too, for if deviance results from interactional labelling processes, then irrespective of whether or not someone 'really' did it, if they have been labelled deviant, they *are* deviant. From Pollner's standpoint Becker wanted to have his cake and eat it. However, we should note that Becker (1974) did review his original position and say that instead of secret deviant he should have used the concept of 'potential deviant'.

While Pollner criticizes Becker's concepts, he approves of the logic of labelling theory which sees deviance as socially constructed. Others, however, have disputed the contention that labelling need occur in order for deviance to exist. In other words, they have insisted that deviance is a quality of the act of breaking strongly sanctioned rules. From this standpoint Maradona did commit a foul. The case for this line of reasoning has been forcefully put by Taylor *et al.* (1973). They agree with Becker, Erikson and Kitsuse that deviance is not an absolute quality intrinsic to an activity, and give as an example the taking of human life: in wartime it can earn a medal, in peacetime a life sentence. Their dispute with writers such as Becker concerns the view that deviance requires a social reaction and labelling in specific cases. For Taylor *et al.* it is quite possible for a secret deviant to exist. To illustrate this they distinguish between 'behaviour' and 'action'. Following Weber, behaviour is simply some physical activity, such as accidently falling off a ladder, whilst action is of sociological significance because it is behaviour to which meaning has been attached. Therefore, even a secret deviant is generally aware that what they are doing is disapproved of, which is why they remain secret. Taylor *et al.* (1973) thus argue that if the individual (secret) deviant attaches this sort of meaning to their action – meanings shared with the rest of society – then at that moment in time deviance *is*, objectively, a quality of the act, and no specific reaction is required.

This concern with the meanings lying behind deviance had, by the late 1960s, become part of a major critical assault whereby labelling theory was accused of treating the deviant as a passive 'underdog'. At the same time, a second critical front opened up which homed in on labelling theory's concentration on 'nuts, sluts and preverts'. Each will be examined in turn.

Underdogs

In a classic paper, Alvin Gouldner (1968) argued that labelling theorists had conjured up an image of the deviant as the innocent victim of the application of labels by control agents such as the police: 'man-on-his-back', rather than 'man-fighting-back'. This, he said, made deviance entirely contingent on the whims of authority. For Gouldner, the labelling theory view of marginalized groups was in fact an expression of the liberal, welfare-oriented ideology of the American establishment, whereby all deviants were victims. They were, however, not seen as victims of the system, so much as victims of petty-minded and illiberal agencies and individuals within it.

This 'fighting back' view of the deviant was also in evidence in a paper published in the following year by Horowitz and Leibowitz (1969). Here they argued that a false dichotomy was made by sociologists (including labelling theorists), law makers, social workers, and so forth. Some forms of 'socially' deviant behaviour, they said, should more properly be viewed as 'politically' deviant. They developed this by arguing that traditional definitions of 'political' were too narrow and inflexible. Thus the views of Horowitz and Leibowitz, as well as Gouldner, were clearly in tune with some of the ideas emanating from the New Left/counter culture configuration at that time. After a decade of riot and protest in the United States, for Horowitz and Leibowitz (1969: 280) an important convergence had occurred in which deviant groups were increasingly using political tactics to further their cause, whilst political groups were increasingly using deviant tactics: 'the result of this trend is estimated to be an increase in the use of violence as a political tactic, and the development of a revolutionary potential among the expanding ranks of deviant sub-groups.'

This attempt to politicize deviance was particularly important as far as the development of the sociology of deviance/crime was concerned over the next few years. Criticizing Becker, Taylor *et al*. (1973: 142), for instance, drew directly on Gouldner's (1968) paper when they wrote:

> Becker's confusion stems from his desire to preserve the category deviant for those people who are labelled deviant, but, to do this, is to imply at the outset

that rule-breakers, and rule-breakers who are labelled (i.e. deviants), are fundamentally different from each other in their self-perceptions . . . this leads to an over-concentration by Becker and other social reaction theorists on the importance of the application of a label in creating self-conscious commitment to deviant acts.

One of Taylor *et al.*'s primary goals was to present deviance not only as meaningful from the point of view of the participants, but also as a form of *political* action. It is not surprising, therefore, that they attack Becker's proposition that people do not choose to engage in deviance, but rather choose to carry out certain acts of rule breaking which may subsequently be labelled deviant. Because of their general theoretical position, it was necessary for Taylor *et al.* to argue that the deviant makes a conscious choice to be deviant, for this was seen as a political action against bourgeois rules.

Eventually, a growing number of writers were criticizing labelling theory for seeing the deviant as a passive victim of the agents of social control, and arguing that as a theory it was just as deterministic as the theories they railed against (e.g. Schervish, 1973; Broadhead, 1974). It was seen as deterministic because it suggested that the reaction caused the deviance. However, sometimes this line of criticism was prone to distort the original claims made by labelling theory. As Plummer (1979: 104) says: 'no labelling theorist seems to espouse the "label creates behaviour" view'. An observation by Akers (1967: 46), for instance, will be familiar to most of those who have studied 'A' level sociology (it certainly cropped up with monotonous regularity in the examination papers that I used to mark): 'One sometimes gets the impression from reading this literature that people go about minding their own business, and then – "wham" – bad society comes along and slaps them with a stigmatized label'. Labelling theorists, however, did not say that rule breakers were blissfully unaware that they were breaking rules, and suddenly realized that they were when they were labelled. Becker's marijuana users, for example, knew full well that what they did was disapproved of, and indeed illegal, and took pains to conceal their activities. The relevance of the label is that it is a public recognition and stigmatization of a 'deviant' and has implications for self-perceptions and subsequent treatment by others in society.

The criticism had, perhaps, more substance when it was directed at labelling theory's tendency to examine forms of deviance where sympathy for the deviant, as a victim of labelling, was relatively easily invoked. In particular, this involved 'crimes without victims' – for example, soft drug users, dropouts, stutterers and prostitutes. Studies of serial killers, racist murderers, rapists and the like were conspicuously lacking. By doing this, the sociologists concerned gave the impression of approaching deviance in general in, as Gouldner put it, 'a spirit of sentimental romanticism'. As a theory, or perspective, it did most strikingly lend itself to a focus on those who seemed to be treated oppressively by control agents.

The moral ambiguity surrounding much of the research by interactionists reached its apotheosis in Becker's (1967) article 'Whose side are we on?'. Here he rejected traditional criminology's condemnatory approach to the study of deviance, and argued instead for an 'appreciation' of the deviant as victim. In some cases this might be appropriate, but, as many commentators have pointed out (e.g. Heidensohn, 1989), it ignores those who are often the deviant's victims.

'Nuts, sluts and preverts'

A second important critical front developed around Liazos's (1972) theme of 'nuts, sluts and preverts' (the misspelling has already been explained). By focusing on marginalized groups with unconventional lifestyles, it was argued that labelling theorists were themselves helping to create deviant labels, and mystifying the reality of deviance and crime; for example:

> The term 'social deviants' . . . does not make sufficiently explicit – as the terms 'scapegoat' or 'victim' do – that majorities usually categorize persons or groups as 'deviant' in order to set them apart as inferior beings and to justify their social control, oppression, persecution, or even complete destruction. (Szasz, 1973: xxv–xxvi)

Thus, the argument ran, even if one accepted the view from labelling theory that deviant status was ascribed by control agents, and that when in full swing the labelling process led to an acceptance of that status and a commitment to a deviant lifestyle by the individual, they none the less ended up *as* deviant. No matter how they got there, we can all recognize who they are. It was this seeming compliance with the ideologies of dominant groups in society that was now being criticized.

Labelling theory had ignored the deviant activities of the powerful in American society; in fact, in the absence of labelling (by the powerful) these activities were, according to labelling theory, not deviant. Critics argued that many of the activities of the powerful and 'respectable' were more socially harmful than were the activities of those labelled 'deviant'. They pointed to the massive amounts of corporate crime committed in the United States, to the violence of the Vietnam war and other imperialistic excursions, and to the corruption of political administrations. In a study of business crime, Conklin (1977: 4), for example, concluded:

> The direct cost of business crime surpasses the cost of such conventional crimes as larceny, burglary, and auto theft. In 1965, the estimated loss from these four crimes was about $600 million; with inflation and rising crime rates, a better estimate as of 1977 would be about $3 to $4 billion a year. This figure pales in significance when compared with an estimated annual loss of $40 billion from

various white collar crimes. Half that amount results from consumer fraud, illegal competition and deceptive practices.

Critical voices questioned the double standards that permeated the culture of American society whereby, for instance, President Nixon could say that abortion was a violation of 'the sanctity of human life', whilst at the same time giving approval to the actions of Lieutenant Calley at My Lai (a Vietnamese village where the civilians were massacred).

Liazos's paper on 'nuts, sluts and preverts' was an important example of this type of critique. He drew attention to the harm done to people as a result of racial disadvantage and discrimination, and to the poverty, ill health, and so on, associated with a capitalist society. In the following year, Thio (1973) produced a similar argument, and castigated the sociology of deviance for failing to disengage itself from the ideological requirements of powerful elites.

Recently the British criminologist, Colin Sumner (1994: 262), has suggested that the 'nuts, sluts and preverts' critique presented by these two papers in 1972 and 1973 could have had a momentous impact on the sociology of deviance in the United States and in Britain, leading to the demise of the concept of deviance itself:

> These two essays took American sociology of deviance to the brink of a dissolution of the field of study, but held back from the crucial theoretical steps of *superseding* the concept of deviance and abandoning the search for a *general* theory of deviance. (original emphasis)

From this perspective the key to understanding deviance lies not in the behaviour itself, but, rather, in the ideologies that define and shape what is thought to be 'deviant'. According to Sumner, though, the sociology of deviance pulled back from the brink because of the ideas set in motion by the 'underdog' critique: Gouldner's 'man-fighting-back' imagery gave the concept of deviance a new lease of life as the 1970s unfolded, and deviance came to be seen as a form of political resistance (these developments will be looked at in Chapter 11):

> This was hardly a time for sociologists to declare that deviance was a dead concept. Far from it, it was all too tempting to take the concept and give it a new behavioural meaning as a political rejection of the established social order. *In this sense, the late sixties gave the concept of deviance a whole new lease of life, a second wind.* (Ibid. 258, original emphasis)

Two further criticisms of labelling theory should also be noted. First, it was argued that it had shown a wilful lack of interest in the original causes of deviance – primary deviation, as Lemert had called it. Although writers such as Schur (1971) had argued that, by definition, this was not the intention of labelling theory, critics saw this neglect of causes, and a concentration on reaction, as one-sided (Bordua, 1970; Mankoff, 1971; Taylor *et al.*, 1973). For them, deviant motivations and a commitment to a deviant lifestyle should not be linked exclusively to social reactions. These, they argued, can result from causal factors that pre-date any reaction by a social audience. In Mankoff's (1971: 211) words: 'one might attribute career deviance and its consequences not to societal reaction but to the continued effects of social structural strains, psychological stress, or disease states which produce initial rule-breaking.'

Secondly, the interactionist approach was criticized for failing to locate the rules themselves, the causes of rule breaking, and reactions to perceived deviance within the wider structures of power in society. Although labelling theory had pointed to the central importance of the power to apply the label, analyses had tended to be confined to the actions of relatively low-level agents of social control, such as police officers, teachers, social workers and psychiatrists. This was a critique that, as we shall see, eventually helped to stimulate the development of the 'new' critical criminology of the 1970s, which attempted to establish a political economy of crime/deviance and control.

Part IV

The 1970s

10 | The discipline of criminology and its context – 3: post-new deviancy

Deviance and politics
The sociology of law: making laws, making deviants
Criminology in the 1970s: other directions
Orthodox criminology
Radical critiques and the growth of the New Right

In this section we will examine some of the main strands in British criminology following the initial impact of new deviancy theory. The tradition of drawing on American sources for ideas and inspiration continued unabated for a while. In retrospect, this period can be compared to the pre-Beatles era when British singers produced hasty cover versions of American hit songs, songs that had been written in an American context, incorporating a stock of cultural items that had at that time only limited availability in this country.

Deviance and politics

As in the United States, various criticisms of labelling theory began to appear among radical sociologists of deviance, and in the first instance it was the 'underdog' critique that stimulated most work.

In an underdeveloped form, labelling theory had introduced the notion of politics into the field of deviance research. By stressing that the power to impress the deviant label was concentrated in the hands of the relatively powerful few, the deviant process was, to this extent, political. Radical sociologists, however, criticized labelling theory for failing to make connections between processes of interaction and the structures of power in which they were rooted.

As we have seen, some writers in the United States began to extend the ideas of labelling theory. In particular, Horowitz and Leibowitz (1968) argued that some deviant groups were engaging in political action. However, in their enthusiasm to politicize deviance, some British sociologists were quick to read into these formulations rather more than the authors originally intended. Horowitz and Leibowitz's position was that whereas in the past deviant minorities had carried out their deviances more or less privately, they were now entering the public realm, and taking up political modes of protest. It was this *new* activity that was seen as political, not the original deviance. Engaging in homosexual acts, for example, was not regarded as political, but the activities of the Gay Liberation Movement were. Geoff Pearson (1975: 96), for instance, seems to have read more into their paper than was actually there:

> But what emerges in the literature of misfit sociology from the analysis provided by Horowitz and Leibowitz is the imperative that one should understand not only the *labelling process* as a politically derived judgement, but also that *deviant behaviour* itself should be accorded political status. Or, more specifically, that deviance should be grasped as a primitive crypto-political action.

From hesitant beginnings, the project of politicizing deviance was to become an important strand of British sociological criminology. Similar developments occurred in other disciplines too: for instance, R. D. Laing's (1967, 1968) 'anti-psychiatry', and efforts to show how the definition and treatment of mental illness were political processes. An early response to Horowitz and Leibowitz came in an article from Stan Cohen (1969), with a fuller version being published in 1973, and from Stuart Hall (1974). Although each of these essentially reiterated the original arguments, they did relate them to events in this country, and also had the merit of recognizing, and endorsing, the limited extension of labelling theory offered by Horowitz and Leibowitz. Such restraint, however, was short-lived, as some radical sociologists moved to a position of arguing that some, or even all, crime/deviance was itself a political act – in simple terms, because it was resistance to bourgeois rules. This entailed delving into earlier precursors of this type of work: for example, Goldman (1959) on school vandalism and truancy. It also involved widening the academic net by trawling among the work of radical historians who had produced accounts of revolts from 'below' in Britain's past. Hobsbawm's (1959) concept of 'primitive rebellion' soon became common currency within this genre.

Ian Taylor (1971) identified soccer hooliganism as a form of political protest and, together with Paul Walton and Jock Young, incorporated the politics of deviance into an ambitious attempt to develop a Marxist theory of deviance in a book entitled (in contradistinction to the new deviancy) *The New Criminology* (Taylor *et al.*, 1973). Here, instead of picking out specific types of (usually working-class) deviance as candidates for the appellation 'political', they suggested that 'much deviance is in itself political'. Unfortunately, the authors failed to define either 'deviance' or 'political'. This was, though, an important and influential, if much criticized, text. However, by 1975, with the publication of a follow up collection of readings (Taylor *et al.*, 1975), Jock Young was already starting to review his position. Whatever the merits of *The New Criminology*, it stands as a supreme example of criminological work nurtured by the twin influences of the New Left and the counter culture: the New Left in its effort to introduce humanistic Marxism into the field, and the counter culture because of its commitment to social diversity, to a celebration of 'difference'. As result of this, a serious criticism of the text was that it owed more to anarchism than it did to Marxism.

Geoff Pearson (1976, 1978) continued to plough the crime-as-politics furrow, in particular in a study of so-called Paki-bashing, where he argued that those involved were engaging in 'crypto-political' action. As early as 1973, though, other National Deviancy Conference members were pointing to the dangers of romanticism which they saw as characterizing the counter culture. Paul Rock (1973: 103), for instance, criticized the 'romanticism which views all criminals as primitive innocents who are engaged in inarticulate political conflict with institutional authority'.

The mid-1970s saw the growth in influence of the Birmingham Centre for Contemporary Cultural Studies, and in much of the work we can detect attempts to politicize crime/deviance. Under the direction of Stuart Hall, the Birmingham Centre drew on the work of the Italian Marxist, Gramsci, and introduced key concepts, such as hegemony and ideology into the criminological discourse. The Centre is particularly associated with radical youth subcultural theory (see Hall and Jefferson, 1976). The main emphasis was on youth subcultural 'styles', and the ways in which these operate as modes of cultural resistance, and therefore, to that extent, represent forms of political action (Clarke and Jefferson, 1973a, 1973b; Jefferson, 1973; Clarke, 1976). The Centre laid down the foundations for future work that examined, and attempted to refine, concepts such as 'style' and 'cultural symbolization' (e.g. Hebdige, 1979).

By the end of the 1970s the crime/deviance-as-politics argument had more or less fizzled out within radical criminology: but then, like a firework that had not quite gone out, in the early 1980s it burst into life again. Instead of *working-class* crime, though it was specifically *black* crime that was characterized as political. It was no coincidence that American versions of this argument had come in the wake of major riots; likewise, the British versions emerged following large-scale urban disorder and resistance in 1980 and 1981 in this country (for a critique, see Tierney, 1988).

So we see that into the 1970s, in spite of the conceptual challenge raised by labelling theory, among radical sociologists the concept of deviance was, albeit in a politicized form, firmly back on the agenda as a quality of the act. Some things really were deviant, and not only that, they were also political.

The sociology of law: making laws, making deviants

As the above discussion shows, the politicization of deviance in the late 1960s gave the concept of deviance, as Sumner puts it, a 'second wind', and set in motion a research agenda that placed the actions of the deviant centre stage. Inevitably, the deviants placed under this spotlight were marginalized, relatively powerless groups. At the end of the 1960s, however, another strand of sociological criminology emerged, again partly contingent on labelling theory and the theoretical problems it raised. This second strand developed along a broad pedigree line that included Liazos's 'nuts, sluts and preverts' critique, as well as Gouldner's 'underdog' critique, and was essentially based upon two propositions. First, that definitions of crime and deviance (and, thus, ultimately, the nature of law itself) were linked to the interests of powerful elites or classes; and secondly, that governments, corporations and 'respectable' members of society were often involved in, and got away with, criminal activities that were much more harmful than so-called deviant activities. In short, rather than concentrate on the nature of officially defined deviant behaviour (as hedonistic, crypto-political, prophetic, or whatever), this strand of criminological thought turned its attention to the powerful in society, either as self-interested rule makers, or as cynical rule breakers, or as both. Indeed, in *Critical Criminology*, Jock Young (1975: 89) attacked the ruling class in terms of both rule making and rule breaking: 'Radical criminological strategy . . . is to show up the law, in its true colours, as the instrument of the ruling class . . . and that the rule-makers are also the greatest rule-breakers.'

In combination with the earlier *The New Criminology* (Taylor *et al.*, 1973) we can see in fact three central elements of what became known generically as critical criminology: a view of deviants as political rebels; an 'instrumentalist' view of law; and a desire to emphasize ruling-class, as opposed to working-class, crime.

Inevitably, *The New Criminology* generated a great deal of debate and criticism when it was published, and criticism was only marginally assuaged following the publication of *Critical Criminology* (Taylor *et al.*, 1975). The most fundamental question raised was whether a specifically Marxist theory of deviance was, from the point of view of Marxism itself, possible. Fellow Marxist, Paul Hirst (1975a: 204), one of the contributors to the second text, argued that Marxists should have nothing to do with deviance: 'there is no "Marxist theory of deviance" either in existence, or which can be developed within orthodox Marxism. Crime and deviance vanish into the general theoretical concerns and the specific scientific object of Marxism.' Hirst's objection essentially revolved around the concept of deviance. For him, the theoretical objects of analysis are, in Marxism, laid down and structured by the concepts that Marx himself devised:

> The objects of Marxist theory are specified by their own concepts: the mode of production, the class struggle, the state, ideology, etc. Any attempt to apply Marxism to this pre-given field of sociology is therefore a more or less 'revisionist' activity in respect of Marxism; it must modify and distort Marxian concepts to suit its own pre-Marxist purposes. (Ibid. 204)

Put into simpler language, from this standpoint, using the concept of deviance is a bit like, for instance, using the concept of 'bad art'. Why should Marxists acquiesce to (bourgeois) definitions and treat some art as if it really was 'bad'?

Shortly after this exchange between Hirst and Taylor *et al.*, the Marxist criminologist Colin Sumner (1976) attempted to provide a solution to the problem posed by Hirst. Sumner argued that deviance should be seen as a type of ideology – as a social censure – rather than as behaviour. As we shall see, this was to become an important theoretical issue for radical criminology.

In his critique, Hirst also attacked Taylor *et al.* for romanticizing crime – the criminal as revolutionary – and for their 'oppositional' stance regarding law: that is, for seeing all law as acting in the interests of the ruling class ('instrumentalism').

We can now look briefly at developments in radical criminology based upon the two propositions mentioned earlier.

Self-interested rule makers

Attempts to develop a political economy of crime – that is, to develop a theoretical criminology based upon analyses of the creation and functions of the law within a political and economic context – encompassed a range of writers from the late 1960s onwards. Some of these were Marxist theorists, some non-Marxist conflict theorists, with the former tending to be products of a European tradition, the latter of an American one. What united them all was a rejection of the conservative view that the law was a neutral and universally beneficial entity. In various ways, and with varying degrees of sophistication, the political economy of crime perspective attempted to show how the law, both in terms of its substance and its administration, acted to protect the interests of those with power.

In this context, some criminologists during the 1970s began to look afresh at the work of social historians such as E. P. Thompson (1975) and Stedman-Jones (1971), who had documented how the law had been used in the past to control the labouring poor. This acknowledgement of the contribution that historians could make to the study of crime, law and the state was something of a breakthrough in British criminology. As Pat Carlen (1980: 13) says:

> The peculiar isolationism of 'criminology' meant that sociologists of crime could plead for more historical studies of crime without acknowledging that histories of labour and political movements have repeatedly been histories of lawbreaking and criminalization.

Other criminologists decided to explore similar themes by excavating the past themselves: for example, Chambliss (1976), with his study of the vagrancy laws of medieval England, and Kolko (1976) with his study of the meat-packing industry in the United States at the beginning of this century. Graham (1976) provided a contemporary example of such research with his study of drugs legislation in the United States. Graham argued that because of their power, pharmaceutical companies were able to have federal laws aimed at controlling amphetamine production and use significantly weakened. Their action, he maintained, was due to the stake that these companies had in the manufacture of this class of drug.

In a way this kind of criminology takes to its logical conclusion the argument derived from labelling theory that deviance (or crime) is not a quality of the act, but rather results from the application of rules by the relatively powerful. However, unlike labelling theory, radical criminologists began to trace the creation and application of the law to the structural arrangements of a specifically capitalist society. This was one way out of the problem of surrendering to the capitalist state's definition of crime and in effect only being allowed to study what the state allowed: that is, legally proscribed behaviour. As a consequence, during the second half of the 1970s there was a shift away from the 'criminal' or 'deviant' towards issues of law, state and social control, and to a large extent criminology became the sociology of law. Theoretical developments were also becoming more sophisticated, and there was in particular a rejection of a simplistic, instrumental model of the law as a tool of the ruling class. This entailed a number of Marxist writers reassessing the work of Marxist theoreticians from the early twentieth century such as Renner and Pashukanis. One text, especially, stands as a culmination of this project: *Capitalism and the Rule of Law*, edited by Bob Fine (1979) for the National Deviancy Conference and Conference of Socialist Economists. The subtitle, *From deviancy theory to Marxism*, aptly summed up the journey taken by radical criminology over that decade.

It was during the second half of the 1970s that the work of the French writer Michel Foucault began to influence British criminologists. Foucault's (1977, 1979) writings are complex and difficult to classify, but his work played a key role in the development of 'post-Marxist' criminology during the 1980s (Reiner, 1988). Foucault's book, *Discipline and Punish*, published in 1977, in which he analyses the phenomenon of punishment in a historical context, was particularly influential, as it seemed to offer, for some criminologists, a more satisfying alternative to the mechanistic models of the state and systems of discipline. For Foucault, discipline was literally everywhere, and was not the exclusive province of coercive formal state institutions.

In a paper originally published in 1970, and then given a wider audience when it was reproduced in Taylor *et al.*'s (1975) *Critical Criminology*, the American criminologists H. and J. Schwendinger attempted to redraw the map of criminality in a way that seemed to free the radical criminologist from the parameters set by the capitalist state. They proposed a 'human rights' definition of crime: criminal activities, they argued, should be defined in terms of certain universal codes of conduct, rather than the legal codes of a particular society:

> The abrogation of these rights certainly limits the individual's chance to fulfil himself in many spheres of life. It can be stated that individuals who deny these rights to others are criminal . . . imperialism, racism, sexism and poverty can be called crimes according to the logic of our argument. (Schwendinger and Schwendinger, 1975: 148)

Another landmark publication in the 1970s that should be noted, and which was also located within this tradition of focusing on the rule makers, was Stuart Hall *et al.*'s (1978) *Policing the Crisis*, a study produced by members of the Birmingham Centre for Contemporary Cultural Studies. Drawing on neo-Marxism and labelling theory, Hall and his colleagues argued that in order to divert attention away from the deep structural economic and social problems afflicting Britain, the state constructed a moral panic during the 1970s regarding so called 'muggings'. According to the authors these crimes of violence were, with the help of the media, linked specifically to supposedly 'black muggers'.

Cynical rule breakers

We can now turn to the other proposition associated with this strand of radical criminology as it developed through the 1970s: that governments, corporations and 'respectable' members of society were often involved in, and got away with, criminal activities that were much more harmful than so-called deviant activities. These are sometimes called 'crimes in the suites' rather than 'crimes in the streets'.

This is the radical end of a criminological tradition that has concerned itself with white-collar crime, a term originally used by the American criminologist Edwin Sutherland (1940). However, as David Nelken (1994) argues, although the term has entered into general usage, and people feel that they know what it means, its use as a descriptive term within criminology is highly problematic. In practice, it functions as a catch-all term encompassing a vast array of criminal activities, involving offenders of high as well as relatively low status:

> If Sutherland merited a Nobel Prize, as Mannheim thought, for pioneering this field of study, he did not deserve it for the clarity or serviceableness of his definition. What, if anything, is there in common between the marketing of unsafe pharmaceuticals, the practice of insider trading, long-firm fraud, computer crime, bank embezzlement and fiddling at work? (Ibid. 361)

From the point of view of radical criminology, of course, the crimes of the powerful (Pearce, 1976) – in the form of corporate crime – are of most interest. Sometimes referred to as exposé criminology, research in this field is attractive to radical criminologists because, as well as providing satisfying ammunition to use against the 'real' criminals in society, on a theoretical level it provides evidence that the capitalist system is in itself criminogenic (Box, 1983). A classic American study in this vein fron the 1970s was carried out in Seattle by W. J. Chambliss (1978), where a criminal network involving many of the great and the good was uncovered. According to Chambliss, significant sections of the business community, together with politicians and police officers, constituted a large crime syndicate in the city.

Criminology in the 1970s: other directions

Whilst radical criminology attempted, along the lines discussed above, to construct a political economy of crime and deviance during the 1970s – and, in Britain, tending to draw on a European Marxist tradition rather than American-style conflict theory – this decade also saw British criminology developing along other pathways. Although some of this work complemented the radical project, overall it reflected the increasingly wide variety of research themes, methodologies, theoretical orientations and political leanings opening up within the discipline of criminology. These alternative pathways will be examined briefly, although not in any particular order of precedence.

Feminism and criminology

The 1970s finally saw the beginning of serious research in Britain on issues of gender, crime and criminal justice from the perspective of feminism. This reflected the growth of feminism in a general sense, in the United States during the 1960s, and in this country during the 1970s. Carol Smart's (1976) book, *Women, Crime and Criminology*, is identified by most commentators as the first British example of a criminological text written from the standpoint of feminism. Since then, a large and influential literature oriented towards feminist concerns has sprung up. However, just as there is no one feminism, so there is no one 'feminist criminology': different schools of thought have developed out of different political and theoretical traditions. The central common element, though, has been a commitment to ending sex-based discrimination in society towards women. Nevertheless, as we shall see in a more detailed discussion later on, debates over the implications of this for criminology, and even whether a specifically feminist criminology (or criminologies) is possible, continue to flourish.

As with other areas of criminological research, the early feminist work in this country drew heavily on American sources (e.g. Klein, 1973; Chesney-Lind, 1973). As the 1970s came to an end four main themes had emerged in Britain. First, the 'invisibility' of women in existing criminological theories. Up to the mid-1970s criminological theory had to a startling degree ignored female offenders. The assumption seemed to be that *if* women were to be considered, then the particular criminological theory involved could somehow accommodate them without too much bother, or, if a theory linked criminality to 'machismo', then the question of female criminality could be simply dispensed with. In fact, some early feminists sought to incorporate their ideas into existing theoretical frameworks as a progressive step (e.g. Shacklady Smith, 1978), though subsequent writers have been more sceptical. The second theme focused on the relatively few examples of criminological work – written by men – that *had* addressed the issue of female criminality. This work was accused of 'distortion', of offering explanations based on crude, sexist stereotypes (Smart, 1976). The third theme concerned itself with the workings of the criminal justice system, in so far as that system was seen to be profoundly sexist (R. Pearson, 1976; Cashburn, 1979). Finally, the fourth theme was that of female victimization, especially sexual assault and violence taking place within the domestic sphere (Hanmer, 1978).

That the bulk of criminological theorizing concerned itself with men rather than women was a corollary of the much higher rates of offending among men. In Britain and in the United States, statistics have consistently shown that around 80 per cent of those found guilty of, or cautioned for, indictable offences are men (self-report studies of offending behaviour, though, put the sex–crime ratio at around two to one). This is reflected in prison populations in Britain: out of a total of around 50,000 prisoners, about 1,500 are women. Thus, it would appear that the best single predictor of future criminality among, say, a group of schoolchildren is the sex of the child, rather than, for example, the child's social class background. This observation, said feminist writers, should logically have placed issues of gender firmly at the centre of the criminological stage: What is it about masculinity that leads to such relatively high levels of crime, especially with respect to violent crime?

Interactionism, phenomenology and ethnomethodology

As we have seen, American-led interactionist approaches to the study of deviance, and in particular the emphasis on labelling, had an enormous impact on British criminology in the late 1960s. The message from labelling theory was that deviance was created by society, which at first glance seems a less than earth shattering revelation. After all, it was commonplace to link deviant, or criminal, behaviour to social factors such as poverty, rough neighbourhoods, urban life, and so forth. However, for the labelling theorists, 'created by society' meant something rather different. In fact, it had two meanings, though the distinction is not always recognized: first, that society creates the rules against which behaviour is judged, and second, that in specific circumstances certain groups are selected and labelled as deviant by those in a position to do so, for example the police or the mass media. It was the first of these meanings that stimulated radical work which focused on the law makers later on in the 1970s. The second meaning was picked up during the late 1960s and early 1970s by a number of sociologists of deviance (by now the preferred term) and applied to a British context, with the addition of the congruent concept of deviancy amplification, devised originally by Leslie Wilkins (1964). Two notable examples of such research are Jock Young's (1971) study of soft drugs use in Notting Hill, London, and Stan Cohen's (1980) study of the Mods and Rockers phenomenon, the latter introducing the term 'moral panic' into the lexicon of 'informed debate' on law and order.

By the early 1970s, though, various critiques of labelling theory, and indeed new deviancy as a whole, were beginning to stack up, first in the United States, and then in Britain. Although this eventually led to more radical criminologists breaking with labelling theory in favour of a harder, Marxist-informed, political economy of crime, a number of the early members of the National Deviancy Conference, together with later adherents, continued to work within an interactionist framework. Thus through the 1970s various writers developed and refined the earlier forms of interactionist theory: Steven Box (1981, first published 1971), for instance, attempted to incorporate labelling theory into yet another American import, control theory.

One result of this was the growth in ethnographic studies of groups defined as deviant. Drawing on the earlier symbolic interactionism of G. H. Mead, labelling theory had argued that it was important to take account of the ways in which those labelled as deviant respond, at both a behavioural level (what they do) and at a mental level (how they think). Under certain circumstances, the argument ran, labelling processes lead to the successful application of the label 'deviant' to a group, and this has fundamental implications for the deviant's self-image. In other words, under appropriate circumstances, labelled groups come to accept the label and see themselves as deviant. Criticisms that this viewed the deviant as mere passive victim (Gouldner, 1968), and was highly deterministic (Akers, 1967) led inter-actionists to develop more refined theoretical formulations as the 1970s progressed, with a stress on labelling as a 'sensitizing' perspective, rather than a heavy-duty theoretical school (Plummer, 1979).

Proponents of interactionism argued that research should be sensitive to the subjective worlds constructed by those labelled as deviant, and indeed, to the subjective worlds of any group being studied. In other words, one of the tasks of the sociologist is to engage in research that will seek to understand the social world from the point of view of the individuals and groups concerned. This was part of a critique of positivism which, it was said, merely imposed the researcher's understandings onto the deviant under the cover of a spurious claim to be 'scientific'. Thus, whilst being sensitive to the subtle changes in meanings that occurred via interactions with control agents, the anti-positivists underlined the importance of providing authentic accounts that the deviant groups would themselves recognize. In this context, ethnography offered the only viable research method. Originally developed by anthropologists, ethnographic research basically involved the researcher joining a group, either covertly or overtly, and, by spending time with the members, gradually building up an in-depth understanding. The 1970s produced a number of important studies of this type, for example, delinquent youth in Liverpool (Parker, 1974); the construction of homosexual identities (Plummer, 1975); and pilferage at work (Ditton, 1977).

These ethnographic studies also reflected the British interest in the phenomenological criminology associated with David Matza. Writing in the 1960s, Matza, whose work came to be known as 'American naturalism', was a strong influence on British new deviancy theorists. His famous injunction to 'tell it like it is', indicates the phenomenologist's commitment to present accounts of human events in their own terms: to adopt an 'appreciative' stance and to see the deviant's world as they see it (Matza, 1969).

Other research during the 1970s also continued to develop some of the elements of interactionist theory, although it did not opt for an ethnographic methodology. Inevitably, where deviant groups were being studied, this involved a rejection of 'correctionalism', that is, a refusal to align criminological research with the practical goal of stamping out the deviance. In the 'sceptical' spirit of new deviancy theory such research was imbued with a strong sense of relativism rather than absolutism (see Taylor and

Walton, 1971). Other research, also expressing some of the central ideas of interactionism, turned the spotlight away from defined deviant groups and towards other players in the criminal justice process, such as police officers (Cain, 1973; Holdaway, 1977) and magistrates (Carlen, 1976).

An interest in the subjective worlds of those labelled as deviant, as well as all other participants in interactive processes of meaning construction, is associated with two other theoretical developments in the late 1960s and 1970s, each of which turned their attention to crime and deviance: phenomenology and ethnomethodology. Within the context of this overview of developments in academic criminology, it is not necessary to embark on a detailed exposition of the respective theoretical positions here; that can be left until we return to an examination of criminological theory. However, some markers can be put down.

From the point of view of phenomenology, no objective social reality exists 'out there' waiting to be discovered. What we perceive to be reality is, from this perspective, merely a version of reality (phenomenal reality), constituted by the subjective meanings that the world has for us. Within this theoretical framework a number of forays were made into the criminological terrain by phenomenologists, for example Cicourel (1968) on juvenile justice in the United States; Coulter (1973) on insanity; and Atkinson (1971) on definitions of suicide in coroner's courts. On a general level, Phillipson (1971) produced a phenomenological critique of the sociology of deviance that questioned the entire stock of theoretical knowledge making up that field. As Bob Roshier (1989: 68) has noted: 'Phenomenological sociology, with its micro-level focus on human meaning construction, has mostly ruled out any specific interest in substantive areas of human action such as crime.' Therefore, because phenomenology is ultimately concerned with shared meanings and the nature of knowledge in the most fundamental sense, and adopts a totally relativistic position, as a perspective it drifted away from the specific concerns of criminology or the sociology of deviance.

Ethnomethodology drew on many of the insights of phenomenology, and directs attention to day-to-day, taken-for-granted methods used by individuals to create a meaningful, ordered social world. The relevance of this to criminology manifests itself in detailed examination of the assumptions used to make sense of what appear to be the 'facts' of crime and deviance. As an example, from an ethnomethodological standpoint, the notion of 'law making' has a quite different meaning to the one that it normally has. Law making is not addressed in terms of the formulation of the law of the land at some point in time, by, say, Parliament. Rather, law making is seen as a process that is acted out each day within the courtroom, as each of the participants comes to understand what 'really happened': 'In contrast to the "finished" conception of criminal law . . . ethnomethodology favours a view of criminal law as a continually contingent production of the *in situ* practices of participants in legal proceedings and settings' (Hester and Eglin, 1992: 75).

Orthodox criminology

Whilst criminology was shooting off in all these various directions during the 1970s, with ideas and debates tumbling forth at a breathless rate, orthodox criminology continued to stalk quietly alongside. Furthermore, much of orthodox criminology was still possessed by new deviancy theory's very own folk devil: positivism. It may not have grabbed the headlines, or excited the brain cells of students (except, perhaps, when they were disparaging it), but in terms of volume of work and influence on policy, positivist criminology remained a powerful force, both in Britain and in the United States. Writing in the mid-1980s, Gottfredson and Hirschi (1987: 18) felt able to report: 'In the light of the pervasive distaste for positivism expressed by many modern criminologists, it is surprising to discover that positivistic criminology may today be healthier than ever.' They see this situation as being a result of positivist criminology's ability to respond to the earlier criticisms and to create 'what is perhaps a healthier and more self-assured positivistic criminology than has heretofore existed' (ibid.). However, as we shall see when discussing criminological theory in detail, and as sometimes happens with medical diagnoses, this confident pronouncement probably coincided with positivist criminology taking a turn for the worse, at least in this country.

In Britain during the 1970s, though, positivist-oriented orthodox criminological research continued unabated. To a large extent this was due to its powerbase in key research institutions, and in particular, the Home Office. At the same time there was an increase in the amount of in-house research carried out by criminal justice agencies, such as the police, the Prison Department and the probation service. Government funded social science research within universities, on the other hand, began to be cut back. Although the grandiose promises of the nineteenth century had by then been scaled down to more modest dimensions, criminological research carried out within the positivist tradition continued to appeal to policy makers more than other approaches did, because it still promised to be useful. As always, positivism was committed to discovering the causes of crime (or at least determining correlational factors) and devising ways of treating offenders so that they cease to be offenders. The dominant conceptual framework within which this proceeded was not seen as problematic – clearly much less irksome to a government than the critical stances adopted by other criminologies at the time. A classic example of this type of orthodox criminological research is the massive longitudinal study conducted by West and Farrington (1973, 1977), where they attempted to link delinquency to a range of salient social factors. In spite of all the developments associated with new deviancy and radical criminology, orthodox criminology – the 'criminological establishment' – still maintained a tenacious hold on powerful institutions. This is a point made by Stan Cohen (1988: 82) in his review of British criminology at the start of the 1980s:

> There are more corners and cavities than ten years ago, but for the most part the institutional foundations of British criminology remain intact and unaltered . . . the establishment saw the new theories as simply a fashion that would eventually pass or as a few interesting ideas that could be swallowed up without changing the existing paradigms at all.

Although the 'institutional foundations of British criminology' may have remained intact, the influence of the various strands that grew out of the new deviancy, and, in particular, the impact made by a specifically sociological criminology, should not be underestimated, at least within the context of academic criminology. Many of the concepts from new deviancy theory had, by the end of the 1970s, permeated through the education system, so that most 'O' level sociology students, let alone undergraduates, would have been introduced to, for instance, moral panics and the amplification of deviance. Theoretical developments over the preceding decade had resulted in a substantial remapping of the terrain of sociological criminology. Questions concerning why people broke the law, and how criminals should be treated, which at one time were taken for granted within criminology, had been replaced by different questions: Why are certain types of behaviour designated illegal? In whose interests do the laws operate? Why are only some people selected as deviant or criminal? And so on. Whatever else we might say about this change of emphasis, for students of criminology the more radical strands did seem to offer something far more interesting than the preoccupations of an earlier orthodox criminology.

Having said this, although interactionism and the various strands of radical criminology had become very influential within the academic world during the 1970s, the limits of this influence have to be recognized. Echoing Stan Cohen's sentiments, Jock Young (1988: 170) has pointed out:

> But what radical criminology did not do to any significant degree is challenge the criminological establishment. For the policy centres in British society were, and remain, remarkably unaffected, both in the Home Office itself and the university institutions which it helps to finance.

Young is specifically referring to positivist criminology in all of its guises (sociological, psychological, biological), and it is important to appreciate that throughout the intellectual turmoil of the 1960s and 1970s, orthodox criminology, with its positivist credentials, lived on, and, significantly, continued to attract official research funding. Its position had, however, been weakened, and, in the next decade, positivism had to contend with a more powerful challenge, though this time from a less obvious source.

At the level of policy, radical criminology had made little impact. Young does refer to its influence on Labour Party thinking, but this occurred just as the Labour Party lost office to a Conservative government, a government still in power in the mid-1990s. However, radical criminology did influence the Labour Party at local government level in some parts of the country. As far as national criminal justice policies were concerned, though, by the end of the 1970s the influence of radical criminology had, not surprisingly, been minimal.

Unlike positivism, which, since its inception, had taken an uncritical stance *vis-à-vis* the concepts of deviance and crime, and offered the promise of discovering the causes and cures of crime, radical criminology had celebrated its disengagement from the requirement to be 'useful' in this sense. Clearly, radical socialist criminology's commitment to the dismantling of capitalism – and, in Taylor, Walton and Young's version, a revolutionary call for 'socialist diversity' – was unlikely to endear it to the main political parties or to the custodians of the criminal justice system. Although feminism was interested in an agenda that confronted official responses to female criminality, women as victims, and the treatment of offenders, its contribution to criminology was still at an underdeveloped stage by the late 1970s.

When attempting to assess the impact of radical criminology on the criminal justice system the tendency, of course, is to expect this impact to be progressive in nature. This has meant that analyses of the period up to the 1980s have usually ignored the possibility that left–liberal thought, inside and outside criminology, may have unwittingly played a part in paving the way for the growth of criminal justice policies with a quite different character.

Radical critiques and the growth of the New Right

The election of a Conservative government in 1979 signalled a decisive shift to the right in British politics and with it the establishment of Thatcherism. A similar political realignment occurred in other European countries and, with the election of a Reagan administration, in the United States too. Soon afterwards, state socialism began to be dismantled across former Eastern Europe and the Soviet Union, and 'the market' took centre stage, both as an economic mechanism and as an ideological symbol.

From 1979 onwards, those on the liberal–left spectrum in Britain found themselves having to fight a rearguard action, as they tried to unravel the precise meaning and impact of what has been variously described as new rightism, right-wing authoritarianism and authoritarian populism.

Obviously, a range of social, political and economic factors would have to be taken into consideration when accounting for the rise of the New Right, factors beyond the scope of this book. However, one ironic dimension to this will be considered: that over the previous decade left-of-centre (described loosely as 'radical') thought unwittingly helped to prepare the ground for the New Right. This can be illustrated by focusing on two central characteristics of radical thought as it developed from the late 1960s, on a general level as well as specifically within the context of criminology:

1. There was much criticism of institutions and processes in capitalist Britain, especially by socialists, though this criticism tended to remain truncated; constructive and convincing alternatives to contemporary arrangements were in short supply.

2. Radical thought came to be riven by internal divisions. Ideological in-fighting created various schisms, with the Labour Party in particular having to cope with a number of disparate factions; one important outcome was the split resulting from the formation of the Social Democrat Party.

Radical criticism on a general level

Clearly, criticism of aspects of life in capitalist Britain is an expected and appropriate response on the part of radicals; what was perhaps not expected was that this criticism would play a part in helping pave the way for the advent of the New Right. The irony of the situation is encapsulated in a letter that appeared in the journal *New Statesman and Society* in 1988. The writer castigated the journal for allowing the phrase 'chattering classes' to be used in its columns, pointing out that the phrase was used by Prime Minister Thatcher as a term of abuse, as a way of ridiculing liberal-minded, middle-class academics and intellectuals. The phrase is, of course, synonymous with 'Guardian reader', with the sort of person who joins CND and Amnesty International, uses 'chair' rather than 'chairman', and until recently reprimanded supermarket managers for stocking South African oranges. If such people are to be treated as a joke, are the causes they support worthy of ridicule too?

The irony is that during the 1970s those so labelled joined in the fun themselves, or laughed at comedians who did the job for them. Some of these comedians would fill theatres with members of the 'chattering classes', who would then be treated to being the butt of the comedian's jokes, with inevitable references to vegetarianism, muesli, stripped-pine furniture and polytechnic angst. Some novels followed the same path; *The History Man* (about a 'trendy', a.k.a. useless, university sociology lecturer) being a classic of the genre. This was made into a television series. If that was what sociologists were like, if that was how they behaved, why should taxpayers support them with their hard-earned money? The fact that the book was meant to be humorous helped to protect it. Any criticism by a sociologist was likely to be written off as sour grapes and confirmation that sociologists did indeed lack a sense of humour. Thus in the 1970s people began to get accustomed to apparently right-on comedians and writers having a go at liberal to left-minded groups and the causes they supported. Who were these chattering, 'middle-class' victims? In the main they were not particularly well-paid public employees. They did not run private corporations or sell arms to right-wing military dictatorships, but they were fair game for radical humour. It is likely that in subtle ways this process contributed to the creation of a climate in which the value of these groups, their work and the causes they subscribed to, came to be questioned.

If this 'softening up' process was going on at a cultural level, using humour as a vehicle, the connections between much more systematic radical social and political criticism and subsequent developments associated with the New Right are even more remarkable. A wide range of critical analyses of key sectors of British society had begun to appear by the late 1960s. The validity of this work is not at issue here; what is at issue is the way in which these critical analyses failed to develop constructive alternatives, beyond, for instance, vague socialist phrases. The result was an opening up of a political space which was readily colonized by the New Right in the 1980s. The Right, then, homed in on the same sectors previously criticized by radicals and were able to put forward concrete solutions (or what purported to be solutions). A cursory glance at the key sectors of British society around which radical critical thought flourished, and which subsequently became locations for Conservative policies, quickly exposes, as Matza would put it, an 'embarrassment of riches'. Here are some examples:

- Nationalized industries were seen as overbureaucratized examples of pseudo-socialism. As far as the workers were concerned, they operated much as private industries did and, in fact, were necessary for capitalism as they could be used by the state to fine-tune the economy. They were privatized by the Conservative government.

- Manual work, for instance in manufacturing industry and mining, was alienating, physically damaging and demeaning. Huge portions of manufacturing have disappeared and most of the coal mines have closed.

- The National Health Service was overbureaucratized and to a large extent run for the benefit of overpaid professionals. The National

Health Service has been increasingly underfunded and organized around strict notions of cost efficiency and effectiveness.

- Mental hospitals, we were told, did more harm than good for the patients; decarceration was the clarion call. Under the guise of 'community care', patients have been decanted from these hospitals out onto the streets.

- Council estates were bleak, standardized and soulless. Large numbers of council houses have been privatized, heralding in a new Georgian front door era.

- When it was not corrupt because of a junket-loving entrenched local political mafia, local government was overstaffed and inefficient. The power of local government has been dramatically reduced.

- By dealing with the system's casualties social workers were in effect propping up a capitalist society. Social work has had to cope with financial stringency and a changed orientation towards the whole welfare process.

- Aid programmes to the 'Third World' were seen as both counterproductive because they postponed a socialist revolution among recipient nations, and futile because the real problem lay in a system of world trade dominated by the developed nations. As a proportion of GNP, British aid has significantly decreased.

- Comprehensive schools were great failures because they were simply secondary modern schools and grammar schools under one roof. The opting out system is gradually recreating a two-tier system.

- The arts were elitist, benefiting only a tiny minority of the population. Here too funding has been significantly reduced.

Radical criticism within criminology

There were similar developments within criminology. While a huge amount of work appeared during the 1970s that was intensely critical of orthodox, establishment approaches to crime, crime control techniques and indeed to the whole criminal justice system, concrete suggestions regarding how things might be improved were relatively thin on the ground. The New Right, however, did at least appear to have strong, confident ideas regarding a supposed better future. A range of ideas, policies and practices relating to crime and criminal justice were, from the late 1960s, routinely criticized by radical criminologists. Again, whatever the validity of these criticisms, the targets were often the same ones subsequently selected by the New Right. Furthermore, and to inject more irony into this, those features of the criminal justice system being criticized by radicals were arguably more liberal, more humane and less draconian than what were to follow in the 1980s and 1990s. The radical criticism that developed within criminology from the late 1960s coalesced around three main themes:

1. The reality and fear of crime.
2. The causes of crime.
3. Prescriptive policies aimed at controlling crime and dealing with the criminal.

The reality and fear of crime

Following labelling theory, it was commonplace during the 1970s for radical criminologists to argue that crime rises were a function of labelling by control agents, with the police simply recording more offences. Reassuring comparisons were sometimes drawn between life today and life in Britain's cities 100 years ago. The fear of crime tended to be equated with moral panics and, looked at objectively, people had to contend with worse things than crime. One outcome of this type of reasoning was that links between crime rises and capitalist development could not be made. If there were no crime rises, then there was nothing beyond 'reaction' to explain. The Right, on the other hand, did offer explanations, unpalatable as these were to left–liberal thought, and appeared to be sympathetic to the worries of the public, who did feel that crime was on the increase. However, if necessary, the Right could appropriate radical reasoning and argue that official crime rises reflected the greater willingness of the public to report crime to the police, which in turn reflected the government's policies in this area.

The causes of crime

Attempts to fathom the causes of crime were attacked by many radical criminologists as deterministic positivism, and futile anyway. Thus, for instance, theories linking crime to poverty, unemployment and deprivation were criticized for being deterministic, especially by those oriented towards an interactionist paradigm. Ironically, as we shall see, with the rise of the New Right there was a significant shift away from trying to identify the causes of crime. The growth of what has been called administrative criminology in the 1980s led to a greater emphasis being placed on control. From the point of view of the Right, if poverty was irrelevant, why waste money on such things as urban aid programmes, which, it was argued, had so obviously failed in the United States anyway?

Prescriptive policies

Among left criminologists and liberal ones within the interactionist tradition, it was not thought proper for criminologists to help the capitalist system, or the forces of law and order, by joining in the fight against crime. There was no desire to line up with the repressive apparatus of the state. The New Right, however, was able to present itself as a force in society that was bothered about crime. Within the context of criminal justice policies, the 'softening up' process was most obviously seen in radical critiques of welfare-oriented treatment models of juvenile justice. Again ironically, those on the right agreed. They attacked what they saw as 'soft', 'kid-gloved' approaches, and argued that people should take full responsibility for their actions and be punished accordingly. Many on the left argued that juveniles should be dealt with on the basis of a 'due process' model of justice, linked to the idea of 'just deserts', rather than the welfare model supposedly enshrined in the 1969 Children and Young Persons Act (e.g. Taylor, Lacey and Bracken, 1980). Interestingly, a similar convergence between left and right occurred in the United States, where rehabilitation through treatment was also criticized: 'The subsequent turn against rehabilitation cannot be explained primarily as a conservative reaction to rising crime rates. It was made possible only by a discrediting of rehabilitation from the Left' (Plattner, quoted by Cullen and Wozniak, 1982: 24).

Divisions within radical thought

The ideological infighting within radical thought in general was paralleled by increasing disunity within radical criminology during the 1970s. The major divisions that opened up encompassed labelling theory, critical criminology and recent debates between 'left realism' and 'left idealism'. No concerted challenge to New Right thinking on crime arose; rather, what we saw was a great deal of sometimes vitriolic disputes within radical criminology.

11 | Post-new deviancy and the new criminology

Interactionism had the rare distinction of having to cope with criticisms from all political directions. Looking back on these criticisms, Becker (1974: 53) has commented:

> Moral problems arise in all sociological research but are especially provocatively posed by interactionist theories of deviance. Moral criticism has come from the political centre and beyond, from the political Left, and from the left field. Interactionist theories have been accused of giving aid and comfort to the enemy, be the enemy those who would upset the stability of the existing order or the Establishment. They have been accused of openly espousing unconventional norms, of refusing to support anti-Establishment positions, and (the left field position) of appearing to support anti-Establishment causes while subtly favouring the status quo.

Irrespective of interactionism's 'true' nature, it did play an important role in generating key criminological debates during the 1970s. The strongest criticisms of interactionism, and in particular of labelling theory, probably came from the left. Already by the beginning of the 1970s labelling theory was being attacked for its lack of politically radical credentials; the British left came to see it as another version of American liberalism. In response, there emerged a much more radical and politically committed criminology based upon varieties of conflict theory. In the United States this was conflict theory of a pluralistic, non-Marxist type – though later on some of it did become infused with Marxist concepts – whilst in Britain there was a more explicit commitment to neo-Marxist formulations in the shape of critical criminology. The enduring influence of labelling theory, though, should not be overlooked. Conflict theorists picked up on the argument from writers such as Becker and Lemert that deviance had to be seen in relative terms, and that the designation of certain acts as deviant was a function of the distribution of power in society. Furthermore, Lemert had stressed that powerful elites were able to influence how deviant behaviour would be dealt with: whether to 'control or de-control'. However, labelling theory had fallen short of an analysis of the deeper sources of the power to label, and conflict theorists, through their attempts to construct a political economy of crime, were concerned to analyze the structural bases of rule creation and rule enforcement.

Two important theoretical themes emerged in the immediate post-new deviancy period and helped pave the way for conflict theory, and each developed out of a critique of labelling theory: one focused on deviance and power, the other on the politicization of deviance.

Deviance and power

This theme is associated with those writers who were critical of labelling theory for concentrating on the least powerful, marginalized groups in society, groups conventionally defined as deviant (Gouldner, 1968; Liazos, 1972; Thio, 1973). They also criticized labelling theory for confining their analyses of the power to label to low-level agents of social control. Liazos argued that the sociology of deviance had only a partial view of deviance. It had, he said, neglected the violence perpetrated by the United States government in Vietnam, and the violent, corrupt and fraudulent activities of large corporations. Thio took a similar line, but also argued that powerful elites protected their interests by defining certain forms of behaviour as deviant and, by maintaining an unequal society, sustained the social and economic conditions that caused deviant behaviour among the powerless.

These were issues taken up by conflict theory in the United States as it developed from the late 1960s and through the 1970s. The theme of powerful elites or classes as self-interested rule makers is particularly apparent in the early work of the conflict theorists. Later on, they turned their attention to the powerful as law breakers, via 'exposé' criminology and a focus on the 'crimes of the powerful' and, under the influence of Marxism, to the criminogenic features of capitalism itself.

American conflict theory

Three criminologists in particular are associated with the early development of conflict theory in the United States: Austin Turk, William Chambliss and Richard Quinney. Although many of their ideas overlapped, summarizing their work is complicated by the fact that their ideas (especially in the case of Quinney) underwent some modification during the 1970s, this reflecting the theoretical ferment within radical criminology at that time.

Coincidently, each of these writers introduced their ideas in books published in the same year, 1969. In general terms, all three followed labelling theory by orienting their analyses towards the criminalization of behaviour, rather than towards the criminal and the sources of criminal behaviour. Thus they adopted a relativistic stance, and rejected the view that deviance/crime was a quality of the act. However, unlike labelling theory, they attempted to explain processes of criminalization from the point of view of the deeper structures of power in American society. Powerful interest groups were seen as imposing their own definitions of crime onto society. Fundamentally, the law was seen as a coercive instrument used selectively by these sectional interests to preserve their power.

Turk (1969) developed a particular form of conflict theory, largely derived from Ralph Dahrendorf (1959, 1968), in which he emphasized the conflict arising from the unequal distribution of authority, rather than from class relationships rooted in the economic system. The model of authority used owed much to Weber's model of power, where authority is equated with legitimized power. For Turk, relationships based upon authority and subordination would always exist – in socialist as well as capitalist societies – though the sources of authority may alter. At a given moment, therefore, there will always be a dominant group able to impose their own normative system onto society in general. Rather than class, Turk saw subordinate status as deriving from sex, 'race'/ethnicity and age. Those occupying subordinate positions were more likely to find their behaviour criminalized, not because it was inherently criminal or 'bad', but because their normative systems were in conflict with the normative system of the dominant group. As a corollary of this, those most likely to experience criminalization in American society were male, black and young.

Chambliss carried out his own empirical research in order to substantiate the theoretical claim that the law operated in favour of the powerful in society. His first study (1964) was of the English vagrancy laws initially introduced in the fourteenth century, where he showed how they directly operated in the interests of the ruling class. He argued that feudal landowners used these laws as a mechanism to compel people to work on their land. From the point of view of the landowners the laws were necessary because of the shortages of labour brought about by the Black Death. The vagrancy laws made it illegal for people to give food or shelter to those defined as vagrants. In addition, vagrants were threatened with imprisonment if they refused work offered by a landowner. As Chambliss (1964: 69) concluded:

> There is little question that these statutes were designed for one express purpose: to force laborers . . . to accept employment at a low wage in order to insure the landowner an adequate supply of labor at a price he could afford to pay.

Later on Chambliss did a study of the introduction of a Poll Tax law by British colonizers in their East African colonies. Again, he made the point that the law was used to further the interests of the class in power. The introduction of the Poll Tax law meant that African migrant workers were forced to work on the colonizers' plantations so as to earn enough money to pay the tax. The establishment of a low-wage economy ensured that the workers stayed on the plantation until the season ended, and prevented them from earning sufficient to pay their taxes mid-season.

By the middle of the 1970s Chambliss had moved towards a more overtly Marxist position, drawing now on key concepts such as ruling class (rather than elite) and class conflict. In his article 'Towards a political economy of crime' (Chambliss, 1975), he was arguing that as capitalism develops, so the gaps between proletariat and bourgeoisie will widen, bringing with it increased social conflict. Under these circumstances he saw it as inevitable that the ruling class would gradually impose a more coercive penal law on the working class in the hope of maintaining social order through their submission. As a consequence, he argued, modern capitalist societies are characterized by increasingly oppressive criminal justice systems as social conditions deteriorate, and the corresponding deprivation suffered by large sections of the working class contributes to rising levels of crime. Thus by the middle of the 1970s Chambliss was giving attention to explanations of criminality, rather than concentrating on processes of criminalization. This engagement with causal questions was also found in the work of another American conflict theorist, David Gordon, at the beginning of the 1970s. Gordon (1971) argued (as Chambliss was to do) that given the selfishness, individualism and competitiveness of a capitalist system, crime represents a perfectly rational response.

Chambliss also took up another theme in his research, a theme that was to be developed further by radical criminologists: namely, the powerful as rule breakers (Chambliss, 1978). For many years he carried out a study of crime and the legal system in Seattle in the United States. His conclusion was that all classes were involved in criminal activities, with the major crime syndicate consisting of both professional criminals and 'respectable', powerful members of the community. In addition, he identified what he called a 'symbiotic' relationship, based upon mutual interdependency, between organized crime and the bureaucratic legal system. Rather than cope with the organizational disequilibrium that would result from bringing those involved in organized crime to justice, powerful players in the legal system preferred to devote most of their resources to the apprehension and punishment of the least powerful criminals, such as drug users and prostitutes. In effect, the criminal justice system and organized crime in the city oiled each other's wheels.

Like Chambliss, Quinney gradually moved towards an explicitly Marxist position, though his own intellectual journey was especially remarkable in that it encompassed earlier on some ideas from phenomenology and, later on, theological considerations. The latest stage on this journey finds Quinney editing a collection of readings entitled *Criminology as Peacemaking* (Pepinsky and Quinney, 1991). His own contribution to this volume is an eclectic mix of radical social science, humanism and a wide range of religious sources. As the title suggests, the book is aimed at mobilizing criminologists not for the traditional 'war against crime', but for a process of reconciliation and healing. Macho cynics are likely to scoff at this enterprise, though there is no evidence that declarations of war on crime in Europe and the United States have been particularly successful.

In his first important contribution, Quinney's (1969) arguments are similar to those found in Turk and Chambliss, in that they stress the powerful as instrumental law makers. In two books published the following year, though, he introduced a phenomenological dimension (Quinney 1970a, 1970b). Here he addressed the social reality of crime: the ways in which those with power were able to construct subjective understandings of crime and criminality that suited their own interests. On this basis he argued that perception of crime – that is, the subjectively understood 'reality' of crime (and, indeed, anything else) – was a 'state of mind'; nothing that constituted 'social reality' existed as an objective entity. Thus the 'problem of crime' is shaped by powerful interests in society. However, by 1974 Quinney was criticizing the perspective of phenomenology, and had embraced an explicitly Marxist position (Quinney, 1974).

This work was strongly influenced by the Frankfurt School, with its emphasis on the manipulation of consciousness by bourgeois ideological formations, such as the mass media. Quinney (1977) described his Marxian criminology as 'critical criminology', and argued that because of its inherent contradictions, the capitalist system created large numbers of unemployed people – surplus populations. The capitalist state, he said, attempts to manage these surplus populations by welfare and criminal justice policies, in an effort to stave off social disruption. In Quinney's view, these attempts were doomed to failure, being unable to prevent increases in crime. The crime associated with surplus populations are described by him as 'survival crime'; it is crime that arises from living in or at the edges of poverty. However, it was also seen as a form of immature political action – the poor fighting back. In Quinney's work, then, we can see a move away from an earlier, purely instrumental view of the law and legal system, with the suggestion of ruling-class conspiracies, towards a more structuralist position, where law and the criminal justice system are locked into the structural imperatives of capitalism as a whole.

The conceptualization of crime as the means by which the poor and marginalized fought back that Quinney subscribed to later on in the 1970s, leads directly to the second theme that emerged in the late 1960s within an embryonic radical criminology: the politicization of deviance.

Politicizing deviance

This theme is associated with the 'man-fighting-back' image of the deviant introduced by Gouldner (1968) as a critique of what he saw as labelling theory's defeated, 'man-on-his-back' image, and also with the work of Horowitz and Leibowitz (1969). These writers pointed the way towards theoretical models that placed the actions of the deviant centre stage. Rather than a pathetic victim of labelling by control agents, the individual was now seen as choosing a specifically deviant path as an expression of resistance. Deviance here becomes linked to political action.

Horawitz and Leibowitz's influential article considerably extended the argument put forward by labelling theorists. Not only was the labelling of certain acts as deviant a political process, they argued, but also some 'socially' deviant acts should more properly be viewed as 'politically' deviant acts. Their charge that traditional definitions of 'political' are too narrow and inflexible was obviously in tune with some of the ideas emanating from the New Left/counter cultural configuration in America and Europe at that time. The labels 'social' and 'political' deviance were, they said, becoming increasingly redundant in modern America. Developments in the 1960s – and in particular, protest based upon the experience of the ghetto – had produced a convergence between the deviant and the political. Thus political minorities were increasingly stepping outside the repertoire of acceptable tactics to further their causes, and adopting methods and lifestyles normally associated with deviant groups. On the other side, in an effort to make their voices heard, deviant groups were increasingly adopting tactics that were normally thought of as political tactics. In Horowitz and

Leibowitz's view, this convergence had occurred because the 'right to dissent', traditionally enjoyed by powerful minorities, had come to be questioned by the elites as these minorities had begun to use deviant tactics. From the other direction, deviant minorities had become less willing to confine their problems to the private sphere, and were using modes of protest traditionally thought of as political. However, powerful interests tended to deny political status to their protests, since they had, so to speak, already been written off as 'social problems'. If, therefore, the actions of political minorities are defined in ways traditionally reserved for deviants, so they will be responded to in similar ways. A classic example of this would be the Stalinist ploy of labelling political dissension in the former Soviet Union as mental illness.

In Britain this theme was taken up by Cohen (1969, 1974) and by Hall (1974). Following Horowitz and Leibowitz, they discussed the tendency of those with power to assign certain kinds of political activity to the 'deviant' category, thereby negating any social criticism informing that activity. It is important to recognize (as Cohen and Hall did) precisely what Horowitz and Leibowitz were saying about *deviance* and politics. They did not argue that deviant acts are, by definition, political, but rather that some deviant groups – the Gay Liberation Movement, for example – were now adopting political modes of protest to further their cause. The original deviance was never seen as political in itself. Unfortunately, on this side of the Atlantic some sociologists (e.g. Pearson, 1976) saw in Horowitz and Leibowitz's article an argument that deviance in general was political.

Critical criminology

I have already described the eagerness with which a generation of young, radical British criminologists seized upon the ideas of new deviancy theory in the late 1960s. This was the beginning of an intensely fertile period, when the foundations for the subsequent development of criminology in this country were laid.

While interactionism had emerged out of a strongly liberal tradition in the United States, in Britain it attracted the attention of academics with more radical aspirations, reflecting the influence of a European Marxist tradition. From the very beginning there was a tension between interactionism, pulled by a 'do your own thing' counter culture, and neo-Marxism, whose sympathizers kept one eye on the barricades and the possibility of socialist revolution. In the early British interactionism-inspired research, though, this political radicalism was still underdeveloped, and only hinted at by the use of phrases such as ruling class or bourgeoisie instead of elites, class conflict instead of culture conflict, and capitalism instead of industrial society. By the beginning of the 1970s the tensions and inevitable splits were surfacing within the National Deviancy Conference, new deviancy's forum in Britain.

Eventually this led to attempts to develop an explicitly Marxist criminology, given the title of critical criminology. Although much criticized – in time by the authors themselves – Taylor, Walton and Young's (1973) *The New Criminology* announced this shift in Britain towards a Marxist-informed political economy of crime and deviance. From the title we can see that the sociology of deviance had been eclipsed by a return to criminology, though the book was subtitled *For a social theory of deviance* and was largely devoted to the phenomenon of deviance, which indicated a lingering ambivalence. Their follow-up book, *Critical Criminology* (Taylor *et al.*, 1975), which they edited, drew on a range of contributors, and tried to answer some of the criticism met by the first book.

These early versions of critical criminology were to a large extent based upon a mixture of radical labelling theory and neo-Marxism, a potent brew that ended up with more than a whiff of anarchism. The two themes (discussed above) of deviance and power, and the politicization of deviance, that emerged in the immediate post-new deviancy period in the United States, and was to some extent incorporated into the work of American conflict theorists (especially Quinney), strongly influenced Taylor, Walton and Young's ideas. The two elements contained in the deviance and power theme were clearly in evidence: 'radical criminological strategy . . . is to show up the law, in its true colours, as the instrument of the ruling class . . . and that the rule-makers are also the greatest rule-breakers' (Taylor *et al.*, 1975: 89). The second theme, the politicization of deviance, was also a key component of their work. Seeing deviants as political rebels, 'much deviance,' they said, 'is in itself political'.

Although a few writers in Britain and the United States had produced work on crime and deviance that was influenced by Marxism, until the advent of *The New Criminology* attempts to construct a Marxist theory of crime and deviance had been rare. In response to Paul Hirst, one of their critics, Taylor *et al.* (1975: 283) wrote:

> We can think of no theorist of crime and deviancy in this country, and only two in the USA (John Horton and Tony Platt) who could be accused of the 'Marxism' in deviancy theory he (Hirst) sees to be prevalent. None of the other 'conflict' theorists of crime . . . borrow in any significant fashion from Marxism.

Indeed, the dearth of Marxist criminology was such that until the early 1970s the prewar work of the Dutch Marxist criminologist, Willem Bonger, was seen by many as definitive (and was much criticized by Taylor, Walton and Young).

Taylor, Walton and Young's ambitious aim was to help construct a Marxist informed theoretical understanding of both the processes of criminalization/deviantization, and the aetiology of criminal/deviant activities, by opening up 'the criminological debate by pointing to certain *formal* and *substantive* requirements of a fully social theory of deviance, a theory that can explain the forms assumed by social control and deviant action in "developed" (capitalist) societies' (Taylor *et al.*, 1973: 269, original emphasis). The main features of their work can be summarized as follows:

1. There was a commitment to a 'normative' criminology. By this they meant a socialist criminology that insisted on the need to eradicate social and economic inequalities inherent in capitalist society. This would be congruent with Marx's view that 'man's' true nature could only be realized in a classless society based upon a spirit of community.

2. The creation of a socialist society would usher in a celebration of 'diversity', though without the need for any activities to be criminalized. Thus they envisaged a future 'crime free' society.

3. They attempted to find a route to understanding human action that avoided the determinism found in positivism, as well as the relativism found in phenomenological accounts of deviance. This was reflected in their endorsement of Gouldner's 'man-fighting-back' image of the deviant, and they advanced the view that deviance had to be seen as the way in which individuals 'actively made' the external world. From this perspective deviance is chosen, and 'much' of it is in fact political. In this context they were critical of Bonger, and of the more recent work of the American conflict theorists for holding on to a deterministic and pathologized view of deviance.

4. Although they stressed voluntarism and choice, they did none the less recognize the structural contexts in which people made decisions, ultimately class society. However, following Marx, they saw the development of class consciousness as the basis for eventual liberation.

5. They spent much time discussing the role of the powerful, via the state and its agencies, in the creation of rules and their enforcement, thereby leaning towards an instrumentalist view of the law. This included those professionals and institutions in advanced capitalist societies concerned with the control of, as they saw it, increasing numbers of people.

Critical responses

Inevitably, *The New Criminology* generated a great deal of criticism and debate – including criticism from other Marxists. The most fundamental issue thrown up by these debates was whether, whilst still retaining Marxist credentials, a Marxist theory of deviance was possible at all. Taylor, Walton and Young's strongest Marxist critic at the time was Paul Hirst (whose critique appeared in *Critical Criminology*). Hirst (1975b) argued that Marxists should have no truck with bourgeois concepts such as crime and deviance; to do so would lead only to revisionism. For Hirst, crime and deviance were not 'real' objects of study; Marxist social theory was already specified by its own conceptual language. Using a concept such as deviance was to assume that deviant behaviour was special, and essentially different to non-deviant behaviour. How, then, can deviance be separated out for study? Unfortunately, in *The New Criminology* the authors did not provide a precise definition of deviance. They seemed to be saying that deviance *is* different to conformity in so much as it is purposive infraction of (ideological) rules. Deviants were thus seen as being committed to modes of behaviour that they know are frowned upon by the wider society. The difficulty here is the implication that there is a consensus in society, a notion that they had thoroughly disapproved of when criticizing orthodox criminology.

In fact, as the 1970s progressed, the focus switched to crime and law, and the concept of deviance was used less often. Colin Sumner (1976) was one Marxist who felt that it could be retained, providing that it was reconceptualized so as to make it compatible with Marxism. He suggested that deviance was best seen as an ideological 'social censure', or adverse judgement. From this standpoint, 'deviance' does not exist because people decide to break rules, or because they have a deviant label impressed upon them. It exists as an objective phenomenon located within the ideological superstructure of capitalism, irrespective of actual behaviour, or the extent of a consensus. In a later discussion, Sumner (1990: 27) points out that social censures 'mark off the deviant, the pathological, the dangerous and the criminal from the normal and the good. They say "stop", and are tied to a desire to control, prevent or punish.' From this perspective, the sociology of deviance should become the sociology of social censures. The focus would therefore be on 'the negative categories of moral ideology', the social censures, rather than on the 'offenders' that they produce.

During the rest of the 1970s a large amount of theoretical work was produced in Britain in varying degrees informed by Marxist ideas. Before we examine that work, it will be useful to return to original sources and see what Marx himself, and his collaborator Engels, had to say about crime.

Marx and Engels on crime

Marxists who return to source to look for detailed analyses of the phenomenon of crime are likely to be disappointed. Marx had little more than a passing interest in crime, and when he did address the subject it was usually treated as part of a wider concern with the political economy of law and right (especially in *The German Ideology* (Marx and Engels, 1965)). Engels spent rather more time specifically on the subject of crime, especially in *The Condition of the Working Class in England* (Engels, 1969).

By modern standards, Marx's writings on crime as such are, arguably, less than adequate. His faith in criminal statistics, his lack of interest in criminal motivations, and his identification of crime with the lumpen-proletariat, are good examples of this.

Taylor *et al.* (1973: 221) argued that criminology should recognize 'in deviance the acts of men in the process of actively making, rather than passively taking, the external world'. This formulation, although it was intended to be 'Marxist', did appear to be at variance with Marx's own writings on crime. In general, he seemed to view the criminal as 'passively taking', rather than 'actively making', the world. They attempted to resolve this problem by arguing that Marx's work on crime was misleading, and that we should utilize his general body of theory rather than rely on those instances where he specifically takes up empirical challenges.

One of the main difficulties to be overcome by Taylor *et al.*, and indeed by all Marxists, was that Marx saw crime as being concentrated in the lumpenproletariat, and this provided Hirst with one of his main criticisms of 'Marxist' criminology. From Hirst's point of view, Marxists should follow Marx and treat the lumpenproletariat with the contempt they deserve. Lying outside the relations of production – that is, as 'non-productive' labour – and living a parasitic mode of life, they were of no interest as far as revolutionary socialist struggle was concerned. Marx and Engels (1970a: 44) said of the lumpenproletariat:

> The 'dangerous class', the social scum, that passively rotting mass thrown off by the lowest layers of old society, may here and there be swept into the movement by the proletarian revolution, its conditions of life, however, prepare it far more for the part of a bribed tool of reactionary intrigue.

This was not a reflection of some grumpy Victorian morality; it was based upon a view of this stratum as being more likely to inhibit than further a revolutionary cause. It was in the context of a discussion of 'productive' and 'unproductive' labour that Marx referred ironically to the 'productivity' of crime (see Chapter 3).

Engels's (1969) *The Condition of the Working Class in England* stands as a denunciation of the life conditions that the working class was subject to at that time (1844–45), and a denunciation of the capitalist mode of production which he saw as producing and sustaining those conditions. He discussed crime within the context of a brutal wage labour system. Out of this system arose economic deprivation and the demoralization of increasing numbers of the working class. Engels contended that crime was an inevitable response, as summed up in this rather deterministic passage:

If the influences demoralizing to the working man act more powerfully, more concentratedly than usual, he becomes an offender as certainly as water abandons the fluid for the vaporous state at 80 degrees, Reaumur. Under the brutal and brutalizing treatment of the bourgeoisie, the working man becomes precisely as much a thing without volition as water, and is subject to the laws of Nature with precisely the same necessity; at a certain point all freedom ceases. (Ibid. 159)

There are, however, more 'voluntaristic' elements to be found in Engels's discussion. Faced with economic deprivation, he argued, the worker either 'merely strives to make life endurable while abandoning the effort to break the yoke' (ibid. 145), or he in some way revolts. Using this reasoning, Engels goes on to outline a number of possible, criminal, responses. These 'conflictual' crimes may sometimes be committed by the working class against the working class, and are seen as representing a caricature of capitalism itself: 'This war of all against all . . . it is only the logical sequel of the principle involved in free competition' (ibid. 162). In some cases, though, crime was directed at the rich:

The working man lived in poverty and want, and saw that others were better off than he. It was not clear to his mind why he, who did more for society than the rich idler, should be the one to suffer under these conditions. Want conquered his inherited respect for the sacredness of property, and he stole. (Ibid. 240)

Engels stresses the inevitability of this conflict, and its potential for development into more mature, class-based economic, then political, struggle against the bourgeoisie: 'The revolt of the workers began soon after the first industrial development, and has passed through several phases... The earliest, crudest and least fruitful form of this rebellion was that of crime' (ibid. 240).

Engels associated different types of criminal activity with different types of consciousness. However, *class* consciousness is not present in any of the three types described above: crime determined by conditions of brutality, crime reflecting capitalist values, and crime based on taking from the rich. *Class* consciousness involves participants having collective class interests: 'As a class, they first manifest opposition to the bourgeoisie when they resisted the introduction of machinery at the very beginning of the industrial period . . . factories were demolished and machinery destroyed' (ibid. 241).

The fifth possibility for Engels was when the working class used crime in the struggle for socialism.

Marx too saw crime as an inevitable response to the conditions of life created by capitalism. Crime arose as a symptom of the contradictions within capitalism, and as capitalism progressed he believed that the total amount of crime would increase. He did not, however, see crime *per se* as revolutionary. Crime was: 'the struggle of the isolated individual against the prevailing conditions' (Marx and Engels, 1965: 367). He was aware that crime covered a spectrum of behaviours, though in each case his overriding concern was with the efficacy of the behaviour in terms of the workers' struggle for socialism. Thus the fact that crime is 'against' the capitalist's law was irrelevant. However, certain types of crime, such as machine smashing, have a special significance for Marx and Engels: they represented forms of criminal activity which presaged a more mature political struggle. This is an important point when we come to consider attempts by more recent Marxists to politicize criminal behaviour. Whilst Marx was aware of the ways in which law functioned in the interests of capital, he was never led into the position of romanticizing crime. Engels, too, in no way romanticized crime. Even crime that involved stealing from the 'rich idler' was described as the 'crudest, least fruitful form of rebellion'.

Taylor, Walton and Young and the politicization of deviance

A central thread running through *The New Criminology*, and latched on to by a number of critical criminologists in the 1970s, was that the deviant was actively committed to breaking bourgeois rules, hence 'much' deviance was in itself political. 'Deviance' and 'political' were therefore seen as qualities of the act. Hirst (1975a: 218) was not alone in his retort that:

> The romanticisation of crime, the recognition in the criminal of a rebel 'alienated' from society, is, for Marxism, a dangerous political ideology. It leads *inevitably* . . . to the estimation of the lumpenproletariat as a revolutionary force.

Obviously, if we adhere to a strict Marx-derived line, and equate criminality with the lumpenproletariat, this does follow. However, this is to assume that all crime has essentially the same qualities, based upon lumpen-type consciousness, which would contradict Hirst's argument that we should not accept bourgeois categories. And, in fact, he referred to crimes such as mob agitation, machine smashing and industrial sabotage as 'having a more obviously "political" quality'. The question remains, though, on what basis do we separate political from non-political crime? Marx's view of the lumpenproletariat as the source of most crime, a view that Hirst endorsed, is problematic in that it ignores the vast amount of law breaking carried out by other sections of society, and Hirst's critique of Taylor, Walton and Young to some extent rests on this understanding of the lumpenproletariat, or some supposed modern-day equivalent.

Politicizing deviance: nuts, sluts, preverts . . . and revolutionaries?

During the 1970s a number of left, critical criminologists focused on what they saw as the political content of deviant/criminal activities. Some saw virtually all such activities, if carried out by the working class, as forms of political action, others concentrated on specific instances. In his review of Marxist criminology during that period, Ronald Hinch (1983: 69) has written:

> The exact meaning given to crime as a political act, of course, varied. For some . . . the act itself constituted a political statement, while for others . . . the act had to be accompanied by a conscious intent to rebel. In most instances the result was a blurring of the relation between the act, the intent of the act, and the class struggle. Indeed, it appeared that for some . . . the class struggle and crime were inseparable.

Basically, the argument was that some (or all) so-called conventional crime, as well as more obvious forms of working-class resistance, such as urban protest, represented a threat to capitalist society, a society whose structural arrangements had shaped the criminality in the first place. Deviance/crime was characterized as proto-revolutionary activity. One of the strongest advocates of this view, Geoff Pearson (1975: 96–7) argued that since the late 1960s various sociologists had attempted to show how deviant behaviour was in itself political: 'Or, more specifically, that deviance should be grasped as a primitive crypto-political action, in the same way that social bandits in peasant societies, or the machine smashing of the Luddites, represented a primitive political force.'

These two terms 'crypto-political' and 'primitive rebellion', derived from Habermas and Hobsbawm respectively, were widely used at this time. Pearson supported his argument by giving examples of research that had broken with traditional approaches and looked at rule breaking in political terms: Goldman (1959) on school vandalism and truancy (an early precursor of this type of work), I. Taylor (1971) on soccer hooliganism, and his own study of 'Paki-bashing' (Pearson, 1976). Often those engaging in these deviant activities were cast in the role of Robin Hood figures striking out against an unjust society. Thus some vandals, truants, soccer hooligans and Paki-bashers were lumped together within the same analytical scheme as representatives of crypto-political action and, sometimes, as 'folk heroes'.

The problems associated with this kind of reasoning are exemplified by Pearson's Paki-bashing study set in a north-east Lancashire cotton town (for a detailed critique of this study see Tierney, 1980). Although carried out in the mid-1970s, the research was based on incidents that occurred in the summer of 1964, when, according to Pearson, a 'flood' of Paki-bashing hit the town. It was, he argued, 'a primitive form of political and economic struggle . . . a rudimentary form of political action' (Pearson, 1976: 69). He also made the unsubstantiated claim that those involved were viewed as 'folk heroes': 'the misdirected heroism of the Paki-basher' (ibid. 80). This, in effect, got uncomfortably near to accusing the town's residents of racist complicity (coincidently, it was my home town, and I was living there in 1964). Pearson compares the actions of the Paki-bashers to the political actions of the machine-smashing handloom weavers from an earlier period in Lancashire's history. It is a complex study which is, unfortunately, consistently misunderstood:

> so that a myth has grown up that he was suggesting that high unemployment during the period referred to in the study led to racist attacks on Pakistanis. Given that unemployment in the town was at that time less than 1%, his argument has to be more sophisticated than that. (Tierney, 1988: 145)

On the basis of Pearson's own sources the so-called Paki-bashing that occurred hardly constituted a 'flood', and on the evidence available it would be stretching credulity to characterize those involved as latter-day Luddites, folk heroes, or crypto-political revolutionaries. Most of those involved seem to have been motivated by the very unromantic desire for revenge.

Youth subcultures and politics

As we have seen, most orthodox studies of adolescent delinquency have reflected the message given by official statistics and assumed that in the main delinquency was a feature of working-class life. On the other hand, orthodox studies of youth culture have minimized or ignored the importance of class, seeing youth culture as a largely classless phenomenon, simply structured around the fact of belonging to a certain age group. By the 1970s, studies of youth were concerned to rectify this.

On a different level, we might question the extent to which orthodox studies of youth culture were able to *understand* those they were studying. Consider this curious example from Cyril Smith's (1970: 28) book on adolescence republished (with corrections) in 1970, and conjuring up an image of Cliff Richard being 'discovered' in the *Two I's* coffee bar, circa 1958: 'Teenage culture in Britain was generated, and is still largely sustained by male entertainers performing in coffee bars in city centres.' And, in a rush of elitism:

> The conformity of the young in Britain is in line with the conformity of the adult population . . . for they are the successful products of a stable family life. They have, most of them, belonged to youth organisations managed by adults permeated with the values of the Establishment and breeding respect in them for

the churches, monarchy, and their aristocracy . . . They have accepted without protest the weight on their young shoulders of tradition in the public schools and grammar schools, and they become charmed by their privileges. (Ibid. 95)

By the 1970s work explicitly linking youth subcultural formations to class were emerging. Partly because researchers were unable to find structured delinquent gangs in Britain of the sort discovered by American researchers, subcultural theory in this country tended to concern itself with youth subcultures and leisure more than delinquency as such. Of particular importance in this respect was the work produced by the Birmingham Centre for Contemporary Cultural Studies. John Muncie (1984: 97) points to the central elements of this research:

On the one hand the meaning of subcultural style was examined through various ethnogaphic and semiological analyses: on the other, the political implications of deviancy were explored through investigations of the structural and class position of various subcultures.

This work, then, provided a further example of that strand of radical thought that sought to politicize deviant activities.

The Birmingham Centre research put class and class conflict at the centre of the stage, whilst examining the impact of social and economic change in the postwar period on working-class youth. This involved research on a range of subcultural styles, for example, Teddy Boys, Mods, and skinheads. To some extent the researchers agreed with Downes (1966) and saw these styles as products of a parent working-class culture, though they represented an 'intense articulation' of that culture. Clarke *et al.* (1976) argued that ruling class culture is the dominant culture in society, and is therefore a dominant ideology. This class will endeavour to shape other, subordinate cultures, so that they conform with this dominant ideology. Working-class youth subcultures, he argued, arose as threats to this ideology, because they developed alternative ideas about what a 'teenager' should be like, what leisure should be used for, what is an appropriate dress style, and so on. Clarke and his colleagues at the Birmingham Centre thus put forward the view that youth subcultures were, at a symbolic level, oppositional.

Phil Cohen's (1972) article on the theme of youth subcultures as solutions to stresses and contradictions existing within working-class communities in the East End of London was being described as 'seminal' by the middle of the 1970s. Redevelopment and rationalization in the East End of London during the postwar period had destroyed traditional neighbourhoods, led to a decline in local job opportunities, and created increasingly privatized families. These changes produced disruptions and dislocations in working-class culture, and Cohen saw the various youth subcultures as providing not 'real' solutions to these problems, but, rather, what he called 'magical' solutions. Young people, he argued, used their subculture as an expression of an 'imaginary relation' (a term he borrowed from the French Marxist Althusser), that is, a relation expressed in terms of symbols (styles of dress, haircuts, etc.) and feelings. Paul Willis (1978) made a similar point in his study of the 'cultural politics' of bike boys and hippies. The view of youth subcultures as attempts to recapture some of the socially cohesive elements of working-class culture destroyed by postwar social change provided an important backdrop to much of the work at the Birmingham Centre.

It is worth pausing to examine the place of consciousness in Cohen's analysis: how did the Teddy Boys, skinheads, and others, understand their actions? This is an important consideration when assessing all attempts to make 'deviant' activities into something political. Cohen's statement that 'The latent function of subculture is . . . to express and resolve . . . contradictions', implies that those involved did not have as a conscious aim the resolution of contradictions, but rather that their actions fulfilled this function. This use of a form of functionalism seemed to get round the problem of consciousness, yet at the same time created its own problems. Clearly, skinheads, for instance, did not consciously devise a programme aimed at recapturing lost working-class community, but the *sort* of consciousness involved is important. As a subcultural theorist, Cohen took consequences and worked backwards. Thus skinheads presented an already existing representation of an 'imaginary solution', which focused the analysis on subcultural consequences, but ignored the subjective intent as an element in the original formation of the subculture.

Also at the Birmingham Centre, John Clarke and Tony Jefferson (1976) drew up a typology of forms of consciousness among working-class youth. This 'ideal type' classificatory scheme was designed to indicate a range of possible responses, at the level of consciousness, to their social worlds. In two of the categories a political dimension was suggested: 'traditional delinquency', where opposition to established authority is limited to illegal activities, and 'deviant youth culture', which was seen as expressing a moment of originality, a creative assertion of deviant consciousness: 'These styles offer a symbolic critique of the established order and, in so doing, represent a latent form of "non-ideological" politics' (ibid. 148). For the authors, this was the nearest that working-class youth got to opposing a dominant ideology, for in their analysis they dispensed entirely with a more mature political consciousness situated in what they classified as the 'oppositional category'. Now, while working-class adolescents tend not to get involved in large numbers with political movements on the left, they do join and actively participate in such movements, and to an extent that does not justify writing them off completely. The methods of research employed in these kinds of studies will, in fact, generally lead to such examples being excluded from consideration, simply because they begin with a 'deviant' subculture and work backwards.

The title of Corrigan and Frith's (1976: 237) article, 'The politics of youth culture', promised to confront head on the question of just how political youth cultures are: 'We are thinking, for example, of the ways in which kids can use the symbols of pop culture as a source of collective power in their struggle with schools or police.' It was working-class culture at its moment of creation that was seen as representing the most potent mode of resistance: youth cultures were described as the 'crystallization' of rebellion at the symbolic level. From this vantage point, they are a manifestation of working-class power to redefine and rework meaning systems. Around this general framework Corrigan and Frith attempted to map out the guidelines for a political reading of working-class youth cultures, but the analysis fizzled out with the comment that 'at present we just don't have the sort of knowledge on which clear answers to these questions can be based' (ibid. 236). I am not sure that that knowledge was ever forthcoming. Again, a basic problem with the material that came from the Birmingham Centre was a failure to come to terms with a clear understanding of 'political', and it is this in particular that dogged subsequent attempts to construct a convincing theoretical framework in this area. The political content of youth subcultures was predicated on their existence as 'struggles' against alternative, dominant, meaning systems, but of interest here are the types of meaning involved, the extent to which the diffusion of youth subcultures weakens this resistance, and the relationship between resistance at a symbolic level and resistance at a concrete material level.

During the 1970s, research continued to be carried out on the theme of youth subcultures and 'style' and 'cultural symbolization' (e.g. Hebdige, 1979; and see Muncie, 1984, for a review). These studies emphasized that the construction of style was an act of creation and a form of resistance. In particular, attention was focused on the ways in which youth subcultures took over and reshaped or redefined the original cultural meaning attached to an object. Items of clothing, signs such as the swastika, safety pins, hair style, and so on, are infused with new symbolic meanings. To this extent, it was argued, some young people are involved in cultural resistance. The task for sociologists was to 'read' the signs, to decode the new meanings (see Hall and Jefferson, 1976). Clarke introduced the concept of 'bricolage' (which he borrowed from Lévi-Strauss) to describe the process of transforming the symbolic meaning of objects.

One of the difficulties with the 'reading the signs' approach to subcultural theory, as Stan Cohen (1980) has pointed out, is that it often seems to distance the perceived meanings of cultural symbols from the subjective intent of the participants. The wearing of a swastika might be decoded as a subversive shock tactic directed at mainstream society, and in the same symbolic universe, therefore, as an unconventional hair style. It might, though, simply mean that the wearer is a supporter of fascist movements.

A further point also needs to be made. Given that, according to the

Birmingham Centre, youth subcultures do not offer 'real' solutions to contradictions or problems, an important question to ask is: To what extent do they provide even an 'imaginary' solution? The political dimension to subcultures was seen as being located in the subculture's control of meaning. The problem with the concept of 'imaginary solution' was that it implied that from the individual's point of view, life actually did become (via his or her 'imaginary relations') exciting, interesting, full of action, or whatever. Thus, although the real problems of life were not altered, it appeared to the participants that, in a sense, they were. Subcultures became a sort of sociological Valium. However, as with Valium, the effects are only temporary, and 'real relations' can break through even in leisure time. The bleaker realities of life are not swept away totally in leisure time, even at the 'imaginary level' and, indeed, are likely to have a strong determining influence on what leisure can offer. To imply that working-class youth subcultures provide a total symbolically constituted resolution of problems is to endow those concerned with unrealistic amounts of power.

Efforts to politicize deviance or the subcultural affiliations of working-class youth did not, at the time, escape criticism. Commenting on his influential study of working-class youth in 'Roundhouse', a neighbourhood of tenements in Liverpool, published in 1974, Howard Parker puts a different slant on 'oppositional' subcultures:

> parents, kids and adolescents basically share so many of the basic structural constraints and social inequalities forced upon them that their world views are consistent and in harmony much more than they are in opposition . . . (this) can be seen to be to a large extent an accommodation to a particular structural situation rather than a perpetuating rejection of dominant values and life styles. (Parker, 1976: 47)

There was, too, an important theoretical debate between Geoff Pearson and Paul Rock. For Rock (1973: 103), the political status of an activity derived from the meaning that it had for the participants, in other words the type of consciousness involved was crucial: 'Politicized deviancy may be defined as that activity which is regarded as expressly political by its participants.'

Pearson, though, objected to this formulation because, as he put it, 'it reduces politics to a "meaning"'. This criticism of Rock implied a rejection of schools of thought which stressed the primacy of subjective intent or 'meaning'. In Rock's view, deviance only became political when those classed as deviants actively worked to change the attitudes and responses of the social audience by redrawing the boundaries between 'moral' and 'immoral'. Thus consciousness and action were inextricably linked, and he refused to make all deviants into political figures, a position he saw as misplaced romanticism. Rock's dourly anti-romantic stance clearly did not accord with Pearson's approach which made the 1964 Paki-bashers into

political activitists. In effect, Rock's solution to the problem of deciding what
was meant by political deviance was to bracket off what are relatively more
obvious forms of political deviance – the protests of the poor in the ghetto,
Black Power, and so on – and to this extent he dealt with the same groups
as Horowitz and Leibowitz, Hall, and Stan Cohen. However, both Pearson
and Rock ultimately met the same problem: Where does the boundary
between political and non-political deviance come?

Critical criminology: deviance, crime and power

The second theme emerging out of the post-new deviancy period – deviance
and power – was also in evidence in *The New Criminology*, along with the
theme of politicizing deviance, as discussed above. The theme of deviance
and power encompassed two elements: the powerful as instrumental rule
makers, and the powerful as cynical rule breakers. It was the first of these
that assumed particular importance among a growing number of critical/
radical criminologists in the 1970s, with the concept of 'crime' being
preferred to that of 'deviance'.

With the qualification that this describes the discipline-based, intellectual
momentum leading to these developments, rather than the sources of the
theoretical concepts, Galliher (1978: 253–4) has summed up radical
criminology's journey from the 1960s as follows:

> the popularity of the labeling perspective with its emphasis on societal reaction
> and created deviance seems to have provided the conditions in the discipline for
> the swift re-emergence of the conflict orientation once it was triggered by the
> political milieu . . . The conflict perspective stressing powerful interest groups'
> control of the law, police, and courts, in turn created the intellectual basis for the
> emergence of Marxism in criminology in the 1970's.

In passing it can be noted that plotting the developments in critical/radical
criminology from the middle of the 1970s is accompanied with certain
difficulties. Theoretical discussions were often complicated, sometimes
obscure, and occasionally turgid and, in addition, given that this was still a
time of intellectual ferment, some writers were adding to the confusion by
vacating theoretical positions with which they had been closely associated
in favour of different schools of thought.

During the first part of the 1970s, conflict theory and early versions of
Marxist criminology had taken an instrumentalist approach to analyses of
rule making. However, by the middle of the decade critical academic work
was increasingly concerned with developing a more sophisticated understanding of the nature of law, one that transcended the fairly crude
instrumentalist approaches. This indicates another important feature of

these developments in critical criminology, namely, that attention switched from the actions of the criminal to the legal order and reactions to the criminal, bringing with it an emphasis on the sociology of law.

The powerful as law makers

In the ensuing debate among Marxist writers, a number of key questions emerged:

- In what ways, and to what extent, does law protect the interests of the ruling class?

- Is law, by definition, 'bad' because it is a product of, or is present in, a capitalist society?

- Is it possible to achieve progressive, socialist-oriented, reform of law within the context of capitalism?

- Is law necessary in a socialist society, or can regulation and order be accomplished without a legal order and the criminalization of some behaviour?

Broadly speaking, critical criminologists saw law as bourgeois law, and therefore the legal order in a capitalist society existed to further the interests of capital by creating appropriate conditions for the pursuit of profit. This required:

- The creation and enforcement of laws, and hence definitions of 'crime', aimed at regulating the workforce and surplus populations.

- The creation of laws pertaining to notions of private property, thereby underpinning the capitalist's right to own the means of production.

- The use of law as an educative device whereby relations between labour and capital are ideologically sanctioned and justified.

- The use of law and penal sanctions against the least powerful who constitute a threat to the system.

However, it was recognized that such formulations raised complex and difficult issues when trying to construct theoretical explanations. The precise nature of the relationship between the state, the ruling class and the legal order was, in particular, an issue that stimulated intense and highly complex debates. Other important issues had to be addressed, and incorporated into theoretical formulations. Some laws, such as those relating to welfare, consumer protection, unfair dismissal and health and safety at work, seemed to act primarily in the interests of the working, rather than ruling, class. Similarly, legislation relating to, for instance, homo-sexuality and abortion seemed not to be acting directly in the interests of capitalists (see Greenberg, 1976).

An instrumental Marxist approach to law owed much to a well-known statement by Marx and Engels (1970b: 37) in the *Manifesto of the Communist Party*, where, referring to political leadership, they wrote: 'The executive of the modern state is but a committee for managing the common affairs of the whole bourgeoisie.' It was an approach based upon an instrumentalist school of thought in political theory which argued that powerful members of the state apparatus were either themselves capitalists, or they strongly identified, at a subjective level, with the goals and interests of the capitalist class (Miliband, 1969; Domhoff, 1970). The study of law, therefore, was based on the premise that law reflects the interests of the ruling class. This was a similar position to that taken by American conflict theorists, except that conflict theorists tended to use the concept of elites, rather than ruling class, and to reduce the relationship between these elites and the legal order to a sort of conspiracy theory. From this perspective, those with economic power are able to exert direct influence on the state and the legal system. At the same time, they will use whatever ideological means are available in order to present an image of law as neutral and even-handed – both 'in the book' and 'in action' – and in the process construct notions such as the 'rule of law'. From a radical instrumentalist standpoint this merely masks the partiality of law. As Bankowski and Mungham (1975: 29) grimly put it, law is a 'means of domination, oppression and desolation'. For other examples, see Takagi (1974); Quinney (1975); Michalowski and Bohlander (1976); Hepburn (1977).

Structural Marxist approaches

By the second half of the 1970s a number of Marxist-influenced writers were criticizing instrumentalist accounts of the legal order. These came to be seen as altogether too neat and tidy and, in the style of conspiracy theory, suggesting that somehow the state and the ruling class form a monolithic whole, working together harmoniously for their own benefit. Thus when dealing with, for instance, the issue of some law appearing to be disadvantageous to the ruling class, instrumentalists argued that it must in some way be advantageous, otherwise it would not have been created (see Thompson, 1975, for a defence of the concept of 'rule of law', and the argument that law is not always oppressive, and is sometimes the result of working-class struggle). Instrumentalist critiques entailed searching for the 'real', nefarious motives lying behind even apparently benign law. Wolfe (1971: 19), for example, has said: 'there are times when sections of the ruling class become sponsors of reform in order to rationalize the system and make it work better.' And, on disputes within the class holding power: 'Superficially, groups within the dominant class may differ on some issues. But they share many interests, and they can entirely exclude members of the other classes from the political process' (Quinney, 1975: 288). This is a view that has permeated into some radical analyses of policing, and is sardonically summed up by Young (1986):

> It is a strange world, bourgeois economists may argue about the logic of capital – as do Marxist economists – but seemingly a local police chief has no problem in understanding what capital requires of him nor does the lone school teacher facing a disruptive class.

Structuralism detaches the workings of the state, the economy and the legal order from the actual individuals concerned. The nature of law, therefore, does not result from the imposition of the will of the powerful as a conscious act, but rather develops as part of the functioning of a total system having reality at a structural level. Put simply, whichever party is in government, capitalism is always in power (Althusser, 1971; Poulantzas, 1973). Furthermore, structuralism sees the institutions of the state as having 'relative autonomy' (Althusser, 1971), although in the final analysis the economy is the determining force. On the basis of this formulation, it logically follows that the state will sometimes introduce laws that do not represent the interests of the ruling class, or that disadvantage certain sections of the ruling class, because of the structural requirement for an ordered, compliant society overall. This is necessary because capitalism is always in a state of tension due to its internal contradictions. It is the capitalist system as a total social formation that is ultimately at stake (Werkentin, Hofferbert and Baurmann, 1974; Beirne, 1979). For a critique of analyses that reduced the nature of law to the demands of the economy see Cain and Hunt, 1979.

By the end of the 1970s a large body of work, with contributions from a wide range of academic disciplines – though usually built around the sociology of law – had been produced. The intention of this work was to develop a theoretical, Marxist-informed explanation of law, and a better understanding of its practical significance. In this context Fine's (1979) *Capitalism and the Rule of Law* was particularly significant. This was a collection of articles by scholars explicitly committed to a multidisciplinary project of constructing a Marxist theoretical framework for the study of the legal order. Drawing on the work of Gramsci, Althusser, Foucault, and the Bolshevik jurist Pashukanis, whose work appeared in the 1920s, the book was seen as marking the triumph of structuralism over instrumentalism. Pashukanis's 'commodity-exchange' theory of law was a major influence, in particular his ideas on the bourgeois *form* of law in capitalist society. Thus he accepted the need for social regulation and order based upon 'rules', but developed a critique of the legal rules specific to capitalism; for these, he argued, functioned to produce bourgeois social order. In a socialist society, he said, the form of law would disappear, so that regulation was no longer based on state-sponsored legal rules, but on informally generated codes of conduct derived from working-class 'social defence', in line with the needs of socialist construction. This had echoes of Taylor, Walton and Young's arguments for 'socialist diversity' in a crime-free society, which adds a touch of irony, for one of the contributors to this book was Jock Young, who by then was distancing himself from many of the ideas contained in *The New Criminology*, ideas he was labelling as 'left idealism'.

Pat Carlen and Mike Collison's (1980) *Radical Issues in Criminology*, also a collection of articles, directed itself towards a Marxist-informed engagement with practical issues of regulation within capitalist societies, with a view to providing a 'counterbalance to recent libertarian, anarchistic and utopian trends in criminology'. Although the contributors did not share the same 'radical political space', this too reflected the growing criticism of the type of criminology associated with *The New Criminology*, and indicates the direction taken by radical criminology in the 1980s, when a serious debate opened up between so-called left-realists and so-called left-idealists. Laurie Taylor's (1980) article in *Radical Issues in Criminology* was, he said, not a defence of 'legalism' – that is, blind faith in the rule of law – but a defence of 'civil liberties' and the use of law to bring power to heel. This was a common thread running through the book: that socialist theory and practice can be applied to bourgeois law in progressive ways. Clearly, this is an issue that is central to socialist action (or inaction) on the part of criminologists. The book supports the idea of intervening and challenging law, as a springboard to, as the authors saw it, greater things, though there was a clear tension between this and 'mere reformism'.

On a general level the book was 'critical' in the sense of attempting to emphasize problems and contradictions in bourgeois law, criminalization and penal practices, and problems within current socialist criminology. The critique of the latter centred on those who seemingly did not wish to sully their hands with intervention aimed at changing 'unjust' laws, or ensuring that law makers and law enforcers themselves kept within the law. Paul Hirst's article in *Radical Issues in Criminology* (Hirst, 1980) stands as a critique of those who would, in his terms, look anarchically towards a crime-free and law-free socialist future. He was, therefore, critical of writers such as Pashukanis and his old adversaries Taylor, Walton and Young.

Policing the crisis

Drawing on the language of warfare, Colin Sumner (1981) has described the onslaught by Marxist theoreticians on the ideas associated with *The New*

Criminology during the 1970s. Hirst's various critiques had worked like a 'defoliant' on the concepts of crime and deviance; 'Parisian B-52s' in the shape of Althusserian structuralism had 'devastated the terrain'. According to Sumner (1981: 277–8), though, by the end of the 1970s there was a silver lining for Marxist studies of crime indicated by:

1. the return to reading Marx,
2. the epistemological dilution of structuralist Marxism through its confrontation with the nasty business of empirical reality in the booming area of cultural studies,
3. the stimulation of 'quality' Marxist studies of crime and law from outside the sociology of deviance, and
4. the deconstruction of the welfare state and an increased significance of criminal law in a period of heightening social tension.

All of these factors, in Sumner's view, were expressed in Hall *et al.*'s (1978) *Policing the Crisis*. Subtitled *Mugging, the state and law and order*, the book addressed what were seen as moral panics over so-called mugging in the early part of the 1970s, and drew on the cultural studies work of the Birmingham Centre for Contemporary Cultural Studies (where Hall was the Director), and Gramsci's writings on hegemony and ideology. The argument was that exaggerated claims were made by control agencies and the mass media regarding an outbreak of mugging. Not only was the amount of mugging inflated, but street robbery was itself incorrectly linked directly to young black males. In a sophisticated analysis the authors argue that the British state was having to cope with considerable social and economic problems, thus creating a 'crisis in hegemony': in other words, the authority of the state was under threat. The response by the state was to deflect attention away from the 'real' bases of the crisis by generating a moral panic over mugging. Although Hall *et al.* never suggested that *no* muggings occurred, what they did argue was that the state overreacted to what was actually going on: special police anti-mugging squads were set up, much space was devoted to 'black muggers' by the mass media, and stiff prison sentences were handed out by the courts. Arguing that the key to support for the established order lies in the creation of 'consent' rather than coercion, Hall *et al.* saw the state tapping into already existing popular stereotypes regarding black youth, and popular explanations of criminality based upon 'permissiveness' and a 'soft' criminal justice system. The 'black mugger' was, therefore, created as a scapegoat for the social anxieties arising from social and economic dislocations.

Powerful law breakers

This is the second strand arising out of the theme of power and deviance, and, as well as featuring in *The New Criminology*, it proved attractive to other writers on the left in the 1970s especially in the United States. This theme is part of a tradition of 'exposé' criminology that can be traced back to Sutherland during the 1940s; the conflict theorist, Chambliss, and his study of law breaking among powerful elites in Seattle, has already been examined.

Studies of white-collar and corporate crime were important in that they directed attention away from the powerless and marginalized, and towards other more powerful groups in society, thereby illustrating how conceptualizations of crime derived from official sources lead to a mystification of reality. In an important study of criminal activities among American business corporations, Frank Pearce (1976) showed that the estimated amount of money involved was far in excess of the monetary value of conventional crime. In spite of this, culprits were rarely brought before the courts. On the basis of a number of case studies, Pearce concluded that the main examples of *organized* crime were to be found among the large business corporations in the United States. Pearce develops his argument by attempting to explain why there were so few prosecutions. In his view, prosecutions were rare because to do otherwise would subvert the ideology that the bulk of crime is carried out by the poor, which would create a crisis of legitimacy for the capitalist system. He also includes an analysis of the links between big business and organized (as normally understood) crime, in which he paints a picture of a history of collusion, graft and complicity: for example, Ford and General Motors' use of gangsters in the 1930s to threaten and intimidate striking workers.

There is not the space here to examine these points in detail, but a number of writers focused their attention on specific, and sometimes spectacular, examples (for a recent, and excellent review, see Nelken, 1994). Dowie (1988) brought to light the now well-known case of the Pinto car made by the Ford Motor Company in the 1970s. According to Dowie, Ford went ahead with the manufacture and sale of the Pinto when they knew that, because of a crucial design fault, it was dangerous. He estimated that by so doing, Ford were responsible for between 500 and 900 unnecessary deaths on American highways. Caudill (1977) documented the case of the Scotia Coal Company in Kentucky which failed to conform with safety requirements, in spite of a record of hundreds of previous violations of safety requirements, and in whose pit 26 miners died in an accident. A study of what he saw as lax attitudes towards safety in the North Sea oil industry by Carson (1981) offered a sobering backdrop to the subsequent destruction of the *Piper Alpha* oil rig in 1988, and with it the loss of 168 lives. The nuclear reactor meltdown at Chernobyl, and the chemical explosion at Bhopal, provide further examples where question marks over safety have arisen.

Although this takes us into the 1980s, it is appropriate to dwell on this theme a little longer at this point. Steven Box (1987) provides one of the few analyses of links between economic recession and not just conventional crime, but corporate crime. He refers to an American study by Clinard and Yeager (1981) which did address this dimension. In their estimation: 'financial performance was found to be associated with illegal behavior . . . firms in depressed industries as well as relatively poorly performing firms in all industries tend to violate the law to greater degrees' (quoted in Box, 1987: 99).

Box then goes on to examine data from various sources in this country concluding that corporate and white-collar crime do seem to correlate with economic recession. Figures from the Health and Safety Executive for the period 1980–84 showed a drop in the number of visits to establishments by inspectors coupled with an increase in enforcement notices (by 16 per cent from 30.9 to 35.9 per 1,000 visits). If local authority enforcement notices are added, then between 1975 and 1982 Box found an increase of over 110 per cent. Looking at the incidence of fatal accidents and serious injuries at work as an indicator of 'corporate violations of regulation', Box writes:

> what has changed markedly during the 1980s is the total number of such incidents. Thus from 1981 when there were 67.9 per 100,000 employees, to 1984 when the figure was 87.0 per 100,000 there was an increase of 28% . . . this is a remarkable increase and it indicates clearly just how far health and safety conditions at work have deteriorated under the impact of recession. (Ibid. 101)

A similar story emerges when figures relating to bankruptcy and underpayment of the (now defunct) Wages Council legal minimum wage are examined.

Three other theoretical strands had become influential among some criminologists by the 1970s – phenomenology, control theory and feminism – and these will be examined here before we move on to the final section.

Phenomenology and criminology

The fundamental message from phenomenology is that those things and activities that make up the social world do not possess absolute, essential meaning. Out of practical necessity, members of society construct shared perceptions of these things and activities, and thus endow them with meaning. Phenomenal reality, therefore, is reality as we perceive it – as it appears to be for us. Social order requires that to a significant extent these meanings are shared. Those aspects of philosophical phenomenology taken up by sociologists were concerned with the production and nature of this practical knowledge shared by members of society. Clearly, these are deep waters. Question marks are placed against all notions of knowledge, for what is 'knowable' is not an essential 'real' social world, but the social world as it is perceived: a taken-for-granted, common-sensically understood world. This is why phenomenological research is oriented towards providing accounts of the social world from the point of view of participants. Conventional social science is criticized for imposing its own, ready-made conceptual reality onto those being studied (what Schutz, 1972, calls 'constructs of the second degree').

Because phenomenology is concerned with the most fundamental processes involved in the production of meaning, it detaches itself from the study of specific substantive areas as such. Thus although a number of writers in the 1960s and early 1970s utilized the ideas of phenomenology when looking at issues of crime and deviance (e.g. Sudnow, 1965; Bittner, 1967; Douglas, 1967, 1971; Cicourel, 1968; Matza, 1969; Phillipson, 1971), by the middle of the 1970s phenomenological studies specifically oriented towards crime and deviance had largely petered out.

However, whilst phenomenology did attract a good deal of criticism from within criminology, especially from structuralists who were unhappy with what they saw as its utter subjectivism, it did have some important influences. This was particularly apparent with respect to official statistics relating to the amount and distribution of crime, and the social categories routinely used by criminal justice agencies, and criminologists, such as 'thief', 'alcoholic', 'victim', and so forth. Jack Douglas's (1967) study of the interpretive processes involved in the construction of suicide rates, for instance, provided a strong challenge to positivist approaches that followed the lead taken by Durkheim in his study of suicide. As Douglas argued, suicide was not a 'real' thing existing 'out there' as an objective event; actual suicide rates were produced by organizations and the individuals working in them according to shared meaning systems (see, also, Atkinson, 1979).

Ethnomethodology

Ethnomethodology grew out of sociological phenomenology during the 1960s, and has shown more durability in terms of a continuing contribution specifically to the sociology of crime and deviance. As a perspective it rests on three assumptions (Jones, 1993: 97):

1. Social life is inherently precarious. Anything could happen in social interaction. However:
2. Actors never realise this, because
3. They unwittingly possess the practical abilities necessary to make the world appear an ordered place.

Literally defined as 'people's methods', ethnomethodology concerns itself with the empirical exploration of the tacitly understood, everyday methods used by society's members to create order through their interactions (Garfinkel, 1967). As Downes and Rock (1988: 199) say:

> But a number of phenomenologists have become empirical of late. Variously referring to themselves as ethnomethodologists, existential sociologists, and sociologists of everyday life, they rely less obviously upon a search within. They have undertaken meticulous examinations of the conduct of conversation, believing that talk makes a social world.

In a recent discussion Hester and Eglin (1992) illustrate how ethnomethodologists see crime/deviance not as an objective, independent entity, but, rather, as a product of subjective interpretation. Ethnomethodologists, therefore, use a 'constitutive' model, rather than a 'mundane' (Pollner, 1974) or common-sense model; crime/deviance is constituted by an audience's perception of it *as* crime/deviance. An example of mundane reasoning given by Hester and Eglin (1992: 129) concerns the remarks made by a police chief following the trial of some strikers. He was unhappy because the judge had 'thrown out' the charges against them, though in the police chief's view they had acted 'unlawfully':

> from the police chief's point of view, for something to be 'unlawful' it is not crucial that a judge finds it so; rather its unlawfulness exists independently of judicial response . . . Judges, in this view, do not constitute crime in their judicial work, rather they merely respond to its already existing criminal character. This is mundane reasoning *par excellence*: it presumes some independent factual domain of criminality against which human perceptions can either correctly or incorrectly correspond.

For ethnomethodologists, then, Becker's concept of the 'secret deviant', referred to in the earlier discussion of labelling theory, is nonsensical; unlabelled deviance cannot exist. Likewise, in my example of Maradona handling the ball, no foul was committed. These insights from ethnomethodology are important in alerting criminologists to the deeply textured interactional processes at work in the characterization of certain activities as 'crime' or 'deviance', and raise the issue of just what is meant by 'reality'. However, there are people out there shooting cashiers during bank hold-ups, or 'secretly' snorting cocaine, or knowingly inflating their expenses claims. In ethnomethodology's terms none of these are crimes, because that social category has not been assigned to them. But, *something* is going on that makes such activities interesting to (some) criminologists. Focusing on the processes that create crime out of such events, whatever its ultimate value, does leave the question of why people do it in the first place, and why there are laws prohibiting such acts, off the agenda.

Control theory

Control theory in its modern form (versions of it can be traced back to Aristotle, see Downes and Rock, 1988) is primarily associated with the American criminologist Travis Hirschi and his book *Causes of Delinquency* (1969). To some extent control theory's thunder was, at the time, stolen by labelling theory, though more recently it has gained in influence. Downes and Rock identify what they see as possible explanations for control theory's lack of impact:

- It was ignored by many sociologists because its explanation of criminality was seen as too obvious, merely serving to confirm common-sense opinion.

- It gave the appearance of supporting 'law and order' style calls for more discipline and punishment, which liberal–radical sociologists found unacceptable.

- In a modified form Hirschi recycled a number of variables linked to delinquency originally introduced by Eleanor and Sheldon Glueck, whose work was heavily criticized for its individualized and pathological approach to criminality.

Unlike traditional criminology, control theory does not seek to discover the impulses that cause people to break the law. Instead of asking, 'Why do we break the law?', the theory asks, 'Why do we *not* break the law?' Following the classical school of criminology to some extent, control theory sees human beings as rational decision makers. However, whereas the classical school assumed that these decisions were based upon free will, control theory makes no such assumption; the free will versus determinism debate is left open-ended. Consequently, the question of what causal factors 'make' people into law breakers is not posed by the theory. Therefore, as criminal motivations are not relevant to the theory, the ultimate source of those motivations ceases to be an issue.

By asking the question, 'Why do we not break the law?', control theory is suggesting that something special happens to prevent people acting out whatever impulses they may possess. In other words, conformity is explained in terms of certain controls, which in varying degrees make people *unfree* to break rules. Without these controls, and left to our own devices, we would do whatever was required, as we saw it, to look after our own interests. Again, this draws on classical criminology's view of the individual as essentially self-seeking. Control theory thus paints a picture in which all members of society are potentially free to behave in ways that will sometimes entail breaking the law. The task, then, becomes one of identifying those controls that operate to prevent people taking up the

assumptions
of theory

option. Hirschi argued that these controls are located in the social and material bonds that tie individuals to society and to law-abiding behaviour. As rational beings, people make decisions according to the costs and benefits of conformity or nonconformity, and conformity is achieved to the extent that nonconformity is perceived of as a social or material cost. This is not seen as fixed for each individual; circumstances and perceptions can change over time. In a 'post-classical' analysis Bob Roshier (1989: 47) summarizes the bonds that Hirschi said tie people to the conventional order:

> He proposes four bonds: attachment (the extent to which individuals have close emotional ties to other people); commitment (the extent to which they see conventional behaviour, for example at school, as offering immediate or long-term rewards); involvement (the extent to which their time is taken up with conventional activities); belief (the extent to which their beliefs about what is permissible or not coincide with conventional ones).

Hirschi's book largely consists of empirical research, based on a self-report study of over 4,000 12 to 17 year olds, aimed at testing the theory, and this triggered a number of similar research projects throughout the 1970s. Most of the work on 'attachment' has concentrated on family relationships. According to the theory, those families where emotional ties between children and parents are weak, so that children are relatively unconcerned about about their parents' feelings towards delinquency, are more likely to contain delinquent children than are families where the reverse is true. Research has tended to support this idea (e.g. Johnson (1979), Poole and Regoli (1979) and Hirschi himself in the United States; and Wilson and Herbert (1978) and Wilson (1980) in this country). Wilson, for instance, in a study of families living in a deprived inner city neighbourhood, found that non-delinquent children tended to live in families where moral upbringing was strict, and where parents had a protective attitude towards their children in what they defined as a non-threatening environment. 'Attachment' in this context derives from the children's concern that delinquency would be frowned upon by parents; it was not simply the result of living in a 'happy' family.

'Commitment' directs attention to the individual's ability to make rational decisions regarding the costs of law breaking. The degree to which we are committed to conforming behaviour is seen to reflect the degree to which we have a stake in society. Those who subjectively feel that their jobs, reputations and standards of living would be placed at an unacceptable risk if they engaged in delinquency, are less free than others who take up this option when tempted. At first glance this reasoning would appear to suggest that delinquency is more likely to occur among the working class than the middle class, simply because they seem to have less at stake materially. However, Hirschi found that the distribution of delinquency did not follow this pattern: there were no class differentials. Hirschi explains this by arguing that 'commitment' has to be seen from a subjective standpoint. What is important is how the individual perceives the nature of their stake in society. In a development of the ideas of control theory, Steven Box (1981, though originally published in 1971) incorporated some of the insights of labelling theory in order to explain why official statistics show delinquency to be largely a working-class activity, whilst self-report studies, such as Hirschi's, show a more even distribution along class lines. Box argues that official statistics deal with 'secondary deviation' (to use Lemert's term), whilst self-report studies uncover 'primary deviation'. In Box's view, it is the nature of the societal reaction which gives the misleading impression that middle-class youngsters are less delinquent.

A good deal of research has been carried out on the relationship between commitment to education, and consequent 'involvement' in the conformist behaviour necessary for academic success. Research indicates a strong correlation between underachievement at school and delinquency (e.g. Hargreaves, 1967; Thomas, Kreps and Cage, 1977).

The fourth 'bond' discussed by Hirschi, 'belief', refers to the extent to which young people have a commitment to the moral values of conventional society. Again, the evidence from research is that rejection correlates with delinquency (e.g. Cernkovich, 1978). Hirschi found that religious beliefs had little effect on delinquency.

Extending the model

As Box points out, this approach to delinquency only addresses the circumstances that make delinquency possible; it does not explain why some actually commit delinquent acts, whilst others under similar circumstances do not. Box develops this further by taking the analysis beyond the situation where an individual is *free* to engage in deviant behaviour, to situations where they are, first, *able* to deviate, and secondly, *wanting* to deviate.

Whether or not an individual is able to deviate depends, says Box, on the following issues:

- *Secrecy*. Although free to deviate, individuals may feel that they cannot conceal what they do. This introduces 'deterrence theory' into the equation, which was central to the classical school of criminology, though it was not part of Hirschi's original formulation. However, as Box points out, proponents of deterrence theory, such as Gibbs (1975), tend to focus on what they see as objective deterrents, when, in his view, it is the individual's subjective understanding of these deterrents that is crucial.

- *Skills*. This refers to the need for individuals to possess the necessary abilities for the various deviant possibilities.

- *Supply*. Here Box is thinking of the need for individuals to possess the necessary equipment, for example a supply of drugs, or a weapon.

- *Social support*. This directs attention to the social groups of which the individual is a member, which may or may not provide encouragement for deviant behaviour. Again, Box stresses the subjective dimension, by arguing that the importance of the group lies in the meaning attributed to it by the individual. He is critical (as Hirschi was) of 'bad company' explanations of delinquency.

- *Symbolic support*. This has been examined by a number of writers sympathetic to control theory (e.g. Hindelang, 1974; Austin, 1977; Cernkovich, 1978), and recognizes the importance of the group *vis-à-vis* the provision of a framework of moral justification for deviance: for example, 'the victim deserved it'.

Box (1981: 144) continues:

The analysis cannot stop at this point . . . Why would an adolescent who perceived a delinquent act to be one without many costs (in terms of attachments, commitments, beliefs, sanctions and supports) none the less *want* to do it?

His answer to this question is derived from Matza and Sykes (1961) and Matza (1964). They outlined four possibilities that might explain what makes delinquency attractive:

1. Individuals get a thrill out of taking risks, perhaps because an activity is banned, and there may, of course, be pleasure in the act itself.

2. Delinquency may provide a means for confirming and acting out gender roles.

3. Sometimes there is material gain.

4. Matza argued that delinquency offered some possibility of acting creatively, of taking control of one's life, albeit in ways that often hurt others.

As we have seen in the earlier discussion of their work, Matza and Sykes do not equate these values with a specifically working-class culture. In their view, they are 'subterranean values' found throughout society.

Control theory in the 1970s

During the 1970s control theory became increasingly influential, especially among more right-wing criminologists (e.g. Wilson, 1975; van den Haag, 1975; Ehrlich, 1975; Hagan, 1977; Nettler, 1978; and, specifically on the theme of gender and criminality, Hagan, Simpson and Gillis, 1979). As it turned out, this work was to constitute the first phase of an upsurge in right-wing criminology in the 1980s, a criminology drawn in varying degrees to notions of control, deterrence and retribution.

Control theory has also been subjected to critical scrutiny. Control theory contends that it is only designed to make modest claims. Instead of seeking out the answers to 'big' causal questions, it simply focuses on circumstances that 'make delinquency possible'. However, as Downes and Rock (1988: 237) say: 'there is a tendency to overdraw the differences between what are presented as the empirically sound but modest claims of control theory and the empirically unsound but more pretentious alternatives.' These modest claims are seen by control theorists as having the virtue of being supported by empirical evidence, though Downes and Rock indicate a number of problems here. In Hirschi's self-report study, for instance, the definition of 'serious delinquency' is described as 'weak in the extreme'. In addition, and speaking from an interactionist, anti-positivist position, control theory, they say, neglects the different motivations lying behind deviant choices: 'Shorn of any meaning, for control theory deprives it of such, deviance is presumably pursued for the sheer gratification of appetites' (ibid. 238).

Downes and Rock are also critical of control theory for assuming that the acceptance of norms and values is totally dependent upon 'attachments'. There are many different and complex sources of norms and values, and many complex reasons, untouched by control theory, why they are, or are not, subscribed to. Many have criticized control theory for ignoring big structural issues such as class, the nature of law and the role of the law makers and law enforcers. 'Commitment' to school, for instance, may be important, but this needs linking to broader social structural issues relating to the organization of schooling in general. Finally, as control theorists admit, the theory can only explain relatively trivial primary forms of deviance. Therefore, it is not relevant to analyses of professional crime, or the crimes of the powerful.

Feminist perspectives and criminology

Although the material in this book has been presented, broadly speaking, within a chronological framework of decades, obviously this is not meant to suggest that paradigm shifts or key developments in criminological thinking conveniently coincide with particular decades. The difficulties involved in this approach are acknowledged, but some organizing principle is necessary. These difficulties are plainly demonstrated in the case of feminism and criminology: obviously there was no sea change in this field as Big Ben heralded in the New Year in 1980, and again in 1990. However, during the 1970s, feminist contributions to criminology were in the early stages of development, and the amount and theoretical sophistication of this work was to increase significantly in the 1980s. Although some American work had preceded it, Carol Smart's *Women, Crime and Criminology*, published in 1976, is generally seen as the first example of British 'feminist criminology', and in common with the rest of the early work, was exploratory, and was subjected to extensive review and re-orientation later on. This early work tended to focus on females as offenders, or as victims (of crime or of the criminal justice system).

Critical analyses during the 1970s addressed four themes: invisibility, distortion, the criminal justice system and victimization.

Invisibility

The discussion so far of the predominant schools of thought in criminology testifies to the neglect of female offenders in the literature. They were not, though, totally absent in criminological theory making – otherwise 'invisibility' would be a misnomer, and the second theme of 'distortion' would be irrelevant. A comparatively small amount of work did attempt to explain female criminality. From a feminist standpoint this was over-influential and wholly unacceptable.

Writers such as Heidensohn (1968, 1985) and Leonard (1982) argued that principal theories such as anomie, differential association and labelling, were aimed at an explanation of male, not female, crime/deviance. This prompted some feminists to pull criminology into the twentieth century by reworking past theories so that they took account of females (e.g. Shacklady Smith, 1978). Others preferred to carry out their own studies on female offenders (e.g. McRobbie and Garber, 1976). The chief contribution of feminism, however, did not derive from a simple desire to achieve some 'balance' by, say, studying more women and fewer men. Fundamentally, feminism made gender, as a social construction, a central issue within criminology, and that obviously involves men as much as women, or, more accurately, 'masculinity' as much as 'femininity'. It is, at the same time, committed to challenging the gender-based discrimination and disadvantage that is characteristic of patriarchal societies.

Various explanations of why females were neglected in criminological research were forthcoming. Heidensohn (1985) points to the fact that the discipline has been dominated by men, which affected such things as access to male gangs, cultural assumptions about masculinity and femininity, and a fascination with the macho, working-class deviant. She also notes that their relatively low crime rates make female offenders more difficult to find. In a sense, though, the gender dimension has always featured in criminological studies. It has been inherent in notions of masculinity and the socio-cultural contexts in which (usually working-class) delinquency-prone masculinity is shaped. These have generally proceeded along fairly stereotypical paths, which not only meant that females were excluded, but also that different understandings of masculinity were ignored.

The lower criminality rates for females, as indicated by official statistics, self-report studies and victim studies, clearly led some criminologists in the past, guided as they were by the imperative to find the 'causes' of crime, to concentrate on those largely responsible for crime – males. Apart from pushing to one side those cases where females *do* break the law (see, for example, Campbell's (1981) study of girl delinquent gang members), this failed to appreciate that an understanding of criminality involves coming to terms with the question of why some people do not break the law. What was missing was a theoretical engagement with the observation that females, as well as males, experienced things such as unemployment, poverty, inner city life, the mass media, unsatisfactory schooling and life as a teenager. Thus one of the most glaring omissions was an analysis of the different ways in which factors such as these impact on females and males. A feminist agenda, according to Smart (1976: 89), had to 'situate the discussion of sex roles within a structural explanation of the social origins of those roles'.

Differences in crime rates for males and females have for many years remained fairly constant at around five or six to one in Britain; other European countries and the United States have similar ratios. Nevertheless, there has been much debate over the accuracy of these figures, hence the use of self-report studies, which purport to give us a better picture of criminality (there is a review of this research in Box, 1983). These studies tend to put the ratio nearer to two to one. As Box observed, though, large amounts of unrecorded crime will be in the categories of corporate crime, domestic violence and sexual assault, and these are either impossible or difficult to pick up in self-report studies. In certain offence categories, of course, women will be overrepresented: for example, prostitution and illegal abortion. Apart from the well-rehearsed problems with self-report studies (sampling, honesty, memory, and so on) some of them fail adequately to differentiate between 'serious' and 'less serious' offences, or to state the frequency with which offences are committed. We will return to this point later.

Distortion

On the theme of 'distortion', the feminist critique was summed up by Smart (1976: xiii) when she argued that the then current stock of criminological explanations of female criminality 'shares an entirely uncritical attitude towards sexual stereotyping of women and girls'. Essentially, the feminist critique emphasized a line of thinking, still around in modern criminology, that stretched back to the genetic theories of Lombroso and Ferrero in the nineteenth century, and in which the assumption was that the normal human being was male, and that the female was therefore an aberration. Combine this with the more specific cultural ideas about women carried around in the heads of these male criminologists and, said feminists, the distorted images of women pervading their work should come as no surprise: 'the majority of these studies refer to women in terms of their biological impulses and hormonal balance or in terms of their domesticity, maternal instinct and passivity' (ibid. xiv).

Even in the postwar period, studies of female offenders tended to have been cut adrift from the main body of criminological theorizing, which had moved away from the crude biological determinism of Lombrosian criminology. Pollak (1950), for instance, thought that women possess two characteristics that not only determined the sorts of offences they committed, but also helped them to cover their tracks more effectively than men: they are naturally deceitful (incredibly, Pollak saw the faking of orgasm as evidence for this), and played social roles based upon privacy (evidence for this was seemingly provided by the concealment of menstruation). It will come as no surprise to learn that feminist writers have reserved particular wrath for Pollak. Later on, Cowie, Cowie and Slater (1968) continued to confuse sex with gender. According to them, because of biologically determined factors boys are less able than girls to cope with stressful situations, hence they are more criminal than girls. However, some girls they argued, are born with 'masculine traits', which explained their criminal behaviour.

Criminal justice

The 'criminal justice' and 'victimization' themes were, in this early period, less in evidence within feminist work than the two themes discussed above. This situation was to change significantly in the 1980s though. Research on the theme of criminal justice looked at the ways in which women were dealt with by the various criminal justice agencies such as the police, the courts and the prisons, though the earlier work tended to concern itself with women's imprisonment (Ward and Kassebaum, 1966; Giallombardo, 1966; Heidensohn, 1969). This research drew attention to the disadvantages experienced by female prisoners compared with male prisoners, due to entering a system that was essentially designed for men (for example, women had fewer educational and recreational facilities).

Some writers explored the widely accepted view that women were treated more leniently by the criminal justice system, because it was largely administered by men, who adopted a chivalrous attitude towards them. This was an idea that had been around for some time in criminology (for example, Mannheim, 1940), and according to some criminologists explained the lower official crime rates for women and, if women were brought before the courts, the supposedly more lenient sentences handed out. Anderson (1976) in a review of this debate, pointed the way to subsequent feminist repudiations of the argument that 'chivalry' had a significant and beneficent impact on the treatment of women by the criminal justice system. In an early study of the British courts, Dell (1971) concluded that while a greater proportion of men than women were sent to prison (though women were only rarely involved in violent crime), women were more likely to be held on remand prior to trial or sentencing. Other research carried out in the 1970s found that the treatment of female juvenile offenders was influenced by considerations of 'moral protection', in addition to the actual offence. With males, the tendency was only to see the offence as relevant. This, it was argued, increased the likelihood of juvenile female offenders being sent to an institution (Chesney-Lind, 1973, 1978; Jay and Rose, 1977).

Feminist writers also argued that because of the stereotypical understandings of gender carried by men, women offenders are seen to have offended twice: once from the point of view of the offence itself, and twice because they have transgressed cultural understandings of 'feminine' behaviour. An important component of this characterization is that women are judged according to particular notions of 'motherly' or 'wifely' roles.

Victimization

Finally, the theme of victimization. Research on this theme grew slowly in the 1970s, then mushroomed rapidly through the 1980s, in line with a growing interest in what is known as victimology. The earlier feminist work on women as victims concentrated on sexual crime (Brownmiller, 1973) and domestic violence (Dobash and Dobash, 1979). Studies of rape, child sexual abuse, and violence in the home highlighted the low levels of reporting, and signalled an end to the complacency surrounding these areas. Gradually this type of research had an influence at the level of practice – for example, the growth in Women's Aid Refuges (Pizzey, 1973) – and, eventually, in police responses to victims of rape.

Part V

The 1980s and 1990s

12 | The discipline of criminology and its context – 4

The shift to the right in British politics
Criminology's external history
Social organization
The growth of policy-oriented research
The nature and context of research
Policy-oriented research and the Left
Contemporary British criminology

We now reach the final phase (in this review) in the historical development of sociological criminology, which takes us through the 1980s and into the 1990s and an impending *fin de siècle*. Being brutally honest, one has to say that the task of plotting the various twists and turns, whilst sketching in some social and political background, now becomes more taxing. Relatively clear-cut theoretical shifts gave way to a high degree of fragmentation. In addition, there was a large increase in the amount of academic work subsumed under the title of criminology. Already by the end of the 1970s developments in non-mainstream criminology, and especially within a specifically radical tradition, were becoming less obvious. For students of criminology, the discipline's development since the reorientations of the 1960s had, for a while, helpfully gone through relatively easily understood chronological stages: new deviancy theory had challenged an earlier positivism; conflict theory had radicalized the liberalism of labelling theory; and critical criminology had attempted to develop a neo-Marxist political economy of crime. There had also been the beginnings of a feminist tradition and the first murmurings of a victimology. In spite of their internal complexities, these could at least be put into reasonably neat theoretical packages, and to a large extent be identified with conventional political

215

affiliations. At the risk of being scandalously vulgar, students could for a while think in terms of theoretical 'camps'. The embracing of a sociology of law, and with it an intense theoretical interrogation by radical scholars of the political economy of rule making during the second half of the 1970s, made the situation less clear-cut. This did not immediately appear to represent an obvious, challenging theoretical 'camp'. Not only was the work highly complex, but it did not seem to conform to the earlier pattern of a chronological series of paradigms – and why should it? Furthermore, 'criminals' had disappeared from the scene, together with the concept of 'deviance', though the former were to reappear shortly afterwards.

Colin Sumner (1990: 15) observed:

> Students still ask 'Whatever happened to the theoretical debate about deviance in the early 1970s?' . . . Perhaps the revulsion for theory and theoretical wrangling, the return of empirical research, the new popularity of historical work and the general air of hard-nosed realism in the late 1970s and early 1980s, have all contributed to the demise of theoretical dynamics in this field.

This pessimistic reading of developments in sociological criminology became necrological in 1994, when Sumner published a book on the sociology of deviance with the subtitle *An obituary*. What had led to this situation? Early theoretical debate seemed to have disappeared. Challenging paradigms no longer followed one after the other. Theorizing seemed to have been supplanted by empirical research. And, on a number of fronts, there was a rush to embrace 'realism'.

The shift to the right in British politics

1979: a political turning point

'Law and order' was a central element of the Conservative Party's election campaign in 1979, though it involved more than a narrowly conceived focus on crime as such. The rhetoric was resplendent with images of militant trade unionists on the rampage; of the dead being unburied and dustbins unemptied; of British culture being 'swamped' by black immigrants; of classrooms in the grip of anarchy; and of a dependency culture, where large sections of the population had grown lazy and undisciplined on the back of a too generous welfare state. At the same time, we were told, the pendulum had swung too far towards the rights of criminals; police officers needed more powers to secure convictions, and the courts were too 'soft'. In the home, an increasing number of parents had abrogated their responsibilities regarding bringing their children up properly. The incoming government was committed to 'getting tough' on law and order.

For the left in Britain, what followed was a drift into an authoritarian law and order society (Hall, 1980, 1988) though as Norrie and Adelman (1989) have pointed out, the sentiments expressed by the Conservatives were in accord with the views of large sections of the working class. Put another way, certain significant common-sense understandings, widespread throughout British society, had found a political voice. However, as various commentators have suggested, the drift in this direction had, in fact, been gathering momentum during the 1970s (see, for example, Pitts, 1988; Norrie and Adelman, 1989). This view acts as a necessary antidote to those who paint a misleading picture of British society in the pre-Thatcher era, as if, for over a decade, the population had dwelt in an age of universal libertinism, where continual saturnalia enveloped everyone in an orgy of decency-sapping permissiveness.

The area of juvenile justice provides a particularly good example. John Pitts shows how a Fabian-influenced Labour Party went some way towards liberalizing the system in the 1960s. However, the 1970s saw a move away from a treatment–welfare model of juvenile justice towards the more punitively oriented justice model. The increasing use of custody – in spite of the intentions of the 1969 Children and Young Persons Act – illustrates this. Thus the 'psychologically impaired' children of the 1960s were gradually transformed into the wicked and irresponsible children of the 1970s: undisciplined products of a welfare state that had supposedly made them take too much for granted. In Pitts's view, this trend was to find its culmination in the Thatcher era of the 1980s.

It is impossible to understand the directions taken by criminology during the 1980s and l990s without taking into consideration the cultural changes in that period, as well as the impact of the social and economic policies of an entrenched Conservative government:

> In practical terms, the government of Margaret Thatcher introduced new legislation to curb the power of sectional interests (including the legal profession as well as the unions); competitive market mechanisms to start to break state monopolies (for example, extending prison privatization); more powers, pay and resources for the police; a major prison rebuilding programme; a 'short, sharp, shock' for recalcitrant, ill-disciplined juveniles; and various measures to make families and communities more self-reliant. (Jefferson and Shapland, 1994: 266–7)

A number of other developments during the 1980s and 1990s should also be noted: rising levels of unemployment; the decline in manufacturing industry and the impact of this on communities; the 1984–85 miners' strike; rising levels of recorded crime; serious outbreaks of urban rioting; widening differentials in the distribution of wealth and income; and pressure on the government to curb public expenditure.

Good old common sense – again

The election of a Thatcher government marked the endorsement of common-sense amateurism. In a way this was a reversion to an earlier, traditionally British approach to social administration – an approach based upon the pragmatic all-rounder – of Cabinets, Committees and civil servants, eschewing the 'expert' and the 'intellectual' in favour of the generalist, who, above all, lay claim to common sense. However, whereas in the past this process had been founded on an explicit elitism, where our 'betters' by definition knew best, the 1980s version celebrated the concordance between the common sense of the political elites and the common sense of 'the people'. In the realm of criminal justice policy, the 1980s offered an opportunity for the views of all right thinking men and women, who 'knew in their hearts' what was wrong, to be put into practice. Well rehearsed during the preceding decade over both lunchtime gin and tonics at the country pub and pints of beer at the working men's club, and underscored daily by the tabloid press, it seemed that the end of the liberal, the do-gooding expert and the intellectual was at hand – the same do-gooding liberals (social workers, teachers, psychologists, and so forth) who, as pointed out earlier, were criticized by radical thought in the 1960s and 1970s. Reviewing Brewer and Lait's *Can Social Work Survive?*, a book exemplifying the New Right's thinking, Geoff Pearson writes:

> Mrs Lait concluded that the whole business of childcare should be taken away from permissive educationalists and do-good social workers, and placed instead 'in the hands of ordinary people who have rejected pretentious, self indulgent and unscientific theorising in favour of their own good sense'. (Quoted in Pitts, 1988: 445)

Just as law enforcement ideologies have presented the police officer as merely a citizen in uniform, so the ideologue of the New Right was merely a citizen in academic dress.

This takes us back to the discussion of common sense in the first chapter, and Becker's distinction between common sense as potentially deluding, tribal gut-feelings, and common sense as practical no-nonsense truth. As always, of course, proponents of the ideas of the New Right saw their common sense as representing the latter.

Criminology's external history

In an illuminating analysis of criminology's historical development, David Garland (1985a) refers to the distinction between an academic discipline's 'external' and 'internal' history, an idea originally put forward from the perspective of the philosophy of science by Imre Lakotos. Briefly, the argument is that all scientific disciplines are established within the context of appropriate external social, political and cultural conditions. Eventually, a discipline becomes internally self-sufficient and continues to develop because of its own resources. One outcome of this is that it is no longer tied to catering for the needs of powerful social and political interests: 'In other words, to the extent that this internal logic asserts itself, the social origins of the science will tend to fade into its pre-history' (Garland, 1985a: 2). In Garland's view criminology in Britain has been unable to cast off its dependence upon these external demands, so that it continues to exist as an ideological, rather than scientific project: 'Precisely because criminology's object is a social problem – defined by policies, ideologies and state practices – its "external" origins will always be internal to it' (ibid. 3). This is an important argument that should at least sensitize us to the on-going connections between the nature of criminology as an academic discipline and the broader social, political and cultural circumstances. The same point is made by Jock Young (1994: 71) when he says:

> the interior dialogue is propelled by the exterior world. The dominant ideas of a period, whether establishment or radical; the social problems of a particular society; the government in power and the political possibilities existing in a society – all shape the interior discourse of the academic.

If the shift to the right at an external level nurtured the development of a much more self-confident and influential right-wing criminology, both in Britain and in the United States, it posed fundamental problems for radical and liberal criminology. The two characteristics of radical thought referred to earlier – negative criticism and internal divisions – that during the 1970s in a sense helped to prepare the ground for the New Right, went through remarkable transformations during the course of the 1980s, though not in all quarters.

First, radical thought pulled back from criticizing such things as publicly owned industries, the teaching profession, social welfare programmes, council housing, the Labour Party, and so on. In the climate of Thatcherism, previous arrangements suddenly looked more attractive than they had at the time. For liberal and left thought, the 1980s and 1990s opened up a period of reclamation and self-appraisal. Within criminology, left realism stands as the main representative of this trend, especially with its close links with the Labour Party (left realism is discussed later). Outside of a critical strand, radical criminology tended to gravitate towards a liberal democratic baseline, heralding a more explicit commitment to empirical research and even a discussion of policy. Left realism in particular represented a move from pitching analyses at the level of the political economy of capitalism with a stress on the need for radical transformation, to a more modest engagement with concrete reforms. Left realists argued that this was necessary in order to challenge the Right's domination of issues of crime and punishment. Importantly, though, it illustrates how many on the liberal–left spectrum did attempt to develop constructive ideas regarding how things might be improved in the short term.

Secondly, the existence of an external enemy in the shape of Thatcherism worked wonders in healing many of the previous divisions among radical factions. Although critical criminologists continued to develop a neo-Marxist agenda, greater account was taken of the realities of street crime, the victimization of women and black people, and the dangers of romanticizing working-class crime. Across a range of liberal–left thought, however, previous bellicosity gradually disappeared. The overriding truculent debate that continued through the 1980s and into the 1990s was between critical criminology (described by their antagonists as left idealism) and self-styled left realists. This was particularly apparent in the area of black criminality, where some critical theorists, recycling an earlier 'working-class crime as politics' theme, argued that black crime was political. As I have said elsewhere: 'If there was a Richter Scale in the social sciences it would have registered maximum points during these vitriolic exchanges' (Tierney, 1988: 133).

As the 1980s progressed, and the New Right celebrated the idea of common sense, among many radicals there was a corresponding rush to 'realism'. Pared down to its basics, the notion of being realistic seemed to bear a strong resemblence to using common sense. The same process was at work within the Labour Party, which, after a series of election defeats, increasingly assessed its policies in terms of realism. Realism came to suggest a set of qualities based upon 'practical views and policy'. This meant, for example, addressing the here and now rather than a utopian future, taking account of what the public says and feels, taking the reality of crime seriously, and being practical rather than hopelessly theoretical or wildly abstract. Clearly, this raises important issues regarding the nature and role of criminology, issues that have always lain awkwardly at the core of the criminological project.

Social organization

Paul Rock's (1994) survey of 'all identifiable British criminologists' provides the most up-to-date information on what he calls the social organization of criminology in this country: demographic patterns, institutional arrangements and social relations. His findings give us a useful starting point for a discussion of the development of criminological thought since the end of the 1970s.

The survey underlines the fact that academic criminology in Britain is dominated by a group of criminologists, now in their forties and fifties, who were products of an expanding higher education system during the late 1960s and early 1970s – the 'fortunate generation'. Predictably, the bulk of them are men rather than women. The beginning of their academic careers also coincided with the advent of the new deviancy and the break with positivism, and, indeed, many played pivotal roles in developing the sociology of deviance in that period. As well as forming the largest group – 68 per cent of criminologists are aged over 40 – they continue to have a powerful presence in terms of professorial posts and published work. Of course from this base their influence on academic criminology will be widespread: for instance, speaking at conferences, being involved in the recruitment of staff, acting as external examiners, helping to establish and validate new courses, and reviewing proposals for books and articles for journals. In short, the influence of the 'fortunate generation' on the shape of British criminology has been, and continues to be, considerable.

Although there has been a growth in the proportion of younger criminologists since the late 1980s, when Rock carried out a similar survey, the overall picture reflects the mixed fortunes of higher education in general, and the social sciences in particular:

> In effect, two demographic waves have moved through post-war British criminology: the greater in the 1970s and the lesser in the latter half of the 1980s; and it was the greater that gave definition to the discipline. Criminologists educated and appointed in the late 1960s and early 1970s form a distinct and self-conscious intellectual generation. (Rock, 1994: 132)

On a note of pessimism, Rock points out that although an expansion may be imminent within departments of law, at the moment the lack of sustained recruitment over the years means that 'Sociological criminology in particular looks somewhat emaciated' (ibid. 132). As I have said previously, one result of this has been the absence of decisive theoretical challenges coming from a younger generation, a generation that had to struggle for hard-earned research funding during the 1980s, under strong pressure to pursue empirical research.

The largest proportion of criminologists is now to be found in departments of law – and they have a variety of subject backgrounds – followed by departments of sociology. This reflects more recent increases in undergraduate demand for places on law degrees. Law departments have the highest proportion of female criminologists. The greatest concentration of criminologists, however, is to be found in the Home Office Research and Planning Unit, an institution that continues to influence profoundly the type of research carried out under the banner of criminology in Britain. Not surprisingly, the majority of this research has been policy-oriented. Research initiatives coming from another important funding source, the Economic and Social Research Council, have taken similar directions.

Interestingly, though, Rock's survey illustrates the enduring influence of sociological criminology when it comes to theoretical allegiances, with interactionists forming the largest proportion. This is strongly reflected in the way that criminology is taught within universities:

> Theoretical criminology may no longer seethe and flow but it is what British criminologists continue to teach. Variously called criminology and the sociology of deviance, it looms over all else. Over half the courses offered were so labelled and, in the main, they survey the accomplishments of the past. (Ibid. 146)

The growth of policy-oriented research

Mapping the terrain

Having briefly discussed the wider political, social and cultural context, and, following Rock, looked at the social organization of criminology, we can now examine how the discipline developed through the 1980s and into the 1990s. In view of the large amount of work emerging during this final period, and the inevitable disputes over the significance of more recent developments, analyses become a little more hazardous.

Drawing out what appear to be the more important and significant examples of criminological work is bound to be an invidious project. Necessarily, the selection is to some extent arbitrary, and cannot but reflect my own interpretation of events. However, the intention is to give an indication of the main contours of developments in British criminology, whilst paying attention to external and internal pressures on the discipline. The selection of material to illustrate these developments has a qualitative and quantitative dimension to it. By definition, making qualitative judgements involves subjective interpretations with regard to notions of 'importance', 'influence', 'academic virtuousity', and so on. Accusations of bias are less likely to follow when choices rest on the sheer volume of work of a certain type that is produced. However, the fact that a particular topic or theme forms the basis for a large amount of research over a given period, does not guarantee, of course, that the work is fundamentally important, of high quality, will have long-term effects, or is even interesting from the audience's point of view. We have to acknowledge that fashions and trends come and go within criminology as much as they do within other disciplines and, indeed, within social life in general. What perhaps seemed desperately fascinating and impressive at one time, can seem banal, silly or irrelevant at some future date. Some of us need only look at old photographs of how we used to dress to appreciate this.

Some of the insights of the labelling perspective can be applied to the social production of criminological work. Whether or not a research proposal is funded, or a book or article gains an audience by being published, is the outcome of a range of social processes. It is not simply a question of the work being 'good' or 'bad'. Publishers are well aware of market trends in criminology, and the harsh reality is that some books will not be published if they are thought to be out of tune with these trends. Furthermore, the status of the author will play a part; like all areas of publishing, criminology has its luminaries. These criminologists will also wield influence over what is published via their role as reviewers of proposals for books and articles. Likewise, the kind of research that is successful in the tendering stakes, and attracts funding, will be linked to the demands set by research councils and agencies.

Research topics

Unlike the situation in the 1960s, no one can complain that contemporary criminology is 'obsessed' with juvenile offenders. Such research has not been abandoned, but now constitutes only a relatively small proportion of the total (e.g. West, 1982; Farrington, 1992b; Fergusson, Horwood and Lynskey, 1992; Robins and Rutter, 1990; Agnew, 1991; Nagin and Farrington, 1992; Riley and Shaw, 1985).

Criticism of this 'obsession' is associated with the new deviancy theorists of the late 1960s who, under the banner of the sociology of deviance, turned their attention to various groups defined as deviant, and the labelling processes involved in the construction of deviant identities. This interest in defined deviant groups continued into the 1970s. From the late 1970s onwards, however, the concept of deviance tended to fall into disuse, and with it there was a corresponding decline in studies of specific groups labelled as deviant. With the evaporation of the sociology of deviance, criminal, rather than deviant, activities moved centre stage. Thus during the 1980s and 1990s there has been little interest in, for example, youth subcultures, new age travellers, or the 'nuts, sluts and preverts' of the 1960s. In fact, as the 1980s wore on, and although there are exceptions, the general trend was to address issues of social control and the victims of crime, rather than criminal (let alone deviant) motivations, lifestyles, and experiences.

In spite of this, David Downes (1988) argues that by the 1980s three key ideas deriving from new deviancy theory had fundamentally changed 'the nature of "taken for granted" criminological inquiry'. First, that the criminal's (or deviant's) subjective understanding of the world should be considered. Secondly, that the nature and extent of crime (or deviance) are to some degree a result of social control responses, rather than products of quite separate factors. And thirdly, that crime (or deviance) is ubiquitous, especially if we consider corporate, occupational and domestic crime. However, Downes does point out that while these ideas informed a great deal of research in the 1960s and 1970s, and may have been generally accepted within academic criminology, their influence on actual research in the 1980s had diminished. Ethnographic research that would attempt to tap into the subjectivities of criminal groups began to dry up. The growth of administrative criminology and versions of control theory (see below) set the clock back by separating processes of social control – seen in terms of labelling – from criminal behaviour. And, while domestic violence has figured strongly in feminist contributions to criminology, other kinds of 'normalized' crime – that is, widespread and more or less tolerated crime, and in particular, white-collar crime – have remained relatively under-developed areas of research. (There are, however, notable examples of such research: e.g. Carson, 1982; Box, 1983; Levi, 1987; Clarke, 1990; Croal, 1992; Nelken, 1994.)

Observations made by a number of contributors to *The Oxford Handbook of Criminology* (Maguire *et al.*, 1994) indicate the lack of recent research in a variety of areas. Nigel South (1994) opens his chapter on illicit drug use by quoting from Downes's (1988) review mentioned above: 'With a few exceptions . . . sociologists were not engaged by the drugs issue.' And, although more work in this field did come on stream during the 1980s and early 1990s (e.g. Dorn and South, 1987; Pearson, 1987; MacGregor, 1989; Dorn, Murji and South, 1992; Strang and Gossop, 1993), South himself concludes by saying: 'However, at present, British criminology and broader policy and practice are ill served by the limited (albeit generally excellent) research upon which we can draw' (South, 1994: 425).

In Michael Levi's (1994: 344) chapter on violent crime we learn: 'By contrast with this focus on "the victim", the causes of violence have received comparatively little criminological attention.' Even in the area of youth crime, which has received much media and legislative attention in the recent past, Geoff Pearson (1994: 1195) makes the point: 'We simply do not have the evidence – in the form of government-sponsored statistics, social surveys, reliable self-report studies, etc. – to state with any confidence the actually existing relationships between "youth" and "crime".'

Criminological research in some areas, then, grew more slowly than might have been expected. But, while emphases changed and research topics were reshuffled, the overall volume of research in Britain continued to grow during the 1980s and 1990s. In terms of amount of research, a number of previously neglected topics came to dominate the field.

One notable example is research on policing. It is interesting that at the end of the 1970s, when a number of polytechnics and colleges were exploring the possibility of mounting degrees in police studies, or criminal justice studies, the Council for National Academic Awards (the now defunct body that in those days validated non-university-sector degree courses) seriously questioned whether there existed a sufficient academic literature on policing in Britain to sustain degree programmes. A decade later, the huge growth in police-related research had dramatically reversed the situation. This trend continued unabated into the 1990s.

The 1980 and 1981 urban riots, and the 1984–85 miners' strike, stimulated research on the topic of public order, and inevitably this frequently overlapped with research on policing. As did an upsurge in research on the themes of 'race', racism and protest, and 'race' and criminality.

Echoing the shift in much of this work away from the offender as such, and towards responses to crime and disorder on the part of criminal justice agencies, the 1980s and 1990s also saw an increase in research on the theme of 'penalty', that is, in the widest sense, prisons, probation and community sanctions. In some cases this was allied to particular pieces of legislation: for instance, the 1984 Police and Criminal Evidence Act and the 1991 Criminal Justice Act.

Research on victims of crime is a particularly good example of a previously neglected topic that came to the fore in this period. Originally associated with a conservative tradition, this type of research began to attract some of the more radical criminologists in Britain, notably those belonging to the left realist school. Since the beginning of the 1980s studies of victims of crime have grown rapidly in number, and developed along a variety of fronts. An important aspect of this research has been the connections between the nature, extent and distribution of victimization and issues of class, gender, age and 'race'. Raw material relating to the experiences of victims has been generated by the periodic large-scale British Crime Surveys, carried out by the Home Office, and the more focused local crime surveys.

Empirical and theoretical research carried out within a feminist framework, and taking in such topics as gender and criminality, women as victims (for example, domestic violence and sexual abuse), and women and their treatment by the criminal justice system, continued to thrive. We might note, though, that according to Tony Jefferson and Joanna Shapland (1994: 282), in spite of feminism being 'by one reckoning . . . *the* growth area in criminology during the 1980s . . . the experience of women remained marginal to the *criminological enterprise*' (original emphasis). They also point to the marginalization of research on Northern Ireland and the crimes of the powerful over this period.

With a pedigree that goes back to the Chicago ecologists, research based on the neighbourhood, and on the social and physical environment, continued to be carried out during the 1980s and 1990s. Although studies concentrating specifically on the inner city were fewer in number than might have been expected, the urban rioting at the beginning of the 1990s did trigger research on the experiences of people living in the more deprived areas of the city. Analyses had to recognize, however, that in many cases these areas were not in fact inner city areas, but rather council estates situated on the outskirts of the city – municipal suburbia. One offshoot of areal studies has been policy-oriented research built around some notion of 'community', and concerning itself with initiatives that would encourage residents to take some responsibility for crime control. This is particularly associated with the Home Office, and has involved developments such as neighbourhood watch schemes.

The Home Office in particular has also been instrumental in carrying out and commissioning research projects organized around the theme of situational crime control. This has encompassed a multiplicity of ideas ranging from better street lighting, to more effective house security, to the Home Secretary's invitation to 'walk with a purpose'. On a general level this kind of research reflects the emergence of what is usually referred to as administrative criminology, itself linked to a rekindling of interest in control theory.

The nature and context of research

As it stands, of course, the above description is of little more than a list of research topics that have become popular over the last fifteen years or so. With this as a backdrop, the next task is to examine the nature of British criminology as it developed as an academic discipline during this period. This will entail a consideration of competing criminological discourses and assumptions, around which research is built, together with the broader context in which research is conducted. Later on we will return to this period for a more detailed analysis of criminological theory.

An expanding academic base

As far as the teaching of undergraduate courses in criminological theory is concerned, Rock (1994) has shown that sociological criminology continues to play a dominant role. On the other hand, the contraction in teaching, postgraduate and research opportunities that befell sociology during the 1980s, albeit to some extent offset by a 'second wave' surge at the end of the 1980s, did have an impact on research activities and the production of theory. This partly explains why, since the early 1980s, criminological research in this country has been carried out from a widening academic base. Increasingly, contributions have been made by criminologists whose roots lie in disciplines other than sociology: for example, political science, law, social history, psychology and economics. Other developments have also played a part. A variety of research projects opened up opportunities for the employment of the specialist knowledge offered by these other disciplines. As an example, a central theme of police-related research in the early 1980s was accountability, and given that this raised complex legal and political issues turning on the constitutional position of the police, it is not surprising that lawyers and political scientists quickly became involved. Following the pattern set in the United States, the establishment of degree courses in criminal justice studies in a number of higher education institutions during the 1980s (Tierney, 1989), provided criminology-related teaching and research opportunities for a range of social scientists. Finally, there has been an increase in the amount of 'in-house' research carried out by practitioners within criminal justice agencies, as well as by various pressure groups such as Liberty (formerly the National Council for Civil Liberties) and NACRO (the National Association for the Care and Resettlement of Offenders). All of these developments encouraged a broadening of the academic base of criminology.

The research focus

According to Tony Jefferson and Joanna Shapland (1994: 267), criminological research during the 1980s was characterized by 'a gradual contraction of the research focus'. They see this process as having two dimensions to it. First, the field of vision was narrowed so that research concentrated on elements of the criminal justice system and the practicalities of crime control: the police, prisons, courts, probation and community sanctions, situational crime control, and complementary community-based initiatives such as neighbourhood watch and police–public consultation. Secondly, analyses tended to lose sight of the broader picture by treating those elements in relative isolation. This contraction in focus has been in evidence among radical as well as mainstream criminologists.

Policy and pragmatism

A number of commentators, including Jefferson and Shapland, have pointed to another characteristic of much criminological research in the 1980s and 1990s: a shift away from theory towards a pragmatic, policy-oriented approach. Indeed, this factor and the narrowing of the research focus noted above can be seen as mutually reinforcing processes and, again, they caught the attention of radical as well as mainstream criminologists. This was in evidence at different levels of theoretical research.

On one level, there was a relative decline in macro research that endeavoured to develop a theoretical understanding of issues of crime and crime control within contemporary political, social and economic contexts. This macro research refused to isolate 'law and order' from such things as economic change, government policy and changing ideologies of control. In spite of a decline, however, this type of theoretical research has continued to appear over the last fifteen years (e.g. Hall (1988) and Scraton (1987) on the nature of the authoritarian state; Dahrendorf (1985) on law and order from a position he describes as 'institutional liberalism'; Box (1987) on crime and economic recession; Sumner (1994) linking this agenda to the rise and fall of the sociology of deviance; and Reiner and Cross (1991)).

On another level, the 1980s also saw less research concerned with theoretical analyses of particular areas of criminal justice-related activity in contemporary Britain. However, again, critical work of this sort did appear, and, more recently, seems to have been on the increase. Some notable examples are: Cohen (1985), Hudson (1987), Lacey (1988), Walker (1991), Garland (1990), von Hirsch (1993), and Hay, Sparks and Bottoms (1994) on the themes of sentencing, punishment and social control; Brogden (1982) and Reiner (1992, 1994) on the police; Pitts (1988) on the politics of juvenile crime; and Harris (1992) on probation. Important theoretical work that addressed historical developments was also in evidence, notably: Garland (1985a) on punishment and social regulation; Harris and Webb (1987) on the treatment of juveniles; and Sim (1990) on the prison medical service.

Some factors influencing the course of research

The narrowing of the research focus, coupled with a shift towards policy-oriented research, can be linked to a number of key factors at work during the 1980s. The government's commitment to financial stringency had a marked impact on the funding of teaching and research in the social sciences. Increasingly the stress was on 'value for money', which inevitably meant that research had to be seen to be useful in terms of policy. Not only did this lead to an expansion in the research carried out by criminologists at the Research and Planning Unit at the Home Office, it also helped to set the parameters of research initiatives funded by the Economic and Social Research Council – the primary source of funds for university social science departments. The stress on 'value for money', though, was essentially directed at criminal justice agencies, and increasingly the task of criminological research was to evaluate the extent to which these agencies were measuring up to the demand to be efficient and effective. Hence the tendency of research to deal with elements of the system in an isolated fashion, measuring their performance against some posited criteria.

Another factor was the growth in research carried out by the criminal justice agencies themselves (who sometimes funded university research) and by various pressure groups. Obviously, such research conformed to agendas set by the agencies or pressure groups, who in general would hardly finance highly abstract, theoretical work. However, even at the policy level there will be in-built limitations. As Roger Hood (1987) has pointed out, setting the research agendas themselves, agendas already circumscribed by central government policy, forecloses on the possibility of radical alternatives. Stan Cohen's (1988: 236) observation made at the beginning of the 1980s now seems prophetic: 'the content of this type of criminology has switched (and is likely to switch even more) in the direction of "criminal justice"; that is to say, an exclusive concern with the operation of the system.'

The introduction of privatization within the criminal justice system is also relevant in this context. After a slow start in the 1980s, the momentum of privatization speeded up in the 1990s, especially with respect to prisons, and although the overall impact in terms of contracts has been small, the principles driving privatization should not be underestimated:

> The real legacy of the privatization debate has not so far been in actual contracts, but in changing expectations. In 1980 the criminal justice system was thought of as a series of state-run agencies which attempted to contain, punish, or sometimes rehabilitate offenders. Today these agencies are to be managed, offenders to be processed, throughput to be controlled, the system to be modelled. The language of industrial production has been adopted. (Jefferson and Shapland, 1994: 279)

Also worth noting is the build-up of pressure on academics and their departments to carry out and publish research: what American academics call the 'publish or perish' syndrome. In the 1990s university departments find themselves subject to period review by external inspectors. On the basis of certain indicators – one of which is research output – they will be given a rating. While public accountability is no bad thing, of course, there is a danger that the pressures placed on staff to publish creates an edge of desperation, and the possibility of being tempted to avoid time-consuming, innovative theorization, especially as funding and/or sabbatical leave for such research is in short supply. As Downes (1988: 49) says: 'work from the late 1970s to the present day, has been conducted with a lower level of theoretical intensity but a greater attentiveness to method and project management.'

A number of commentators have suggested that internal theoretical squabbles have largely disappeared, with the bulk of criminologists hovering around a consensus, which might also partly explain this diminution in 'theoretical intensity'. It is acknowledged, though, that these placid waters are still disturbed by a handful of 'combative' radicals:

> The second generation of the 1980s consists chiefly of a smaller and younger group of professional scholars. It is a group that missed the period of major recruitment to teaching posts, having to turn instead to research contracts in applied criminology. Their work has necessarily been empirical and policy-oriented . . . there is apparent agreement that many of the earlier problems of theoretical definition and identity have grown stale or have been resolved for most practical purposes. (Rock, 1988: 63)

Or, alternatively, perhaps these theoretical disputes have been swept under the carpet.

These, then, are some of the key factors influencing the shape of criminological research during the 1980s and 1990s. All of them, of course, have to be seen within the context of economic recession, consistently high levels of unemployment, growing gaps between rich and poor, pressure on the government to cut public expenditure, rising levels of recorded crime, decreasing police clear-up rates and their seeming lack of impact, beyond a certain point, to control criminal behaviour, over-crowding and rioting in the prison system, major examples of urban disorder, and increasing fears about crime.

Policy-oriented research and the Left

The interest in questions of policy that characterized mainstream criminology over this period, was also apparent within areas of radical criminology. As indicated earlier, criminologists on the Left had to come to terms with the impact of Thatcherism/Majorism, especially in relation to criminal justice policies. Research associated with the left realist school in particular concerned itself with practical policies pertaining to 'law and order'. Here political sights were lowered. Relatively modest, 'realistic' aspirations based upon an explicitly reformative programme replaced a more radical commitment to major social transformations, though the reforms were, and are, seen as progressive and aimed in the direction of an (unexplicated) socialist future. Embracing the idea of reform manifested itself in developing close links with the Labour Party, especially at local government level, and (traditionally anathema to the Left) cooperating with the police in order to develop strategies for reducing levels of crime. And why not? Because, say 'critical' opponents, criminology should not surrender to a conceptual framework and research agenda determined by outside interests, and especially those of the capitalist state.

Although the left realists have advocated the development of a broadly based criminology that will encompass all relevant micro and macro dimensions, according to Jefferson and Shapland (1994: 269) their work has in the main been narrowly focused, because of the central role given to victims' accounts: 'victims' experiences . . . have came to define the new (left) realist project (coupled with, almost by way of a postscript, demands for a more democratically accountable police force . . .) – a more narrow approach.'

Jefferson and Shapland argue that this tendency partly results from the 'crisis of Marxism' during the 1980s, and the influence of the French writer Foucault. While one important strand of Foucault's work – based on analyses of the totality and ubiquity of discipline – has inspired radical research pitched at a societal level, and often of a historical nature, a second strand of Foucauldian thought examines the day-to-day manner in which specific institutions exercise power. It is this strand, they argue, that has influenced the left realists.

The desire to link criminological research to the administration of justice carries echoes of what Garland calls the 'governmental project' of classicial criminology. Given the close relationship forged with the Labour Party, if there is a change of government at the next general election left realism might become the literal embodiment of the governmental project.

Although rejecting this move towards narrowly focused, policy-oriented research, critical criminology, does, none the less, address concrete issues relating to the operation of the criminal justice system. This is not new, but the impact of Thatcherism/Majorism stimulated an increase in research of this type. Arguing that the 1980s and 1990s have witnessed the growth of an increasingly coercive, authoritarian state, and a narrowing down of areas of freedom, critical criminology has emphasized what are seen as the harmful effects of government policy and the injustices permeating the criminal justice system. This type of research is, in fact, a continuation of two traditions already well established within radical criminology (and discussed earlier): one based on the theme of 'self-interested rule makers', the other on the theme of 'cynical rule breakers'. During the 1980s, critical criminology picked up on the first of these by scutinizing the effects on civil liberties and justice that the implementation of government policy was having. The second theme was originally associated with white-collar crime, but during the 1980s the spotlight was turned on such things as miscarriages of justice, corruption, and abuses of power. Research by critical criminologists into substantive criminal justice issues was seen by them as part of a wider critique of a capitalist society characterized by profound inequalities based on class, gender and 'race'. For left realists, the critical criminologists' insistence that criminal *justice* can only be achieved via a radical transformation of society – which leads them to be sceptical of the value of research aimed at devising practical measures for reducing crime – means that they are unable to offer a realistic and constructive alternative to the 'law and order' policies of the Right.

However, by concentrating simply on the question of *why* research should be carried out, there is a danger of reducing the debate between these two schools of radical criminology to a dispute between 'reform' and 'revolution'. As we shall see when examining criminological theory in more detail, the debate between left realism and critical criminology encompasses a range of theoretical issues concerning the production, meaning, and uses of knowledge. In short, the debate raises core questions regarding the nature of academic criminology.

Contemporary British criminology

This examination of the historical development of criminology began with Marx's observation that 'hasn't the Tree of Sin been at the same time the Tree of Knowledge ever since the time of Adam?' The imagery was meant to capture the ironic fact that the livelihoods and reputations of both 'goodies' and 'baddies' (though the distinction is not always clear) were owed to the existence of crime. In the same context Marx refers to 'the inevitable compendium in which this same professor throws his lectures onto the general market', and it is certainly true that the Tree of Knowledge that constitutes British criminology has grown enormously during this century.

One of the obvious difficulties when plotting criminology's historical development is in identifying those movements and ideas that have been particularly significant and influential. The French historian Pierre Vilar (1985: 47) has written: 'The history business has one thing in common with selling soap powder: mere novelty in both can easily pass as innovation.' The same can be said of the 'criminology business'. However, looking at the past has one advantage over looking at the present: with the passage of time, and an opportunity to reflect and take stock, certain key patterns do begin to emerge. Describing and assessing the current state of British criminology, when the dust from very recent developments has not yet settled, are more problematic. With this qualification, and prior to a closer examination of contemporary criminological theory, certain key features can be outlined.

The backdrop

Criminology has both an 'internal' and an 'external' history. Over the period under review we have seen how changes in the nature of criminology – its discourses, institutional settings, and projects – have been shaped by intellectual processes at work within the discipline as well as by wider social, political, economic and cultural factors. The recent history of criminology, therefore, has to be seen against the backdrop of a panoply of 'external' events and movements.

The growing influence of the New Right, and the policies of an (up to now) entrenched Conservative administration, are particularly important. Continuing economic recession, high levels of unemployment and deprivation, and changes in the taxation system, have all helped to sharpen social divisions within British society. The 1995 United Nations international audit of children's rights in Britain provides one illustration. The report accuses the British government of violating the UN convention on the rights of children, to which it was a signatory four years previously. A number of areas are pointed to, including what are defined as inadequate benefit allowances, which the report links to teenage pregnancies and a high divorce rate, and the large number of children living in poverty. According to the Child Poverty Action Group around one-third of Britain's children now lives in poverty; twenty years ago the figure was one in ten. For gypsies and black and Asian people there has been the added burden of racism in its various forms, including an upsurge in racially motivated violence. In addition, the 1980s and 1990s have seen spectacular outbreaks of urban disorder, such as occurred in Brixton in 1981 and on Tyneside in 1991. It did not escape the notice of some commentators that serious rioting had taken place during the 1930s and 1880s; these were also periods of severe economic recession. The recent past has also seen large-scale protest relating to specific pieces of legislation, such as the Poll Tax and the 1994 Criminal Justice and Public Order Act. The 1984–85 miners' strike brought a range of issues to the surface concerning the role of the state, and in particular the way in which the strike was policed. Finally, give or take a few year-on-year fluctuations, levels of recorded crime have continued to rise inexorably. One response to this has been the greater use of imprisonment; as a proportion of the population, Britain imprisons more people than most other Council of Europe members (Morgan, 1994; Muncie and Sparks, 1991; Vagg, 1994). One consequence of this policy, in spite of a recent large prison-building programme, is severe overcrowding. Furthermore, over the same period there have been serious outbreaks of rioting in prisons.

Some of the main features of contemporary British criminology

Not surprisingly, these developments have had a profound impact on criminology in this country, irrespective of the political affiliations of the various participants. Left realism represents an attempt to construct a radical criminology that is prepared to address both the causes of crime and practical policies aimed at reducing the victimization of vulnerable sections of society. The intention is to put forward a radical alternative to the rhetoric of the Right. While rejecting this as mere reformism, critical criminologists have still felt the need to engage with substantive criminal justice issues in the face of what is seen as a closing down of areas of freedom by the capitalist state. It can also be noted that critical criminology has provided fertile ground for the ideas associated with the abolitionist school of thought (e.g. Bianchi and van Swaaningen, 1986). Originating during the 1960s in some of the Scandinavian countries, abolitionism essentially argues that prisons and other punitive elements of the criminal justice system do more harm than good, and that they should therefore be replaced by more humane and effective systems of conflict settlement. Liberal democratic thought has also had to come to terms with the increased influence of the New Right, and the implementation of what are seen as illiberal criminal justice policies, though unlike critical criminology, solutions are pitched at a more modest, reforming level. For 'establishment' criminology, and especially that associated with the Home Office, rising levels of recorded crime, and the seeming inability of various forms of penality to either deter or rehabilitate offenders, have led to a disenchantment with positivism's promise to (scientifically) discover the causes and cures of crime. Thus we have seen a growth in administrative criminology. This approach incorporates a rational choice model of human behaviour and elements of control theory, and the emphasis is switched to such things as situational crime prevention, the mobilization of the community, and efforts to improve the efficiency and effectiveness of policing (Heal and Laycock, 1986).

The growing influence of New Right criminology is particularly significant. This has occurred in both Britain and the United States (though a discussion of developments in American criminology will be reserved until later) and has to be seen as not one, homogeneous school of thought, so much as a number of strands clustering around certain key themes.

Traditional conservatives attack what they see as the catastrophic failure of liberal welfare-oriented criminal justice policies, and in so doing lay claim to the practical no-nonsense common sense of 'ordinary' people (Brewer and Lait, 1980; Brewer et al., 1981). They are all Sancho Panzas. The ideas of the traditional conservatives are based upon supposed fundamental traditional values. Another strand of New Right criminology is composed of economists whose view of the world derives from the free market principles of nineteenth-century liberalism (Veljanovski, 1990). Drawing to some extent on classical criminology, crime from this perspective is much the same as any other business activity; criminals make rational choices to break the law, and therefore the aim of criminal justice policies should be to make such 'business' decisions irrational. The new (or right) realists reject the traditional punitive law and order policies of the Right, though they also reject the liberal explanations of criminality offered by sociological positivism (Coleman, 1988). Biological positivism, however, is introduced, and linked to the notion of a 'culture of poverty'. Finally, there are those who describe themselves as right-wing libertarians. Here there is strong support for decentralization and an unregulated free market, together with an ideological commitment to the privatization of public agencies such as the police and the prisons. The libertarians argue that 'victimless' crimes, for example illegal drug use, should be decriminalized. The source of social order, they say, should be moral education and the exercise of self-discipline (Elliot, 1990).

An interesting, and sometimes confusing, aspect of recent developments in academic criminology is that the various schools of thought do not always represent neat and tidy expressions of expected theoretical or political positions. Thus, for instance, criminologists sympathetic to interactionism are conjoined with those on the Right who stress voluntarism rather than determinism when explaining criminal motivations; the treatment model of juvenile justice, linked derogatorily by the Right to the 'excuse making industry', has also been criticized by many on the Left; an interest in the victims of crime has been embraced by representatives of the Left and the Right; and arguments in favour of the legalization of drugs unite some on the Left with the libertarian Right.

While radical and liberal criminology had to consider how best to respond to the movement to the Right in Britain, and in the process cope with pressure to conduct research according to the demands of the funding agencies, feminist work relating to crime and criminal justice has tended to enjoy more independence. This has been double edged in that although funding for research into specifically feminist concerns has not been in generous supply, and thus perhaps illustrates the marginalization of feminism in terms of the criminological enterprise, it has allowed alternative research agendas to be set and, importantly, allowed space for theoretical development. Clearly, as far as the world of academic criminology is concerned, feminism has been very influential, which has helped it to build up its own resources and power bases.

There are two other features of contemporary British criminology that are worth noting, and each concerns the status of theory. First, in tandem with a strong emphasis on narrowly focused, policy-oriented research carried out by highly competent, professional researchers, criminological work, as Downes (1988: 49) puts it, 'has been conducted at a lower level of theoretical intensity'. This is not to say that contemporary criminology in Britain ignores theoretical analysis, but rather that theoretical analysis tends to have a contracted research focus, concerning itself with specific crime or crime control issues. Thus compared to the late 1960s and 1970s, there are relatively few texts that address wider, more fundamental debates. Although some criminologists will undoubtedly feel that these debates have already been settled, or that they are irrelevant, the chief explanation for this is probably related to the pressures involved in seeking out research funds, and working to agendas set by the funding agencies. As a consequence, 'major keynote articles and books have become perhaps a rarer, and more endangered species' (Jefferson and Shapland, 1994: 284). The point is well made by Sumner (1990: xi):

criminology cannot be limited to policy-oriented studies and must retain its integrity as an area of independent, critical enquiry of interest to scholars from a variety of disciplinary backgrounds. A criminology that wants to remain dynamic and worthy of its complex subject matter must therefore constantly renew theoretical debate, explore current issues, and develop new methods of research. To allow itself to be limited by the often narrowly political interests of government departments or the funding agencies' need for parochial 'relevance', especially in an age when 'realism' is so often defined by short-run philosophies, is to promote its own destruction as an intellectual enterprise.

There are, though, examples of work that attempt to develop a wider theoretical discourse, especially within the field of radical criminology (e.g. Cohen, 1988; Sumner, 1990, 1994; Garland, 1992; Scraton and Chadwick, 1991; Newburn, 1992), and notably, on the part of feminist writers (e.g. Gelsthorpe and Morris, 1990; Smart, 1989; Cain, 1990; Young, 1990; Carlen, 1992; Campbell, 1992).

The second feature has been a significant trend towards an eclectic, 'pick and mix' approach to the use of theory, in the sense that criminologists have, where they feel it is appropriate, drawn on a variety of models and insights from the past, thereby eschewing a commitment to a single school of thought. This is often associated with postmodernism. The postmodern world, it is argued, is one that rejects the 'grand narrative', that is, an all-encompassing, all-explaining intellectual source. However it is described, it does appear that within criminology the certainties that nourished the bravado and panache of earlier theoretical work have evaporated somewhat.

Plus ça change

One final observation regarding criminology's historical development is prompted by the growth of the New Right. New Right thinking has one thing in common with much of the British and American criminology that has emerged since World War Two: it concentrates on the crimes of the 'powerless' as opposed to the crimes of the 'powerful'. In so doing, New Right criminology has invoked concepts such as the 'underclass' and the 'culture of poverty', and, along the way, has constructed various folk devils such as the 'yob', the 'single mother' and the 'trendy' social worker. In many ways it is reminiscent of a school of thought that was around during the 1930s and 1940s, and was well represented by Claude Mullins's (1945) book, *Why Crime?* discussed earlier. This alone should make us wary of a 'march of progress' view of history.

Like the New Right, Mullins concentrated on the criminality of the less well-off, singling out what he called the 'low grade' and the 'mentally deficient'. His discussion of remedies lays before us in stark terms the dichotomy between, on the one hand, welfare/treatment, and on the other, social control/punishment. Lamenting the general drift towards welfarism, Mullins in effect labelled those who emphasized the social bases of crime (and especially deprivation) as 'excuse makers'. The parallels with New Right criminology are obvious. Like Mullins, the New Right has come down on the side of social control. In 1945 it was a pre-emptive strike against an imminent social welfare programme, today it is an attack on the supposed failure of that programme. As we have seen, Mullins's preferred instrument of social control was sterilization; those sections of society prone to commit crime should be prevented from producing a new generation of criminals. Thankfully, in the year that marks the fiftieth anniversary of the liberation of Auschwitz, this view is less palatable than it used to be.

13 | Criminological theory

In the last chapter we looked at the social and political context in which the discipline of criminology continued to develop in the 1980s and 1990s. With this as a backdrop, in this final chapter we examine in more detail the main currents in criminological theory at the present time: feminism; administrative criminology; right-wing classicism; neo-positivism; and radical criminology.

This is not an exhaustive list of contemporary theoretical work in criminology, but it does indicate the more recent developments.

Mainstream criminology

One omission is what is usually termed 'mainstream' criminology. The name is not used to suggest that it plays a prominent role nowadays, but rather that it continues the empirically grounded, positivist tradition associated with pre-new deviancy criminology. However, it should not be confused with recent New Right versions of positivism discussed later. The principle features of mainstream criminology have been well summarized by Barbara Hudson (1993: 3):

> Mainstream criminology may itself now be on the theoretical margins, but it continues. It can be identified primarily by an absence of concern with the role of the state in producing crime, an absence of concern with the part played by social reactions in producing criminal identities, and absence of any appreciation of crime and criminal justice as contingent outcomes of socio-political configurations. In mainstream criminology there is no deconstruction of definitions of crime and no fundamental challenge to state punishment strategies or practices: its concern is to assist state correctional policies by providing information about criminals which will facilitate fine-tuning of penal practices.

This summary of the characteristics of mainstream criminology points to its unreconstructed nature, in the sense that it has tended to remain true to a particular understanding of what criminology should essentially be seeking to achieve. Although theoretical developments from the new deviancy period onwards are acknowledged, and sometimes incorporated into research, mainstream criminologists are in general terms committed to a core orthodoxy as indicated above. This has entailed, first, a concentration on the amount and distribution of so-called conventional crime, such as burglary, theft, criminal damage and certain sorts of violence, in other words, offences that make up the bulk of recorded crime; they are also the types of offences that members of the general public are most likely to worry about. Secondly, there is a continuing interest in young offenders, reflecting the message from official statistics and self-report studies that this age group is disproportionately involved in crime. Thirdly, there is a strong positivist orientation, expressed in attempts to identify the factors that cause or predict crime.

Although the concerns of mainstream criminology, in particular the search for causal factors, are out of favour with government funding agencies at the present time, these concerns do coalesce around questions that continue to dominate public debate, notably: Who commits crime and why do they do it? In view of this it will be useful to extend this discussion of mainstream criminology via an examination of the concept of 'criminal career'.

Longitudinal research and criminal careers

Criminal career research involves plotting the amounts and types of offending of a sample of individuals as they go through life; because of the relatively large time periods covered they are referred to as longitudinal studies. The variables that appear to be associated with the offending are then noted. Proponents point out that longitudinal studies are superior to cross-sectional studies (which provide a 'snapshot' of a number of individuals at a given moment) because changes in behaviour can be linked to changes in relevant variables. As Farrington (1994: 539) says in a recent, comprehensive review of criminal careers:

> Cross-sectional studies make it impossible to distinguish between indicators and causes, since they can merely demonstrate correlations between high levels of one factor (e.g. unemployment) and high levels of another (e.g. offending). However, longitudinal studies can show that offending is greater (within individuals) during some periods (e.g. of unemployment) than during other periods (e.g. of employment).

However, as Farrington acknowledges, longitudinal studies still have to cope with the problem of disentangling dependent from independent variables, that is, causes from symptoms.

Criminal career research does not, in itself, produce criminological theories; rather it is empirical research which aims to provide resources for the testing or development of criminological theories. Historically, such research has concerned itself with conventional, rather than white-collar, crime and has often relied on information from official statistics, although self-report studies are used. The following is a brief discussion of the kind of data generated by criminal career research.

Age and criminality

Research in Britain and other European countries, and in the United States, has shown that by the time they reach their thirties a large proportion of males have been convicted of a criminal offence (see Home Office (1985) and Farrington and West (1990) in Britain; Stattin, Magnusson and Reichel (1989) in Sweden; Wolfgang *et al.* (1987) in the United States). Farrington and West, for instance, found that over one-third of males in London aged up to 32 years had been convicted of at least one criminal offence serious enough to be recorded in the Criminal Records Office. This study is part of an ongoing longitudinal research project called the Cambridge Study in Delinquent Development. Using a sample of four hundred males born in 1951–54, the project was set up at the beginning of the 1960s by D. J. West; D. P. Farrington has been the major collaborator. When self-report studies are used, over 90 per cent of adult males admit to having committed at least one criminal offence (Farrington, 1989). Obviously raw data such as these need to be carefully scrutinized so that such things as frequency and seriousness are taken into account. The comparable figures for females, it should be noted, are much lower (gender and crime is discussed later). The build-up of offences as an individual moves through adolescence and adulthood is referred to as the 'cumulative prevalence' of offending.

According to official statistics and self-report data, there is a much greater prevalence of offending among teenagers than among other age groups. Currently the peak age for offending, based on cautions and convictions, is 18 years. The Home Affairs Committee (1993) reported that of the indictable offences committed by juveniles, and for which they were cautioned or convicted in 1990, 60 per cent involved theft or handling stolen goods, 17 per cent burglary, 10 per cent violence and 4 per cent criminal damage. Evidence from research, though, indicates that offenders are not specialized: known offenders tend to be involved in different types of offence (Farrington *et al.*, 1988). There is some evidence that specialization increases with age; sex offenders being the most specialized (ibid.). A significant finding is that a very large proportion of teenagers commit offences, but in the main these are relatively trivial and rarely lead to a caution or court appearance (most avoid getting caught). Of those arrested and prosecuted, most will have ceased or significantly reduced their offending by the time they are into their twenties (Belson, 1975; West, 1982). Studies from various countries show that offending usually begins at age 13-15 years, and shoplifting and criminal damage seem to be the typical offences committed in the early teenage years. Farrington (1992a) found that the 'take off' age for an acceleration in offending was 14 years, and for a decrease, 23 years. His self-report study (Farrington, 1989) discovered that certain types of offences, basically theft, burglary and criminal damage, declined as individuals went through their teens into their twenties, though the decrease was much less for theft from work, assault, drug use and fraud.

It was also discovered that first convictions occured on average at 17.5 years of age, with those convicted during an earlier pre-adolescence stage most likely to persist in offending (Farrington, 1992a). Many studies point to the link between late onset of offending and early desistance (e.g. Home Office, 1987). Whether the link between early onset and later persistence is a result of the behaviour in itself encouraging further offending, the labelling process, or the unfolding of a 'criminal potential', is in dispute. A Home Office (1987) study suggested that if burglary or theft were the onset offences, then persistent offending could be predicted. Desistance from offending seems to be associated with the development of a close relationship with a partner (unless the partner is also an offender), job statisfaction, worries about getting caught and a sense of 'maturity' (Shover, 1985).

Socio-economic status and criminality

The link between low socio-economic or low social class status and criminal behaviour has been the subject of much research activity within criminology. As we have seen, many criminological models take this as given. Although this link is reflected in official statistics, data from self-report studies are less conclusive (see Box, 1981, 1987; Rutter and Giller, 1983; Farrington, 1995, for reviews). Certainly in the case of more trivial offences, self-report studies indicate that offending is widespread among all social classes, although in Britain low social classes are still overrepresented (less so in the United States). With respect to more serious offences, studies tend to point to a correlation between rates of offending and low socio-economic status (Rutter and Giller, 1983). However, some writers (e.g. Box, 1981, and Hindelang, Hirschi and Weis, 1981) have disputed this.

As measures of criminal activity, there are a number of difficulties with self-report studies, in addition to the obvious ones such as getting respondents to tell the truth. First, they are usually carried out on youths, and therefore exclude many serious offences in the white-collar and corporate crime categories. Secondly, as Roshier (1989) says, because such studies are generally conducted in school, the serious and frequent offenders are more likely to be absent because of truanting. Thirdly, and again following Roshier, when more detailed indicators than, for instance, being a manual worker are used, then links between social and economic disadvantage and criminality become more apparent. Fourthly, the crudity of questionnaires means that they often fail to distinguish between fairly and very frequent offending (Wilson and Herrnstein, 1985).

The Cambridge Study was one attempt to deal with detailed indicators. The study found that juvenile and adult offending – official and self-reported – could be predicted on the basis of low family income, poor housing and large family size (Farrington, 1992a, 1992b). One of the benefits of criminal career research is that the same individual can be followed through life. Thus the Cambridge Study found that an unstable (unskilled) work record on the part of a boy's father was a predictor of offending by the boy when aged 18 years, and an unstable (unskilled) work record at 18 years predicted offending between 21 and 25 years. In this study conviction rates were found to increase when individuals were unemployed (Farrington, 1986).

Anti-social tendencies

Criminal career research has very often tried to identify various 'anti-social' tendencies in early life that are associated with offending later on, or, as West and Farrington (1977) argue, form a totality of which delinquency is one element. Clearly, a term such as anti-social will mean different things to different people, and within criminal career research the term has encompassed a very wide range of activities: for example, smoking, bullying, sexual intercourse, lying, poor concentration and truanting. Often the focus has been on the escalation of anti-social/offending behaviour as an individual develops. A large body of research has pointed to links between various clusters of anti-social behaviour and offending:

In the Cambridge Study, delinquents tended to be troublesome and dishonest in their primary schools, tended to be aggressive and frequent liars at age 12–14, and tended to be bullies at age 14. By age 18, delinquents tended to be anti-social in a wide variety of respects, including heavy drinking, heavy smoking, using prohibited drugs, and heavy gambling. In addition, they tended to be sexually promiscuous, often beginning sexual intercourse under age 15, having several sexual partners by age 18, and usually having unprotected intercourse. (Farrington, 1992b)

I sense some readers of this book shuffling uncomfortably in their seats. Some have traced so-called anti-social tendencies to an even earlier age. In an American study of 3 and 4 year olds in kindergarten, Spivack, Marcus and Swift (1986) argue that misbehaviour at that age predicted trouble with the police in later life. An even more startling revelation comes from a piece of research by Bates et al. (1991) which purported to show that six-month-old baby boys whose mothers judged them to be 'difficult' in terms of temperament, were likely to exhibit anti-social tendencies at age 8. Some studies, for example, Eron and Huesmann (1990) and Farrington (1993) have found that aggression during boyhood is associated with assaults on spouses and bullying in adulthood, and such men are very likely to have sons who themselves carry out these behaviours when they are adults. However, longitudinal studies do show that around a half of the children defined as anti-social are not so defined by the time that they reach adulthood.

Family context

Longitudinal studies have paid particular attention to family factors, with a view to discovering those factors that predict offending during adolescence. Typically, this research points to the following as predictive factors: irregular and harsh discipline, lax supervision, large family size, lack of parental interest in, and involvement with, the child, parents who exhibit anti-social tendencies, and conflict between parents (West and Farrington, 1973; McCord, 1979; Wilson, 1980; Loeber and Stouthamer-Loeber, 1986).

According to McCord (1979), rejection or lack of interest on the part of the mother predicted the child's later involvement in property crime, whilst violent crime was linked to having been brought up in a family where parental conflict and aggression were in evidence.

The Cambridge Study found that a relatively small number of families were responsible for a very large proportion of criminal behaviour. Indeed, having a convicted parent or sibling was an important predictor of later offending by a child (West and Farrington, 1973, 1977). Having a convicted parent, however, was a predictor of persistence in offending in later life, rather than a predictor of early onset of offending.

Lone-parent families have recently come under the spotlight in debates about juvenile crime (see, for example, the remarkable convergence between Conservative ministers and self-styled 'ethical socialist' in Dennis, 1993). On a general level, longitudinal studies do tend to show that children brought up in homes broken by divorce or separation (but not death) are more likely to become juvenile and adult offenders than are children brought up in two-parent families (Wadsworth, 1979; Farrington, 1992b), though this is not the case if parental divorce or separation occurs before the child is 5 years old. However, these research findings do not show that family structure, and in particular the lone-parent family, is *per se* criminogenic. Longitudinal researchers acknowledge that abstracting 'lone parent' as a single causal factor is far too simplistic, and ignores factors such as economic and social deprivation and the nature of relationships between spouses and between parents and children. McCord (1982) took a sample of families where the childen's natural father had (because of death, divorce or separation) left the home and, for comparison, a sample of unbroken families. She reported that the prevalence of serious offending on the part of the children was as follows:

Lone-parent families:
   62 per cent where the mother failed to give the child affection.
   22 per cent where the mother was affectionate.

Two-parent families:
   52 per cent where parental conflict existed.
   26 per cent where there was little parental conflict.

A Home Office study by Riley and Shaw (1985: 45) in the mid-1980s concluded: 'The notion that one-parent families are . . . "criminogenic" receives no support from the results of the present survey.' For a brief, but useful overview see Rodger, (1995).

Moral panics?

In the light of the issues raised during the above discussion of mainstream criminology, and before examining contemporary criminological theory, we can complete this section by discussing briefly some current debates on the specific theme of juvenile offending and criminal justice policies.

A striking feature of the juvenile justice legislation introduced between the beginning of the 1980s and the middle of the 1990s is its lack of consistency. To what extent, one might ask, is this a reflection of political expediency or knee-jerk reactions, as opposed to a careful consideration of what might actually 'work'? Importantly, government policy has to be seen against the backdrop of a desire to present a tough law and order stance, and pressure to cut costs via 'value for money' (currently over £7 billion per year is spent on the criminal justice system).

At the beginning of the 1990s Home Office ministers were congratulating themselves on the apparent success of their juvenile justice policies. Official statistics showed that between 1985 and 1991 the number of offenders aged 17 or under convicted or cautioned had more than halved – 264,000 in 1985 compared with 149,000 in 1991. In 1992 the figure decreased further to 99,000. This contrasted with an increase of 150 per cent in the number of male juvenile offenders convicted or cautioned in the period 1959 to 1977. The decrease from the mid-1980s is only partly explained by a reduction in the juvenile population. There was, too, during the 1980s a significant decrease in the number of juveniles being given custodial sentences. In 1979 the number was 7,900, and in 1984 it was 6,700, falling to 1,500 in 1990, and then rising to 2,000 in 1991.

An optimistic reading would conclude that over the period in question there really was a fall in the number of juveniles who offended. On the other hand, more juveniles may have escaped apprehension; or (which is highly likely) police may have preferred to issue informal cautions rather than formal cautions or setting in motion prosecution procedures. During the 1980s amounts of recorded crime in general continued to increase and, given the disproportionate involvement of juveniles in offending, the apparent decreases seem anomalous. A serious difficulty with all this, of course, is that we cannot know the ages of those committing the majority of recorded offences. As Maguire (1994: 271) points out:

> not many more than one in ten offences recorded by the police result in a caution or conviction . . . only about one in fifty of the comparable crimes identified by the BCS (British Crime Survey) result in a conviction – a figure which drops to as low as one in 200 where 'vandalism' (criminal damage) is concerned.
>
> This being the case, it can obviously not simply be assumed that the characteristics of 'offenders' as a whole can be inferred from those of adjudicated offenders.

In spite of the optimistic glow induced in some quarters by the juvenile crime figures, the early 1990s witnessed a significant upsurge of interest in the 'youth crime problem'. The *Daily Star* in November 1992 pulled no punches, arguing that:

> hardcore child super-crooks are bringing fear to Britain's streets . . . they are our number one crime problem, tearaways just out of primary school who have learned their lessons in motor theft and housebreaking so well they account for *90 per cent* of offences. (Quoted in Hagel and Newburn, 1994: 97; emphasis in original)

The mass media provided a rich diet of young thugs 'laughing at the law', 'rat boys', 'criminal tots' in balaclavas who terrorized certain neighbourhoods, and rampaging rioters. The James Bulger case provided a particularly potent image. For many media commentators this was not merely an isolated, idiosyncratic and tragic event (which was how the Mary Bell case in the 1960s, which contained similar features, seemed to be interpreted). Rather, it tended to be presented as a symbol of something having gone profoundly wrong with Britain's children. As public and political debate focused increasingly on youngsters as a generalized threat, a parallel concern was growing which stressed the role of children as victims. In her ongoing study of 11 to 16 year olds in Cleveland, Browne (1994) for instance, found that for many children the world was a frightening and dangerous place. It was not uncommon for weapons to be carried for self-defence, bullying in schools was endemic and a large number of girls spoke of sexual harassment from male teachers (see also Anderson *et al.*, 1991; Hartless *et al.*, 1995). At the same time various child sex abuse scandals appeared in the media, and there were numerous references to parents being increasingly worried about their younger children playing outdoors and walking home from school alone.

Meanwhile, the judiciary and the police argued that the official statistics were misleading, and that the 1980s had seen not a decrease, but an increase in juvenile crime. This was the dominant view within the mass media, and it was not contradicted by the evidence from academic research. In July 1995, under the headline 'Thatcher's children turn to crime', the *Observer* carried a front page story by Hugill that drew on the findings from three recent pieces of research. In particular that by James who, linking crime to Thatcherism, argued that there had been 'an unprecedented increase in violent crime by and against young people. He reports a 41 per cent increase since 1987 . . . [He] has found that since 1987 juvenile crime figures have risen at a rate of 12,000 crimes a year, three times faster than the average of 4,000 for 1979–86' (Hugill, 1995: 1).

The government, on the other hand, believed that their policies were bearing fruit and amounts of juvenile crime were decreasing. One of their policies had been to divert juveniles from custody, hence the huge decreases in custodial sentences. More recently, however, the use of custody has increased (for all ages), and the 1994 Criminal Justice and Public Order Act introduced, among other things, secure training centres for 12 to 14 year olds convicted of serious offences. This was a significant turnaround from the philosophy underpinning the 1991 Criminal Justice Act, and signalled a reversal to a more punitive 'law and order' stance that might satisfy those who believed that the criminal justice system was 'soft' on criminals. It did, however, appear to contradict government celebrations of earlier decreases in recorded offending. The way out of this quandary was for the Home Office to join with judiciary and police and argue that the real problem lay with a hard core of persistent young offenders, and these were now to be targeted. Kenneth Clarke, the Home Secretary who framed the Act, spoke of 'really persistent, nasty little juvenile offenders', and the Prime Minister urged that 'we should understand less and condemn more'. The size of this group of 'persistent' offenders has been the subject of much controversy during the 1990s. The Home Office identified boys in their mid-teens who had been given many informal warnings by the police and who were responsible for the lion's share of juvenile crime. Persistent juvenile offending was one of the issues looked at by the Home Affairs Committee (1993) of the House of Commons. Agencies giving evidence to the Committee, such as the Association of Chief Police Officers (ACPO), the National Association of Probation Officers (NAPO) and Chief Officers of Probation, all agreed that a small group of persistent offenders did exist, and each offered an estimate of the numbers involved (NAPO, for example, thought that there might be 12 to 20 in Newcastle upon Tyne; ACPO suggested around 600 for England and Wales). ACPO also argued that during the decade of the 1980s, and contrary to what official statistics said, juvenile offending had actually increased by 54 per cent. As they saw it, the decrease in the statistics was misleading, and reflected a decline in the proportion of juveniles in the population coupled with a lower police detection rate. Therefore, if these two factors had remained constant, during the 1980s there would have been an increase of 54 per cent in juvenile crime.

Persistent offenders

Clearly, given the nature of the debate, there is plenty of scope for statistical manipulation and astonishing conjecture. In the case of a so-called hard core of persistent offenders, efforts to define and quantify them are fraught with a range of difficulties. For instance, offenders 'known' to the police may subsequently experience greater police scrutiny (for example, when searching for stolen property), leading to them being continually sucked into the system. Although multiple offending may come to light among these groups, such offending among others will go unrecorded. This is particularly important if research is extended into an examination of socio-cultural and other factors associated with offending behaviour, for it cannot be assumed that known offenders constitute a representative sample of all offenders.

The most recent British study of so-called persistent young offenders is that carried out by Hagel and Newburn (1994) and commissioned by the Home Office Research and Planning Unit. This research took a sample of 531 10 to 16 year olds in two geographical areas – London and the Midlands – who were selected on the basis of having been arrested at least three times during 1992. The authors acknowledge the view that because self-report studies show that offending by young people is widespread, it is fruitless to search for individual and family characteristics. However, most of this is trivial and infrequent; thus Hagel and Newburn (1994: 78) argue: 'The issue of reoffending refocuses attention on such work, however, for although *most* young people may engage in criminal acts at one time or another, persistent offenders by any definition are a small minority.' They prefer to label their overall sample 'reoffenders', rather than persistent offenders.

Offending profiles

In line with other studies referred to earlier, the research found that reoffenders who specialized in one type of crime were in a minority; only one-fifth were, on the basis of known offending, in this category. However, those who had committed the widest range of offences were also those who had committed the most offences. Lone offenders were in a minority: over three-quarters of offences were committed in the company of others, and the indications were that many of the offenders knew each other. A majority of reoffenders – 60 per cent – had committed their offences whilst on police or court bail, a finding that provides ammunition for those who have complained about 'bail bandits'. The researchers, though, found that there was often a long gap between offence and final sentence, and the bulk of offenders had spent most of the year on bail.

Violent offences were more common among the sample than among juvenile offenders in general: one-third had committed a violent crime. More serious violence, in the form of grievous bodily harm, was rare, and no offences of rape, manslaughter or murder were recorded. The majority of offences involved property, with the largest proportion covering the range £10–£100 in value.

Not surprisingly, the self-report element of the study showed greater amounts of offending than did police records. Illicit drug use, in particular, was underrecorded: 'drug use among the group was very frequent' (ibid. 70).

Offender profiles

Hagel and Newburn's study included interviews with 74 of the sample, and although this was a relatively small response rate, as the authors say: 'the survey still provides a unique source of illustrative information about a group that is very hard to interview' (ibid. 78). Of the reoffenders, 32 of those interviewed lived with their mothers only, and five with their fathers, while 22 lived with both parents. Most said that they got on well or fairly well with their mothers. Where there was a father figure, expressions of loyalty were only slightly weaker, though relationships with fathers appeared to become less close with the passage of time. Eleven per cent of the interviewed sample were girls, compared with 14 per cent for the total sample of reoffenders.

Closer examination of family circumstances pointed to some

inconsistencies: for example, half of those interviewed said that they had run away from home at least once. A further source of information was social services departments. Although gathering together the relevant evidence was quite difficult, the researchers say that the data suggest that a high proportion had experienced social services care in the past, with the vast majority first entering the system because of welfare problems, rather than because of offending behaviour. Half of those interviewed had at one time been referred for counselling or psychological help.

Two out of three of the group were no longer at school, and many had left before they officially should have done. Over half had been permanently excluded. Views on school were generally negative, and truanting was commonplace.

Few of those interviewed had jobs, and lack of money was clearly an important factor in their lives, especially as they were ineligible for state benefits. When asked why they committed crime, money was often mentioned, as were boredom and the excitement experienced from crime, being influenced by others, and wanting to act tough.

Half of the group were living in households where the head of the household was either unemployed or not working. Only a tiny minority lived in a household where the head was in a non-manual job.

Who are persistent offenders?

Obviously, in any given year there will be enormous variation in frequency of offending within the juvenile population – from never to a great deal. There will also be enormous variation in the seriousness of this offending: some will commit a lot of very trivial offences, whilst others will commit relatively few yet extremely serious offences. The central theme of Hagel and Newburn's research was how the notion of 'persistent offender' might be defined and the extent to which those so defined possessed certain common characteristics. Of particular importance was an assessment of the number of offenders in their sample who would be classified as persistent offenders eligible for what at the time of the research was a proposed secure training order. This, together with plans to build secure training centres, became part of the 1994 Criminal Justice and Public Order Act. The secure training order was one of three criteria used as a basis for defining 'persistent'. The main conclusions can be summarized as follows:

- Although Hagel and Newburn's (1994) sample represented, as they put, the 'heavy end' of juvenile offending, it was difficult to identify a distinct group of very frequent offenders. Frequent reoffending coupled with offending over lengthy periods of time were rare. Applying the three different criteria produced three groups of 'persistent offenders'. However, in terms of the individuals comprising these groups, little overlap was found. Put another way, the different measures of 'persistent' did not lead to the identification of one distinct group: 'Only three children out of the full sample of 193 Midlands reoffenders aged 12–14 were defined as "persistent" by all three sets of criteria, whereas a total of 36 were persistent according to one definition or another' (ibid. 131).

- There were 'no striking differences' (from the point of view of, for example, seriousness of offence) between those identified as persistent by any of the sets of criteria and the rest of the overall sample, apart from the former having committed three or more offences that year.

As Hagel and Newburn (1994: 123) say:

not only is the process of attempting to define persistence deeply problematic, but because there is a degree of arbitrariness in the way some offenders rather than others become defined as persistent, creating a custodial sentence for that group raises issues both about equality and about efficient resource use.

The historical roots of contemporary criminology

In the words of Lilley, Cullen and Ball (1989: 194): 'Rather than being a period of new theories cut from the whole cloth, the 1980s were primarily a time that witnessed the revitalization of old theories.' With the exception of feminism, each of the theoretical perspectives or paradigms looked at in this chapter has a direct link with either eighteenth-century classicial criminology, nineteenth-century positivism, or interactionism/neo-Marxism from the 1960s and early 1970s. Classical criminology emphasized 'free will', conceiving of human beings as rational creatures able to weigh up the costs and benefits of crime. Described by Vold (1958) as 'administrative criminology', classicism was primarily concerned with establishing effective and efficient deterrents that would control crime by making the pain of punishment outweigh the pleasure of the offence. Having said that, a recent rereading of early classical texts by Beirne (1993) suggests that although unrecognized in historical accounts, classicism also contained strong elements of psychological determinism. Positivism concentrated on the offender rather than the offence, and was committed to the application of scientific method. The aim was to discover the causes of criminality – in the earlier period located in the individual's genetic/biological make-up, but later on traced to psychological or social factors. Unlike classical criminology, positivism drew a sharp distinction between criminals and non-criminals. Interactionism shifted attention away from the deterministic search for the causes of crime, and focused instead on the nature of social reactions to behaviour perceived as deviant. Through labelling processes, deviance/crime was thus socially constructed, and was not seen as an inherent quality of the act. Neo-Marxist approaches attempted to develop a political economy of crime through analyses of law making and control within the context of a capitalist mode of production. The links between these approaches and contemporary criminology can be briefly indicated as follows:

- *Administrative criminology.* A direct descendant of the classical tradition, with a primary interest in deterring crime and a lack of interest in the causes of criminality. There are elements of control theory.

- *Right-wing classicism.* This too explores ways of deterring people from breaking the law, laying stress on 'rational choice' and the individual's personal responsibility for their actions. With an explicit commitment to the politics of the New Right, there is an acceptance of punishment as retribution. There are libertarian and conservative versions of right-wing classicism.

- *Neo-positivism.* Some versions are associated with the New Right and have close links with the earlier forms of positivism. Other versions have been influenced by control theory.

- *Radical criminology.* Broadly speaking, radical criminology contains two strands. On the one hand, critical criminologists who see themselves as the true carriers of the radical tradition, and on the other, self-styled left realists committed to 'taking crime seriously'. Critical criminology's roots lie in interactionism and neo-Marxism, whilst left realism has a more eclectic base, drawing, for instance, on subcultural theory and anomie. From the perspective of critical criminology, left realism is essentially reformist liberalism dressed up as radicalism, and has been seduced by the belief that criminal *justice* can be achieved in a fundamentally unjust society. From the other direction, left realism attacks critical criminology for being woefully utopian and ignoring the real concerns of working-class people.

- *Feminist perspectives.* These are less obviously linked to the main criminological traditions, as feminist perspectives on crime and social control arose out of broadly based feminist concerns. It is feminism and criminology that will be discussed first.

Feminism and criminology

Although 'feminism and criminology' is, I think, a reasonable signifier of the theoretical field under review, choosing a title for this part of the chapter was less straightforward than it might appear. The early contributions from feminist writers in the 1970s stimulated a wave of intense theoretical work as the 1980s and 1990s unfolded. Given the increasing complexity of the debates, and the different theoretical and political directions from which writers were coming, it was inevitable that a number of different strands began to emerge. In the context of these debates, not only is the definition of 'feminism' problematic, but so too is the definition of 'criminology'. Although on a general level feminists may have a common commitment to 'the elimination of gender inequalities' (Dominelli, 1992: 85), it is probably more correct to speak of feminisms rather than feminism. Adamson *et al.* (1988) identify liberal, radical, socialist and black feminisms; Gregory (1986) refers to radical, socialist and bourgeois versions. Different theoretical and political orientations have also developed within the field of criminology. Thus the question of whether or not a feminist criminology exists, is desirable, or is possible, remains unsettled. In their review of feminism and criminology in Britain up to the late 1980s, Gelsthorpe and Morris (1988) mention a range of opinion on this. Greenwood (1981) and Brown (1986) support the idea of an extant feminist criminology, whilst Smart (1981) is sceptical in view of the divisions existing at the level of theory and practice. According to Gelsthorpe and Morris (1988: 97): 'just as we had to talk of "feminisms", we have to talk of feminist criminolog*ies*, or, better still, feminist perspectives within criminology.'

They do add, however, that feminist perspectives share 'certain core elements': they are anti-positivist, critical of stereotypes, place women centre stage and are concerned to develop methodologies which are 'sympathetic to these concerns'. Different, and often competing, strands, though, exist within this broad framework and there have been complex debates about precisely what a feminist analysis of crime and social control would look like. Some writers, such as Cousins (1980), Cain (1989, 1990) and Smart (1990) have rejected the idea of linking feminism to the discipline of criminology itself. Using the notion of deconstruction associated with postmodernism, they argue that by attaching themselves to 'criminology', as a taken-for-granted 'given', feminists unwittingly fall into a conceptual trap. This is because criminology is crime-inology – that is, the study of what is assumed to be special behaviour, qualitatively different to non-criminal behaviour, when in fact it has no meaning beyond ideological and institutional contexts. It is rather like feminists studying seventeenth-century 'witches', but defining them in exactly the way that a male witchfinder from that century defined them. Put another way, why should feminists surrender to an already existing 'essentialist' conceptualization of 'crime', as if the concept itself was not problematic? This is an aspect of doing criminology that has been alluded to in earlier discussions, and does raise important and complex issues. These issues, though, have not been ignored by radical writers, feminist or otherwise (see Sumner, 1990, 1994; Hester and Eglin, 1992). As Pat Carlen (1992: 62) has pointed out:

> fear of the ideological and already institutionalized meanings of the empirical referent is not new among social scientists or political theorists attempting radical critique. Yet the very task of theory is to engage in a struggle for power over the 'meaning of things' (including all material and ideological constructs). The purpose is to produce new meanings that will empower.

Smart (1990) is also critical of efforts by feminists to develop a 'feminist criminology' committed to 'useful', policy-oriented research that is ostensibly aimed at, say, improving the treatment of women by the criminal justice system. Again, this is a familiar theme within radical thought, often turning on the 'reformism' versus 'revolution' debate (see the later discussion of left realism), and is certainly not a view shared by all radical feminists. Moulds (1980) argues that feminist research should be directed towards the creation of a criminal justice system that treats men and women equally, whilst Heidensohn (1986) points to cultural differences between male and female offenders that necessitate different types of dispositions by the courts. And Carlen (1990) has argued for the abolition of imprisonment for all but a small minority of female offenders.

Heidensohn (1994: 1029) has recently stated: 'something of an epistemological crisis has affected social science and feminism, and studies of crime are implicated.' Put simply, there are still important questions to be answered regarding *what* is to be studied and *how* it is to be studied. Should the focus be on female offenders, or on the concept of gender and its explanatory power with respect to female and male offending? To what extent should studies of social control and jurisprudence be a part of this? Should the main business of feminism be to illuminate the continuing injustices experienced by females in the criminal justice system? Or should it concentrate on the various ways in which women are victimized? And, from the point of view of methodology, can only women study women (see Harding, 1991 and the concept of 'standpointism' – which suggests that only researchers who share the feelings and experiences of the subject can carry out meaningful research)? Which returns us to the central question: What makes a piece of research distinctly 'feminist'?

In a useful review of some of these debates, Carlen defends the view that feminists should study 'women and crime', but at the same time does not accept that 'a "feminist criminology" is either desirable or possible' (Carlen, 1992: 53). It is not *desirable*, she says, because it suggests that a universal theory which reduces female (and by implication, male) criminality to distinctive biologies can be constructed. The biological fact of being female, and the social context of patriarchy, have, therefore, to be seen in conjunction with a host of other possibilities when explaining criminality, such as, poverty, affluence, unemployment, racism, upbringing, education, and so on. A feminist criminology is not *possible*, says Carlen, because:

1. Apart from patriarchy, criminological knowledge has not developed distinctly 'feminist' explanatory concepts.

2. Those things that interest feminists merge into issues of class, racism and imperialism.

3. No single theory can explain:
    (a) why women's crimes are in the main crimes of the powerless;
    (b) why there is a disproportionate number of ethnic minority women in prison; and
    (c) why most women in prison are poor.

Making females visible

As we have seen, early feminist writers complained that traditional criminology had to a large extent made females invisible. Stanley and Wise (1983) argued that in addition to using non-sexist methodologies, and a commitment to the production of practical knowledge, feminist research in criminology should 'make women visible'. Feminist explanations of 'invisibility' highlighted the male domination of the discipline. However, the fact that males appeared to commit most crime (and certain sorts of males at that) cannot be overlooked as a factor shaping the focus of research. After all, the crimes of aristocratic men were also made invisible:

> It so happens that criminological theory has been crime-led, and that the subjects around whom theorizing has been formed have been predominantly white, urban, lower-class, and usually adolescent males in advanced industrial capitalist societies. (Downes and Rock, 1988: 289)

Since the 1970s there has been a growth in research that has attempted to measure the gaps between male and female crime rates. This was largely triggered by the argument in some quarters (e.g. Adler, 1975; Simon, 1975) that as women became more 'liberated', we could expect their crime rates to move nearer to those of men. Relying on official data is, of course, fraught with a range of well-known problems: for example, the extent to which they reflect organizational practices, rather than criminal activities as such and, in the case of females, how small increases can appear in an exaggerated form because of the small numbers comprising the original base. Box and

Hale (1983) found a proportionate increase in conventional property crime for females during the 1970s, but not with respect to burglary or robbery; also, there were no increases for violent offences. According to Home Office figures for England and Wales, the proportion of violent offences attributable to females rose from 9.0 per cent to 11.2 per cent between 1979 and 1989. For other indictable offences proportions varied widely. Self-report studies, as mentioned earlier, tend to put males and females closer together, but seriousness of offence and frequency of offending are not always carefully controlled for. One recent self-report and victim study of school-age children in Edinburgh (Anderson *et al.*, 1991) attempted to be sensitive to one of these aspects by asking the children themselves to rank various offences in terms of perceived seriousness. The self-report data show that three to four times as many boys as girls have committed serious offences based on dishonesty and violence, whilst in the case of drug-related offences, the proportion was only slightly higher for boys. When it came to offences ranked as 'less serious', the ratio again varied according to type of offence, as follows:

Offence	Ratio of boys to girls
Rowdy/rude	1.06 to 1
Fighting	1.96 to 1
Shoplifting	1.33 to 1
Broken into car	2.50 to 1
Vandal car	3.00 to 1
Vandal property	1.36 to 1

Source: Based on Anderson *et al.*, 1991: 107.

This still leaves, though, the problem of distinguishing between different *types* of vandalism, shoplifting, and so forth.

In her pioneering book, Smart (1976) referred to the possible danger of a moral panic accompanying feminist efforts to make female crime visible, and the attempt by some writers to equate increased offending with women's liberation would seem to bear this out. Much feminist work has been devoted to counteracting this kind of reasoning. Smart (1979), for example, argued that what increases there were in female crime rates in fact pre-dated the impact of the women's liberation movement. More recently, Carlen (1990) puts forward the view that any increases in property crime among women are more likely to be explained by economic recession and deprivation.

There is a double edge to the project of making female crime 'visible'. Those feminists who are unhappy at traditional characterizations of women as passive, and resigned to their fate, whilst men 'rebel' through crime (as 'proto-revolutionary' Paki-bashers or football hooligans, say), may be tempted to present female crime in a positive light. On the other hand, those who wish to underline masculinity as the primary basis for criminality, could find this approach subverted if large amounts of female crime suddenly materialized. Quite a few important studies have been carried out, from a feminist standpoint, which concentrate specifically on female criminals; for example, Campbell (1984) on girl members of delinquent gangs in New York; Campbell (1986), a self-report study of girls and violence; Browne (1987) on female murderers (of their husbands); McLeod (1982) and Miller (1986) on prostitutes; Carlen (1985) on a small group of 'criminal women'; Parton (1992) on the role of mothers in family child sex-abuse cases; MacDonald (1991) on women terrorists; Player (1989) on female burglars.

Challenging 'distortion'

When feminist work on female criminality began to emerge in the 1960s, one of the main arguments was that when women and girls had been made 'visible' within criminology, explanations of their criminality were usually based on versions of biological determinism or psychological reductionism, and their offences tended to be 'sexualized' and presented as 'irrational'. This approach, it was argued, created a climate where responses to female offenders tended to be based on assumptions of 'sickness' or mental illness (Carlen, 1983).

Some feminist writers, such as Leonard (1982), pressed for the modification of important sociologically oriented criminological theories, where women were neglected, so that they took account of gender. Others, such as Smart (1990), have argued against the idea that feminists should simply 'insert' women into already existing theoretical frameworks. Clearly, this is a complex issue, which turns on the question of whether existing theories contain the potential both to explain female crime, and draw out the gender dimension to criminal behaviour and reactions to it in general. In a vigorous defence of what some might call 'pre-feminist' criminology, and criticizing the 'stark terms' in which gender has been presented by some feminists, Downes and Rock (1988) argue that there is plenty of mileage in the work of major theorists and concepts such as drift, labelling and stigma. They also point to subcultural theories and control theories as explicitly providing explanations of the lower crime rates for females:

> Subcultural theories have assumed that females pursue less criminogenic and more attainable goals than men, namely marriage and family life, and are therefore insulated from the social sources of delinquency, the main exception

being the strain to sexual deviance. Control theories specify with some precision the far more intensive informal controls that are brought to bear on girls rather than boys, which constitute powerful inhibitors against criminality. (Ibid. 283)

If we look at some of the directions taken by recent feminist research on female criminality, certain tensions become apparent, indicating that it is more appropriate to speak of feminist criminolog*ies*:

1. Some theorists seek to accentuate the gender-based differences between males and females, and the implications of these differences for criminality. Gilligan (1982), for instance, argues that women possess a different personality to that of men.

2. Some theorists point out that female offenders have more characteristics in common with male offenders than was traditionally thought. Campbell (1986) argues that gangs composed of boys *and* girls do exist, and although less collective in nature, the girls are involved in more fighting than is commonly assumed. Another example of this is Naffine's (1987) critique of control theories for making females too passive.

3. Some theorists, though, have emphasized that the behaviour of both males and females has to be seen as mediated by other factors such as class or 'race'. Carlen (1988), in her ethnographic study of female offenders, discusses how the women were constrained in their choices by both gender and class. Likewise, Miller (1986), in a study of prostitutes, drew attention to the interrelationship between class and gender.

Heidensohn (1994) indicates three themes around which feminist research has been conducted during the 1980s and 1990s: patriarchy, economic and social marginalization, and control.

The concept of *patriarchy* – defined basically as male power – is particularly associated with radical feminism, and has tended to be employed when examining the treatment of women by the criminal justice system and the issue of victimization, rather than female criminality.

Explanations of crime based upon *economic marginalization*, and the resultant poverty and deprivation, have, as Heidensohn points out, been around in critical Marxist criminology for some time, although for much of that time issues of gender were ignored. Chapman (1980) links increases in recorded female property crime to economic recession and poverty, which she sees as having a greater impact on women than men. In particular, she points to the growth in the number of single mothers, who as a group are especially vulnerable to economic deprivation. *Social marginalization* arises because of women's 'child care role and their dependency on men or the state for welfare' (Heidensohn, 1994: 1027). This dimension is used to explain the types of offences available to women. Heidensohn is critical of the explanatory power of these approaches, seeing them as essentially positivist, and providing only a partial explanation of female criminality. Not all poor people, for instance break the law. 'Marginalization' explanations, though, have been popular with some feminists because they offer a way of challenging the argument that women's liberation leads to more crime (Adler, 1975; Simon, 1975).

Explanations based on *control* theory have become increasingly influential among feminists in the recent past. One reason is that by asking why people don't break the law, rather than why they do, a theoretical space is opened up into which the concept of gender can be inserted. Thus, as far as female criminality is concerned, the fundamental research question becomes: what social controls are at work that can explain the lower crime rates for females (e.g. Hagan, Simpson and Gillis, 1979; Stanko, 1993)?

Research of this sort has pointed to the significance of informal modes of control experienced by women, especially in terms of family and community sanctions and commitments. As a result, men are 'allowed' more freedom to explore deviant routes. According to Hagan *et al.* (1979), even 'career' women are locked into traditional roles *vis-à-vis* the family. Feminist critics of the view that women's liberation leads to more crime, in addition to stressing the links between poverty and crime, have also questioned the extent to which women in Britain are 'liberated'. However, if the lower crime rates for females are seen as a function of greater control, and if those controls were to be lessened, then, according to the logic of control theory, females would have more freedom to engage in crime. The opportunity to commit crime is an important element of this. In a Home Office self-report study of teenage girls, Riley (1986: 38) concluded that: 'given equal opportunities, sex differences in crime participation by young people – as offenders or victims – are minimal.'

Feminists have quite rightly argued that a fully social explanation of crime has to include a consideration of gender issues. This means addressing the range of social processes at work whereby male and female understandings of 'masculinity' and 'femininity' are constructed, and the ways in which these are linked to specific forms of law breaking. These understandings, however, should also be situated within a broader structural context linking gender to such things as class, 'race' and generation.

The criminal justice system

From the standpoint of radical feminism, women's experiences of the criminal justice system have to be seen within the context of patriarchy. For socialist feminists, the criminal justice system has to be seen as part of a capitalist mode of production. As Gelsthorpe and Morris (1988) argue, though, whatever the merits of these analyses, there is a need to explore in more detail precisely how the various elements of the system operate, and to appreciate that a whole range of mediating factors have to be taken into consideration: 'neither men nor the capitalist mode of production can be singled out as chief conspirators in a plot against women. However ideas about women have been shaped, there is no one unified motivational force underlying that shaping' (ibid. 99).

As we have seen, one central issue for feminists has been the debate about whether females are treated more leniently by the criminal justice system than men are. Proponents of the view that they are, have usually pointed to what they see as the 'chivalry' of the male administrators of the system. Again, this is a difficult area, where evidence either way is inconclusive. However, a large and growing body of feminist work has sought to challenge the leniency argument through detailed empirical studies (e.g. Worrall, 1981; Eaton, 1983, 1985, 1986; Carlen, 1983; Edwards, 1984). Research from the 1970s on this theme has already been discussed.

The police

According to Gregory (1986: 55): 'There is some evidence of leniency towards women both in the different cautioning rates for male and female offenders and in the different incarceration rates of those found guilty.' She then argues that 'paternalism', rather than chivalry, is a more appropriate term; but paternalism, as a form of sexism, could still operate in one's favour, of course. Put another way, it is possible that the police treat women more favourably than men, though for the worst reasons. In fact, Morris (1987) argues that it is at this point in the criminal justice process that chivalry is most likely to be in evidence.

It is important to recognize that the nature of street-level interactions between police and public, and the sorts of decisions that result, involve many other factors than gender, and it is not always easy to assess the relative importance of these various factors. As far as the decision to make an arrest is concerned, research in Britain and the United States shows that the prime factor is seriousness of offence. In line with other research, Harris (1992) found that an offender's demeanour was important (for example, showing respect and being apologetic), as was the offender's previous record. Females, however, were more likely to be cautioned than males. In his review of what is mainly American research, Box (1983) concludes that among those who have committed serious offences, older women, especially if they are white, are treated less aggressively than their male counterparts by the police. In her North American research, Player (1989) found that black women experienced significantly worse treatment than did white women.

Measuring the extent to which sexist attitudes exist among police officers is not easy, though what evidence there is does suggest that a combination of background and occupational culture does tend to produce sexist stereotyping. The Policy Studies Institute report on the Metropolitan Police (Smith and Grey, 1985) found that policemen would often joke and boast about their sexual activities, sometimes in the presence of female officers, and they enjoyed apocryphal tales involving sexist fantasies. The word 'plonk' was used as a term of abuse to refer to female officers. None of this is peculiar to policing as an occupation, of course, and it is important to understand how attitudes reflected in locker-room banter get translated into actual street-level behaviour (see also Young, 1993).

Clearly, it is difficult to make generalizations about the nature of (male) police–female (or male) relationships, There is, for instance, a distinction between women as victims and women as offenders, though Jones (1987) argues that negative attitudes towards women, based upon their supposed inferiority, found among officers influence their treatment of both victims and offenders. In the case of domestic violence, a large amount of feminist research has been critical of the reluctance of the police to make an arrest (Edwards, 1989), and for defining 'domestics' as not real policework (Faragher, 1981). (See Dunhill, 1989, for a detailed examination of this subject.) Prostitutes in particular have complained of unfair treatment by the police, though British research indicates a degree of ambivalence on the part of the police: 'Harassment and entrapment were reported, but also a degree of accommodation. Evidence given by police representatives themselves to a parliamentary committee showed disparaging views of women who prostitute themselves' (Heidensohn, 1994: 1008).

Sentencing

Evidence regarding the lenient, or otherwise, treatment of females by the courts is, according to Smith (1988), in a detailed analysis of available research, inconclusive. On a general level, a number of research findings can be noted. Home Office figures show that throughout the 1980s there was a gradual decrease in the use of fines for women offenders, and compared to men, a faster growth in the use of imprisonment. Recent Home Office statistics show that about 5 per cent of females convicted of an indictable offence are given a custodial sentence, whilst the figure for males is 20 per cent. Convicted female offenders are more likely than males to be put on probation, though they are less likely to be given a community service order. On the other hand, and echoing earlier research in the 1970s, as well as showing the complexities involved in interpreting the evidence, British research continues to point to the higher proportion of women than men held in custody, either awaiting trial or sentencing (Greenwood, 1983).

In a significant number of cases, sentencing delays for women arise because the court requires a medical report. Edwards (1984) found that females were much more likely than males to be subject to 'medicalized' interventions by the criminal justice system. In the case of young girls especially, decisions by the courts are strongly influenced by considerations of sexual morality and being 'at risk' (Chesney-Lind, 1986). One outcome is that a higher proportion of girls than boys are taken into care (Eaton, 1986). In an extensive investigation of 'chivalry' within the context of sentencing, Farrington and Morris (1983) came to the conclusion that the apparently more lenient sentences handed out to female offenders were explained by them having fewer previous convictions, and committing less serious offences. On the other hand, Allen (1987) found that women were treated more sympathetically than men when they had committed more serious violent offences.

A number of studies have indicated the particular stereotypes involving non-deviant lifestyles and culturally prescribed family roles that influence sentencing decisions. Eaton (1986) argues that both men and women who appeared to conform to conventional standards of 'normality' were more likely to benefit from a lighter sentence. Research by Daly (1989) in the United States supports this, pointing in particular to the benefits of having children and apparently stable family relationships. Carlen's (1983) study of Scottish Sheriffs underlined the more punitive responses to those women defined as 'failed mothers'. On the theme of leniency, feminists who have researched the area of domestic violence have argued that violent male partners have traditionally enjoyed a high degree of leniency by the courts (e.g. Dobash and Dobash, 1979, 1992).

In a study of the women of Greenham Common, Young (1990) draws out two particularly relevant issues. First, that the police and the courts were here dealing with women who were not involved in run-of-the-mill 'ordinary' crime, and were themselves defined as 'unconventional' (with a media campaign of degradation). Secondly, that an analysis of sentencing decisions has to get behind mere surface appearances. The Greenham women who found themselves in court could potentially have been charged with a broad range of offences, and the choices made reflected the wide discretionary powers of the police (and later on the Crown Prosecution Service). As Young says, on the whole the women were charged with minor offences carrying light sentences. This 'chivalrous' response is seen as resulting from the desire of the courts to maintain a good public image, an image that would have been threatened if many prison sentences were handed out. According to Young, though, there were other considerations at work. One was that the courts were concerned that if Greenham women were imprisoned, they would continue their campaigning within the prison. Furthermore, in some cases the seriousness of the offence was such that defendants could have opted for a jury trial. This was seen as providing the women with dangerous publicity, and consequently the tendency was to charge them with lesser offences. However, Young (1990: 24) does acknowledge that in some cases very severe sentences were passed by the courts:

> Thus, the response of the criminal justice agencies has combined trivialisation with severe criminalisation. Despite the attempts of women to retain some control of the situation through disruption of court procedure and through the positive use of the law as litigants, it would appear that the legal system has lent itself most profitably to the aims of the 'authorities'.

Finally, Matthews (1981) has pointed out that if chivalry is a significant feature of British courtroom justice for women, then those women who are given custodial sentences must have been found guilty of particularly serious crimes. In fact, the majority of female prisoners are in prison for non-payment of fines or stealing.

Imprisonment

As many writers have observed, in a society such as ours, males are, in a sense, 'allowed' to behave in 'deviant' ways much more than females are: that is, certain activities, such as fighting, have traditionally been associated with masculine values. Thus female offenders are more likely to be viewed as doubly deviant, in that they have committed some offence *and* deviated from cultural expectations regarding 'feminine' behaviour. Especially important in this context are dominant understandings of female roles within the family. It is against this cultural backdrop that the imprisonment of women has to be understood. Dobash, Dobash and Gutteridge (1986), for example, express the view that the rehabilitative ideal figures much more prominently for women than it does for men, with rehabilitation strongly shaped by notions of domesticity. Zedner (1991) argues that as a result, women tend to experience prison regimes that are designed to foster dependency status and received understandings of 'femininity', with less emphasis placed on learning useful skills for use in the world outside. Studies such as those by Carlen (1983) and Dobash *et al.* (1986) continue to stress the relative lack of educational and recreational facilities for women prisoners. However, some recent studies of women in prison, especially in the United States, have documented certain improvements with respect to family visits and styles of regime.

Studies of the effects of imprisonment on women (e.g. Carlen, 1985) suggest that it is more traumatizing and generates more resentment than is the case with men. Partly because of this: 'A high proportion of women are charged with disciplinary offences, doses of tranquillizers prescribed are higher, and there is a significant incidence of self-mutilation' (Heidensohn, 1994: 1021). In Carlen's (1990) view, there should be an end to the imprisonment of women, except for a small number who commit the more serious offences.

Victimization

Feminist research on women and children as victims of male violence has grown enormously since the beginning of the 1980s. This was paralleled by the growth of a broadly based 'victim movement' and the development of a field of research known as victimology. Studies of victims had been around in criminology for some time – the term 'victimology' was first introduced by an American psychiatrist, Wertham (1949), though the most important early work is credited to another American, Von Hentig (1948). (For good reviews of this field see Walklate, 1989, and Zedner, 1994.) Contemporary research on the theme of victimology, though, and especially feminist research, has been critical of the narrow social–psychological focus of the earlier work, and its emphasis on 'victim precipitation', which many have criticized for blaming the victim. Contemporary interest in crime victims, it should be noted, encompasses both academic research and campaigning or pressure group activities such as those associated with Victim Support.

Research by feminists on women as victims of crime, already building up in the 1970s, has had a particularly strong influence on recent developments in the field. This, more than any other area perhaps, illustrates the impact of feminist perspectives in criminology. Left realists, for instance, have acknowledged the debt that they owe to this work, as this comment indicates:

> Women bear the brunt of crime. For a long time it was supposed that they were irrational about crime, having, according to official statistics, a high fear of crime compared to men, but in reality a much lower chance of being victims . . . women are, in fact, more likely to be victims of crime than men. (Lea, Matthews and Young, 1987: 15)

The dominant message from feminist research was that very large amounts of interpersonal violence, where the victims are women, has remained hidden from view. Thus official information had distorted actual patterns of victimization, and criminology had failed to recognize that the fear of crime expressed by women was a reflection of their real experiences. Furthermore, when violence towards women did come to the attention of criminal justice agencies, and in particular the police, responses were less than satisfactory. One of the main complaints was that the police were reluctant to treat domestic violence in the same way that they treated other forms of assault, especially assaults by strangers (Dobash and Dobash, 1979; Stanko, 1985; Edwards, 1986). Up until the second half of the 1980s, when police attitudes and policies began to change, research pointed to a tendency for the police to categorize cases of domestic violence as 'family disputes' (see police evidence to the 1975 Parliamentary Select Committee). In fact, Dobash and Dobash (1979) in their study of domestic violence in Scotland, found that only 2 per cent of women victims reported their assaults to the police; the rest went to friends or relatives for support. Of the women who pursued a prosecution, only a small minority – 6 per cent – subsequently dropped the complaint. This is important in that police officers very often argue against prosecution on the grounds that victims of domestic violence usually drop their complaint. In the case of victims of rape and sexual assault, there have been significant changes in police responses since the 1980s, partly as a result of bad publicity and partly as a result of a body of research highly critical of the police. As Brogden, Jefferson and Walklate (1988: 121) put it:

> These police attitudes reflect a victim precipitation view of such incidents, one which sees the victim's behaviour as being responsible for inviting a sexual response. This has been translated in the courts as 'contributory negligence'.

Because of its nature, it is not surprising that the interpersonal violence experienced by women has been largely unrecorded by official crime statistics. Although victim surveys were introduced to bring unrecorded crime to light, in the case of female victimization they have not always been successful. The large-scale sweeps of the British Crime Surveys, for instance, have been notably unsuccessful. One reason is that because British Crime Surveys are householder-based, it is quite possible for victims of violence to be sitting next to their assailants when answering the questionnaire. Smaller, localized surveys appear to have overcome some of these difficulties, though feminists have preferred more intense ethnographic studies. As Zedner (1994: 1215) points out with reference to sexual assaults:

> The first two British Crime Surveys revealed only one (unreported) case of attempted rape and seventeen and eighteen cases of sexual assault respectively in the 1983 and 1985 reports . . . In stunning contrast, the first Islington Crime Survey estimated 1,200 cases of sexual assault in Islington during the period under review.

Stanko (1988) is critical of victim surveys such as these because they usually ask respondents to give details of their victimization over the past twelve months. She argues that is it more satisfactory to follow the example set by the American research of Russell (1982), where women were not tied to a short time span, but were asked about their experiences over a lifetime.

This, says Stanko, would allow surveys to be sensitive to the long-term effects of violence, and its impact on daily routines. In her sample of nearly 1,000 women, Russell found that 22 per cent had been raped at some time in their life, and a further 22 per cent had experienced an attempted rape.

British feminist studies have produced quite large variations in the number of women admitting to having been raped or sexually assaulted. Hall (1985) found that one-third of the women surveyed had in their lifetime been raped or sexually assaulted. Asking women about their experiences over the past twelve months, Hanmer and Saunders (1984) discovered that 59 per cent of respondents had been sexually assaulted, whilst in Radford's (1987) research the figure was 76 per cent. These variations will partly be explained by researcher's and respondent's definitions of these terms, and everyday understandings may not correspond with legal definitions. In fact, one of the important contributions made by feminist writers has been to show how legal categories will probably be incapable of capturing a women's real experience of male intimidation and aggression; for example:

Sexual harassment of women on the street is one form of intimidation. Ranging from leers to physical touching (and in some cases actual assault), sexual harassment reminds women that they are and can be targets for sexual assaults. It creates a climate of unsafety. (Stanko, 1988: 45)

Anderson et al.'s study of school-age children in Edinburgh published in the early 1990s, sheds some light on the extent to which children, and especially girls, experience harassment by adults. Although often defined as frightening by the children, many of these incidents would not per se be categorized as criminal:

For girls, the most common forms of adult harassment were being stared at (32%), being followed on foot (27%) and being 'asked things' (26%). For boys the most common were being asked things (17%) and being threatened (15%). Overall 52% (of) the girls had been harassed in some way during the previous nine months by an adult as had 36% of boys. (Anderson et al., 1991: 155)

In addition to this, 17 per cent of the girls (compared with 4 per cent of the boys) had experienced men trying to 'touch them', and 12 per cent (4 per cent boys) had experienced indecent exposure by men.

Large-scale victim surveys will tend not to pick up examples of domestic violence; however, small-scale local surveys are more successful. The first Islington Crime Survey, for instance, found that nearly one-quarter of all assaults took place within the home. From research into domestic violence it is clear that in the bulk of cases the victims are women. Out of the nearly 1,000 respondents in Dobash and Dobash's study, there were only ten cases where a wife had assaulted her husband; in three-quarters of the cases a husband had assaulted his wife. Worrall and Pease (1986) and Mawby (1987) have shown that in most cases of assaults on women their assailant is known to them, and this creates pressure not to inform the police. Stanko (1985) argues that further pressure from friends and neighbours to keep these events private, combined with the victim's apprehension about how the police will respond, helps to create a situation where violence in the home remains concealed.

Gender and crime

As we have seen, during the 1960s and 1970s, attempts to develop feminist perspectives within the discipline of criminology involved various critiques of existing criminology. Earlier criminology was criticized for the 'distortion' of women in analyses; later criminology for the 'neglect' of women. In an effort to remedy the situation, this was followed by research that focused specifically on female criminals and their experiences of the criminal justice system. A further development was to examine the issue of patriarchy and the social control of women, thus giving prominence to the question, 'why do women not break the law?' More recent work, while acknowledging the important contribution made by those feminist writers who have helped redress the gender balance by addressing the theme of women, crime and criminal justice, has shifted the nature of the debate by stressing that the label 'gender and crime' should not be read, as it sometimes is, to mean women and crime. In other words, recent feminist work has looked at issues of criminality and social control from the point of view of men *and* women, in addition to continuing to challenge both the view that the criminal justice system is gender neutral and, on a broader level, the male assumptions underpinning discourses in the social sciences (for a detailed review see Walklate, 1995).

Brown (1986) points out that one of the dangers associated with equating gender and crime with women and crime is that a bifurcated, two-tier criminology is created, where (feminist) women are left to study women, and (non-feminist) men carry on studying men. In this situation, she argues, feminist research and ideas would become marginalized because men would continue to study the 'real' criminals, more or less immune from feminist critiques. This is likely to perpetuate the assumption made by mainstream criminology (sometimes referred to as 'malestream' – the penchant for puns among some feminist writers has been noted by Carlen, 1992) that although female offenders are neglected, analyses of male criminality are veracious. This is one of the reasons why recent feminist writing has explored the concept of masculinity, or, more accurately, masculini*ties*.

Masculinities and crime

It is certainly the case that criminology has traditionally homed in on male rather than female offenders, and in the process often made reference to what are seen as essential masculine attributes: for example, toughness, daring and 'machismo'. Strong criticisms of this body of work have surfaced in feminist writing (as an aside, it should be noted that feminist writing does not necessarily come from the pens, or word processors, of women):

- Although based on research into male offenders, explanations of male criminal behaviour within mainstream criminology have, paradoxically, been put forward as explanations of criminal behaviour in general. Thus male criminality is equated with human criminality.

- Mainstream criminology has not problematized notions of femininity and masculinity. Analyses have tended to view femininity and masculinity as polar opposites, conceptualized around normative ideal types. Feminists argue that analyses should be sensitive to the different understandings and expressions of 'femininity' and 'masculinity' found within the same society. This is part of a critique of what is called essentialism, which is seeing the world in terms of two fundamentally different genders, each the product of universal and irreducible biological and/or socio-cultural factors.

- Mainstream criminology has failed to explore gender relationships in terms of structured relationships based upon both difference and power.

- There is insufficient appreciation of the multiplicity of socio-cultural contexts in which men and women construct their understandings of what it means to be a 'man' and a 'woman'. This requires a consideration of those factors (for example, poverty, a lack of respect, the mass media) that impact on men and women in gender specific ways, as well as other situations where variables such as class, 'race' and age may be equally, or more, relevant.

- Little attention has been given to the actual ways in which groups and individuals via their interactions and interpretations of the social world come to understand themselves as men and women. Although acknowledging that men and women are caught up in wider structures and ideological forces pertaining to notions of 'proper' male and female behaviour, recent feminist writers have rejected deterministic theories in favour of those that allow individuals some freedom to make choices. As far as crime is concerned, this, as Jefferson (1993) argues, allows the idea of pleasure (derived from, for instance, the risk involved, the approval of the group, or the behaviour in itself) as well as mere opportunity, to be introduced into the reckoning.

What should be obvious from even the above brief discussion is that feminist work on the theme of gender has stimulated highly complex theoretical debates that are central not just to sociological criminology, but to sociology in general. Unlike a large amount of criminological research which has, during the 1990s, concentrated on narrower questions linked to social policy, feminism has opened up a space within which deeper theoretical questions have been addressed. Thus although the impact on policy and the criminological project may have been limited, resources have been available for the development of a feminist theoretical discourse.

The causes of crime

Much criminology is still, implicitly or explicitly, concerned with attempting to fathom the causes of crime. However, any attempt to uncover the salient causal factors associated with criminal behaviour will, to understate the case rather, have to grapple with a complex web of variables. At the same time certain variables may appear to operate at the level of causation, when they in fact can only be understood as correlations. Lombroso, for example, found that male criminals very often had tattoos; clearly, tattoos do not cause crime, no more than, on a different level, being unemployed or male causes crime.

For feminism a central issue has been the extent to which gender can be prioritized as a variable when explaining criminal behaviour, and reactions to that behaviour on the part of the criminal justice system. Put another way, what is the relative importance of gender compared to other variables such as class, 'race' and age? Before we examine this in a little more detail it should also be noted that criminology, of course, still has to cope with the ever-present difficulty that 'crime' is not an absolute behavioural category, and 'criminals'/'non-criminals' do not exist as two discrete types of human being. It may be reasonable for a criminologist to take an interest in, say, male violence in the street or in a domestic setting on the grounds that it causes human misery, or, if directed against women, on the grounds that it is an expression of patriarchy and is therefore of theoretical interest as well. However, male (and female) violence occurs at many levels and takes many forms, and sometimes is not actually criminal. This transports us back into the realms of ideology and the moral evaluation of harmfulness, and so forth, and reminds us that violence in the form of oppression or terror may be carried out on behalf of big business or the state.

As a Walklate (1995: 161) points out:

The literature on masculinity has increased markedly in recent years. However, whilst an increasing number of both academic and media commentators have endeavoured to draw attention to the relationship between maleness and crime, little work . . . has applied these developments systematically to either criminology or victimology.

As a result, discussions of masculinities and crime have to draw on a broader range of sources than those that are, strictly speaking, criminological in nature. One writer who has specifically discussed the relationship between maleness and criminal behaviour is Grosz (1987), and she is not alone in putting forward the view that the problem of crime is fundamentally the problem of men. A similar position is taken by Campbell (1993: 319), who argues that: 'Crime and coercion are sustained by men.' Huge amounts of research in Britain and the United States, as well as the picture painted by official statistics, do little to contradict this kind of assertion, especially with respect to violent crime. Victim surveys underline the fact that the fear of crime among women is largely the fear of male crime. In general, women do not expect to have their homes burgled by other women; or to have their cars stolen and raced around an estate by girls; or to be attacked in the home or on the street by other women. Importantly, and sometimes forgotten in this context, men too fear crime carried out by men. It is this fear that encourages individuals to join Neighbourhood Watch schemes, buy extra bolts for their doors and give considerable attention to how they manage their lives in terms of risk avoidance. As an example, residents in any town who wish to stay clear of trouble on a Saturday night usually know which pubs and other public spaces to avoid. Conversely, of course, there will be those who actively seek out such places, and because the police will also have this local knowledge, elements of a self-fulfilling prophesy may be present. Significantly, though, all parties will be aware that any trouble is likely to involve men, usually young men, and that drinking is heavily implicated. However, many men will avoid these places, and there will be pubs where, in spite of heavy drinking, trouble rarely occurs. Clearly, there is no simple causal connection between being male and, say, fighting. None the less, the much greater likelihood that it will be men rather than women who end up fighting has to be taken seriously.

Power

Feminism has stressed that gender relations are based on power rather than mere 'difference'. Thus, gender relations are not conceptualized simply in terms of socialization processes through which men and women learn their respective masculine/feminine roles according to the particular culture. Not only does this 'role playing' model tend to stereotype and polarize gender divisions, it also ignores the existence of power, thereby sidestepping issues of inequality and oppression; men and women are characterized as different but equal.

A large amount of research has shown that 'women's crimes are the crimes of the powerless' (Carlen, 1992: 52; see also Messerschmidt, 1986; Worrall, 1990). In the case of men, much research, and especially that of a radical tradition, has suggested 'that the powerful (in both the gender and class spheres) do the most criminal damage to society' (Messerschmidt, 1986: 56). In his analyses of masculinity and crime, Messerschmidt argues that the power deriving from an integration of gender and class provides men wlth much greater opportunities than women to engage in corporate and white-collar crime. At the same time, the opportunity to commit different sorts of crime is distributed unequally among men: 'Just as the powerful have more legitimate opportunities, they also have more illegitimate opportunities' (ibid. 56).

An important dimension to Messerschmidt's work is his discussion of the ways in which different men construct their own understandings of masculinity according to their 'access to power and resources' (ibid. 119). These understandings are expressed in behavioural terms within three primary locations: the street, the place of work, and the home. This type of approach, therefore, posits the existence of a range of masculinities, which find expression in various sorts of sometimes criminal behaviour, the nature of which will depend upon access to power and resources. Thus there is an attempt to pinpoint the continuities and discontinuities in masculine behaviour within a particular society. This is well summed up by Walklate (1995: 174):

> All of these accounts are offered as a means of demonstrating the ways in which men display their manliness to others and to themselves. So whilst the business executive might use his position and power to sexually harass his female secretary in perhaps more subtle ways than the pimp controls his women, the effects are both the same. In this particular example, the women concerned are subjugated and the men concerned are affirmed as normatively heterosexual men.

Walklate takes up a similar theme when she writes:

> Put simply, the following question should be asked: what makes the often rude and belligerent *behaviour* of the old boys' network of the House of Commons any different from the lads who shout, whistle and jostle hanging about on the street corner? The reply has to be very little. As expressions of masculine behaviour, the reply also has to be very little. What differs, of course, is their public and political *acceptability*. (Ibid. 178)

This draws out the continuities in behavioural terms between the 'yob' on the street and the 'yob' in Parliament, yet also acknowledges the discontinuities because of differential access to power and resources. For Walklate these turn on public and political reactions. However, we have to recognize that the unwillingness to accept this behaviour when carried out on the street is often because of the fear that it might (as it sometimes does) escalate into violence; this is unlikely to occur in the House of Commons.

The discussion so far indicates that analyses of masculinity and crime need to consider the social contexts within which different men construct their understandings of masculinity, together with the opportunities available for law breaking. Furthermore, it is important to recognize that these social contexts will heighten the likelihood of *certain sorts* of offending and victimization. For instance, young men living on tough housing estates, who have to use late-night public transport if they have a night out, are more likely to encounter and have to deal with threats of violence than those whose lives are more insulated (the victim studies carried out by Anderson *et al.*, 1991, and Hartless *et al.*, 1995, give an idea of the extent to which some young people have to cope with threats of violence).

In a recent and influential study, the journalist Campbell (1993) addresses the theme of masculinity and crime among the least powerful men in our society. Focusing on a number of socially deprived housing estates that experienced outbreaks of rioting in 1991, Campbell examines the social contexts in which young men develop their understandings of masculinity. She notes that most analyses by the mass media and politicians concentrated on the familiar images of the 'underclass', lone female parents and undisciplined youngsters, but overlooked other important aspects. In particular, that the rioting involved young men, rather than women and, she argues, it is the young men on these estates who are responsible for the day-to-day crime and coercion. On the other hand, efforts to develop community-based projects, in the face of enormous difficulties (including a lack of support from central and local government and the police) mainly involve women. For Campbell, therefore, it is the women who make a positive effort to maintain a degree of stability and cohesion.

High levels of unemployment since the end of the 1970s have meant that a generation of young men has been denied the traditional working-class male anchor points of the workplace, the pub and the home. For an earlier generation of men, she argues, these provided the structures around which particular understandings of masculinity were developed. To a large extent traditional understandings of what it means to be a 'proper man', based on the integrated roles of breadwinner, workmate and settled father, have been lost. These have been replaced by new understandings shared by others who inhabit the same social space of the street. Rioting, burglary, car theft, and so on, have become ways of expressing this altered definition of manliness. From this perspective, their social situation offers few alternative sources of inspiration and strongly predisposes them to certain sorts of criminal behaviour. There are echoes here of Messerschmidt's argument, in that masculinity and crime are linked to the exercise of different types of power. Thus the possibilities regarding criminal activities will, for both men and women, be constrained by available opportunities. As Campbell points out, many of the young men living on Britain's run-down estates – 'dangerous places' as she calls them – can create fear. Some of them look and act tough, and intimidate so that witnesses are afraid to come forward, and yet, as the title of her book – *Goliath* – suggests, this power is severely circumscribed. Ultimately they meet the power of the state, at which point other young men, in blue uniforms, will act out their own understandings of masculinity.

Campbell's work has not escaped criticism, however. Some have felt that it can add fuel to a hard-line 'law and order' position which equates Britain's crime problem with the problem of a stereotypical 'yob culture' and 'underclass' (Coward, 1994; Walklate, 1995). Furthermore, a complete analysis of life in Britain's 'dangerous places' has to account for the existence of young men in a similar situation to those discussed above who do not riot, abandon their partners and children, carry out burglaries, or pick fights on a Saturday night. The emphasis on *constructing* masculinities implies some notion of choice and creativity and a corresponding rejection of determinism.

Administrative criminology

Administrative criminology is a product of research carried out by, or on behalf of, the Home Office, and has superseded postwar liberal positivism to become 'the major paradigm in establishment approaches to crime' (Young, 1994: 91; for more detailed reviews see also Young, 1988; Downes and Rock, 1988; Roshier, 1989; Jefferson and Shapland, 1994). Clearly, as indicated in the last chapter, this development has to be seen as part of more general social and political trends, and in particular within the context of the Conservative government's ideologies and policies.

Administrative criminology grew out of a critique of positivist-inclined attempts to discover the causes of criminality, whether pitched at the level of individual pathology, or at the level of socio-cultural factors. These approaches were not criticized for being 'wrong', so much as for failing to deliver the goods in terms of manageable explanations. Administrative criminology provides an alternative and, what is seen as, a more realistic approach to crime by focusing on its prevention rather than its causes. Thus even if causal connections (or correlationships) were established between, say, deprivation and certain forms of criminality, the magnitude of the problem is so great that solutions would require sweeping social transformations, and the political will to carry them through. Administrative criminology argues that it is better to concentrate on more manageable crime control activities (for examples of this argument see Clarke and Mayhew, 1980; Clarke, 1980, 1984, 1992; Cornish and Clarke, 1986a, 1986b). Looked at from this perspective, administrative criminology clearly *is* 'realistic' – but it does raise the issue of what criminology as an academic discipline is for. This version is situated within a fairly narrow framework, where the primary concern is with the prevention of crime rather than the construction of broader criminological theory. Debates about, for instance, free will versus determinism are left off the agenda because they are made irrelevant. So too are fundamental theoretical questions pertaining to the nature of law and the role of the state in defining criminal behaviour and so on – certainly, whether or not Maradona did commit a foul is singularly irrelevant.

Administrative criminology modestly addresses issues of situational crime control, that is, those measures that can be taken at a local level: for example, surveillance cameras, better house and shop security, Neighbourhood Watch, and the like. To some extent there are links here with the classical school of criminology, in that the aim is to deter people from committing offences. There are also links with control theory given the central concern with factors that prevent law breaking. However, in each case there are important dissimilarities. For classicism, deterrence was seen as a function of the punishment handed out by the criminal justice system, whereas for administrative criminology deterrence is situationally based within the neighbourhood. In the case of Hirschi's control theory, the focus is on those controls that prevent individuals from being disposed to break the law, whilst administrative criminology focuses on those controls that prevent individuals breaking the law irrespective of their dispositions:

> This narrowing down of the focus of the original control theory seems to constitute a switch of attention from *offenders* to *situations*. Offenders are assumed to make rational choices . . . Consequently, the offenders are not important; what matters is that opportunities must be reduced and risks increased and this requires that attention be given to the situations in which offences may occur. (Roshier, 1989: 49)

Furthermore, as Young (1994) has pointed out, although administrative criminology does draw on the notion of rational choice (and sometimes likes to be known as 'rational choice theory' (cf. Cornish and Clarke, (1986a)), as classical criminology did, there is a recognition that individuals are subject to various constraints that limit their rationality when making decisions.

Administrative criminology is, *par excellence*, a representative of what Garland (1994) calls the 'governmental project' within criminology. This is apparent in two important and interrelated respects:

1. It is entirely congruent with the government's commitment to what is described as efficiency and effectiveness and 'value for money' in the public sector, and also with the view of the public as 'consumers' of criminal justice services:

    > Consumerism has also had a certain pay-off economically. If the costs of controlling a rising crime rate were apparently spiralling out of reach, demonstrating consumer satisfaction might just prove a more feasible (cheaper) alternative. Similarly, crime prevention initiatives which involved the community – the advent of which paralleled the new victim focus – were cheaper and maybe even more effective than increasing police establishments. (Jefferson and Shapland, 1994: 274)

2. It also provides a type of criminological theorizing that can be used to counteract criticism of the government's 'law and order' record as measured by rises in amounts of recorded crime since 1980. In particular, the government has consistently resisted suggestions that rising crime is connected to economic recession and increasing gaps between rich and poor (for a review see Box, 1987; and for a less accommodating example of Home Office research on this theme, see Field, 1990).

A key element of this symbiotic relationship between administrative criminology and government has been the introduction of national victim-based studies through the Home Office British Crime Surveys. Gaining the approval of the government for the first survey at the beginning of the 1980s required some cogent arguments from the Home Office researchers, illustrating that all 'rational decision making' takes place within specific contexts. From the government's point of view the difficulty was that similar victim-based surveys carried out in the United States and other countries had, because of the 'dark figure' of crime, brought to light much more crime than was shown in official criminal statistics. The obvious worry was that this would both reflect badly on the government and lead to increased fears about crime. Although the research value of a national victim survey was to many self-evident because of the knowledge it would generate, its political utility had to be considered too. As it happended, Home Office researchers argued convincingly that although surveys in other countries had exposed large amounts of 'hidden' crime, all subsequent surveys, carried out at regular intervals and allowing trends to be plotted, had shown that crime was increasing at a *lower* rate than shown by official criminal statistics. This, indeed, was the case with the British Crime Surveys during the 1980s – however, the predictions were confounded for the period 1991–93 when, for the first time, acquisitive crime as measured by the British Crime Survey had increased at a faster rate than indicated by official, police-generated figures (though the opposite was true for violent crime).

Concerns about the first British Crime Survey increasing the fear of crime among the public was reflected in the extraordinary statistical gymnastics used to allay any fear. Although (as predicted) things looked bad, we were told that they were not really *that* bad, and helpful comparisons were provided between the chances of being burgled or robbed and the chances (apparently much greater) of being certified as insane, or having one's house burn down. A further point about victim surveys is that they focus attention on the range of conventional crime, where householders are aware that they have been victimized, at the expense of corporate crime, and fail to pick up on sexual crime and domestic violence where women are the chief victims.

On a more complex level, administrative criminology has political utility because of its emphasis on the *crime* rather than the *criminal*. Rising levels of recorded crime are largely explained as being a function of police effectiveness and recording policies, coupled with the greater willingness of the public to report crime (due, for instance, to Neighbourhood Watch schemes). With the spotlight on situational crime control, crime is characterized as opportunistic, and the requirement, therefore, is to reduce opportunities for crime, through better locks, surveillance cameras, improved street lighting, and so forth. The assumption seems to be that a more or less constant proportion of the population is always at the ready to commit 'conventional' crime, though why they should be motivated to break the law in the first place is irrelevant. For administrative criminology the trick is to close down opportunities available for law breaking. Along with other criminologies that became popular in the 1980s and 1990s, administrative criminology represents an impatient reaction to earlier social democratic approaches that saw their central task as one of illuminating the socio-cultural or psychological bases of criminality. It thus offers a theoretical framework that can seemingly deflect critical analyses of rising crime, to some extent blame the public for a lack of community vigilance, and obviate any need to consider the causes of criminal behaviour.

Right-wing classicism

As with administrative criminology, right-wing classicism has a pedigree that goes back to the classical school of criminology of the eighteenth century, and is associated with the growth of the New Right in Britain and the United States (although there are some differences in emphases: for an overview of New Right criminology see Tame, 1991). There is, therefore an insistence on free will and personal responsibility for one's actions. Attempts to explain criminal behaviour in terms of socio-cultural or psychological factors are rejected if they carry any suggestion that the individual is not to blame. Thus although the notion of an 'underclass' is important, with particular disapprobation being reserved for lone-parent families (Murray, 1990), such things as unemployment, poverty and deprivation are seen as products of the 'culture of poverty'. In other words, there is a repudiation of liberal democratic approaches linking certain forms of criminality to deprivation, and seeing those involved as victims of wider social and political structures. For right-wing classicists, these formulations have permeated social scientific thought and become part of the 'excuse making industry'. In this respect, social work is seen as being particularly culpable, and notions of rehabilitation are treated with some distaste (e.g. Morgan, 1978, 1981). Discussions of corporate, white-collar and state-level crime are left off the agenda. The chief source of criminal behaviour is seen to be the underclass, along with elements of a so-called 'yob culture', such as 'lager louts' who, like the underclass, have seemingly had their minds polluted with 'permissiveness' and 'moral relativism'. Under these circumstances, it is argued, crime control must proceed along two broad fronts. First, there is a need to instil self-discipline into those sections of society at fault, and this should involve a programme of moral education. Secondly, in view of the perceived failure of the rehabilitative model, the penal system should be used as a deterrent and as the basis for retribution; if individuals are responsible for their actions, then there should be no qualms about punishing them.

This view of crime and crime control has harmonized well with common-sense understandings, and was incorporated into the popularist political ideology of Prime Minister Thatcher:

> The more orthodox conceptions of crime are broadly accepted and prioritized by the criminal justice agencies, mainstream politicians, the news media, Hollywood and other organs of popular culture. These social institutions legitimate each others' notions of what crime is, and which crimes are most worthy of attention, in mutually reinforcing and self-fulfilling circles. (Stenson, 1991: 9)

There are, however, 'libertarian' and 'conservative' versions of right-wing classicism. As Tame (1991) says, right-wing libertarianism covers a spectrum of thought from types of anarchy to that associated with nineteenth-century liberalism (when 'liberal' had a different meaning to the meaning that it has today). Unlike in the United States, right-wing libertarianism has lacked credibility within academic criminology in Britain (but see Davies, 1987, 1991). One of its hallmarks is a commitment to an unfettered, free-market economy, and a non-interventionist, though strong, central state. Not surprisingly, therefore, there is much enthusiasm for the privatization of criminal justice agencies. There is also a belief in the idea of 'natural rights', and the freedom of the individual to pursue any actions providing that they do not harm others. This has led to right-libertarian support for the decriminalization of illicit drug use and pornography, and in the United States a vociferous defence of the citizen's right to own a firearm.

Conservative versions of right-wing classicism are less indulgent regarding these freedoms, and stress the need for the state to intervene via the law in order to achieve social tranquillity, even at the expense of justice (see van den Haag, 1975, 1985). Efforts are made to mobilize the community around posited traditional moral values. In addition, and in a classical spirit, there is an emphasis on deterrence through punishment. This overlaps with the work of a number of right-wing economists who, in recent years, have turned their attention to crime and crime control. Essentially, this has meant applying economic models based upon rational choice ('econometric' models) to crime. From this perspective, engaging in crime is the same as engaging in business-oriented behaviour and, following the classical school, the prevention of crime has to proceed on the basis of deterrents: that is, choosing crime has to be made irrational. In the United States, Posner's (1986) econometric approach to the analysis of law has been particularly influential.

All of these right-wing classicists are united in the desire to deter criminal behaviour by having strong punishments available. In a critical discussion, Lilley *et al.* (1989: 200–1) make the point:

> For the most part, these commentators have focused on how increased punishment – scaring people straight – will reduce crime. It is instructive that these theorists have overlooked how increasing the rewards of conformity (e.g. more lucrative employment) can achieve similar gains in crime control.

Neo-positivism

Broadly speaking, criminologies under this heading can be placed into two separate 'schools'. They each continue a positivist tradition, and also contain elements of control theory, but one is associated with the New Right, whilst the other contains a wide range of academic criminologists committed to what they see as the scientific study of criminality.

New Right neo-positivism is particularly associated with James Wilson and Richard Herrnstein (1985) (see also Wilson, 1975). Their approach has also been labelled 'right realism', 'new realism' and 'neo-conservative' (Wilson was for a spell an adviser to the Reagan administration). The label 'realist' does indicate one aspect of their work: a rejection of the liberal democratic belief that welfare-oriented social reform will significantly reduce the crime rate. Needless to say, radical solutions based upon a total transformation of American society along socialist lines are also rejected. Interestingly, though, they agree that major transformations would be required if crime rates were to be reduced to low levels, but reject this scenario on the grounds that it would also bring with it a loss of freedoms, which they see as worth preserving, even at the cost of more crime. As they see it, the liberal policies introduced in the 1960s (poverty programmes) did not lead to lower crime rates; in fact, crime continued to rise, even though America was becoming more affluent. Crime for them does not result from social inequality. Rather, it is connected to the growth of 'permissiveness', and a 'dependency culture' among those existing on welfare benefits. Wilson and Herrnstein's 'realism' derives from a view that governments should seek to make modest, manageable, gains as far as crime control is concerned. 'Crime', for them, however, means street crime (including burglary): they admit that they are not concerned with other types of offences.

Wilson and Herrnstein's approach to criminality involves a complex interplay between social conditions and individualized constitutional factors. Thus they discuss the importance of children being properly socialized in the family so that they develop a conscience which leads them to reject criminal behaviour. This stress on social conditioning is combined with the argument that the deterrent effect of imprisonment will only operate if there is a strong certainty of being caught. However, they also introduce a biological dimension by arguing that some individuals are born with 'character defects', and this makes socialization into law-abiding behaviour difficult: 'Crime cannot be understood without taking into account predispositions and their biological roots' (Wilson and Herrnstein, 1985: 103). They also draw on earlier criminological work linking criminality to body shape.

In a debate between Wilson and the liberal American criminologist Elliott Currie (reproduced in Stenson and Cowell, 1991) a number of important critical points are made by Currie that could be applied to a range of New Right criminology. In essence, Currie says that although Wilson's views, and the views of others on the Right, may appeal to common sense, and be widely agreed with among the general population (especially as these views are often carried by the popular media), this does not mean that they are correct. Two elements of this critique will be briefly outlined.

Leniency and permissiveness

In common with other representatives of the New Right, Wilson sees individuals as weighing up the costs and benefits of crime. A frequent complaint is that in the United States during the postwar period the courts have become too lenient, and society in general has become too permissive. Currie accepts the view that as far as serious offenders are concerned, the police are not particularly efficient, and therefore the certainty of punishment is lacking. However, he argues that the accusation of leniency when offenders are brought to trial does not square with the fact that the United States has much higher rates of imprisonment than most other industrialized nations, and in most cases these other nations have lower crime rates. Furthermore, as the rate of imprisonment rose in the 1980s, so too did the crime rate. As far as general permissiveness is concerned, Currie (1991: 55) makes the point that:

> in recent years . . . we were, again by comparison with many other advanced industrial countries, extraordinarily punitive in many of our cultural values and institutional practices – as evidenced by such things as our continued support for the death penalty – and for corporal punishment of the young.

Human nature

Currie also makes the point that by seeing criminality as being connected to some immutable 'human nature', so that a certain proportion of the population will be resistant to 'proper' socialization, Wilson ignores the links between criminality and general social conditions. Thus Wilson is unable to account for the different crime rates in different cities in the United States (where there will be varying levels of unemployment, deprivation, racism, and so on). At an international level, there are industrialized countries with relatively low levels of crime, for instance Denmark, Switzerland and Japan.

Neo-positivism and free will

After a period of anti-positivism resulting from a barrage of criticism from interactionism and conflict theory, since the 1980s there has been a renewal of interest in positivist criminology in the United States. Some examples of positivism have attempted to trace criminal behaviour to in-born 'biological predispositions' (e.g. Wilson and Herrnstein, 1985), and they sustain a tradition that goes back to nineteenth-century Lombrosian criminology. These individualized explanations of criminality have proved attractive to many on the Right because they offer an alternative to other approaches that focus on such things as social inequality, class conflict and racism (see Lilley et al., 1989 for a discussion of the political context of these developments). Other examples of neo-positivism, although they celebrate the eclectic approach, are largely based on the disciplines of sociology and social psychology. The resurgence of this type of criminological positivism is well represented by Positive Criminology, edited by Gottfredson and Hirschi (1987). The book consists of a collection of readings that attempt to map out the defining features of a reconstructed positivist criminology, which Gottfredson and Hirschi confidently describe as the 'dominant paradigm within criminology'.

One of the main arguments is that standard depictions of classical and positivist criminology, in which the differences between the two are polarized around 'free will' and 'determinism', are no longer valid. Indeed, positivism's incorporation of Hirschi's control theory indicates a degree of compatibility between the two traditions. However, Gottfredson and Hirschi also argue that, for the following reasons, the free will–determinism debate is now defunct:

- In the classical model, punishment should work to deter individuals from breaking the law. It was, though, acknowledged that not everyone would be deterred, and so the punishment that was there as a deterrent would sometimes actually be inflicted on an individual. There must, therefore, be certain variables determining the decision to offend, and a concern with those variables takes us into positivism.

- Control theory's contribution to positivism focuses attention on social deterrents (for example, losing the respect of others), whilst classical criminology concentrates on legal penalties as deterrents. Neo-positivism acknowledges that in either case individuals may exercise 'free will': they can choose to ignore the feelings of others, and they can ignore the legal penalties. However, there are always deterministic factors shaping the choices made. Thus, say neo-positivists, whatever their relative importance, free will and determinism apply equally to the two schools of thought.

Even if this reasoning is accepted, it is still, of course, essentially about perceived overlaps between classicism and positivism, and does not provide a solution to the free will versus determinism debate. Neo-positivism is strongly committed to so-called scientific research: to the gathering of 'hard facts' and plotting correlates. Roshier (1989: 68) is sceptical about its success:

> It has failed to establish clear-cut causal variables that differentiate offenders from non-offenders . . . The best it has been able to achieve is loose, probabilistic associations which sometimes, in all but the terminology used, have treated individual offenders as at least partially free, rational and choice-making (and in so doing has to some extent converged with classical criminology).

Radical criminology

In spite of the rise of the New Right, the growing influence of administrative criminology at the level of policy, and much recent soul searching regarding Marxist social theory, radical criminology has continued to have a prime influence on academic criminology in Britain. Although it encompasses a range of perspectives, taking in Marxism, anarchism and versions of feminism, for the purposes of this discussion radical criminology will refer to criminological work that is part of a Left/socialist tradition. As such, it draws on interactionism and neo-Marxism, together with elements of other strands in criminology: for example, anomie and subcultural theory.

Although there exist various schisms, on a general level the main features of radical criminology are as follows:

- The nature and extent of crime are analyzed within the context of a specifically capitalist society.

- Such a society is seen as characterized by inherent class conflict, and other conflictual divisions based upon, notably, patriarchy and racism.

- Crime, law and social control are to be understood by locating them within material and ideological contexts.

- The ultimate goal is the transformation of society along 'socialist' lines.

- Individualized, positivist explanations of criminality are rejected.

Identifying broadly based common features, however, provides only a vague indication of the nature of radical criminology. The question is: what do these things *mean*? To some extent this question has already been addressed in the discussion of radical criminology during the 1970s, but in this final section, and taking us up to the 1990s, subsequent developments need to be looked at. In order to do this, the discussion will be structured around a consideration of two important and competing paradigms that emerged in the 1980s, and continue to provide the basis for intense theoretical debate among radical criminologists. These are left realism (or radical realism as it is sometimes called) and critical criminology (or left idealism, as it is called by left realists). Some of the principal writers associated with left realism in Britain are Richard Kinsey, John Lea, Roger Matthews, Geoff Pearson and Jock Young. Critical criminology is represented by, for example, Kathryn Chadwick, Paul Gilroy, Paul Gordon, Tony Jefferson, Phil Scraton, Joe Sim and Colin Sumner. The picture is complicated, however, because there are other criminologists on the left who, whilst being sympathetic to the left realist position, are nevertheless critical of some or much of the work (and some of those listed above may complain about this labelling exercise). The debate between these two paradigms does raise a number of important issues relating to the response of radical criminology (in terms of theory and practice) to the growth of the New Right and the dismantling of state socialism in the former Soviet Union and Eastern Europe. It also reintroduces questions of general interest to criminology, such as: what is criminology *for*?

What are left realists saying?

According to left realists, socialist criminology should 'take crime seriously'. This means that it should mount a 'realistic', practical challenge to those on the right who have traditionally colonized the 'law and order' terrain. In order to accomplish this, left realism seeks to

- Build up an accurate picture of crime and its impact on victims.

- Develop causal explanations of criminality.

- Trace the relationship between offenders, victims, and formal and informal controls.

- Develop 'progressive', yet realistic policies aimed at the reduction of victimization rates, especially among more vulnerable poorer groups.

Crime and its impact

Although left realists have argued that the project of 'taking crime seriously' should include both 'conventional' crime such as burglary and robbery, and white-collar and corporate crime, in practice they have concentrated on the former (see Pearce and Tombs, 1992). This was perhaps inevitable given the reliance on localized victim surveys for generating data on amounts and distribution of crime.

According to left realism, the fear of crime among working-class people is based upon their real experiences, and is therefore rational. It is not the result of false consciousness created by media-induced moral panics, as, say the realists, critical criminologists seem to believe. Poorer people, in particular, have to contend with double victimization: as victims of crime and as victims of poverty. Furthermore, in answer to the criticism of taking a ready-made conceptual category – 'crime' – left realists argue that across a range of criminal activities there exists a large consensus regarding its harmfulness. They also acknowledge, though, that the nature of crime is to some extent 'mystified' by, for example, mass media accounts; one of the tasks of criminology, then, is to demystify these stereotypes.

Explanations

Criminology is seen as a discipline that should concern itself with the development of explanations of crime; however: 'The trouble with criminology is that it cannot explain crime' (Young, 1987: 237). And, as far as left-wing versions are concerned: 'on crime, more than on most matters, the left seems bereft of ideas' (Gross, 1982: 51). Young (1994) in particular has argued that within criminology there has been an 'aetiological crisis', that is, the discipline has been perplexed by the curious fact that crime rises correlate with both affluence and recession. Critical criminology and administrative criminology are both censured for a lack of interest in a causal explanation of crime. The former is seen as focusing on criminalization (that is, the construction and application of the law), whilst the latter focuses simply on crime control. Left realists support the view that the postwar period has seen real increases in amounts of crime, coupled with greater sensitivity on the part of victims to its effects. This is the worst of all worlds: official statistics show an increase in the crime rate, the fear of crime has increased, and there are real increases in the crime rate.

Critical criminologists are accused of refusing to recognize the harmfulness of predatory crime carried out by working-class males, because they concentrate mainly on the crimes of the powerful. When they do discuss working-class crime, say the left realists, they either approach it in a spirit of misplaced sympathy for the offender as victim, or romanticize it as proto-revolutionary action. The left-realist position is that conventional crime is, in the main, carried out by poorer working-class males, and that the bulk of this is intra-class rather than inter-class. However, there is a rejection of the positivist view that unemployment or poverty *causes* crime. Jock Young, who has been the most prominent proponent of left realism, draws on Merton's concept of anomie, defined as a lack of opportunity to achieve cultural expectations, and it is poorer working-class people who experience a lack of opportunity most acutely. Thus social class position is important in that it creates a situation where, because of relative deprivation, there are greater pressures to commit property crime. He also points to the importance of working-class male subcultures as carriers of macho, patriarchal values. Focusing on the offender, though, is seen as offering only a partial explanation of crime. Left realists have stressed the need for analyses to recognize that offenders are only one element of a set of relationships out of which is created the 'crime problem'. Young (1994), for instance, speaks of the 'square of crime': offenders, victims, formal controls and informal controls. Richard Kinsey and his colleagues favour a pentagon: offender, victim/witness, public, the city, police (Anderson *et al.*, 1991).

Policies

In an effort to seize the 'law and order' debate from the Right, left realists have attempted to develop concrete, practical policies involving, for example, local authorities and police, and aimed at reducing crime levels and the unequal victimization of the working class. This engagement with policy is not seen as mere 'reform', traditionally associated with liberal thought, but as progressive 'reformism', with the ultimate prize being the creation of a socialist society. Ian Taylor (1982) uses the phrase 'transitional socialist criminology'; others have spoken of 'pre-figurative socialism'. There are echoes here of what other socialists have argued for some time: E. P. Thompson, for example, took the view that historically the rule of law had to some extent protected the working class from the excesses of the ruling class, and Alan Hunt (1980) has argued that law will always be necessary, even in a socialist society. Such sentiments have not always gone down well with others on the Left (see the earlier discussion of the 1970s).

A common theme among left realists is the notion of 'community' and a stress on responses to crime at the local level (see, for example, Gross, 1982; Matthews, 1992; McMullan, 1986; Taylor, 1981, 1982). This appeal to localism is seen as forging links with the historical struggle of the working class to improve their lot, and pitches progressive reform at a more manageable level. Gross (1982) argues for the establishment of self-help groups and 'citizen defence squads'; similarly, Einstadter (1984) proposes crime prevention programmes based upon 'supportive neighbourhood networks'; Michalowski (1983) argues for the democratization of policing and 'authentic' forms of popular justice; Taylor (1981) points to the need for the participation of working-class people and 'marginalized groups' in such things as community homes and magistrates' courts. Broader-based 'progressive' state intervention has also been suggested: for example, victim-offender mediation schemes, target-hardening, better youth facilities, and victim and family support schemes (see Matthews, 1992).

Critical criminology and left realism

The left realist criticism of 'left idealism'

Criticism of critical criminology, or 'left idealism' has centred on the following themes:

- They have failed to recognize the real harm caused by conventional crime, and to this extent have failed to 'take crime seriously'. Concentrating on *criminalization* and moral panics, rather than on actual offenders (the exception being the criminality of the powerful), and highlighting what they see as other, more harmful problems faced by the working class, critical criminologists have ignored causal explanations of crime and at the same time allowed the Right to dictate the terms of the 'law and order' debate.

- They have taken a stance based upon utopianism – that is, an all or nothing commitment to a crime-free socialist future – instead of

engaging with practical problems of crime control in the
This has entailed a rejection of 'reformism', and any atte
work constructively with agencies such as the police.

- They have tended to romanticize working-class crime, seeing it as proto-revolutionary action. Furthermore, there has been a strong element of moral ambivalence regarding certain forms of expressive deviance: for example, drug use.

- Some critical writers have opted for a naive 'abolitionist' stance: for example, arguing for the dismantling of the prison system, or for a declaration of peace, rather than war, on crime (see Pepinsky and Quinney, 1991).

- There is a rejection of the idea that real increases in crime have occurred. Amounts of recorded crime are seen as a function of reporting and recording processes, rather than as a register of increases in the crime rate.

Criticisms of left realism by critical criminology

Some of the main criticisms of left realism will be used to provide a framework within which to explore some of the wider criminological issues raised by this intra-Left debate.

The concept of crime

> One of the strongest attacks on left realism has been that it is essentialist . . . that it attributes to the commonsense phenomenon 'crime' – a phenomenon that consists of many different types of lawbreaking and many different modes of criminalization – a unitary existence known to all people of good will and common sense. (Carlen, 1992: 59)

Clearly, this is an issue that raises major epistemological questions concerning the nature of criminology (for discussions within the context of left realism see Brown and Hogg, 1992; Carlen, 1992; Hogg, 1988). According to critical criminologists, being 'realistic' has meant surrendering to popular stereotypical conceptions of crime. Thus, left realism is seen as merely paying lip service to the requirement to consider white-collar and corporate crime, and has concentrated on certain conventional forms of working-class crime, thereby helping to perpetuate dominant ideological understandings of the 'crime problem': 'I am not convinced that this emphasis of left realism is deserved. In my opinion, *inter-class* crime is an equally serious and real problem that exploits and victimizes working class people' (McMullan, 1986: 190).

Defending left realism, Young (1987) has argued that popular fears and understandings have a 'rational kernel', and Rafter (1986: 12) has written: 'It is time to face the fact that a core of consensus does lie at the heart of the criminal law and to consider the aetiology of serious offending in this light.' This, say critical criminologists, may be correct, but references to 'kernels' and 'cores' of rationality do not explicate those understandings that are 'irrational', and avoids a confrontation with the role of ideology. However, debates over the concept of crime involve more than the issue of focusing on only some forms of offending. While left realists acknowledge the contribution made by labelling theory, they contend that critical criminologists have exaggerated the importance of the 'reaction' in the creation and shaping of criminal behaviour. Left realists, therefore, have underlined what they see as a real, objective crime problem with it own genesis. For critical writers, though, this is to return to an earlier, uncritical and common-sensical view of 'crime', where both criminals and their behaviour are special:

> People who are involved in 'criminal' events do not appear in themselves to form a special category of people. Those who are officially recorded as 'criminal' constitute only a small part of those involved in events that legally are considered to require criminalisation. Among them young men from the most disadvantaged sections of the population are heavily over-represented. (Hulsman, 1986: 65)

Hulsman then makes the point that the working class, towards whom left realists orientate their work, experience a whole range of non-criminal events in their lives that are harmful or distressing: for example, matrimonial difficulties, difficulties between parents and children, and housing problems. However, for those involved there is 'nothing which distinguishes those "criminal" events intrinsically from other difficult or unpleasant situations' (ibid. 65). The task for criminology is, he says, to 'debunk' the conceptual category of 'crime' as it exists within the context of the criminal justice system, and to focus instead on 'problematic situations'.

In a similar vein, Steinhert (1985: 329) has written:

> To 'take crime seriously' in this situation means that we take troubles seriously, but not as 'crimes.' That people are mugged in the streets, that women are raped and beaten . . . that environments are poisoned by irresponsible production, that people who live together are alienated from each other – all this is undesirable irrespective of whether it is 'crime' or not.

On this basis, Steinhert discusses 'socialist' policy interventions that are not tied inherently to a criminal justice frame of reference, for example, into the area of public transport. As Brown and Hogg (1992: 144) have said:

The most fundamental problem in the realist theory, programme and methodology lies in the diminution of concern with the concept of 'crime' itself. This is not a theoretical luxury, but a strategic relaxation with important political effects.

Critical criminologists, then, stress the political and ideological bases of crime and crime control. The essential argument is that left realism has simply drifted back towards a traditional liberal position, though it is now graced with a progressive gloss, and in the process ditched many of the theoretical advances made by radical criminology:

> By their overall commitment to 'order through law' . . . [left realists] have retreated far from the theoretical gains of twenty years ago. Their regresssion into the assumptions of the standard criminal law model of social control – criminalization and punishment – is premature. (Cohen, 1986: 131)

This comment by Stan Cohen, and other criticisms of left realism are addressed by John Lea (1987). In the course of his discussion he refers to the 'abolitionism' of Hulsman mentioned above and in the process touches on some important points regarding the nature of the criminological project. In Lea's view, to speak of 'problematic situations' begs the question of how do we identify them, especially as they will be so wide ranging? Thus he argues the case for taking 'crime' as the central concept on the basis of there being a large consensus of agreement regarding its harmfulness. Critics of this view, however, would say that not only does it fail to question the ideological sources of popular understandings, on which basis draconian criminal justice policies may be introduced (for example, the 1994 Criminal Justice and Public Order Act and its impact on travelling people), it also leads to what we might call a 'particularistic' criminology: a criminology empirically tied to a specific society at a specific moment. The result is that the criminologist is able to study *only* those activities that have been criminalized, with the assumption that they are 'bad'. This contrasts with the, at least potentially, 'universalistic' approach of critical and other criminologies. *In extremis*, the distinction between the two approaches can be illustrated if we imagine the criminological project within the context of Nazi society in Germany. 'Crime' here could not be equated with 'problematic situations' or 'badness' as these are understood by Lea, though from the point of view of the Nazi state they were. To say that Britain in the 1990s is not the same as Germany in the 1930s, misses the point, and does not eradicate the intellectual problem for criminology. Even if we all agreed that currently defined criminal events really are 'bad', it still leaves criminology as an academic discipline tied to definitions of crime that happen to coincide with its moment in history. Interestingly, in the recent study of offending and victimization among school-age children in Edinburgh carried out by a leading proponent of left realism, Richard

Kinsey, and colleagues, the researchers do in fact stray from a focus on 'crime' as such, and deal with 'problematic situations'. Although the text is littered with references to 'the impact of crime', 'caused by crime', and 'contact with crime', many of the events referred to are not actually crimes (Anderson *et al.*, 1991). Focusing simply on current definitions of 'crime' is to ignore the point that in Britain today, in Britain's past and in other societies, there are examples of 'crime' that many of us, including the left realists, would not wish to conceive of as 'bad' and in need of eradication. As Carlen (1992: 58) says: 'Whereas the realism of Durkheim and Popper was aimed at subverting common sense, left realists appear to call for a theory of crime that will fit the facts of crime as popularly conceived of in common sense.'

Victims

Critical criminologists, along with others, have frequently based their critiques of left realism on the theme of the uses and abuses of local victim surveys. Some have argued that concentrating on the victims of crime in certain working-class neighbourhoods gives criminology too narrow a focus, and in effect surrenders to conceptualizations of the social world provided by survey respondents: 'Arguably, the advocacy of inner city victims, and an ill-concealed contempt shown for "suburban souls", constitutes a narrow platform for a socialist strategy dealing with crime' (Mugford and O'Malley, 1991; but see Young and Matthews, 1992, for a defence).

As has been indicated earlier, one of the biggest difficulties with victim surveys is that they fail to register instances of victimization by big business and white-collar criminals. This raises the general point that the validity of a victim survey rests on the respondent's knowledge. Clearly, in some cases – for example, illegal currency dealing on the money markets – respondents will be far removed from the status of victim. However, in other cases – for example, the illegal use of antibiotics by a beef farmer – they may be direct victims, though they will not be aware of it. Furthermore, some left realists, such as Young, have suggested that some people have a low tolerance of crime, and are therefore more victimized than are those with a high tolerance. It is an important point, but raises huge theoretical problems that have yet to be resolved. On a methodological level, Walklate (1989) discusses a number of difficulties with local victim surveys: for example, that they do not always support the idea that working-class people are more likely to be victims of property crime than the middle class.

One of the primary tasks of victim surveys for left realism is to show that crime really is a problem for many working-class people, and that to a significant degree they worry about it (more than, for instance, housing or public transport). While this is valuable in terms of exposing the damage done by crime, it does reintroduce the notion of 'problematic situations' into the debate. What, we might ask, would be the relative importance of other problems not on the list in the lives of respondents? And, their significance is likely to change over time anyway.

Ruggiero (1992: 135) argues that left realists proceed as if there is a convenient split between victims (that is, 'respectable' people) and offenders within the working class – or any social class:

> They imply a notion of working class centred on values such as ethical integrity, productivity, social merit and fairness. One is induced to think that what they describe as a neat divide between offenders and victims corresponds to a similar divide between legality and illegality.

In a study of the East End of London, Hobbs (1988) has stressed the need to recognize that criminal activities cannot inevitably be equated with universal 'harm':

> By concentrating almost exclusively on intra-class crime, left realism is in danger of going the same way as its predecessors. For it is essential to stress the variety of criminal opportunities that are available to the working class and how, on occasions, these opportunities can enhance rather than encumber inner city life. (Quoted in Ruggiero, 1992: 136)

Crime control policies

Left realists have been accused of 'idealism' in their characterizations of working-class 'community', and an overabundance of faith in the willingness of existing organizations to radically alter their structures and policies. Some of the main arguments are as follows:

- Closer attention needs to be paid to the nature of so-called 'communities', and to the allocation of resources that would underpin local action.

- Hulsman (1986) raises the issue of what the agency of reform will be. In other words, which individuals or groups will actually be willing and able to implement reformist policies? Extending this further, Stan Cohen (1988: 229) has noted the wider social and political context: 'the essence of state power is not just the particular way it deploys its forces of criminalization and punishment but its initial normalizing power, that is, its radical monopoly to define what is right.'

- Jefferson (1986) suggests that left realists have failed to appreciate the limitations to police effectiveness, and that a closer involvement with the community on the part of the police will have implications for civil liberties.

- The call to mobilize the community around the idea of 'popular justice' has been seen as highly problematic. If this occurred, then 'justice' might become more punitive and draconian than it is at present. When discussing popular justice, left realists do acknowledge the danger that those involved may resort to exemplary punishment or violent direct action against 'offenders' on the basis of moral panics and misinformation. Thus they logically argue that popular justice presupposes an appropriate information system is in place, that the education system should adjust accordingly, and that the mass media should be reformed to suit. Interestingly, this line of reasoning pushes left realism towards critical criminology, in that it fairly soon arrives at what appears to be a socialist transformation of society. This returns us to one of the central issues: the extent to which justice can be achieved within an unjust society.

As is frequently the case with competing criminological paradigms, as time passes the debate between left realism and critical criminology has become increasingly polarized. One outcome of this might be an implication that radical criminologists have to make a choice and accept one of the paradigms whole cloth. However, this ignores areas of disagreement within each paradigm, as well as areas of agreement between them. It also ignores areas of agreement between them and other criminological paradigms.

Critical criminology's agenda emphasizes the political, economic and ideological structures within which processes of criminalization and deviantization, especially of vulnerable and marginalized groups, occur (see Scraton and Chadwick, 1991; Sumner, 1994). Out of this arise studies of apparatuses of state control and regulation seen within the context of class conflict, patriarchy and racism. This, though, does not mean that critical criminologists are disinterested in the victimization of working-class people. There are, however, different sorts of victims, and different sorts of victimization resulting not just from certain criminal offences, but from a range of experiences and events. Left realism's agenda emphasizes the social reality of crime in terms of the criminal victimization of, in particular, working-class people. Thus causal explanations of 'conventional' crime and an engagement with reformist policies become paramount. This, though, does not mean that left realists are disinterested in processes of criminalization and the role played by ideology in constructing the 'crime problem'. The debate between the two flows naturally from rather different primary agendas.

Final remarks

This book has been about criminology as an academic discipline and the various ways in which the criminological project has been conceived and socially organized; it has also been about criminological theory and the different ways in which issues of crime, deviance and control have been studied. A very broad array of criminological theories have been discussed in this text and, whatever their particular merits, each did at least for a period capture the imagination of some academic criminologists; occasionally they even influenced criminal justice policy. And then something else came along. Out of the discipline's internal and external history have come many different types of criminology, and here at the end of the twentieth century, thank goodness, intense, complex and sometimes vitriolic debates continue. Whatever their personal preferences, it is hoped that readers of this book who are new to the subject will find these debates both important and interesting. In the next century it is from their ranks that books such as this will draw their inspiration.

These debates have sprung from the diverse ways in which criminologists have answered certain fundamental questions:

- *What to study?* For example, offending behaviour, social control reactions, the meaning of 'crime', 'harmful' activities whether criminal or not, etc.

- *Who to study?* For example, 'typical' offenders, corporate criminals, the poor, the rich, the state, etc.

- *How to study?* For example, library-based theoretical work, 'hands on' ethnography, from a feminist standpoint, by using advanced computer facilities, etc.

- *Why study?* For example, to find the causes of crime, to help in the fight against crime, to hasten a socialist revolution, to create gender equality, to fight racism, to bring in departmental funds, etc.

The specific ways in which these are answered will shape the theories and research methodologies constituting the discipline of criminology. Clearly, the range of possibilities is enormous, and one principle aim of this book has been to make problematic the issue of what criminology *is*. The fact that no universal agreement exists is no bad thing; the time to worry is when academic freedom has been so constrained that intellectual disputes no longer exist.

If we look at the general direction taken by criminological research in Britain since the 1980s, the overall impression is that there has been a trend towards more narrowly focused, policy-oriented approaches, though these are not *per se* to be criticized. However, such research has tended to take precedence over the 'big' theoretical debates, although, as we have seen, these debates still continue. This trend, and a degree of theoretical stasis, is partly accounted for by the institutional pressures surrounding criminology and the demands made on researchers by funding agencies.

Where, in the light of these developments, is criminology heading? A pessimistic (for some) prediction would conjure up the scenario of a post-theoretical version of criminology. More optimistic crystal gazing would note the enduring commitment to a theoretical discourse among many criminologists in this country, and the continuing importance of criminological theory for those teaching the discipline (and noted by Rock, 1994, in his survey of the social organization of criminology).

In this context it is important that criminology does not drift away from a *critical* engagement with issues of crime and control. This is one of the dangers if criminology is locked into, as Garland puts it, a 'governmental project': uncritically aiding the government/administrators of the day in the achievement of efficient and effective methods of crime control. A rejection of this does not, however, mean that criminology embraces a 'Lombrosian project': 'scientifically' seeking out the causes of crime. There are other possibilities, such as a criminological project rooted in academic freedom that:

- aims to develop a critical understanding of not just the 'causes' of crime (an interesting and important theme), but also of the equally important processes involved in constructing, defining and responding to the 'crime problem';

- is willing to engage with epistemological questions regarding the nature of crime itself; and

- would not flinch from squaring up to fundamental and ever-present political issues.

Picking up on Foucault's discussion of knowledge and power, Stenson (1991: 11) makes the important point that:

in many ways, conflicts about the definition of crime and how to control it are central to criminology as a discipline, and there can be no simple escape into a world of antiseptic science. Science provides no refuge from politics.

Conventional crime

Over the years, for many criminologists the answers to the core questions posed above have coalesced around the types of offences and offenders that we are familiar with from the criminal statistics. We might say that the mainstay of criminological research has been 'conventional' crime, crime which, the evidence suggests, is disproportionately committed by lower-working-class males. Furthermore, and being 'realistic', it has to be acknowledged that these are the crimes that the public, understandably, worries about most. Not surprisingly, because of the lack of immediate personal impact, they are less worried about expense account fiddles, illegal arms deals, and so forth – the crimes of the powerful.

When a criminologist is invited into a television studio to participate in a programme on, for instance, 'crime today', or 'vandalism in the city', there is the same focus, and the criminologist is usually expected to explain why they, the criminals involved, do it. Certainly, he or she will not be expected to entertain the viewers with an exposition on the conceptual conundrums surrounding definitions of crime and deviance. Significantly, the same criminologists are not usually in the studio when issues such as pollution, nuclear testing in the South Pacific, bullying by employers, or the collapse of an international bank due to fraudulent practices is being discussed. Typically, criminologists get sucked into a milieu structured around common-sense understandings of the 'crime problem', and inevitably this means a preoccupation with the crimes of the powerless.

That the media concentrates on certain sorts of conventional crime is one thing, but to make it the *raison d'être* of academic criminology is something else. Obviously, when we consider that the criminal statistics are dominated by conventional crime, that victim surveys show that this is what people fear, and that such things as stealing cars, breaking into homes and engaging in randon violence causes real misery and suffering, criminology's interest in conventional crime is understandable and important. The social distribution of different types of offending is partly accounted for by the different opportunities available. Those working in professional or managerial occupations are more likely to have access to less risky (and often more socially acceptable) criminal acts than are unskilled manual workers or the unemployed. Those owners of small businesses inclined to 'skim off' a few tax-free pounds from the day's takings, or the builders who for cash in hand will ignore VAT, or employees who add an extra mile or two to a mileage claim, have no need to take the risk of breaking into a house, or robbing someone on the street in order to top up their income. And the opportunities available at a corporate level take us into another league of criminality. Is behaviour such as this 'abnormal' or a function of 'disorganization' as some versions of positivism suggest? The main point to make, though, is that a crude reading of the criminal statistics can give a rather misleading picture of the social distribution of crime and criminal motivations. Although no criminologist would argue that non-conventional crime should be ignored, in some quarters of criminology this is precisely what has happened, with the result that the 'underclass' (or some functional equivalent) becomes *de facto* the source of Britain's crime problem.

At the present time, as we have seen, it is not positivism but administrative criminology that has most influence in government circles. The attention is still on conventional crime, but the search for causes has been displaced by the search for ways of preventing offences taking place. The motivation to commit crime is taken as given; its aetiology, although interesting, is not under consideration.

Winning the fight against crime?

In September 1995, as part of what was called a 'good news on crime' tour, the Home Secretary, Michael Howard, was interviewed on a local radio station in Birmingham. He reported that government crime prevention policies were now beating crime, and he gave particular prominence to the value of security video cameras. Howard's 'good news' message made the front page in a number of national newspapers. Although this is not strictly relevant, it is impossible to resist the temptation to mention that as the Home Secretary was being escorted by police and security staff from the studios through a back entrance, two youths came in by the front door and stole a large number of pictures of DJs off the wall. Ironically, they were filmed doing this by security cameras in the studio. At the time of writing they are still at large.

Although Howard based his argument on official statistics (with all the problems that that involves), supposing we took what was said at face value – that the number of offences committed had, because of various crime prevention initiatives, been significantly reduced – what does this really tell us? To learn that fewer houses are being burgled, cars stolen, or individuals beaten up on a Saturday night, *is*, in itself, obviously 'good news'. However, presenting the issue in this restricted format is misleading. The Home Secretary's fight against crime is based upon administrative criminology's search for ways of controlling criminally motivated individuals. Thus *control* is the key concept. People are still wanting to commit crime, but the project has become one of somehow preventing them doing it. Attractive as this project at first glance might seem, no one would argue that crime control at *any* cost is a good thing. Therefore, a 'real' reduction in crime, if that could be established, does not of itself mean that the quality of life (which, arguably, should involve such things as freedom, justice and rights) has necessarily improved. At a hypothetical level, one could imagine a situation where crime really did plummet to very low levels, but where, because of controls on behaviour, everyday life had became intolerable. The political, and in some quarters criminological, commitment to situational crime control involves a range of preventive measures: physical security (steering locks on cars, bars on windows, security cameras, etc.); personal and community-based strategies (risk avoidance, Neighbourhood Watch, etc.);

different modes of policing. If, after consulting with security companies (and some companies have no qualms about using telephone marketing to inform householders that they are threatened by a crime wave), homes become virtual fortresses, if 'risk avoidance' means that the elderly imprison themselves in their houses and many people do not go into city centres in the evening, levels of crime may go down, but social life has clearly suffered. So although a reduction in crime may appear to be something that we should applaud, the overall circumstances in which it occurs need to be considered.

It is not, though, just a matter of how effective or draconian situational crime control measures are. The entire project pushes to one side the issue of criminal motivations and their socio-cultural contexts, whether relating to the crimes of the powerful or the crimes of the powerless. The existence of individuals who want to commit crime is simply taken as given: the trick is to prevent them doing it. Variations in levels of crime between one society and another are accounted for, therefore, simply in terms of the effectiveness, or otherwise, of the sorts of controls mentioned above. However, in itself 'successful' crime control tells us nothing about the nature, extent and sources of criminal motivations. Simply taking crime levels as an index of, for instance, the 'quality of life' in different societies is thus highly misleading. Equating a reduction in crime, however measured, with 'good news', and therefore implying that there has been a qualitative improvement in social life, is one-sided in the extreme. If the phenomenon of crime is used as an indicator of the quality of life within a society, then the nature and extent of criminal motivations cannot be ignored. This means examining the whole nature of that society in order to piece together and understand the structural roots of criminality. Indeed, rather than 'good news' from the front regarding the 'fight against crime', we would be better served if we had good news from the front regarding the fight against inequality, injustice, oppression and greed.

Postscript

MIGHT

> They are tough now
> And so sure of themselves
> That we even begin to accept it
> Because they don't try to hide
> And they don't care who sees.
> They are confident
> And that's what makes us weak
> But when the change comes
> (and it will)
> The truth will shift
> Because they are wrong
> It just happens that
> For a time
> They have the power.
>
>   Nigel Mellor (1989), *For the Inquiry*, London: Dab Hand Press

References

Adamson, M., Briskin, L. and McPhail, M. (1988), *Feminist Organising for Change: A contemporary women's movement in Canada*, Toronto: Oxford University Press.

Adler, F. (1975), *Sisters in Crime*, New York: McGraw-Hill.

Agnew, R. (1991), 'The interactive effects of peer variables on delinquency', *Criminology*, **29**, pp. 47–72.

Akers, R. L. (1967), 'Problems in the sociology of deviance: social definitions and behavior', *Social Forces*, **46** (4).

Allen, H. (1987), *Justice Unbalanced! Gender, Psychiatry and Judicial Decisions*, Milton Keynes: Open University Press.

Althusser, L. (1971), *Lenin and Philosophy and Other Essays*, London: New Left Books.

Amir, M. (1971), *Patterns of Forcible Rape*, Chicago: University of Chicago Press.

Anderson, E. (1976), 'The "chivalrous" treatment of the female offender in the arms of the law: a review of the literature', *Social Problems*, **23** (3).

Anderson, N. (1975; first pub. 1923), *The Hobo: The story of Chicago's Prohibition era*, London: Hutchinson.

Anderson, P. (1968), 'Components of the National Culture', *New Left Review*, **50**.

Anderson, S., Kinsey, R., Loader, I. and Smith, C. (1990), *The Edinburgh Crime Survey*, Edinburgh: Scottish Office.

Anderson, S., Kinsey, R., Loader, I. and Smith, C. (1991), *'Cautionary Tales': A study of young people in Edinburgh*, Edinburgh: Centre for Criminology, University of Edinburgh.

Atkinson, J. M. (1971), 'Societal reactions to suicide: the role of coroners' definitions', in S. Cohen (ed.), *Images of Deviance*, Harmondsworth: Penguin.

Atkinson, J. M. (1979), *Discovering Suicide*, London: Macmillan.

Austin, A. L. (1977), 'Commitment, neutralization and delinquency', in T. N. Ferdinand (ed.), *Juvenile Delinquency*, London: Sage.

Bagot, J. H. (1941), *Juvenile Delinquency: A comparative study of the position in Liverpool and England and Wales*, London: Cape.

Baldwin, J. and Bottoms, A. (1976), *The Urban Criminal*, London: Tavistock.

Bankowski, Z. and Mungham, G. (1975), *Images of Law*, London: Routledge & Kegan Paul.

Bates, J. E., Bayles, K., Bennett, D. S., Ridge, B. and Brown, M. N. (1991), 'Origins of externalizing behaviour problems at 8 years of age', in D. J. Pepler and K. H. Rubin (eds), *The Development and Treatment of Childhood Aggression*, Hillsdale, NJ: Erlbaum.

Becker, H. S. (1963), *Outsiders: Studies in the sociology of deviance*, London: Macmillan.

Becker, H. S. (1967), 'Whose side are we on?', *Social Problems*, **14** (3).

Becker, H. S. (1974), 'Labelling theory reconsidered', in P. Rock and M. McIntosh (eds), *Deviance and Social Control*, London: Tavistock.

Beirne, P. (1979), 'Empiricism and the critique of Marxism on law and crime', *Social Problems*, **26** (4) (April), pp. 373–84.

Beirne, P. (1993), *Inventing Criminology: Essays on the rise of 'homo criminalis'*, Albany: State University of New York Press.

Belson, W. (1975), *Juvenile Theft: The casual factors*, London: Harper & Row.

Bianchi, H. and van Swaaningen, R. (eds) (1986), *Abolitionism: Towards a non-repressive approach to crime*, Amsterdam: Free University Press.

Biderman, A. D. and Reiss, A. J. (1967), 'On exploring the "dark figure" of crime', *Annals of the American Academy of Political and Social Science*, **374**, pp. 1–15.

Bilton, T., Bonnett, K., Jones, P., Stanworth, M., Sheard, K. and Webster, A. (1981), *Introductory Sociology*, Basingstoke: Macmillan.

Bittner, E. (1967), 'The police on skid row: a study of peacekeeping', *American Sociological Review*, **32** (5), pp. 699–715.

Block, A. (1991), *Perspectives on Organising Crime*, Boston/London: Kluwer.

Bordua, D. (1970), 'Recent trends: deviant behavior and social control', in C. Bersani (ed.), *Crime and Delinquency*, London: Collier Macmillan.

Bottomley, A. K. and Pease, K. (1986), *Crime and Punishment: Interpreting the data*, Milton Keynes: Open University Press.

Bottoms, A., Mawby, R. I. and Walker, M. A. (1987), 'Localised crime survey in contrasting areas of a city', *British Journal of Criminology*, **27**, pp. 125–34.

Bottoms, A. and Wiles, P. (1986), 'Housing tenure and residential community crime careers in Britain', in A. J. Reiss, Jr. and M. Tonry (eds), *Communities and Crime*, Chicago: Chicago University Press.

Box, S. (1981), *Deviance, Reality and Society*, 2nd edn, Eastbourne: Holt, Rinehart & Winston.

Box, S. (1983), *Power, Crime and Mystification*, London: Tavistock.

Box, S. (1987), *Recession, Crime and Punishment*, Basingstoke: Macmillan.

Box, S. and Hale, C. (1983), 'Liberation and female criminality in England and Wales', *British Journal of Criminology*, **23** (1).

Braithwaite, J. (1989), *Crime, Shame and Integration*, Cambridge: Cambridge University Press.

Brewer, C. and Lait, J. (1980), *Can Social Work Survive?*, London: Temple Smith.

Brewer, C., Morris, T., Morgan, P. and North, M. (1981), *Criminal Welfare on Trial*, London: Social Affairs Unit.

Broadhead, R. R. (1974), 'A theoretical critique of the societal reaction approach to deviance', *Pacific Sociological Review*, **17**, pp. 287–312.

Brogden, M. (1982), *The Police: Autonomy and consent*, London: Academic Press.

Brogden, M., Jefferson, T. and Walklate, S. (1988), *Introducing Policework*, London: Unwin Hyman.

Brown, B. (1986), 'Women and crime: the dark figures of criminology', *Economy and Society*, **15**, pp. 355–402.

Brown, D. and Hogg, R. (1992), 'Law and order politics – Left realism and radical criminology: a view from down under', in R. Matthews and J. Young (eds), *Issues in Realist Criminology*, London: Sage.

Browne, A. (1987), *When Battered Women Kill*, London: Collier Macmillan.

Browne, S. (1994), *Whose Challenge? Youth Crime and Everyday Life in Middlesbrough*, Middlesbrough: Middlesbrough City Challenge Partnership.

Brownmiller, S. (1973), *Against Our Will*, Harmondsworth: Penguin.

Burgess, E. (1925), 'The growth of the city', in R. E. Park and E. Burgess, *The City*, Chicago: University of Chicago Press.

Burt, C. (1925), *The Young Delinquent*, London: University of London Press.

Cain, M. (1973), *Society and the Policeman's Role*, London: Routledge & Kegan Paul.

Cain, M. (1989), *Growing Up Good*, London: Sage.

Cain, M. (1990), 'Towards transgression: new directions in feminist criminology', *International Journal of the Sociology of Law*, **19**, pp. 1–18.

Cain, M. and Hunt, A. (eds) (1979), *Marx and Engels On Law*, London: Academic Press.

Campbell, A. (1981), *Girl Delinquents*, Oxford: Blackwell.

Campbell, A. (1984), *The Girls in the Gang*, Oxford: Blackwell.

Campbell. A. (1986), 'Self-report of fighting by females', *British Journal of Criminology*, **26**.

Campbell, B. (1993), *Goliath: Britain's dangerous places*, London: Virago.

Campbell, K. (ed.) (1992), *Critical Feminism: Argument in the discipline*, Buckingham: Open University Press.

Carlen, P. (1976), *Magistrates' Justice*, Oxford: Martin Robertson.

Carlen, P. (1980), 'Radical criminology, penal politics and the rule of law', in P. Carlen and M. Collison (eds), *Radical Issues in Criminology*, Oxford: Martin Robertson.

Carlen, P. (1983), *Women's Imprisonment*, London: Routledge & Kegan Paul.

Carlen, P. (1985), *Criminal Women*, Oxford: Polity Press.

Carlen, P. (1988), *Women, Crime and Poverty*, Milton Keynes: Open University Press.

Carlen, P. (1990), *Alternatives to Women's Imprisonment*, Buckingham: Open University Press.

Carlen, P. (1992), 'Criminal women and criminal justice', in R. Matthews and J. Young (eds), *Issues in Realist Criminology*, London: Sage.

Carlen, P. and Collison, M. (eds) (1980), *Radical Issues in Criminology*, Oxford: Martin Robertson.

Carr-Saunders, A. M., Mannheim, H. and Rhodes, E. G. (1942), *Young Offenders*, Cambridge: Cambridge University Press.

Carson, W. G. (1970), 'White collar crime and the enforcement of factory legislation', *Bristish Journal of Criminology*, **10**, pp. 383–98.

Carson, W. G. (1982), *The Other Price of Britain's Oil*, Oxford: Martin Robertson.

Carson, W. G. and Wiles, P. (eds) (1971), *The Sociology of Crime and Delinquency in Britain*, vol. 1, *The British Tradition*, Oxford: Martin Robertson.

Carter, M. P. and Jephcott, P. (1954), 'The social background of delinquency', unpublished, University of Nottingham.

Cashburn, M. (1979), *Girls Will Be Girls*, London: Women's Research and Resources Centre.

Caudill, H. M. (1977), 'Dead leaves and dead men', *Nation*, **226**, pp. 492–7.

Cernkovich, S. A. (1978), 'Value orientation and delinquency involvement', *Criminology*, **15**, *pp.* 443–57.

Chambliss, W. J. (1964), 'A sociological analysis of the law of vagrancy', Social Problems, **12** (1), pp. 67–77, repr. in W. G. Carson and P. Wiles (eds) (1971), *The Sociology of Crime and Delinquency in Britain*, vol. 1, *The British Tradition*, Oxford: Martin Robertson.

Chambliss, W. J. (1975), 'Towards a political economy of crime', *Theory and Society*, **2**, pp. 152–3.

Chambliss, W. J. (1976), 'The state and criminal law', in W. J. Chambliss and M. Mankoff (eds), *Whose Law, What Order?*, New York: Wiley.

Chambliss, W. J. (1978), *On the Take: From petty crooks to presidents*, Bloomington, Ind.: Indiana University Press.

Chapman, J. (1980), *Economic Realities and the Female Offender*, Lexington, Mass.: Lexington Books.

Chesney-Lind, M. (1973), 'Judicial enforcement of the female sex role: the family court and the family delinquent', *Issues in Criminology*, **8**, pp. 51-69.

Chesney-Lind, M. (1978), *Chivalry Re-Examined: Women and the criminal justice system*, Lexington, Mass.: Lexington Books.

Chesney-Lind. M. (1986), 'Women and crime: the female offender', *Signs*, **12** (1), pp. 78-96.

Cicourel, A. V. (1968), *The Social Organization of Juvenile Justice*, New York: Wiley.

Clarke, J. (1976), 'The skinheads and the magical recovery of community', in S. Hall and T. Jefferson (eds), *Resistance through Rituals*, London: Hutchinson.

Clarke, J. and Jefferson, T. (1973a), 'Politics of popular culture: cultures and subcultures', Occasional Paper No. 14, Centre for Contemporary Cultural Studies, University of Birmingham.

Clarke, J. and Jefferson, T. (1973b), 'Down these mean streets: the meaning of mugging', Occasional Paper No. 17, Centre for Contemporary Cultural Studies, University of Birmingham.

Clark, J. and Jefferson, T. (1976), 'Working class youth cultures', in G. Mungham and G. Pearson (eds), *Working Class Youth Culture*, London: Routledge & Kegan Paul.

Clarke, J., Hall, S., Jefferson, T. and Roberts, B. (1976), 'Subcultures, cultures and class: a theoretical overview', in S. Hall and T. Jefferson (eds), *Resistance through Rituals: Youth subcultures in post-war Britain*, London: Hutchinson.

Clarke, M. (1990), *Business Crime: Its nature and control*, Cambridge: Polity Press.

Clarke, R. (1980), 'Situational crime prevention: theory and practice', *British Journal of Criminology*, **20** (2), pp. 136–47.

Clarke, R. (1984), 'Opportunity-based crime rates', *British Journal of Criminology*, **23** (1), pp. 74–83.

Clarke, R. (1992), *Situational Crime Prevention: Successful case studies*, New York: Harvard & Heston.

Clarke, R. and Mayhew, P. (eds) (1980), *Designing Out Crime*, London: HMSO.

Clinard, M. B. and Yeager, P. C. (1981), *Corporate Crime*, New York: Free Press.

Cloward, R. and Ohlin, L. (1960), *Delinquency and Opportunity*, London: Collier Macmillan.

Cohen, A. K. (1955), *Delinquent Boys*, London: Free Press.

Cohen, A. K. and Short, J. F. (1958), 'Research in delinquent subcultures', *Journal of Social Issues*, **14** (3).

Cohen, P. (1972), 'Subcultural conflict in working class community', Working Papers in Cultural Studies, No. 2, Centre for Contemporary Cultural Studies, University of Birmingham.

Cohen, S. (1969), 'Ideological and criminal violence', *Phalanx*, Issue 2, University of Durham.

Cohen, S. (ed.) (1971), *Images of Deviance*, Harmondsworth: Penguin.

Cohen, S. (1973), 'Protest, unrest and delinquency: convergences in labels and behaviours', *International Journal of Criminology and Penology*, **1**, pp. 117–28; repr. in P. N. P. Wiles (ed.) (1976), *The Sociology of Crime and Delinquency in Britain*, vol. 2, *The New Criminologies*, Oxford: Martin Robertson.

Cohen, S. (1974), 'Criminology and the sociology of deviance in Britain', in P. Rock and M. McIntosh (eds), *Deviance and Social Control*, London: Tavistock.

Cohen, S. (1980), *Folk Devils and Moral Panics*, 2nd edn, Oxford: Martin Robertson.

Cohen, S. (1981), 'Footprints in the sand: a further report on criminology and the sociology of deviance in Britain', in M. Fitzgerald, G. McLennan and J. Pawson (eds), *Crime and Society: Readings in history and theory*, London: Routledge & Kegan Paul/Open University Press; repr. in S. Cohen, (1988), *Against Criminology*; New Brunswick, NJ: Transaction Books.

Cohen, S. (1985), *Visions of Social Control*, Cambridge: Polity Press.

Cohen, S. (1986), 'Community control: to demystify or to reaffirm?', in H. Bianchi and R. van Swaaningen (eds), *Abolitionism: Towards a non-repressive approach to crime*, Amsterdam: Free University Press.

Cohen, S. (1988), *Against Criminology*, New Brunswick, NJ: Transaction Books.

Cohen, S. and Taylor, L. (1972), *Psychological Survival: The experience of long-term imprisonment*, Harmondsworth: Penguin.

Cohn-Bendit, D. and Cohn-Bendit, G. (1968), *Obsolete Communism: The Left-wing alternative*, London: Deutsch.

Coleman, A. (1988), *Altered Estates*, London: Adam Smith Institute.

Conklin, J. E. (1977), *Illegal but not Criminal: Business crime in America*, Englewood Cliffs, NJ: Prentice Hall.

Cornish, D. and Clarke, R. (eds) (1986a), *The Reasoning Criminal*, New York: Springer-Verlag.

Cornish, D. and Clarke, R. (1986b), 'Situational prevention, displacement of crime and rational choice theory', in D. Heal and G. Laycock (eds), *Situational Crime Prevention: From theory into practice*, London: HMSO.

Corrigan, P. and Frith, S. (1976), 'The politics of youth culture', in S. Hall and T. Jefferson (eds), *Resistance through Rituals*, London: Hutchinson.

Coulter, J. (1973), *Approaches to Insanity: A philosophical and sociological study*, London: Martin Robertson.

Cousins, M. (1980), 'Mens rea: a note on sexual difference, criminology and the law', in P. Carlen and M. Collison (eds), *Radical Issues in Criminology*, Oxford: Martin Robertson.

Coward, R. (1994), 'Whipping boys', *Guardian Weekend*, 3 September.

Cowie, J., Cowie, V. and Slater, E. (1968), *Delinquent Girls in London*, London: Heinemann.

Crawford, A., Jones, T. Woodhouse, T. and Young, J. (1990), *Second Islington Crime Survey*, London: Middlesex Polytechnic.

Croal, H. (1992), *White Collar Crime*, Milton Keynes: Open University Press.

Cuff, E. C. and Payne, G. C. F. (eds) (1979), *Perspectives in Sociology*, London: Allen & Unwin.

Cullen, F. and Wozniak, J. (1982), 'Fighting the appeal of repression', *Crime and Social Justice*, Winter, pp. 23–33.

Currie, E. (1991), 'The politics of crime: the American experience', in K. Stenson and D. Cowell (eds), *The Politics of Crime Control*, London: Sage.

Dahrendorf, R. (1959), *Class and Class Conflict in an Industrial Society*, London: Routledge & Kegan Paul.

Dahrendorf, R. (1968), 'Towards a theory of social conflict', *Journal of Resolution of Conflict*, **2**, pp. 170–83.

Dahrendorf, R. (1985), *Law and Order*, London: Stevens.

Daly, K. (1989), 'Rethinking judicial paternalism: gender, work, family relations and sentencing', *Gender and Society*, **3** (1), pp. 9–36.

Davis, F. (1967), 'Why all of us may be hippies someday', *Transaction*, **15** (2), pp. 10–18.

Davis, S. (1987), 'Towards the remoralization of society', in M. Loney (ed.), *The State of the Market: Politics and welfare in contemporary Britain*, London: Sage.

Davies, S. (1991), *The Historical Origins of Health Fascism*, London: FOREST.

Dell, S. (1971), *Silence in Court*, London: Bello.

Dennis, N. (1993), *Rising Crime and the Dismembered Family*, London: IEA, Health and Welfare Unit.

Ditton, J. (1977), *Part-Time Crime*, London: Macmillan.

Ditton, J. (1979), *Controlology: Beyond the new criminology*, London: Macmillan.

Dobash, R. E. and Dobash, R. P. (1979), *Violence Against Wives*, New York: Free Press.

Dobash, R. E. and Dobash, R. P. (1992), *Women, Violence and Social Change*, London: Routledge.

Dobash, R. E., Dobash, R. P. and Gutteridge, S. (1986), *The Imprisonment of Women*, Oxford: Blackwell.

Domhoff, G. W. (1970), *The Higher Circles: The governing class in America*, New York: Random House.

Dominelli, L. (1992), 'More than a method: feminist social work,' in K. Campbell (ed.), Critical Feminism: Argument in the discipline, Buckingham: Open University Press.

Dorn, N. and South, N. (eds) (1987), *A Land Fit for Heroin? Drug Policies, Prevention and Practice*, London: Macmillan.

Dorn, N., Murji, K. and South, N. (1992), *Traffickers: Drug markets and law enforcement*, London: Routledge.

Douglas, J. D. (1967), *The Social Meaning of Suicide*, Princeton: Princeton University Press.

Douglas, J. D. (ed.) (1971a), *Understanding Everyday Life*, London: Routledge & Kegan Paul.

Douglas, J. D. (1971b), *American Social Order: Social rules in a pluralistic society*, New York: Free Press.

Douglas, J. W. B. (1964), *The Home and the School*, London: MacGibbon & Kee.

Dowie, M. (1988), 'Pinto madness', in S. Hill (ed.), *Corporate Violence: Injury and death for profit*, Totowa, NJ: Rowman & Littlefield.

Downes, D. (1966), *The Delinquent Solution*, London: Routledge & Kegan Paul.

Downes, D. (1978), 'Promise and performance in British criminology', *British Journal of Sociology*, **29** (4).

Downes, D. (1988), 'The sociology of crime and social control in Britain, 1960–1987', *British Journal of Criminology*, **28** (2), Spring.

Downes, D. and Rock, P. (1988), *Understanding Deviance*, 2nd edn, Oxford: Oxford University Press.

Drapkin, I. (1983), 'Criminology: intellectual history', in S. Kadish (ed.), *Encyclopedia of Crime and Justice*, vol. 2, New York: Free Press, pp. 546–56.

Dunhill, C. (ed.) (1989), *The Boys in Blue: Women's challenge to the police*, London: Virago.

Durkheim, E. (1970), *Suicide: A study in sociology*, London: Routledge & Kegan Paul.

Durkheim, E. (1982), *Durkheim: The rules of sociological method*, ed. S. Lukes, London: Macmillan.

Eaton, M. (1983), 'Mitigating circumstances: familiar rhetoric', *International Journal of the Sociology of Law*, **11**, pp. 385–400.

Eaton, M. (1985), 'Documenting the defendant', in J. Brophy and C. Smart (eds), *Women in Law*, London: Routledge & Kegan Paul.

Eaton, M. (1986), *Justice for Women?*, Milton Keynes: Open University Press.

Edwards, S. S. M. (1984), *Women on Trial*, Manchester: Manchester University Press.

Edwards, S. S. M. (1986), *The Police Response to Domestic Violence in London*, London: Polytechnic of Central London.

Edwards, S. S. M. (1989), *Policing 'Domestic' Violence*, London: Sage.

Ehrlich, I. (1975), 'The deterrent effect of capital punishment: a question of life or death', *American Economic Review*, **65**.

Einstadter, W. J. (1984), 'Citizen patrols: prevention or control?', *Crime and Social Justice*, pp. 199–212.

Elliot, N. (1990), *Making Prison Work*, London: Adam Smith Institute.

Engels, F. (1969), *The Condition of the Working Class in England*, London: Panther.

Erikson, K. T. (1962), 'Notes on the sociology of deviance', *Social Problems*, **9**, Spring, repr. in H. S. Becker (ed.) (1964), *The Other Side: Perspectives on deviance*, New York: Free Press.

Erikson, K. T. (1966), *Wayward Puritans*, New York: Wiley.

Eron, L. D. and Huesmann, L. R. (1990), 'The stability of aggressive behaviour – even unto the third generation', in M. Lewis and S. M. Miller (eds), *Handbook of Developmental Psychopathology*, New York: Plenum.

Faragher, T. (1981), 'The police response to violence against women in the home', in J. Pahl (ed.), *Private Violence and Public Policy*, London: Routledge & Kegan Paul.

Farrington, D. P. (1986), 'Age and crime', in M. Tonry and N. Morris (eds), *Crime and Justice*, vol. 7, Chicago: University of Chicago Press.

Farrington, D. P. (1989), 'Self-reported and official offending from adolescence to adulthood', in M. W. Klein (ed.), *Cross-National Research in Self-Reported Crime and Delinquency*, Dordrecht: Kluwer.

Farrington, D. P. (1992a), 'Explaining the beginning, progress and ending of antisocial behaviour from birth to adulthood', in J. McCord (ed.), *Advances in Criminology Theory*, vol. 3, *Facts, Frameworks and Forecasts*, New Brunswick, NJ: Transaction Books.

Farrington, D. P. (1992b), 'Juvenile delinquency', in J. C. Coleman (ed.), *The School Years*, 2nd edn, London: Routledge & Kegan Paul.

Farrington, D. P. (1993), 'Childhood, adolescent and adult features of violent males', in L. R. Huesmann (ed.), *Aggressive Behavior: Current perspectives*, New York: Plenum.

Farrington, D. P. (1994), 'Human development and criminal careers', in M. Maguire, R. Morgan and R. Reiner (eds), *The Oxford Handbook of Criminology*, Oxford: Clarendon Press.

Farrington, D. P. and Morris, A. M. (1983), 'Sex, sentencing and reconviction', *British Journal of Criminology*, **23** (3), pp. 229–48.

Farrington, D. P., Snyder, H. N. and Finnegan, T. A.A (1988), 'Specialization in juvenile court careers,' *Criminology*, **26**, pp. 461–87.

Farrington, D. P. and West, D. J. (1990) 'The Cambridge study in delinquent development: a long-term follow-up of 411 London males', in H. J. Kerner and G. Kaiser (eds), *Criminality: Personality, behaviour and life history*, Berlin: Springer-Verlag.

Ferguson, T. (1952), *The Young Delinquent in His Social Setting: A Glasgow study*, Oxford: Oxford University Press.

Ferguson, T. and Cunnison, J. (1951), *The Young Wage-Earner: A study of Glasgow boys*, London: Oxford University Press.

Ferguson, T. and Cunnison, J. (1956), *In Their Early Twenties: A study of Glasgow youth*, London: Oxford University Press.

Fergusson, D. M., Horwood, L. T. and Lynskey, M. T. (1992), 'Family change, parental discord and early offending', *Journal of Child Psychology and Psychiatry*, **33**, pp. 1059–75.

Ferri, E. (1895), *Criminal Sociology*, London: Unwin.

Field, S. (1990), *Trends in Crime and Their Interpretation: A study of recorded crime in post-war England and Wales*, Home Office Research Study No. 119, London: HMSO.

Fine, B. (ed.) (1979), *Capitalism and the Rule of Law: From deviancy theory to Marxism*, London: Hutchinson.

Fine, B. and Millar, R. (eds) (1985), *Policing the Miners' Strike*, London: Lawrence & Wishart.

Finkelhor, D. (1979), *Sexually Victimized Children*, New York: Sage.

Foucault, M. (1977), *Discipline and Punish*, London: Allen Lane.

Foucault, M. (1979), *The History of Sexuality: An introduction*, London: Allen Lane.

Fyvel, T. R. (1961), *The Insecure Offenders*, London: Chatto & Windus.

Galliher, J. F. (1978), 'The life and death of liberal criminology', *Contemporary Crises*, **12** (3), pp. 245–63.

Garfinkel, H. (1967), *Studies in Ethnomethodology*, Engelwood Cliffs, NJ: Prentice Hall.

Garland, D. (1985a), 'Politics and policy in criminological discourse: a study of tendentious reasoning and rhetoric', *International Journal of Sociology of Law*, **13**, pp. 1-33.

Garland, D. (1985b), *Punishment and Welfare*, Aldershot: Gower.

Garland, D. (1990), *Punishment and Modern Society: A study in social theory*, Oxford: Oxford University Press.

Garland, D. (1992), 'Criminological knowledge and its relation to power', *British Journal of Criminology*, **32** (4), pp. 403–22.

Garland, D. (1994), 'The development of British criminology', in M. Maguire, R. Morgan and R. Reiner (eds), *The Oxford Handbook of Criminology*, Oxford: Clarendon Press.

Garofalo, R. (1968; first pub. 1914), *Criminology*, Boston: Little, Brown; Patterson-Smith.

Gelsthorpe, L. and Morris, A. (1988), 'Feminism and criminology in Britain', *British Journal of Criminology*, **28** (2), Spring, pp. 93–109.

Gelsthorpe, L. and Morris, A. (eds) (1990), *Feminist Perspectives in Criminology*, London: Routledge & Kegan Paul.

Giallombardo, R. (1966), *Society of Women: A study of a woman's prison*, New York: Wiley.

Gibbs, J. P. (1966), 'Conception of deviant behaviour: the old and the new', *Pacific Sociological Review*, **14** (1), pp. 20–37.

Gibbs, J. P. (1975), *Crime, Punishment and Deterrence*, New York: Elsevier.

Giddens, A. (1978), *Durkheim*, Glasgow: Fontana.

Giddens, A. (1993), *Sociology*, 2nd edn, Cambridge: Polity Press.

Gill, O. (1977), *Luke Street*, London: Macmillan.

Gilligan, C. (1982), *In a Different Voice*, Cambridge, Mass.: Harvard University Press.

Goldman, N. (1959), 'A socio-psychological study of school vandalism', Final Report on Office of Education Contract No. SAE 181 (8453), Syracuse, NY: University Research Institute.

Gordon, D. M. (1971), 'Class and the economics of crime', *Review of Radical Political Economy*, **3**, pp. 51–75.

Goring, C. (1919), *The English Convict*, London: Methuen.

Gottfredson, M. R. and Hirschi, T. (eds) (1987), *Positive Criminology*, London: Sage.

Gouldner, A. W. (1968), 'The sociologist as partisan: sociology and the welfare state', *The American Sociologist*, May, pp. 103–16.

Gouldner, A. W. (1971), *The Coming Crisis of Western Sociology*, London: Heinemann.

Gove, W. (ed.) (1975), *The Labelling of Deviance*, London: Wiley.

Graham, J. M. (1976), 'Amphetamine politics on Capital Hill', in W. J. Chambliss and M. Mankoff (eds), *Whose Law? What Order?*, New York: Wiley.

Greenberg, D. (1976), 'On one-dimensional Marxist criminology', *Theory and Society*, **3**, pp. 610-21.

Greenwood, V. (1981), 'The myths of female crime', in A. M. Morris with L. R. Gelsthorpe (eds), *Women and Crime*, Cropwood Conference Series, No. 13, Cambridge: Cambridge Institute of Criminology.

Greenwood, V. (1983), 'The role and future of female imprisonment', mimeo, Middlesex Polytechnic.

Gregory, J. (1986), 'Sex, class and crime: towards a non-sexist criminology', in R. Matthews and J. Young (eds), *Confronting Crime*, London: Sage.

Gross, B. (1982), 'Some anti-crime proposals for progressives', *Crime and Social Justice*, Summer, pp. 51–4.

Grosz, E. A. (1987), 'Feminist theory and the challenge to knowledge', *Women's Studies International Forum*, **10** (5), pp. 208–17.

Haag, E. van den (1975) *Punishing Criminals: Concerning a very old and painful question*, New York: Basic Books.

Haag, E. van den (1985), *Deterring Potential Criminals*, London: Social Affairs Unit.

Hagan, J. (1977), *The Disreputable Pleasures*, Toronto: MacGraw-Hill.

Hagan, J., Simpson, J. H. and Gillis, A. R. (1979), 'The sexual stratification of social control: a gender-based perspective on crime and delinquency', *British Journal of Criminology*, **30**.

Hagel, A. and Newburn, T. (1994), *Persistent Young Offenders*, London: Policy Studies Institute.

Hall, R. (1985), *Ask Any Woman*, London: Falling Wall Press.

Hall, S. (1974), 'Deviance, politics and the media', in P. Rock and M. McIntosh (eds), *Deviance and Social Control*, London: Tavistock.

Hall, S. (1980), 'Popular-democratic vs authoritarian-populism: two ways of "taking democracy seriously"', in A. Hunt, *Marxism and Democracy*, London: Lawrence & Wishart.

Hall, S. (1988), 'The hard road to renewal', *British Journal of Criminology*, **34** (3), Summer.

Hall, S., Critcher, C., Jefferson, T., Clarke, J. and Roberts, B. (1978), *Policing the Crisis: Mugging, the state and law and order*, London: Macmillan.

Hall, S. and Jefferson, T. (eds) (1976), *Resistance through Rituals: Youth subcultures in post-war Britain*, London: Hutchinson.

Hanmer, J. (1978), 'Male violence and the social control of women', in G. Littlejohn, B. Smart, J. Wakefield and N. Yuval-Davies (eds), *Power and the State*, London: Croom Helm.

Hanmer, J. and Saunders, S. (1984), *Well Founded Fears: A community study of violence to women*, London: Hutchinson.

Harding, S. (1991), *Whose Science? Whose Knowledge?*, Buckingham: Open University Press.

Hargreaves, D. H. (1967), *Social Relations in a Secondary School*, London: Routledge & Kegan Paul.

Hargreaves, D. H., Hester, S. and Mellor, F. (1976), *Deviance in Classrooms*, London: Routledge & Kegan Paul.

Harris, R. (1992), *Crime, Criminal Justice and the Probation Service*, London: Routledge.

Harris, R. and Webb, D. (1987), *Welfare, Power and Juvenile Justice*, London: Tavistock.

Hartless, J. M., Ditton, J., Nair, G. and Phillips, S. (1995), 'More sinned against then sinning: a study of young teenagers' experience of crime', *British Journal of Criminology*, **35** (1), Winter.

Hay, W., Sparks, R. and Bottoms, A. E. (1994), *Prisons and the Problem of Order*, Oxford: Oxford University Press.

Heal, L. and Laycock, G. (eds) (1986), *Situational Crime Prevention: From theory into practice*, London: HMSO.

Hebdige, D. (1979), *Subculture: The meaning of style*, London: Methuen.

Heidensohn, F. (1968), 'The deviance of women: a critique and an enquiry', *British Journal of Criminology*, **19** (2).

Heidensohn, F. (1969), 'Prison for women', *The Criminologist*, **4** (12), pp. 113–22.

Heidensohn, F. (1985), *Women and Crime*, London: Macmillan.

Heidensohn, F. (1986), 'Models of justice: Portia or Persephone? Some thoughts on equality, fairness and gender in the field of criminal justice', *International Journal of the Sociology of Law*, **14**.

Heidensohn, F. (1989), *Crime and Society*, Basingstoke: Macmillan.

Heidensohn. F. (1994), 'Gender and crime', in M. Maguire, R. Morgan and R. Reiner (eds), *The Oxford Handbook of Criminology*, Oxford: Clarendon Press.

Henry, S. (1978), *The Hidden Economy*, Oxford: Martin Robertson.

Hepburn, J. R. (1977), 'Social control and the legal order: legitimated repression in a capitalist state', *Contemporary Crises*, **1**, pp. 77–90.

Hester, S. and Eglin, P. (1992), *A Sociology of Crime*, London: Routledge.

Hinch, R. (1983), 'Marxist criminology in the 1970s: clarifying the clutter', *Crime and Social Justice*, Summer, pp. 65–73.

Hindelang, M. J. (1974), 'Decisions of shoplifting victims to invoke the criminal justice process', *Social Problems*, **21**, pp. 580–91.

Hindelang, M. J., Hirschi, T. and Weis, J. G. (1981), *Measuring Delinquency*, Beverly Hills, Calif.: Sage.

Hirsch, A. von (1993), *Censure and Sanctions*, Oxford: Oxford University Press.

Hirschi, T. (1969), *Causes of Delinquency*, Berkeley, Calif.: University of California Press.

Hirst, P. Q. (1975a), 'Marx and Engels on law, crime and morality', in I. Taylor, P. Walton and J. Young (eds), *Critical Criminology*, London: Routledge & Kegan Paul.

Hirst, P. Q. (1975b), 'Radical deviancy theory and Marxism: a reply to Taylor, Walton and Young', in E. Taylor, P. Walton and J. Young (eds), *Critical Criminology*, London: Routledge & Kegan Paul.

Hirst, P. Q. (1980), 'Law, socialism and rights', in P. Carlen and M. Collison (eds), *Radical Issues in Criminology*, Oxford: Martin Robertson.

Hobbs, D. (1988), *Doing the Business: Entrepreneurship, the working class, and detectives in East London*, Oxford: Clarendon Press.

Hobsbawn, E. J. (1959), *Primitive Rebels*, Manchester: Manchester University Press.

Hogg, R. (1988), 'Taking crime seriously: Left realism and Australian criminology', in M. Findlay and R. Hogg (eds), *Understanding Crime and Criminal Justice*, Sydney: Law Book.

Holdaway, S. (1977), 'Changes in urban policing', *British Journal of Sociology*, **28** (2).

Holdaway, S. (ed.) (1979), *The British Police*, London: Edward Arnold.

Home Affairs Committee (1993), *Juvenile Offenders*, Sixth Report, London: HMSO.

Home Office (1985), *Criminal Careers of Those Born in 1953, 1958, 1963*, Statistical Bulletin No. 5/89, London: Home Office Statistical Department.

Home Office (1987), *Criminal Careers of Those Born in 1953: Persistent offenders and desistance*, Statistical Bulletin No. 35/89, London: Home Office Statistical Department.

Hood, R. (1987), 'Some reflections on the role of criminology in public policy', Address to the British Society of Criminology, 28 January.

Horowitz, I. L. and Leibowitz, M. (1969), 'Social deviance and political marginality: towards a redefinition of the relation between sociology and politics', *Social Problems*, **15** (3), pp. 280–96.

Hough, J. M. and Mayhew, P. (1985), *Taking Account of Crime: Key findings from the second British crime survey*, Home Office Research Study No. 85, London: HMSO.

Hudson, B. (1987), *Justice Through Punishment*, Basingstoke: Macmillan.

Hudson, B. (1993), 'Racism and criminology: concepts and controversies', in D. Cook and B. Hudson (eds), *Racism and Criminology*, London: Sage.

Hugill, B. (1995), *Observer*, 23 July.

Hulsman, L. (1986), 'Critical criminology and the concept of crime', *Contemporary Crises*, **10**, pp. 63–80.

Hunt, A. (1980), 'The radical critique of law: an assessment', *International Journal of the Sociology of Law*, **8**, pp. 33–46.

Jay, P. and Rose, B. (1977), *Children and Young Persons in Custody*, Working Party Report, London: NACRO.

Jefferson, T. (1973), 'The Teds: a political resurrection', stencilled occasional papers, No. 22, Centre for Contemporary Cultural Studies, University of Birmingham.

Jefferson, T. (1976), 'Cultural responses of the Teds: the defence of space', in S. Hall and T. Jefferson (eds), *Resistance through Rituals*, London: Hutchinson.

Jefferson, T. (1986), 'Unpopular perceptions: a reply to Richard Kinsey', *Marxism Today*, July, p. 39.

Jefferson, T. (1993), 'Theorising masculine subjectivity', plenary address, Masculinities and Crime Conference, University of Brunel, September.

Jefferson, T. and Shapland, J. (1994), 'Criminal justice and the production of order and control', *British Journal of Criminology*, **34** (3), Summer.

Jeffery, C. (1960), 'The historical development of criminology', in H. Mannheim (ed.), *Pioneers in Criminology*, London: Stevens.

Johnson, R. E. (1979), *Juvenile Delinquency and Its Origins*, Cambridge: Cambridge University Press.

Jones, H. (1958), 'Approaches to an ecological study', *British Journal of Delinquency*, **18** (4), pp. 277–93.

Jones, P. (1993), *Studying Society: Sociological theories and research practices*, London: Collins.

Jones, S. (1987), 'Women's experience of crime and policing', mimeo, Centre for the Study of Community and Race Relations, Brunel University.

Jones, T., Maclean, B. and Young, J. (1986), *The Islington Crime Survey*, Aldershot: Gower.

Jupp, V. R. (1989), *Methods of Criminology Research*, London: Unwin Hyman.

Kinsey, R. (1984), *The Merseyside Crime Survey: First report*, Liverpool: Merseyside County Council.

Kitsuse, J. I. (1962), 'Societal reaction to deviant behavior: problems of theory and method', *Social Problems*, **9**, Winter, pp. 247–56. Reprinted in E. Rubington and M. S. Weinberg (eds) (1968), *Deviance: The interactionist perspective*, Basingstoke: Macmillan.

Kitsuse, J. I. and Dietrick, D. (1959), 'Delinquent boys', *American Sociological Review*, **24**.

Klein, D. (1973), 'The etiology of female crime', *Issues in Criminology*, **8** (2), pp. 3–30.

Kolko, G. (1976), *Railroads and Regulations*, Princeton, NJ: Princeton University Press.

Kroeber, A. L. (1952), *The Nature of Culture*, Chicago: University of Chicago Press.

Lacey, N. (1988), *State Punishment*, London: Routledge.

Laing, R. D. (1967), *The Politics of Experience and the Bird of Paradise*, Harmondsworth: Penguin.

Laing, R. D. (1968), 'The obvious', in D. Cooper (ed.), *The Dialectics of Liberation*, Harmondsworth: Penguin.

Landesco, J. (1968), *Organized Crime in Chicago*, Chicago: University of Chicago Press.

Lea, J. (1987), 'Left realism: a defence', *Contemporary Crises*, **11**, pp. 357–70.

Lea, J., Matthews, R. and Young, J. (1987), *Law and Order Five Years On*, London: Middlesex Polytechnic, Centre for Criminology.

Lemert, E. M. (1951), *Social Pathology*, New York: McGraw-Hill.

Lemert, E. M. (1967), *Human Deviance, Social Problems and Social Control*, Englewood Cliffs, NJ: Prentice Hall.

Leonard, E. B. (1982), *A Critique of Criminological Theory: Women, crime and society*, New York: Longman.

Levi, M. (1987), *Regulating Fraud*, London: Tavistock.

Levi, M. (1994), 'White-collar crime', in M. Maguire, R. Morgan and R. Reiner (eds), *The Oxford Handbook of Criminology*, Oxford: Clarendon Press.

Liazos, A. (1972), 'The poverty of the sociology of deviance: nuts, sluts and preverts', *Social Problems*, **20**, pp. 103–20.

Lilley, J. R., Cullen, F. T. and Ball, R. A. (1989), *Criminological Theory: Context and consequences*, London: Sage.

Little, W. R. and Ntsekhe, V. R. (1959), 'Social class background of young offenders from London', *British Journal of Delinquency*, **16** (2), pp. 130–5.

Loeber, R. and Stouthamer-Loeber, M. (1986), 'Family factors as correlates and predictors of juvenile conduct problems and delinquency', in M. Tonry and N. Morris (eds), *Crime and Justice*, vol. 7, Chicago: University of Chicago Press, pp. 29–49.

Lombroso, C. (1876), *L'Uomo Delinquente*, 5th edn, Turin: Bocca; first pub. Milan: Hoepli.

Lowson, D. (1960), 'Delinquency in industrial areas', *British Journal of Criminology*, **1** (1), July, pp. 50–5.

Lukes, S. (1973), *Emile Durkheim, His Life and Work: Historical and critical study*, Harmondsworth: Penguin.

MacDonald, E. (1991), *Shoot the Women First*, London: Fourth Estate.

MacGregor, S. (ed.) (1989), *Drugs and British Society: Responses to a social problem in the 1980s*, London: Routledge.

McCord, J. (1979), 'Some child rearing antecedents of criminal behaviour in adult men', *Journal of Personality and Social Psychology*, **37**, pp. 1477–86.

McCord, J. (1982), 'A longitudinal view of the relationship between paternal absence and crime', in J. Gunn and D. P. Farrington (eds), *Abnormal Offenders, Delinquency and the Criminal Justice System*, Chichester: Wiley.

McLeod, E. (1982), *Women Working: Prostitution now*, London: Croom Helm.

McMullan, J. L. (1986), 'The "law and order" problem in socialist criminology', *Studies in Political Economy*, Autumn, pp. 175–92.

McRobbie, A. and Garber, J. (1976), 'Girls and Subcultures', in S. Hall and T. Jefferson (eds), *Resistance through Rituals*, London: Hutchinson.

Maguire, M. (1994), 'Crime statistics, patterns and trends: changing perceptions and their implications', in M. Maguire and R. Reiner (eds), *The Oxford Handbook of Criminology*, Oxford: Clarendon Press.

Maguire, M., Morgan, R. and Reiner, R. (eds) (1994), *The Oxford Handbook of Criminology*, Oxford: Clarendon Press.

Mankoff, M. (1971), 'Societal reaction and deviant career: a critical analysis', *Sociological Quarterly*, **12**, Spring, pp. 204–18.

Mannheim, H. (1940), *Social Aspects of Crime in England Between the Wars*, London: Allen & Unwin.

Mannheim, H. (1965), *Comparative Criminology*, London: Routledge & Kegan Paul.

Manning, P. (1977), *Police Work: The organisation of policing*, Cambridge, Mass.: MIT Press.

Marx, K. (1969), *Theories of Surplus Value*, vol. 1, London: Lawrence & Wishart.

Marx, K. and Engels, F. (1965), *The German Ideology*, London: Lawrence & Wishart.

Marx, K. and Engels, F. (1970a), *Selected Works*, London: Lawrence & Wishart.

Marx, K. and Engels, F. (1970b), 'Manifesto of the Communist Party', in K. Marx and F. Engels, (1970a), *Selected Works*, London: Lawrence & Wishart.

Matza, D. (1964), *Delinquency and Drift*, New York: Wiley.

Matza, D. (1969), *Becoming Deviant*, Englewood Cliffs, NJ: Prentice Hall.

Matza, D. and Sykes, G. (1961), 'Juvenile delinquency and subterranean values', *American Sociological Review*, **26**, pp. 712–19.

Matthews, J. (1981), *Women in the Penal System*, London: NACRO.

Matthews, R. (1992), 'Replacing "broken windows": crime, incivilities and urban change', in R. Matthews and J. Young (eds), *Issues in Realist Criminology*, London: Sage.

Mawby, R. I. (1987), 'From victimization rates to the crime experience', mimeo, Plymouth Polytechnic.

Mayhew, P., Elliot, D. and Dowds, L. (1989), *The 1988 British Crime Survey*, London: HMSO.

Mayhew, P. and Hough, M. (1983), 'Note: the British crime survey', *British Journal of Criminology*, **23**, pp. 394–5.

Mayhew, P. and Maung, N. A. (1993), *The 1992 British Crime Survey*, London: HMSO.

Mays, J. B. (1954), *Growing Up in the City*, Liverpool: Liverpool University Press.

Mays, J. B. (1959), *On the Threshold of Delinquency*, Liverpool: Liverpool University Press.

Mays, J. B. (1975), *Crime and Its Treatment*, 2nd edn, London: Longman.

Merton, R. K. (1993; first pub. 1938), 'Social structure and anomie', in C. Lemert (ed.) *Social Theory: The multicultural readings*, Boulder, Colo.: Westview Press.

Messerschmidt, J. (1986), *Capitalism, Patriarchy and Crime: Towards a Socialist–Feminist Criminology*, Totowa, NJ: Rowman & Littlefield.

Messerschmidt, J. (1993), *Masculinities and Crime*, Lanham, Md.: Rowman & Littlefield.

Michalowski, R. J. (1983), 'Crime control in the 1980s: a progressive agenda', *Crime and Social Justice*, **20**.

Michalowski, R. J. and Bohlander, E. W. (1976), 'Repression and criminal justice in capitalist America', *Sociological Inquiry*, **46** (2), pp. 95–106.

Miles, I. and Irvine, J. (1981), 'The critique of official statistics', in J. Irvine, I. Miles and J. Evans (eds), *Demystifying Social Statistics*, 2nd imp., London: Pluto Press.

Miliband, R. (1969), *The State in Capitalist Society*, London: Weidenfield & Nicolson.

Miller, E. (1986), *Street Women*, Philadelphia: Temple University Press.

Miller, W. B. (1958), 'Lower class culture as a generating milieu of gang delinquency', *Journal of Social Issues*, **14** (3).

Moore, S. (1995), 'Barking up the family tree', *Guardian*, 9 March.

Morgan, P. (1978), *Delinquent Fantasies*, London: Maurice Temple Smith.

Morgan, P. (1981), 'The Children's Act: sacrificing justice to social worker's needs?',

C. Brewer, T. Morris, P. Morgan and M. North, *Criminal Welfare on Trial*, London: Social Affairs Unit.

Morgan, R. (1994), 'Imprisonment', in M. Maguire, R. Morgan and R. Reiner (eds); *Criminal Welfare on Trial*, London: Social Affairs Unit.

Morris, A. (1987), *Women, Crime and Criminal Justice*, Oxford: Blackwell.

Morris, T. P. (1957), *The Criminal Area: A study in social ecology*, London: Routledge & Kegan Paul.

Moulds, E. (1980), 'Chivalry and paternalism: disparities of treatment in the criminal justice system', in S. Datesman and F. Scarpitti (eds), *Women, Crime and Justice*, New York: Oxford: University Press.

Mugford, S. and O'Malley, P. (1991), 'Heroin policy and deficit models: the Limits of Left realism', *Crime, Law and Social Change*, **15**, pp. 19–36.

Mullins, C. (1945), *Why Crime? Some causes and remedies from the psychological standpoint*, London: Methuen.

Muncie, J. (1984), *The Trouble With Kids Today*, London: Hutchinson.

Muncie, J. and Sparks, R. (eds) (1991), *Imprisonment: European perspectives*, London: Harvester Wheatsheaf.

Murray, C. (1990), *The Emerging British Underclass*, London: Institute of Economic Affairs, Health and Welfare Unit.

Naffine, N. (1987), *Female Crime*, Sydney: Allen & Unwin.

Nagin, D. S. and Farrington, D. P. (1992), 'The onset and persistence of offending', *Criminology*, **30**, pp. 501–23.

Nelken, D. (1994), 'White-collar crime', in M. Maguire, R. Morgan and R. Reiner (eds), *Oxford Handbook of Criminology*, Oxford: Clarendon Press.

Nettler, G. (1978), *Explaining Crime*, New York: McGraw-Hill.

Newburn, T. (1992), *Permission and Regulation: Law and morals in post-war Britain*, London: Routledge.

Norrie, S. and Adelman, S. (1989), ' "Consensual authoritarianism" and criminal justice in Thatcher's Britain', *Journal of Law and Society*, **16** (1), Spring.

Nuttall, J. (1970), *Bomb Culture*, St Albans: Paladin.

Park, R. E. (1937), 'Human Ecology', *American Journal of Sociology*, **42**(1), pp. 1–15.

Parker, H. (1974), *View From the Boys*, Newton Abbot: David & Charles.

Parker, H. (1976), 'Boys will be men: brief adolescence in a down-town neighbourhood', in G. Mungham and G. Pearson (eds), *Working Class Youth Culture*, London: Routledge & Kegan Paul.

Parton, N. (1992), *Governing the Family*, Basingstoke: Macmillan.

Pearce, F. (1976), *Crimes of the Powerful*, London: Pluto Press.

Pearce, F. and Tombs, S. (1992), 'Realism and corporate crime', in R. Matthews and J. Young (eds), *Issues in Realist Criminology*, London: Sage.

Pearson, G. (1975), *The Deviant Imagination*, London: Macmillan.

Pearson, G. (1976), 'Cotton town: a case study and its history', in G. Mungham and G. Pearson (eds), *Working Class Youth Culture*, London: Routledge & Kegan Paul.

Pearson, G. (1978), 'Social work and law and order', *Social Work Today*, **9** (30).

Pearson, G. (1983), *Hooligan: A history of respectable fears*, London: Macmillan.

Pearson, G. (1987), *The New Heroin Users*, Oxford: Blackwell.

Pearson, G. (1994), 'Youth, crime and society', in M. Maguire, R. Morgan and R. Reiner (eds), *The Oxford Handbook of Criminology*, Oxford: Clarendon Press.

Pearson, R. (1976), 'Women defendants in magistrates' courts', *British Journal of Law and Society*, **3**, pp. 265–73.

Pepinsky, H. E. and Quinney, R. (eds) (1991), *Criminology As Peacemaking*, Bloomington, Ind.: Indiana University Press.

Phillipson, M. (1971), *Sociological Aspects of Crime and Delinquency*, London: Routledge & Kegan Paul.

Pitts, J. (1988), *The Politics of Juvenile Crime*, London: Sage.

Pizzey, E. (1973), *Scream Quietly or the Neighbours Will Hear*, Harmondsworth: Penquin.

Player, E. (1989), 'Women and crime in the city', in D. Downes (ed.), *Crime in the City*, London: Macmillan.

Plummer, K. (1975), *Sexual Stigma*, London: Routledge & Kegan Paul.

Plummer, K. (1979), 'Misunderstanding labelling perspectives', in D. Downes and P. Rock (eds), *Deviant Interpretations*, Oxford: Martin Robertson.

Pollak, O. (1950), *The Criminality of Women*, New York: Barnes/Perpetuo.

Pollner, M. (1974), 'Mundane reasoning', *Philosophy of Social Sciences*, **4** (1).

Poole, E. D. and Regoli, R. M. (1979), 'Parental support, delinquent friends and delinquency', *Journal of Criminal Law and Criminology*, **70**, pp. 188–93.

Posner, R. A. (1986), *Economic Analysis of Law*, Boston: Little, Brown.

Poulantzas, N. (1973), 'The problem of the capitalist state', in J. Urry and J. Wakeford (eds), *Power in Britain*, London: Heinemann.

Quinney, R. (1969), *Criminal Justice in American Society*, Boston: Little, Brown.

Quinney, R. (1970a), *The Social Reality of Crime*, Boston: Little, Brown.

Quinney, R. (1970b), *The Problem of Crime*, New York: Dodd, Mead.

Quinney, R. (1974), *Critique of the Legal Order: Crime control in capitalist society*, Boston: Little, Brown.

Quinney, R. (1975), *Criminology: Analysis and critique of crime in America*, Boston: Little, Brown.

Quinney, R. (1977), *Class, State and Crime: On the theory and practice of criminal justice*, New York: McKay.

Radford, J. (1987), 'Policing male violence', in J. Hanmer and M. Maynard (eds), *Women, Violence and Social Control*, London: Macmillan.

Radzinowicz, L. (1961), *In Search of Criminology*, London: Heinemann.

Rafter, N. H. (1986), 'Left out by the Left: crime and crime control', *Socialist Review*, **16**, pp. 7–23.

Reiner, R. (1984), 'Crime, law and deviance: the Durkheim legacy', in S. Fenton (ed.), *Durkheim and Modern Sociology*, Cambridge: Cambridge University Press.

Reiner, R. (1988), 'British criminology and the state', *British Journal of Criminology*, **29** (1), pp. 138–58.

Reiner, R. (1992), *The Politics of the police*, 2nd edn, Hemel Hempstead: Wheatsheaf.

Reiner, R. (1994), 'Policing and the police', in M. Maguire, M. Morgan and R. Reiner (eds), *The Oxford Handbook of Criminology*, Oxford: Clarendon Press.

Reiner, R. and Cross, M. (eds) (1991), *Beyond Law and Order*, London: Macmillan.

Rex, J. and Moore, R. (1967), *Race, Community and Conflict*, London: Institute of Race Relations/Oxford University Press.

Riley, D. (1986), 'Sex differences in teenage crime: the role of lifestyle', Research Bulletin No. 2, Home Office Research and Planning Unit, HMSO, London, pp. 34–80.

Riley, D. and Shaw, M. (1985), *Parental Supervision and Juvenile Delinquency*, Home Office Research Study No. 83, London: HMSO.

Robins, L. N. and Rutter, M. (eds) (1990), *Straight and Devious Pathways From Childhood To Adulthood*, Cambridge: Cambridge University Press.

Rock, P. (1973), *Deviant Behaviour*, London: Hutchinson.

Rock, P. (1988), 'The present state of criminology in Britain', *British Journal of Criminology*, **28** (2), pp. 188–99.

Rock, P. (1994), 'The social organization of British criminology', in M. Maguire, R. Morgan and R. Reiner (eds), *The Oxford Handbook of Criminology*, Oxford: Clarendon Press.

Rodger, J. (1995), 'Family policy or moral regulation?', *Critical Social Policy*, **43**, Summer.

Roshier, B. (1977), 'The function of crime myth', *Sociological Review*, May.

Roshier, B. (1989), *Controlling Crime*, Milton Keynes: Open University Press.

Ruggiero, V. (1992), 'Realist criminology: a critique', in J. Young and R. Matthews (eds), *Rethinking Criminology: The realist debate*, London: Sage.

Russell, D. E. H. (1982), *Rape in Marriage*, New York: Macmillan.

Rutter, M. and Giller, H. (1983), *Juvenile Delinquency*, Harmondsworth: Penguin.

Sainsbury, P. (1955), *Suicide in London*, London: Institute of Psychiatry.

Schervish, P. G. (1973), 'The labelling perspective', *American Sociologist*, **8**, pp. 47–56.

Schlossman, S., Zellman, G. and Shavelson, R., with Sedlak, M. and Cobb, J. (1984), *Delinquency Prevention in South Chicago: A fifty-year assessment of the Chicago area project*, Santa Monica, Calif.: Rand.

Schur, E. M. (1971), *Labelling Deviant Behaviour*, New York: Harper & Row.

Schutz, A. (1972), *The Phenomenology of the Social World*, London: Heinemann.

Schwendinger, H. and Schwendinger, J. (1975), 'Defenders of order or guardians of human rights?', in I. Taylor, P. Walton and J. Young (eds), *Critical Criminology*, London: Routledge & Kegan Paul.

Scott, P. (1956), 'Gangs and delinquent groups in London', *British Journal of Delinquency*, **7**, July, pp. 8–21.

Scraton, P. (1985), *The State of the Police*, London: Pluto Press.

Scraton, P. (ed.) (1987), *Law, Order and the Authoritarian State*, Milton Keynes: Open University Press.

Scraton, P. and Chadwick, K. (1991), 'The theoretical and political priorities of critical criminology', in K. Stenson and D. Cowell (eds), *The Politics of Crime Control*, London: Sage.

Shacklady Smith, L. (1978), 'Sexist assumptions and female delinquency: an empirical investigation', in C. Smart and B. Smart (eds), *Women, Sexuality and Social Control*, London: Routledge & Kegan Paul.

Shaw, C. R. (1930), *The Jack-Roller: A delinquent boy's own story*, Chicago: Chicago University Press.

Shaw, C. R. and McKay, H. D. (1942), *Juvenile Delinquency in Urban Areas*, Chicago: Chicago University Press.

Shaw, C. R., McKay, H. D. and MacDonald, J. F. (1938), *Brothers in Crime*, Chicago: Chicago University Press.

Shaw, C. R. and Moore, M. E. (1931), *The Natural History of a Delinquent Career*, Chicago: Chicago University Press.

Short, J. F. and Strodtbeck, F. (1965), *Group Process and Delinquency*, Chicago: University of Chicago Press.

Shover, N. (1985), *Aging Criminals*, Beverly Hills, Calif.: Sage.

Sim, J. (1990), *Medical Power in Prisons: The Prison Medical Service in England 1774– 1989*, Milton Keynes: Open University Press.

Simon, R. J. (1975), *Women and Crime*, Toronto: Lexington Books.

Smart, C. (1976), *Women, Crime and Criminology: A feminist critique*, London: Routledge & Kegan Paul.

Smart, C. (1979), 'The new female criminal: reality or myth?', *British Journal of Criminology*, **19** (1).

Smart, C. (1981), 'Response to Greenwood', in A. M. Morris and L. R. Gelsthorpe (eds), *Women and Crime*, Cropwood Conference Series, No. 13, Cambridge: Institute of Criminology.

Smart, C. (1989), *Feminism and the Power of Law*, London: Routledge.

Smart, C. (1990), 'Feminist approaches to criminology, or postmodern woman meets atavistic man', in L. R. Gelsthorpe and A. M. Morris (eds), *Feminist Perspectives in Criminology*, London: Routledge & Kegan Paul.

Smith, C. (1970), *Adolescence*, 2nd edn, London: Longman.

Smith, D.J. and Grey, J. (1985) *Police and People in London: The PSI Report*, Aldershot: Gower.

Smith, L. J. F. (1988), 'Image of women: decision-making in courts', in A. M. Morris and C. Wilkinson (eds), *Women and the Penal System*, Cropwood Conference Series, No. 10, Cambridge: Institute of Criminology.

South, N. (1994), 'Drugs: control, crime and criminological studies', in M. Maguire, R. Morgan and R. Reiner (eds), *The Oxford Handbook of Criminology*, Oxford: Clarendon Press.

Sparks, R., Genn, H. G. and Dodd, D. J. (1977), *Surveying Victims*, Chichester: Wiley.

Spencer, J. L. *et al.* (1961), 'Preliminary report of the British social project', unpublished.

Spivack, G., Marcus, J. and Swift, M. (1986), 'Early classroom behaviour up to age 30', *British Journal of Criminology*, **29**, pp. 124–31.

Stanko, E. (1985), *Intimate Intrusions*, London: Routledge & Kegan Paul.

Stanko, E. (1988), 'Hidden violence against women', in M. Maguire and J. Pointing (eds), *Victims of Crime: A new deal?*, Milton Keynes: Open University Press.

Stanko, E. (1993), *Men and Crime*, Milton Keynes: Open University Press.

Stanley, L. and Wise, S. (1983), *Breaking Out*, London: Routledge & Kegan Paul.

Stattin, H., Magnusson, D. and Reichel, H. (1989), 'Criminal activity at different ages: a study based on a Swedish longitudinal research population', *British Journal of Criminology*, **29**, pp. 368–85.

Stedman-Jones, G. (1971), *Outcast in London*, Oxford: Oxford University Press.

Steinhert, H. (1985), 'The amazing New Left law and order campaign', *Contemporary Crises*, **9**, pp. 327–33.

Stenson, K. (1991), 'Making sense of crime control', in K. Stenson and D. Cowell (eds), *The Politics of Crime Control*, London: Sage.

Stenson, K. and Cowell, D. (1991), *The Politics of Crime Control*, London: Sage.

Strang, J. and Gossop, M. (eds) (1993), *Responding to Drug Misuse: Treatment and control in Britain*, London: Tavistock.

Sudnow, D. (1965), 'Normal crimes: sociological features of the penal code in a public defender office', *Social Problems*, **12**, Winter.

Sumner, C. S. (1976), 'Marxism and deviancy theory', in P. Wiles (ed.), *The Sociology of Crime and Delinquency in Britian*, vol. 2, *The New Criminologies*, Oxford: Martin Robertson.

Sumner, C. S. (1981), 'Race, crime and hegemony', *Contemporary Crises*, **5** (3), pp. 277–91.

Sumner, C. S. (ed.) (1990), *Censure, Politics and Criminal Justice*, Buckingham: Open University Press.

Sumner, C. S. (1994), *The Sociology of Deviance: An obituary*, Buckingham: Open University Press.

Sutherland, E. H. (1937), *The Professional Thief: By a professional thief*, Chicago: University of Chicago Press.

Sutherland, E. H. (1940), 'White-collar criminality', *American Sociological Review*, **5**, February, pp. 1–12.

Sutherland, E. H. (1983; first pub. 1949), *White-Collar Crime*, New York: Holt, Rinehart & Winston.

Sykes, G. and Matza, D. (1957), 'Techniques of neutralization: a theory of delinquency', *American Sociological Review*, **22**, pp. 664–70.

Szasz, T. S. (1973), *The Manufacture of Madness*, St Albans: Paladin.

Takagi, P. (1974), 'A garrison state in a "democratic" society', *Crime and Social Justice*, **1**.

Tame, C. R. (1991), 'Freedom, responsibility and justice: the criminology of the "New Right" ', in K. Stenson and D. Cowell (eds), *The Politics of Crime Control*, London: Sage.

Tannenbaum, F. (1938), *Crime and the Communtiy*, New York: Columbia University Press.

Taylor, I. (1971), 'Soccer consciousness and soccer hooliganism', S. Cohen (ed.), *Images of Deviance*, Harmondsworth: Penguin.

Taylor, I. (1981), *Law and Order: Arguments for socialism*, London: Macmillan.

Taylor, I. (1982), 'Against crime and for socialism', *Crime and Social Justice*, Winter, pp. 14–15.

Taylor, I. and Walton, P. (1971), 'Hey, mister, this is what we really do; some observations of vandalism in play', *Social Work Today*, **2** (12), pp. 25–7.

Taylor, I., Walton, P. and Young, J. (1973), *The New Criminology: For a social theory of deviance*, London: Routledge & Kegan Paul.

Taylor, I., Walton, P. and Young, J. (eds) (1975), *Critical Criminology*, London: Routledge & Kegan Paul.

Taylor, L. (1971), *Deviance and Society*, London: Michael Joseph.

Taylor, L. (1980), 'Bringing power to particular account: Peter Rajah and the Hull Board of Visitors', in P. Carlen and M. Collison (eds), *Radical Issues in Criminology*, Oxford: Martin Robertson.

Taylor, L. (1984), *In the Underworld*, Oxford: Blackwell.

Taylor, L., Lacey, R. and Bracken, D. (1980), *In Whose Best Interests?*, London: Cobden Trust/Mind.

Thio, A. (1973), 'Class bias in the sociology of deviance', *American Sociologist*, **8**, pp. 1–12.

Thomas, C. W., Kreps, G. A. and Cage, R. J. (1977), 'An application of compliance theory to the study of juvenile delinquency', *Sociology and Social Research*, **61**, pp. 156–75.

Thompson, E. P. (1975), *Whigs and Hunters: The origins of the Black Act*, London: Allen Lane.

Thrasher, F. M. (1963; first pub. 1927), *The Gang*, Chicago: Phoenix Press.

Tierney, J. (1980), 'Political deviance: a critical commentary on a case study', *Sociological Review*, **28** (4), November, pp. 829–50.

Tierney, J. (1987), 'Police discretion: raising the age of consent', *The Police Journal*, **60** (4), Oct.–Dec.

Tierney, J. (1988), 'Viewpoint: romantic fictions: the re-emergence of the crime as politics debate', *Sociological Review*, **36** (1), February, pp. 133–45.

Turk, A. T. (1969), *Criminality and the Legal Order*, Chicago: Rand McNally.

Vagg, J. (1994), *Prison Systems: A comparative study of accountability in England, France, Germany and the Netherlands*, Oxford: Oxford University Press.

Veljanovski, C. (1990), *The Economics of Law: An introductory test*, London: Institute of Economic Affairs.

Vilar, P. (1985), 'Constructing Marxist history', in J. le Goff and P. Nora (eds), *Constructing the Past: Essays in historical methodology*, Cambridge: Cambridge University Press.

Vold, G. (1958), *Theoretical Criminology*, New York: Oxford University Press.

Von Hentig, H. (1948), *The Criminal and His Victim*, New Haven, Conn.: Yale University Press.

Wadsworth, M. (1979), *The Roots of Delinquency*, Oxford: Martin Robertson.

Walker, N. (1965), *Crime and Punishment*, Edinburgh: Edinburgh University Press.

Walker, N. D. (1991), *Why Punish?*, Oxford: Oxford University Press.

Walklate, S. (1989), *Victimology: The victim and the criminal justice process*, London: Unwin & Hyman.

Walklate, S. (1995), *Gender and Crime*, Hemel Hempstead: Harvester Wheatsheaf.

Walsh, D. and Poole, A. (eds) (1983), *A Dictionary of Criminology*, London: Routledge & Kegan Paul.

Ward, D. A. and Kassebaum, G. G. (1966), *Women's Prison*, London: Weidenfield.

Werkentin, F., Hofferbert, M. and Baurmann, M. (1974), 'Criminology as police science or "How old is the new criminology?" ', *Crime and Social Justice*, Autumn–Winter, pp. 24–41.

Wertham, F. (1949), *The Show of Violence*, Garden City, NY: Doubleday.

West, D. J. (1982), *Delinquency: Its roots, careers and prospects*, London: Heinemann.

West, D. J. and Farrington, D. P. (1973), *Who Becomes Delinquent?*, London: Heinemann.

West, D. J. and Farrington, D. P. (1977), *The Delinquent Way of Life*, London: Heinemann.

Whyte, W. F. (1955; first pub. 1943), *Street Corner Society*, 2nd edn, Chicago: University of Chicago Press.

Wiles, P. N. P. (1976a), 'Criminal statistics and sociological explanations', in P. N. P. Wiles (ed.), *The Sociology of Crime and Delinquency in Britain*, vol. 2, *The New Criminology*, Oxford: Martin Robertson.

Wiles, P. N. P. (ed.) (1976b) *The Sociology of Crime and Delinquency in Britain*, vol. 2, *The New Criminologies*, Oxford: Martin Robertson.

Wilkins, L. (1964), *Social Deviance: Social policy, action and research*, London: Tavistock.

Willcock, H. O. (1949), *Mass Observation Report on Juvenile Delinquency*, London: Falcon Press.

Willis, P. (1977), *Leaning to Labour: How working class kids get working class jobs*, Farnborough: Saxon House.

Willis, P. (1978), *Profane Culture*, London: Routledge & Kegan Paul.

Willmott, P. (1966), *Adolescent Boys of East London*, London: Routledge & Kegan Paul.

Wilson, H. (1980), 'Parental supervision: a neglected aspect of delinquency', *British Journal of Criminology*, **20**, pp. 203–35.

Wilson, H. and Herbert, G. (1978), *Parents and Children in the Inner City*, London: Routledge & Kegan Paul.

Wilson, J. Q. (1975), *Thinking About Crime*, New York: Vintage.

Wilson, J. Q. and Herrnstein, R. (1985), *Crime and Human Nature*, New York: Simon & Schuster.

Wolfe, A. (1971), 'Political repression and the liberal state', *Monthly Review*, **23**, 20 December.

Wolfgang, M. E. (1958), *Patterns in Criminal Homicide*, Philadelphia: University of Pennsylvania Press.

Wolfgang, M. E., Thornberry, T. P. and Figlio, R. M. (1987), *From Boy to Man, from Delinquency to Crime*, Chicago: University of Chicago Press.

Worrall, A. (1981), 'Out of place: female offenders in court', *Probation Journal*, **28**, pp. 90–3.

Worrall, A. (1990), *Offending Women*, London: Routledge.

Worrall, A. and Pease, K. (1986), 'The prison population in 1985', *British Journal of Criminology*, **26** (2), pp. 184–7.

Yeager, P. C. (1991), *The Limits of Law: The public regulation of private pollution*, Cambridge: Cambridge University Press.

Young, A. (1990), *Femininity in Dissent*, London: Routledge.

Young, J. (1971), *The Drugtakers: The social meaning of drug use*, London: MacGibbon & Kee/Paladin.

Young, J. (1975), 'Working class criminology', in I. Taylor, P. Walton and J. Young (eds), *Critical Criminology*, London: Routledge & Kegan Paul.

Young, J. (1986), 'The failure of criminology: the need for a radical realism', in R. Matthews and J. Young (eds), *Confronting Crime*, London: Sage.

Young, J. (1987), 'The tasks facing a realist criminology', *Contemporary Crises*, **11**, pp. 337–56.

Young, J. (1988), 'Radical criminology in Britain: the emergence of a competing paradigm', in P. Rock (ed.), *A History of British Criminology*, Oxford: Oxford University Press.

Young, J. (1994), 'Incessant chatter: recent paradigms in criminology', in M. Maguire, R. Morgan and R. Reiner (eds), *The Oxford Handbook of Criminology*, Oxford: Clarendon Press.

Young, J. and Matthews, R. (eds) (1992), *Rethinking Criminology: The realist debate*, London: Sage.

Young, M. (1993), *In the Sticks: An anthropologist in a shire force*, Oxford: Oxford University Press.

Zedner, L. (1991), *Women, Crime and Custody in Victorian England*, Oxford: Blackwell.

Zedner, L. (1994), 'Victims', in M. Maguire, R. Morgan and R. Reiner (eds), *The Oxford Handbook of Criminology*, Oxford: Clarendon Press.

Name index

Adamson, M., 252
Adelman, S., 217
Adler, F., 254, 258
Agnew, R., 223
Akers, R. L., 148, 165
Allen, H., 261
Althusser, L., 197
Amir, M., 33
Anderson, E., 212
Anderson, N., 92
Anderson, P., 68
Anderson, S., 36, 43, 246, 265, 271, 283, 288
Atkinson, J. M., 135, 166, 202
Austin, A. L., 207

Bagot, J. H., 72
Baldwin, J., 73
Ball, R. A., 78–9, 250, 277, 279
Bankowski, Z., 196
Bates, J. E., 243
Baurmann, M., 197
Bayles, K., 243
Becker, H. S., 7–8, 14–15, 128, 129, 138,
    139–41, 144, 145, 146, 149, 175, 176,
    203, 218
Beirne, P., 197, 150
Belson, W., 241
Bennett, D. S., 243
Bianchi, H., 233
Biderman, A. D., 31
Bilton, T., 20
Bittner, E., 29, 202
Block, A., 38
Bohlander, E. W., 196

Bonnett, K., 20
Bordua, D., 151
Bottomley, A. K., 24, 35, 40–1
Bottoms, A. E., 73, 228
Box, S., 32, 38, 85, 102, 104, 164, 200–1,
    206–7, 210, 224, 228, 242, 254–5, 259,
    274
Bracken, D., 174
Braithwaite, J., 22
Brewer, C., 234
Briskin, L., 252
Broadhead, R. R., 148
Brogden, M., 228, 264
Brown, B., 252, 266
Brown, D., 285, 286–7
Brown, M. N., 243
Browne, A., 256
Browne, S., 246
Brownmiller, S., 212
Burgess, E. W., 91
Burt, C., 54, 55, 68

Cage, R. J., 206
Cain, M., 166, 197, 236, 252
Campbell, A., 210, 256, 257,
Campbell, B., 269, 271–2
Campbell, K., 236
Carlen, P., 8, 160, 166, 198, 236, 253–4, 255,
    256, 257, 259, 261, 262–3, 266, 270, 285,
    288
Carr-Saunders, A. M., 72
Carson, W. G., 72, 135, 200, 224
Carter, M. P., 72, 111, 112
Cashburn, M., 163

317

Subject index

abolitionism, 233
administrative criminology, 224, 251, 272–5
adolescents, *see* juvenile delinquency; young
    offenders
anomie, 80, 84–5, 96, 98
    see also Durkheim, E.; Merton, R. K.
anti-social tendencies, 242–3
'appreciative' studies, 92, 94, 165

Birmingham Centre for Contemporary
    Cultural Studies, 119, 161, 190–3, 199
British Crime Surveys, 34, 35–6, 274–5

Chicago School, 75–7, 89–95
classical criminology, 47–8, 250, 275
collective conscience, 83, 84, 86
conflict theory, in the United States, 176–80
control theory, 204–8, 224, 258, 273
counter culture, the, 130–2
crime
    definition of, 13–15, 18–19
    functions of, 86–8
    measuring, 15–18, 24–43
    official data on, 16, 24–6, 40–2
    see also self-report studies; victim studies
crime statistics
    'class conflict' approach, 40
    and the 'dark figure' of, 26
    'institutionalist' approach, 9–10
    and public reporting, 26–7
    'realist' approach, 9, 31–2
criminal area, 89, 108–9, 111, 112–13,
    225–6
criminal careers, 239–44

criminology
    definition of, 11, 47, 65–71
    'external' history, 134, 218–20, 232–3
    and the 'governmental' project, 48, 62, 70,
        231, 273–4
    'internal' history, 222–8, 232
    social organization of, 220–2
    and the 'Lombrosian' project, 48, 62, 70
critical criminology, 181–4, 194–6, 231, 233,
    281, 284–90
    see also new criminology; left idealism
cultural diversity theory, 92, 114–18
cultural transmission, *see* cultural diversity
    theory
cynical rule breakers, 161–2, 199–201
delinquency, *see* juvenile delinquency; young
    offenders
deviance
    definition of, 13–15, 20–3
    politics of, 129, 147–8, 155–8, 180–1,
        187–94
    as a social censure, 22, 184
    see also labelling theory; new deviancy
        theory; primary and secondary
        deviation; secret deviance
deviancy amplification, 143
differential association, 92–3
domestic violence, 224, 263–4

Edinburgh Crime Survey, 36, 287–8
education and delinquency, 118–19
ethnography, 91–2, 93, 164–5, 224
ethnomethodology, 166–7, 202–3
eugenics, 56–7

322